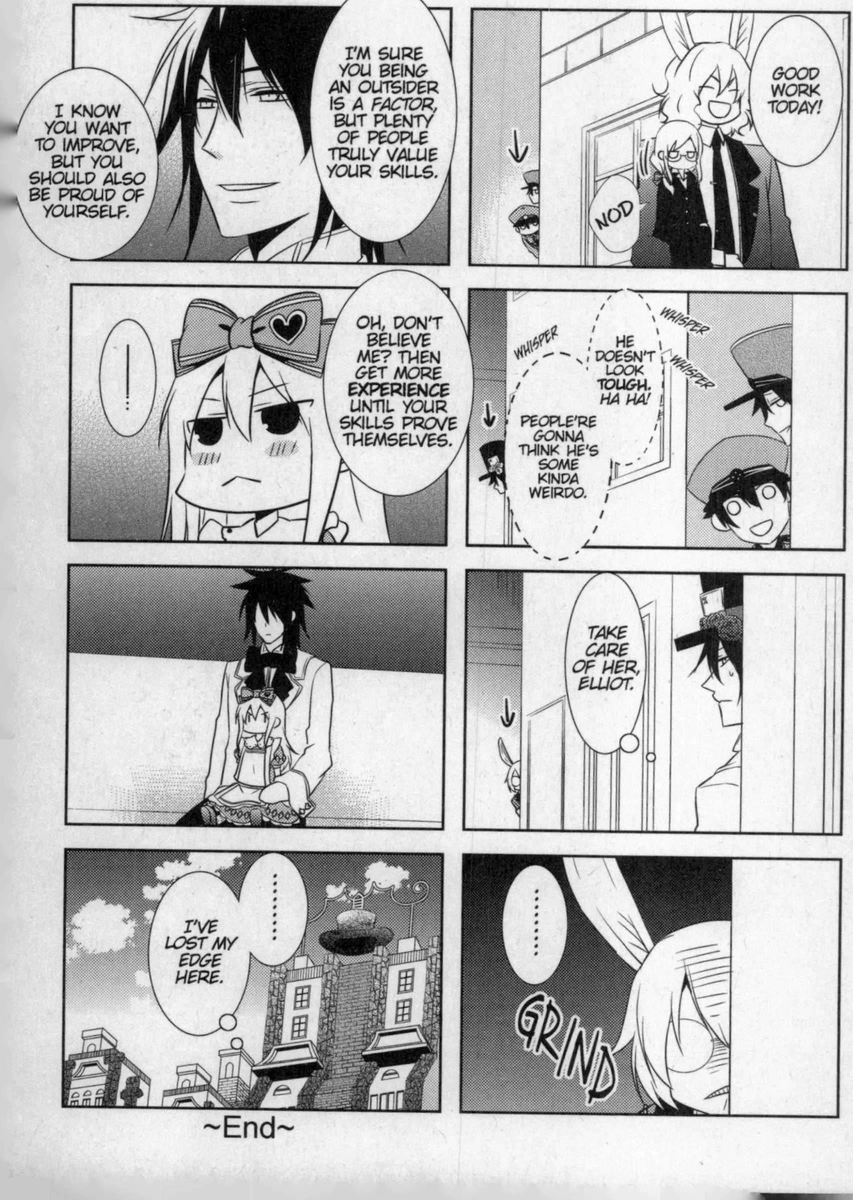
GOOD WORK TODAY!
NOD
I'M SURE YOU BEING AN OUTSIDER IS A FACTOR, BUT PLENTY OF PEOPLE TRULY VALUE YOUR SKILLS.
I KNOW YOU WANT TO IMPROVE, BUT YOU SHOULD ALSO BE PROUD OF YOURSELF.
WHISPER
HE DOESN'T LOOK TOUGH. HA HA!
WHISPER
WHISPER
PEOPLE'RE GONNA THINK HE'S SOME KINDA WEIRDO.
OH, DON'T BELIEVE ME? THEN GET MORE **EXPERIENCE** UNTIL YOUR SKILLS PROVE THEMSELVES.
!...
TAKE CARE OF HER, ELLIOT.
......
GRIND
......
I'VE LOST MY EDGE HERE.

~End~

If Alice Was Small
~Final Episode~

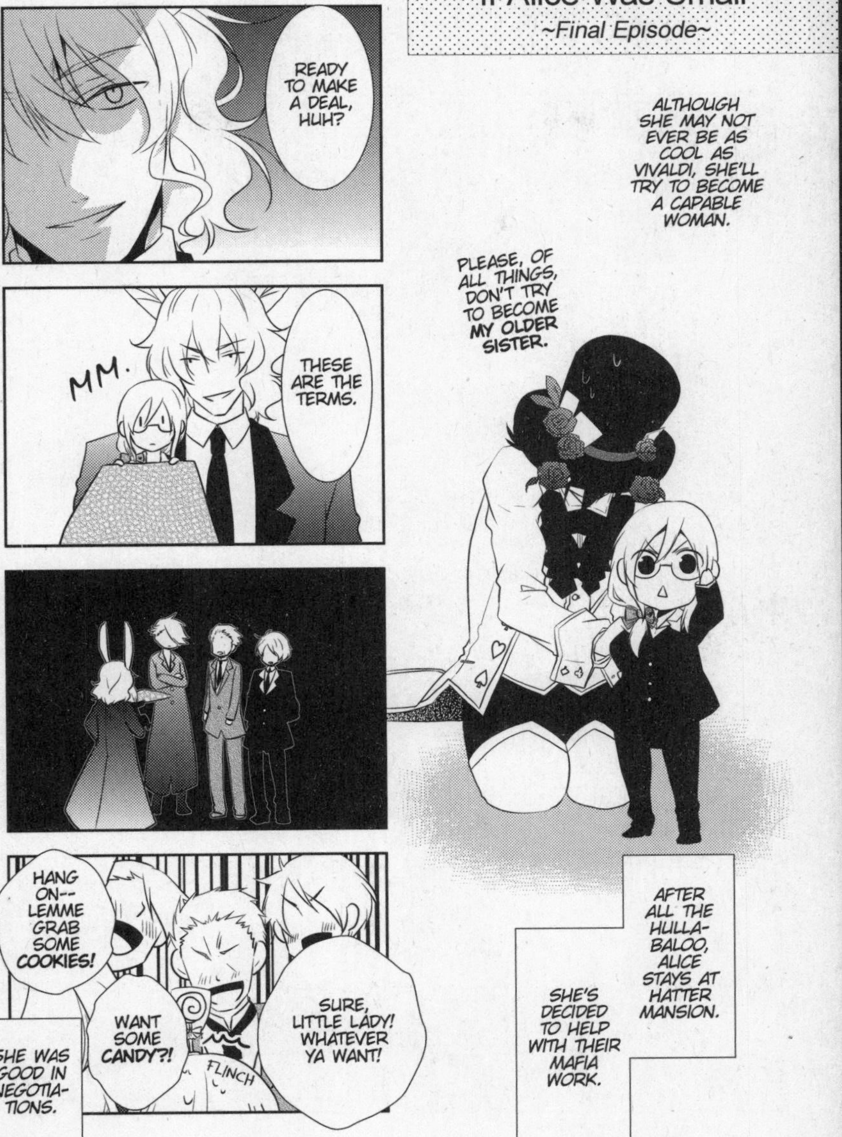
ALTHOUGH SHE MAY NOT EVER BE AS COOL AS VIVALDI, SHE'LL TRY TO BECOME A CAPABLE WOMAN.
PLEASE, OF ALL THINGS, DON'T TRY TO BECOME MY OLDER SISTER.
AFTER ALL THE HULLA-BALOO, ALICE STAYS AT HATTER MANSION.
SHE'S DECIDED TO HELP WITH THEIR MAFIA WORK.
READY TO MAKE A DEAL, HUH?
THESE ARE THE TERMS.
MM.
SURE, LITTLE LADY! WHATEVER YA WANT!
HANG ON-- LEMME GRAB SOME COOKIES!
WANT SOME CANDY?!
FLINCH
SHE WAS GOOD IN NEGOTIA-TIONS.

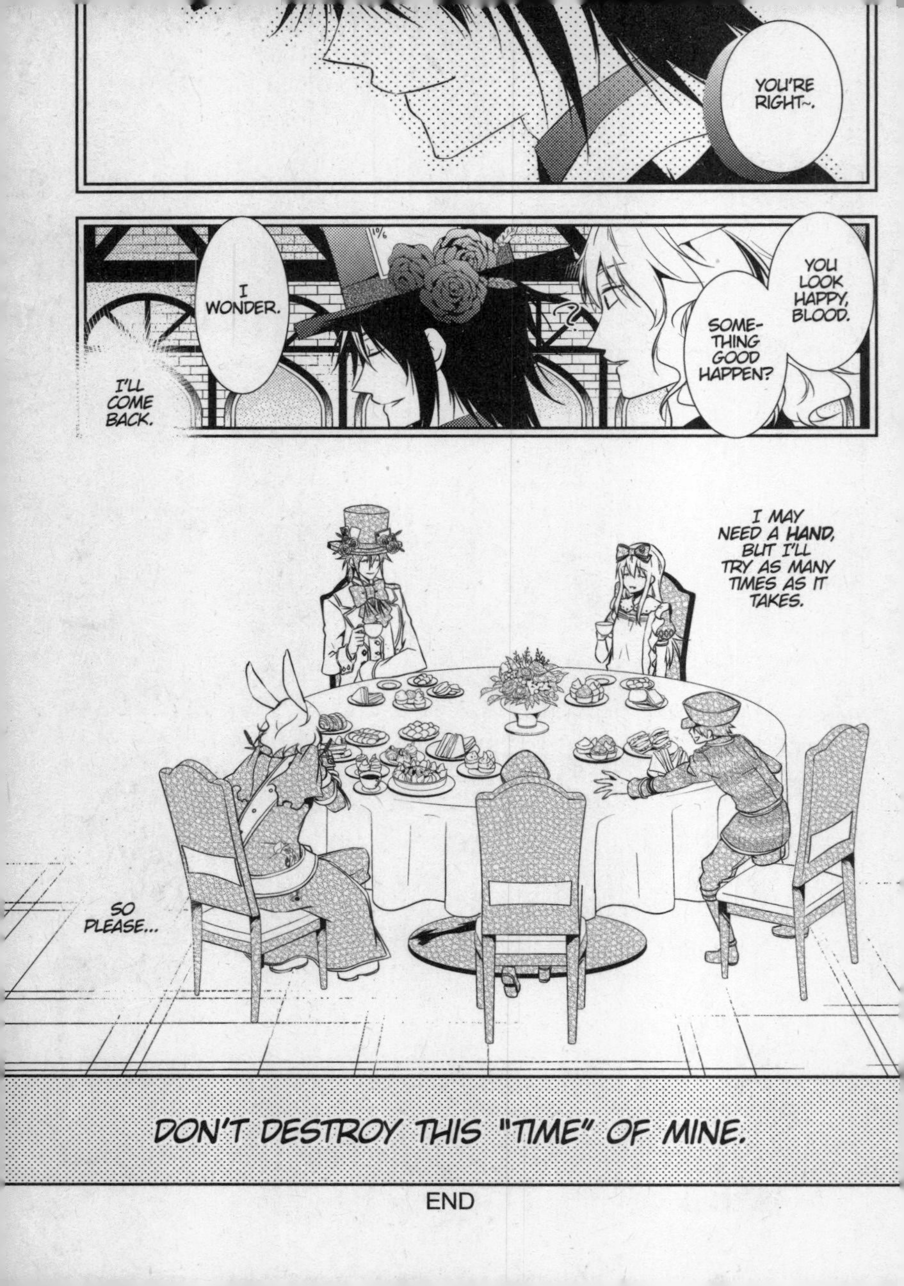
YOU'RE RIGHT~.
YOU LOOK HAPPY, BLOOD.
SOME-THING GOOD HAPPEN?
I WONDER.
I'LL COME BACK.
I MAY NEED A HAND, BUT I'LL TRY AS MANY TIMES AS IT TAKES.
SO PLEASE...
DON'T DESTROY THIS "TIME" OF MINE.
END

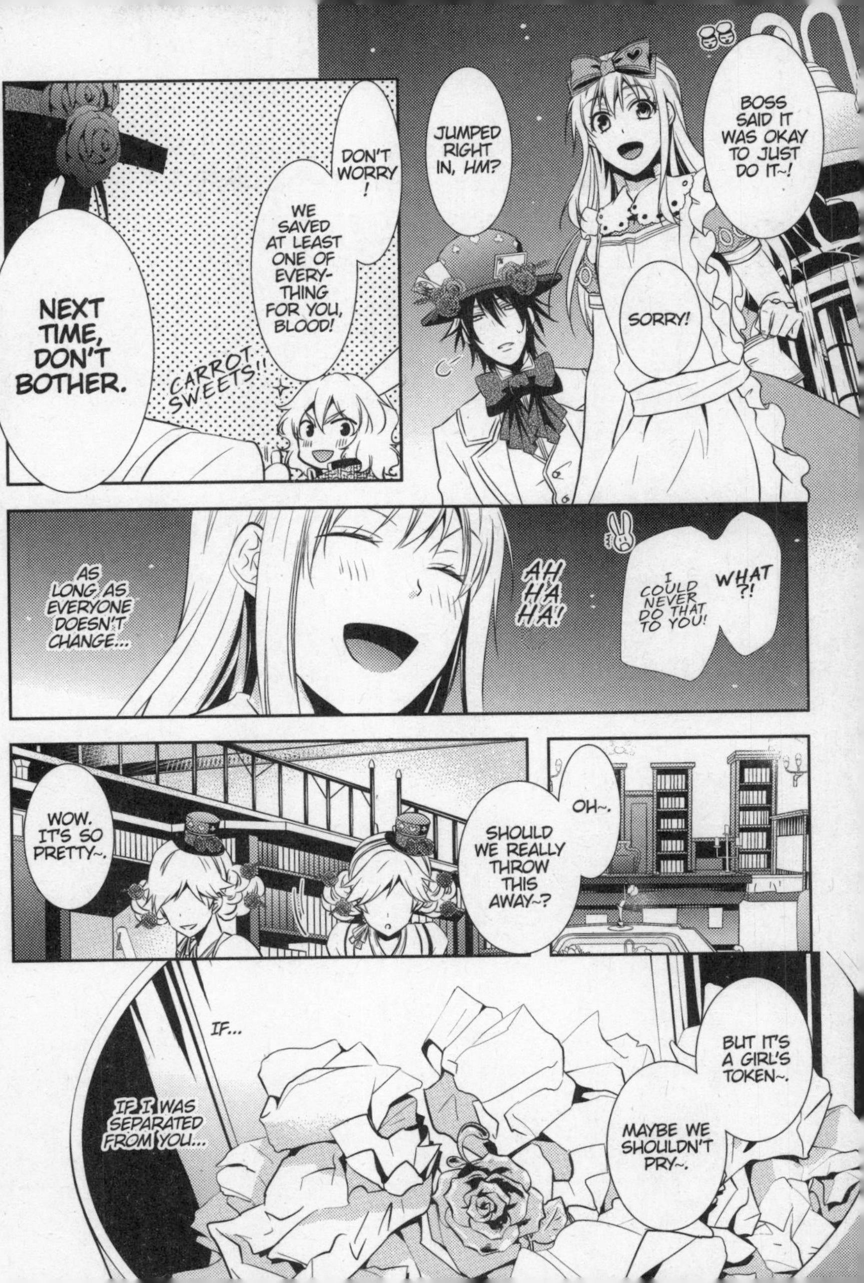
BOSS SAID IT WAS OKAY TO JUST DO IT~!
JUMPED RIGHT IN, HM?
SORRY!
DON'T WORRY!
WE SAVED AT LEAST ONE OF EVERYTHING FOR YOU, BLOOD!
CARROT SWEETS!!
NEXT TIME, DON'T BOTHER.
WHAT?!
I COULD NEVER DO THAT TO YOU!
AH HA HA!
AS LONG AS EVERYONE DOESN'T CHANGE...
OH~.
SHOULD WE REALLY THROW THIS AWAY~?
WOW. IT'S SO PRETTY~.
BUT IT'S A GIRL'S TOKEN~.
MAYBE WE SHOULDN'T PRY~.
IF...
IF I WAS SEPARATED FROM YOU...

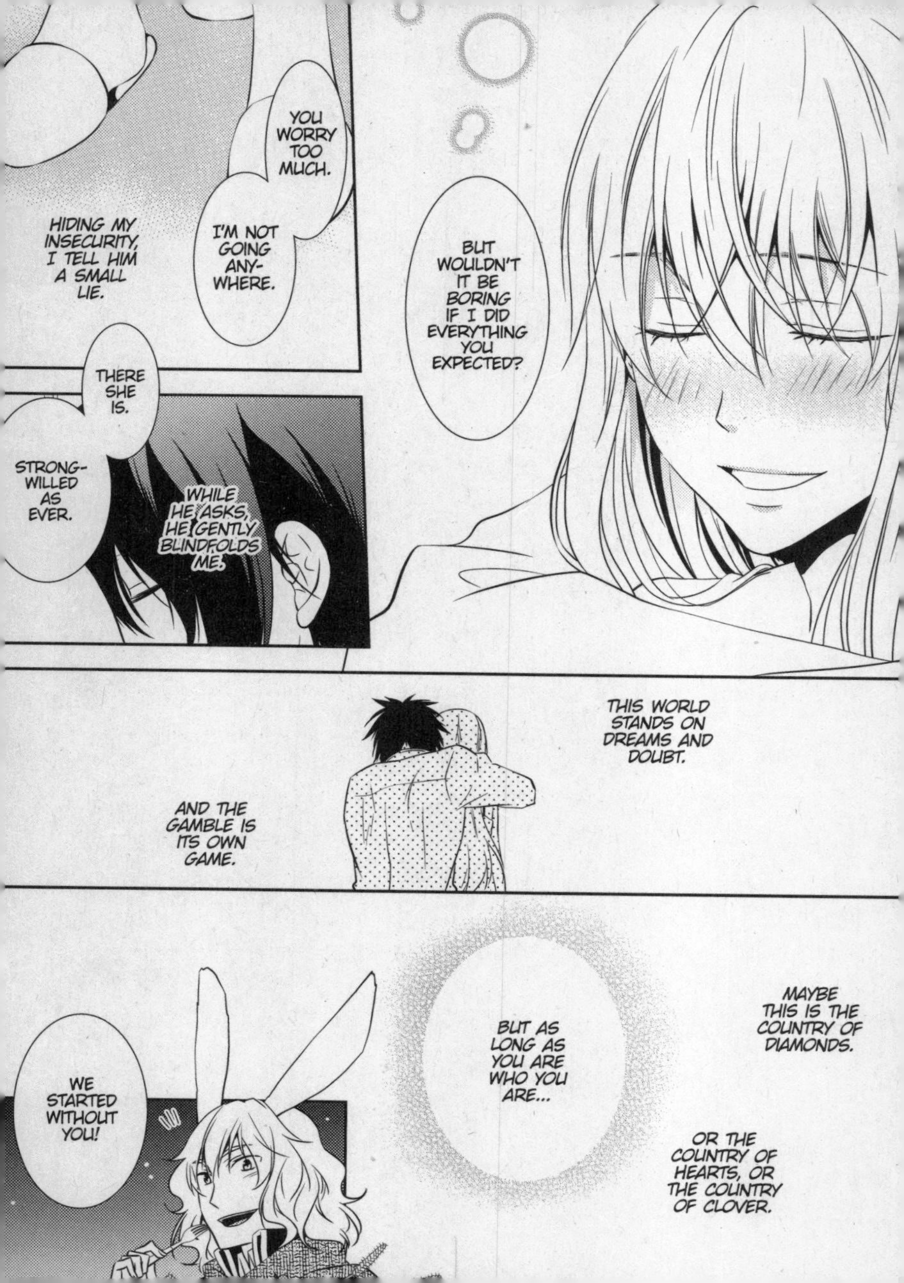
BUT WOULDN'T IT BE BORING IF I DID EVERYTHING YOU EXPECTED?
YOU WORRY TOO MUCH.
I'M NOT GOING ANY-WHERE.
HIDING MY INSECURITY, I TELL HIM A SMALL LIE.
THERE SHE IS.
STRONG-WILLED AS EVER.
WHILE HE ASKS, HE GENTLY BLINDFOLDS ME.
THIS WORLD STANDS ON DREAMS AND DOUBT.
AND THE GAMBLE IS ITS OWN GAME.
MAYBE THIS IS THE COUNTRY OF DIAMONDS.
OR THE COUNTRY OF HEARTS, OR THE COUNTRY OF CLOVER.
BUT AS LONG AS YOU ARE WHO YOU ARE...
WE STARTED WITHOUT YOU!

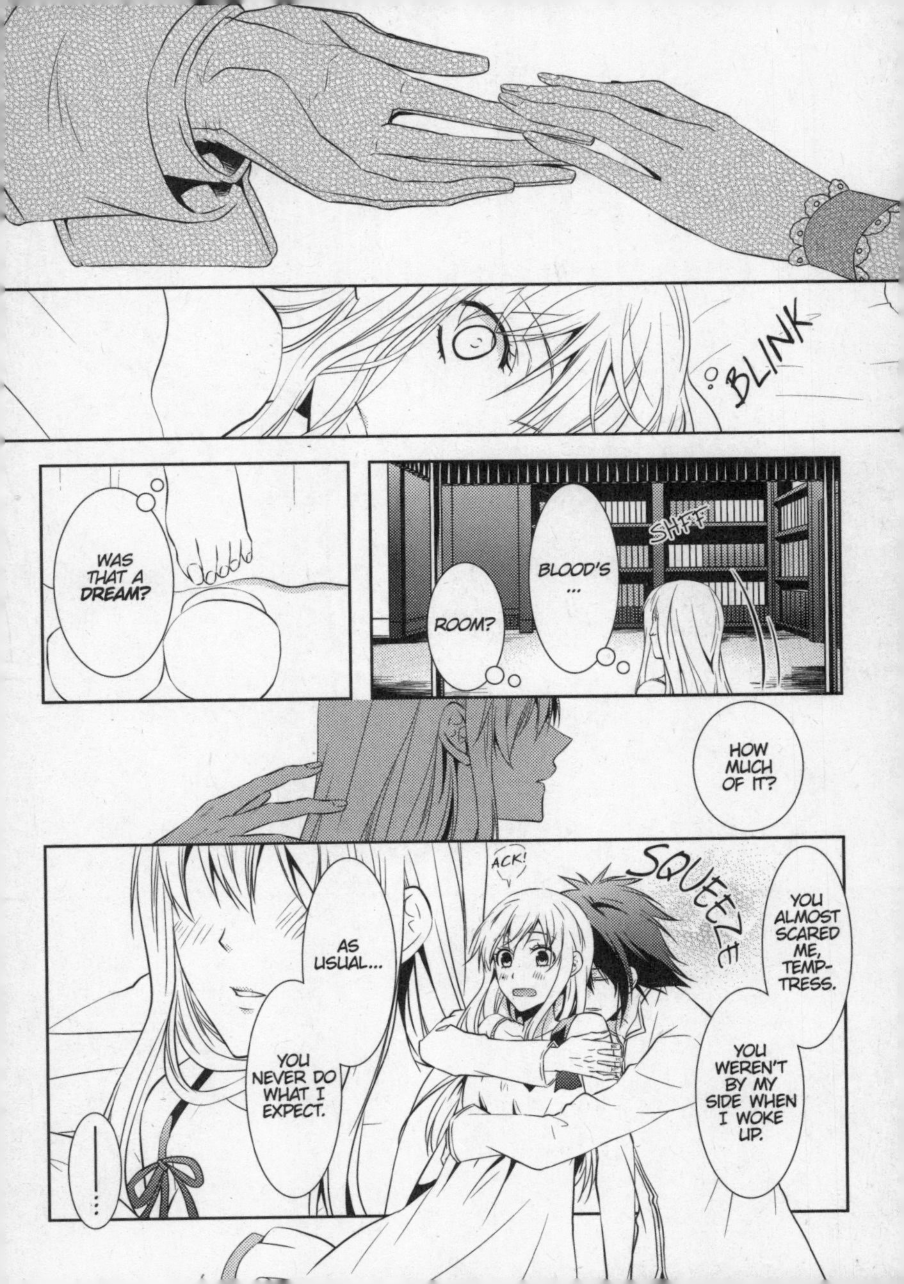
BLINK
SHFF
BLOOD'S ...
ROOM?
WAS THAT A DREAM?
HOW MUCH OF IT?
YOU ALMOST SCARED ME, TEMP-TRESS.
SQUEEZE
YOU WEREN'T BY MY SIDE WHEN I WOKE UP.
ACK!
AS USUAL...
YOU NEVER DO WHAT I EXPECT.
!...

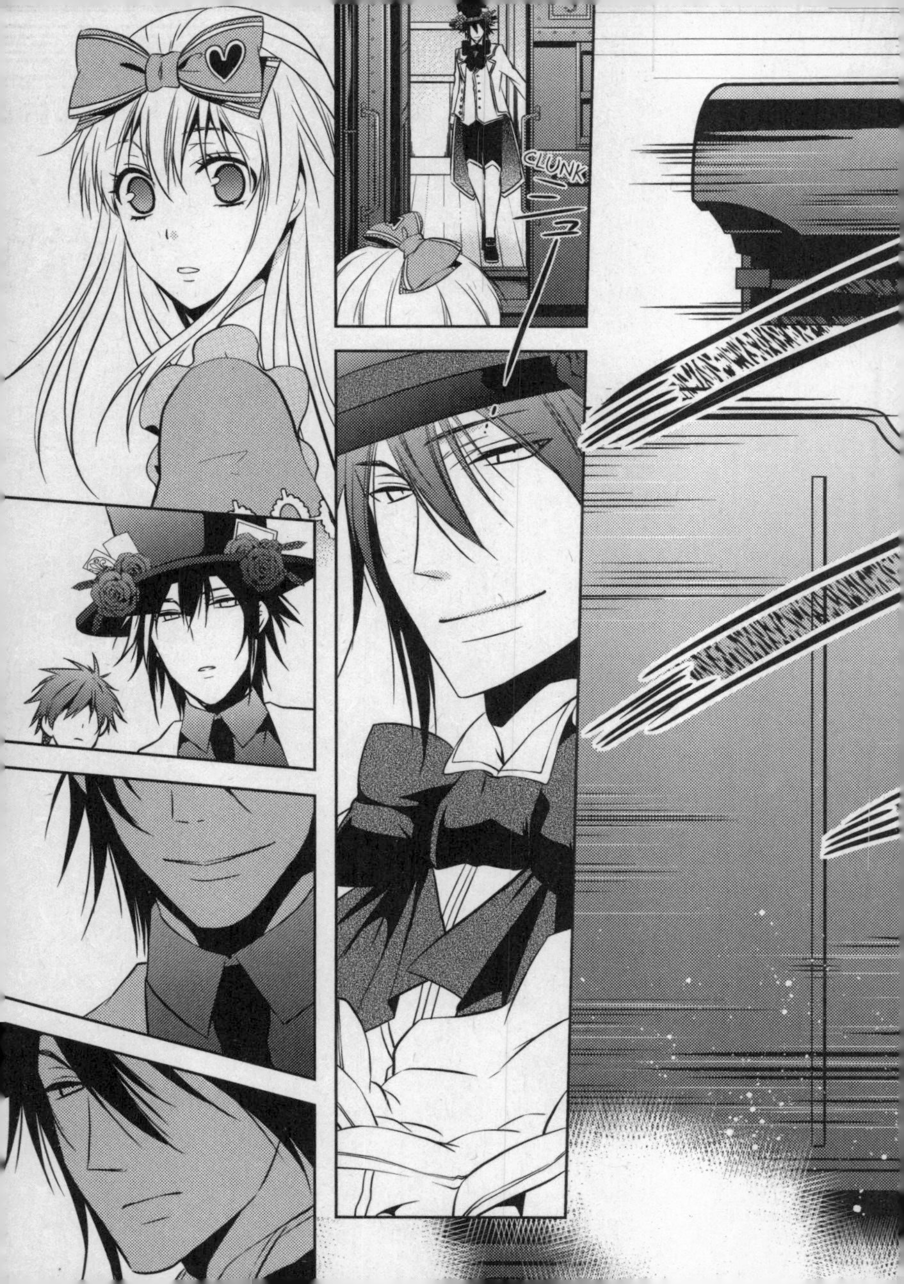
CLUNK

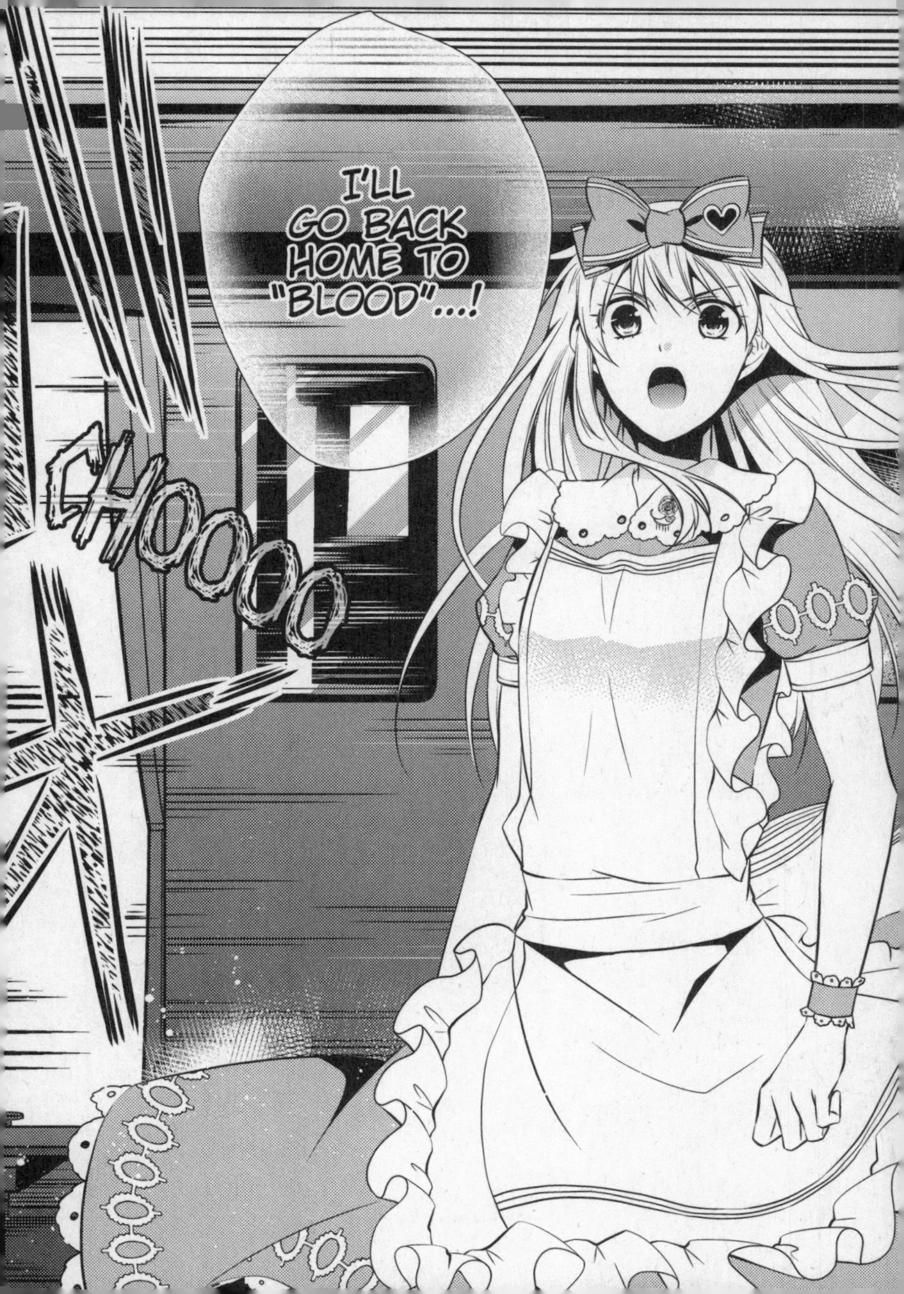
I'LL GO BACK HOME TO "BLOOD"...!
CHOOOO

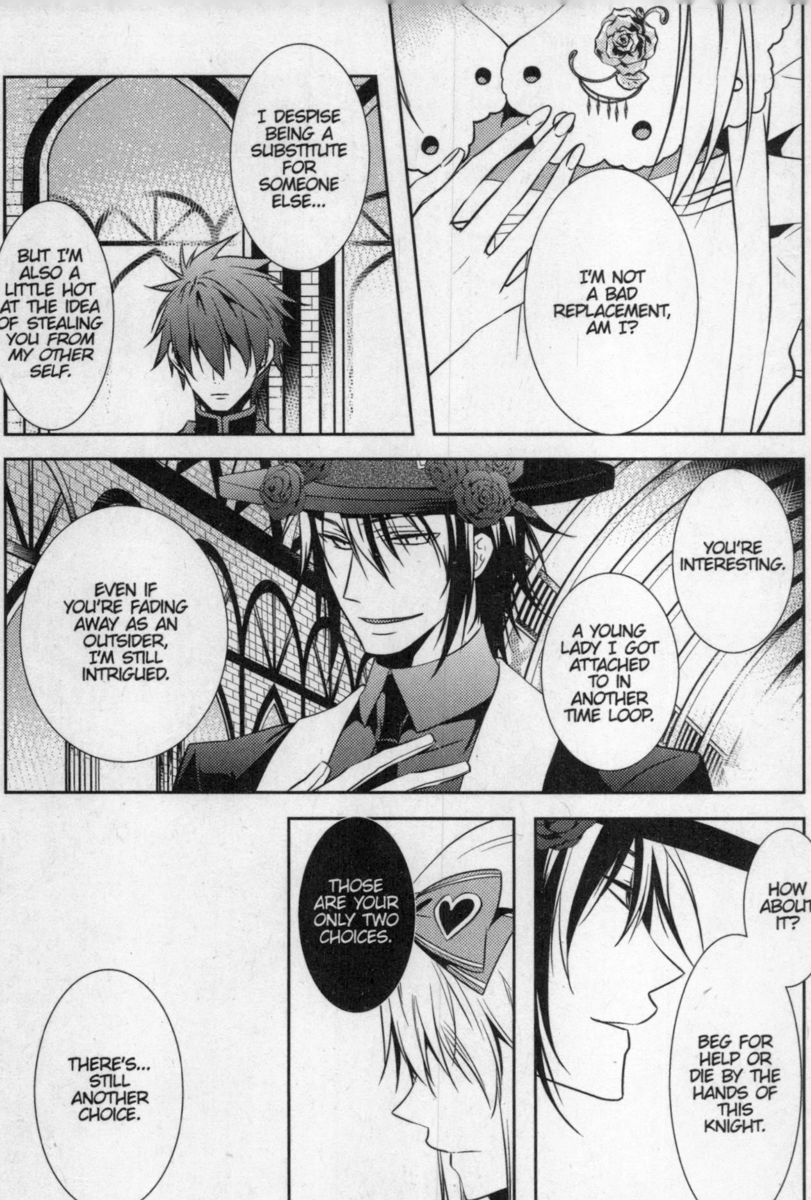
I'M NOT A BAD REPLACEMENT, AM I?
I DESPISE BEING A SUBSTITUTE FOR SOMEONE ELSE...
BUT I'M ALSO A LITTLE HOT AT THE IDEA OF STEALING YOU FROM MY OTHER SELF.
YOU'RE INTERESTING.
A YOUNG LADY I GOT ATTACHED TO IN ANOTHER TIME LOOP.
EVEN IF YOU'RE FADING AWAY AS AN OUTSIDER, I'M STILL INTRIGUED.
HOW ABOUT IT?
BEG FOR HELP OR DIE BY THE HANDS OF THIS KNIGHT.
THOSE ARE YOUR ONLY TWO CHOICES.
THERE'S... STILL ANOTHER CHOICE.

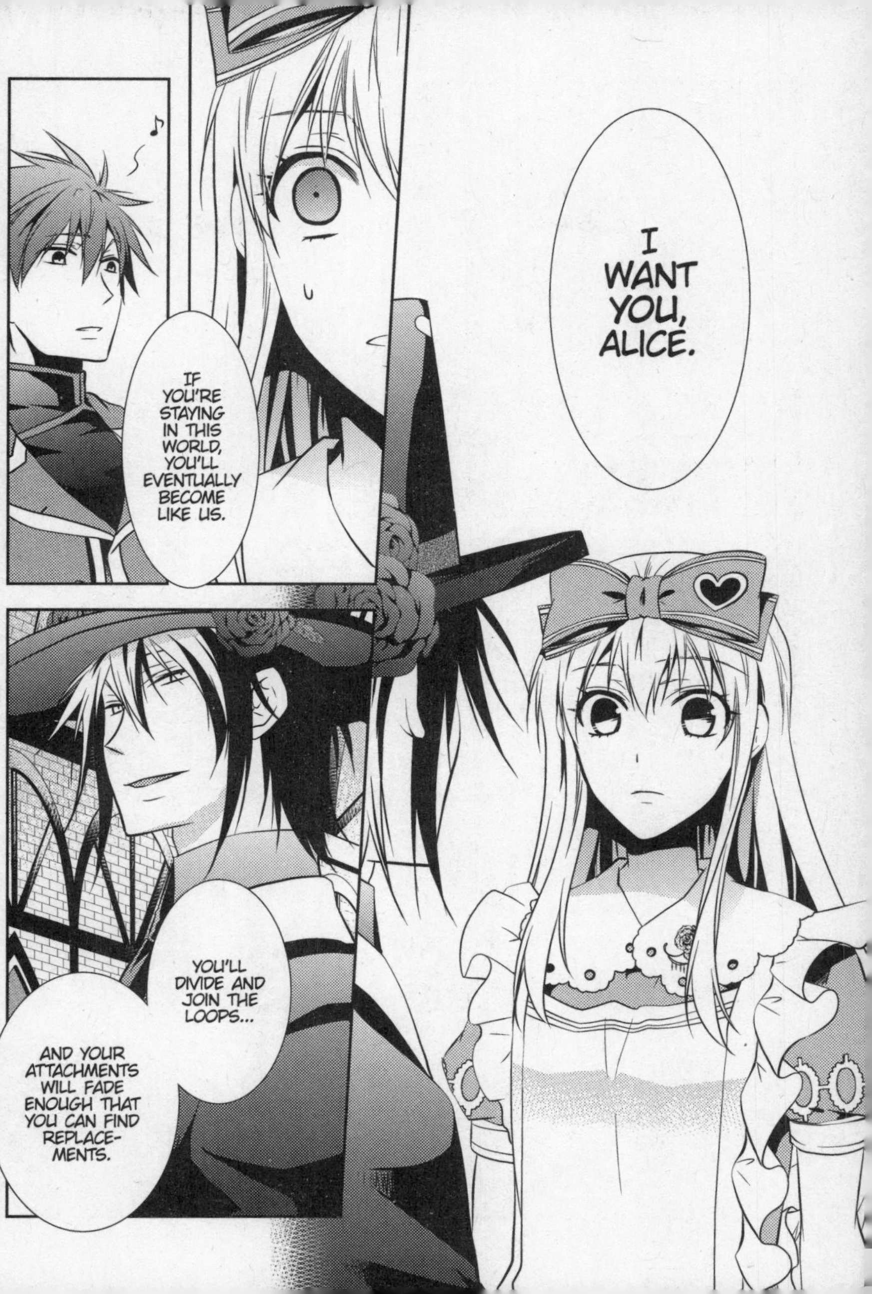
I WANT YOU, ALICE.
IF YOU'RE STAYING IN THIS WORLD, YOU'LL EVENTUALLY BECOME LIKE US.
YOU'LL DIVIDE AND JOIN THE LOOPS...
AND YOUR ATTACHMENTS WILL FADE ENOUGH THAT YOU CAN FIND REPLACE-MENTS.

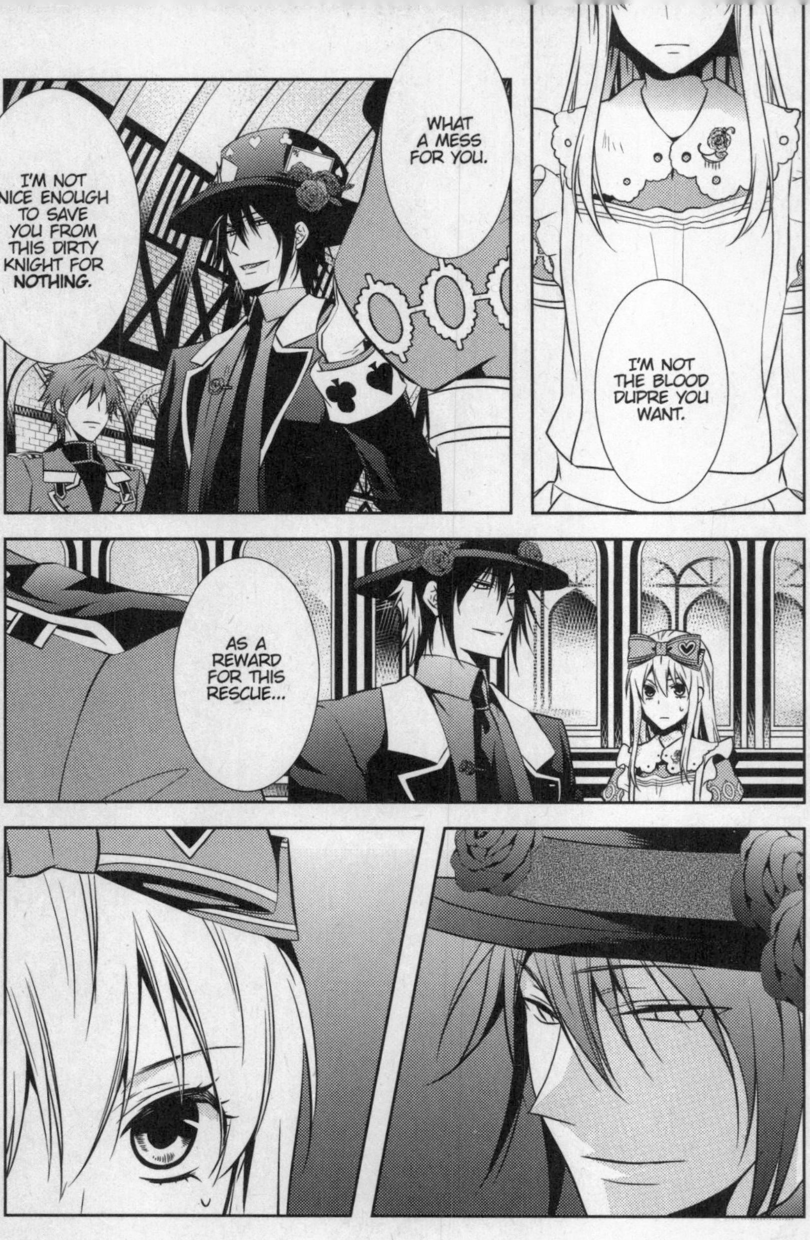
I'M NOT THE BLOOD DUPRE YOU WANT.
WHAT A MESS FOR YOU.
I'M NOT NICE ENOUGH TO SAVE YOU FROM THIS DIRTY KNIGHT FOR NOTHING.
AS A REWARD FOR THIS RESCUE...

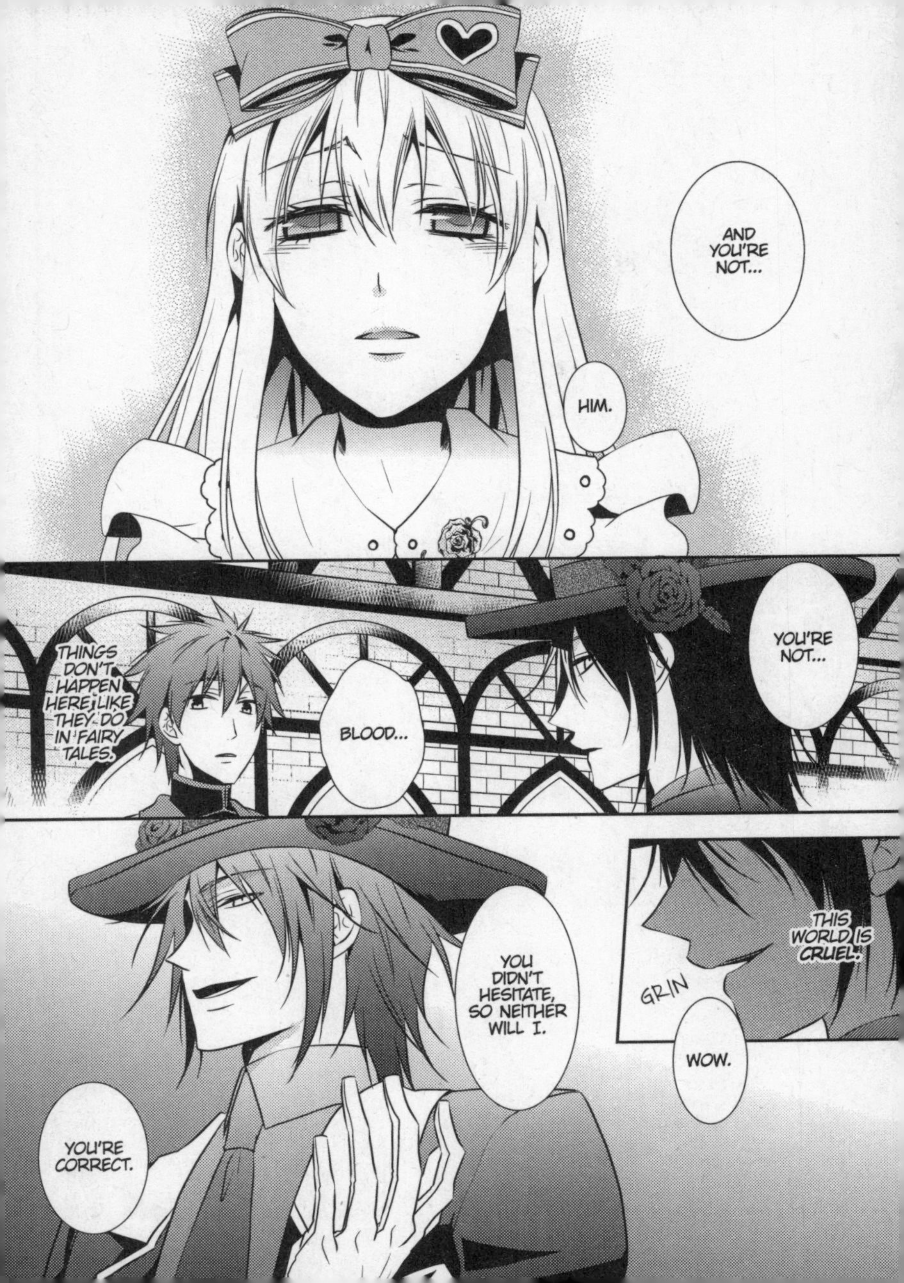
AND YOU'RE NOT...
HIM.
YOU'RE NOT...
BLOOD...
THINGS DON'T HAPPEN HERE LIKE THEY DO IN FAIRY TALES.
THIS WORLD IS CRUEL.
GRIN
WOW.
YOU DIDN'T HESITATE, SO NEITHER WILL I.
YOU'RE CORRECT.

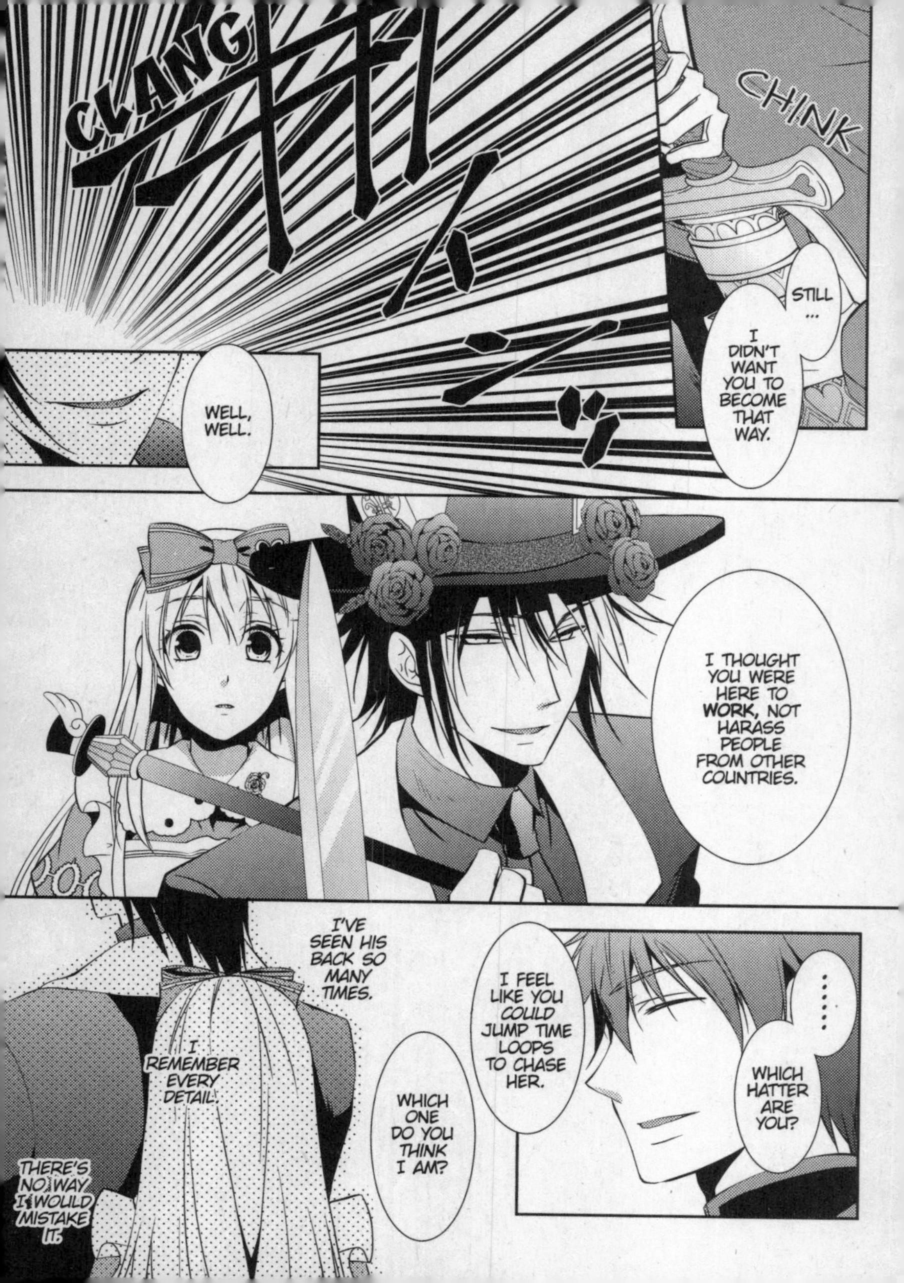
CHINK
STILL...
I DIDN'T WANT YOU TO BECOME THAT WAY.
CLANG
WELL, WELL.
I THOUGHT YOU WERE HERE TO **WORK,** NOT HARASS PEOPLE FROM OTHER COUNTRIES.
......
WHICH HATTER ARE YOU?
I FEEL LIKE YOU COULD JUMP TIME LOOPS TO CHASE HER.
WHICH ONE DO YOU THINK I AM?
I'VE SEEN HIS BACK SO MANY TIMES.
I REMEMBER EVERY DETAIL.
THERE'S NO WAY I WOULD MISTAKE IT.

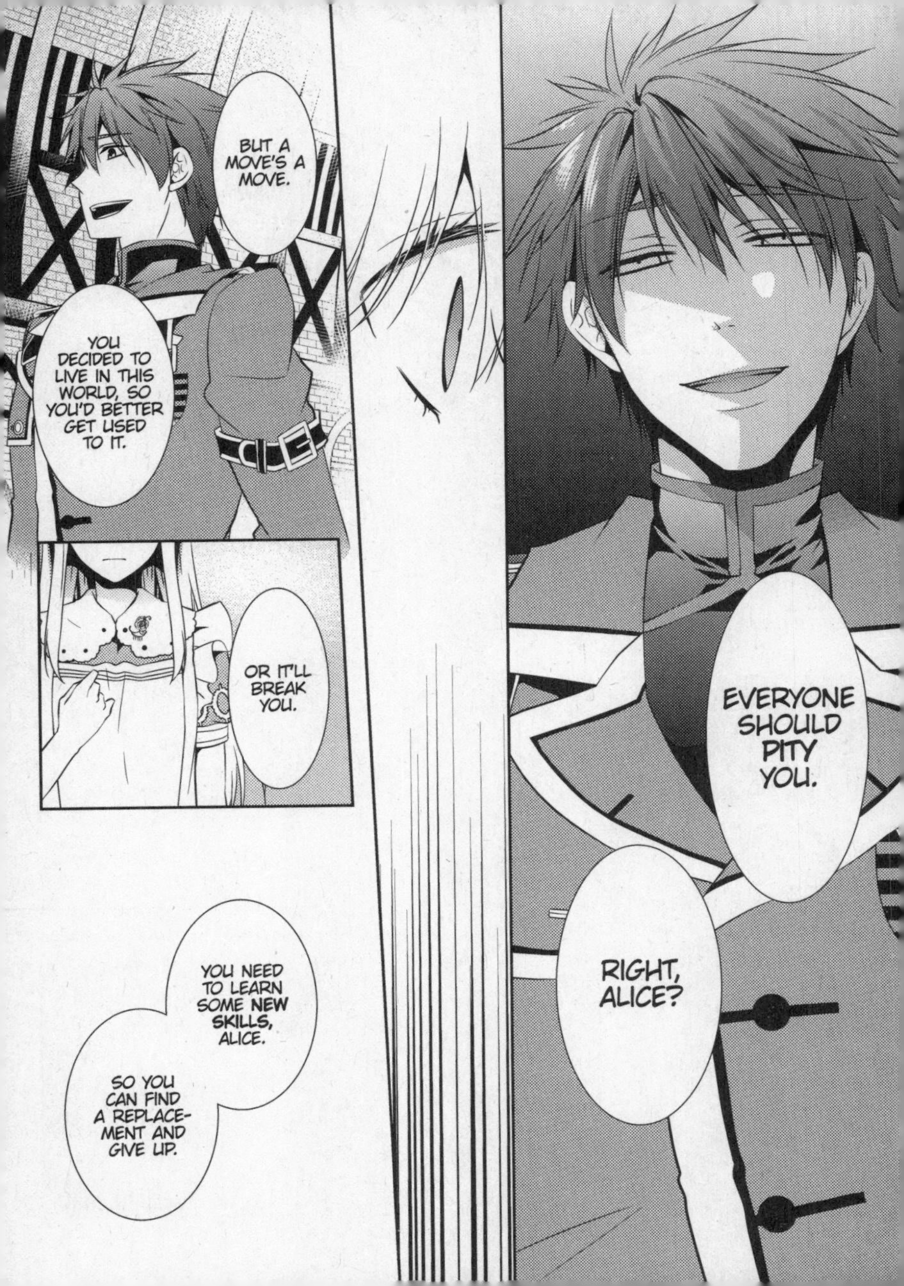
EVERYONE SHOULD PITY YOU.
RIGHT, ALICE?
BUT A MOVE'S A MOVE.
YOU DECIDED TO LIVE IN THIS WORLD, SO YOU'D BETTER GET USED TO IT.
OR IT'LL BREAK YOU.
YOU NEED TO LEARN SOME NEW SKILLS, ALICE.
SO YOU CAN FIND A REPLACE-MENT AND GIVE UP.

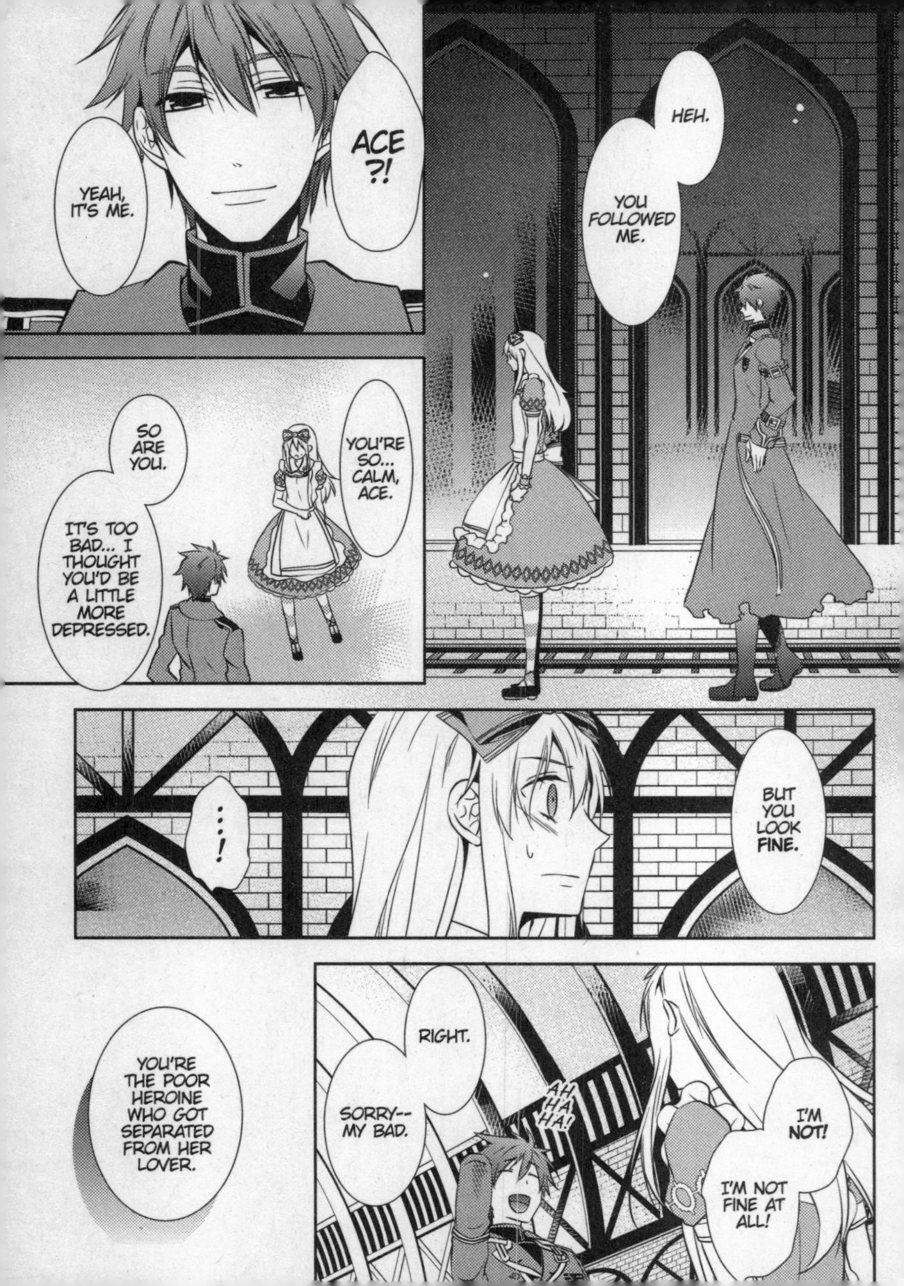
HEH.
YOU FOLLOWED ME.
ACE?!
YEAH, IT'S ME.
YOU'RE SO... CALM, ACE.
SO ARE YOU.
IT'S TOO BAD... I THOUGHT YOU'D BE A LITTLE MORE DEPRESSED.
BUT YOU LOOK FINE.
...!
I'M NOT!
I'M NOT FINE AT ALL!
RIGHT.
AH HA HA!
SORRY-- MY BAD.
YOU'RE THE POOR HEROINE WHO GOT SEPARATED FROM HER LOVER.

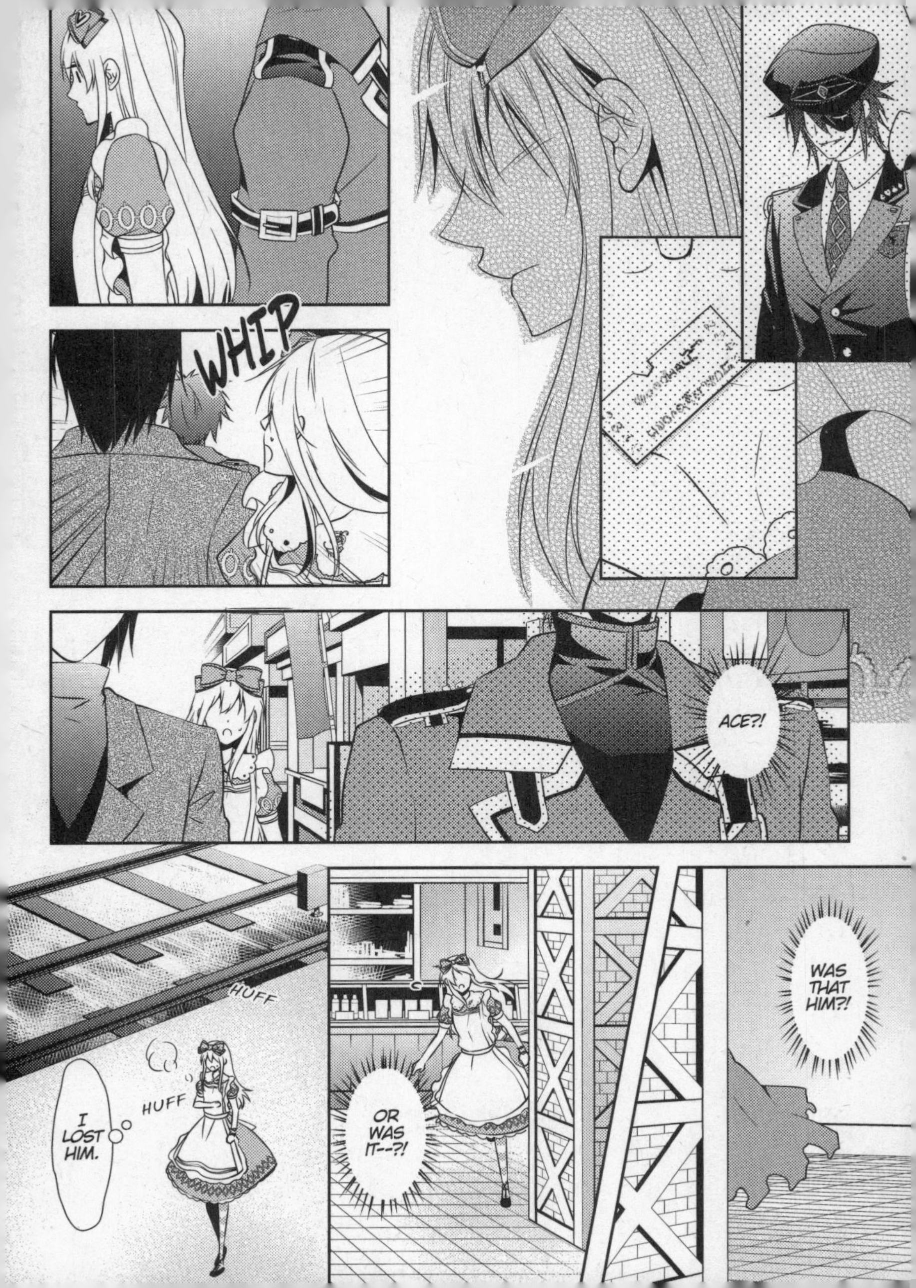
WHIP
ACE?!
WAS THAT HIM?!
OR WAS IT--?!
HUFF
HUFF
I LOST HIM.

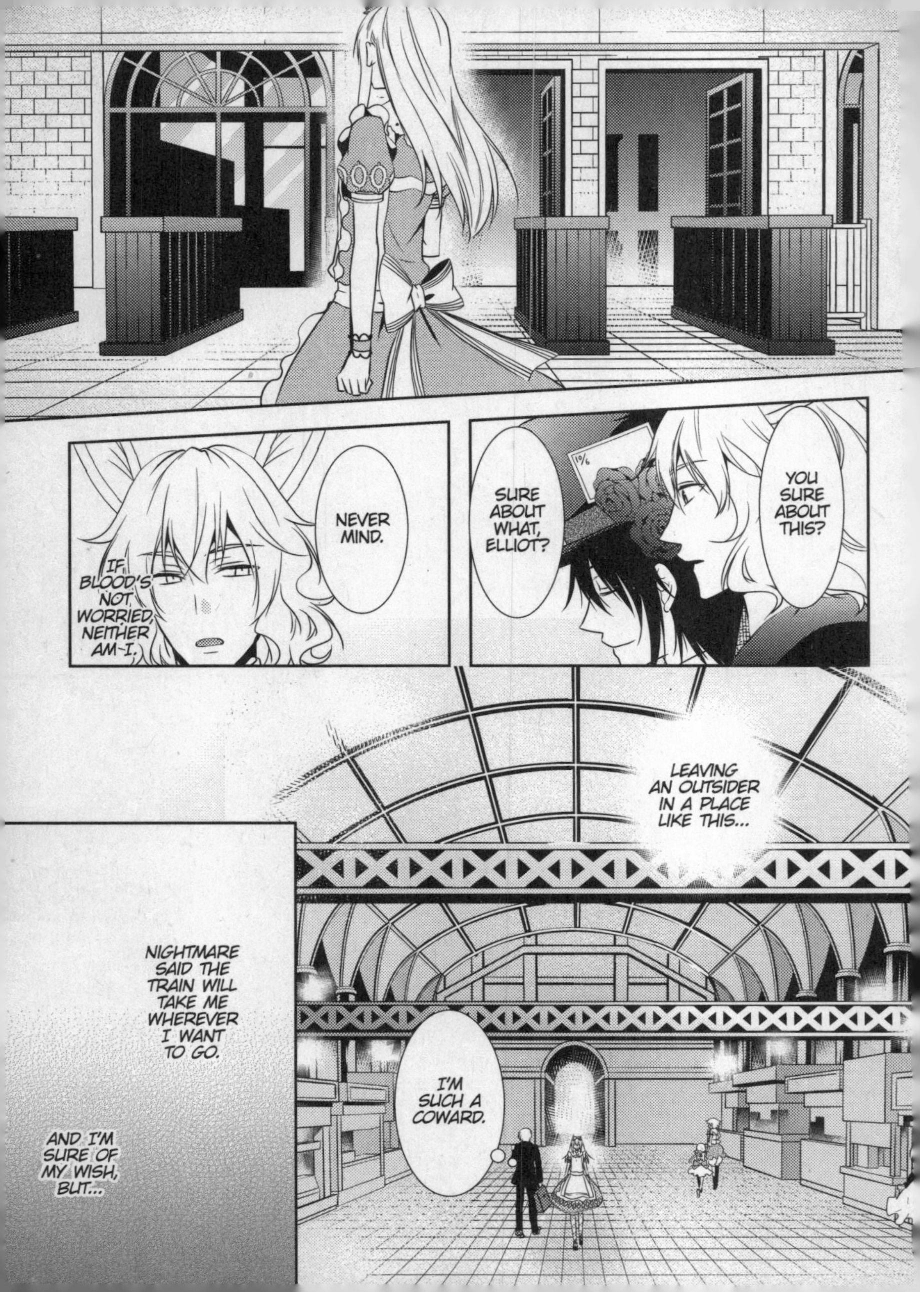
YOU SURE ABOUT THIS?
SURE ABOUT WHAT, ELLIOT?
NEVER MIND.
IF BLOOD'S NOT WORRIED, NEITHER AM I.
LEAVING AN OUTSIDER IN A PLACE LIKE THIS...
I'M SUCH A COWARD.
NIGHTMARE SAID THE TRAIN WILL TAKE ME WHEREVER I WANT TO GO.
AND I'M SURE OF MY WISH, BUT...

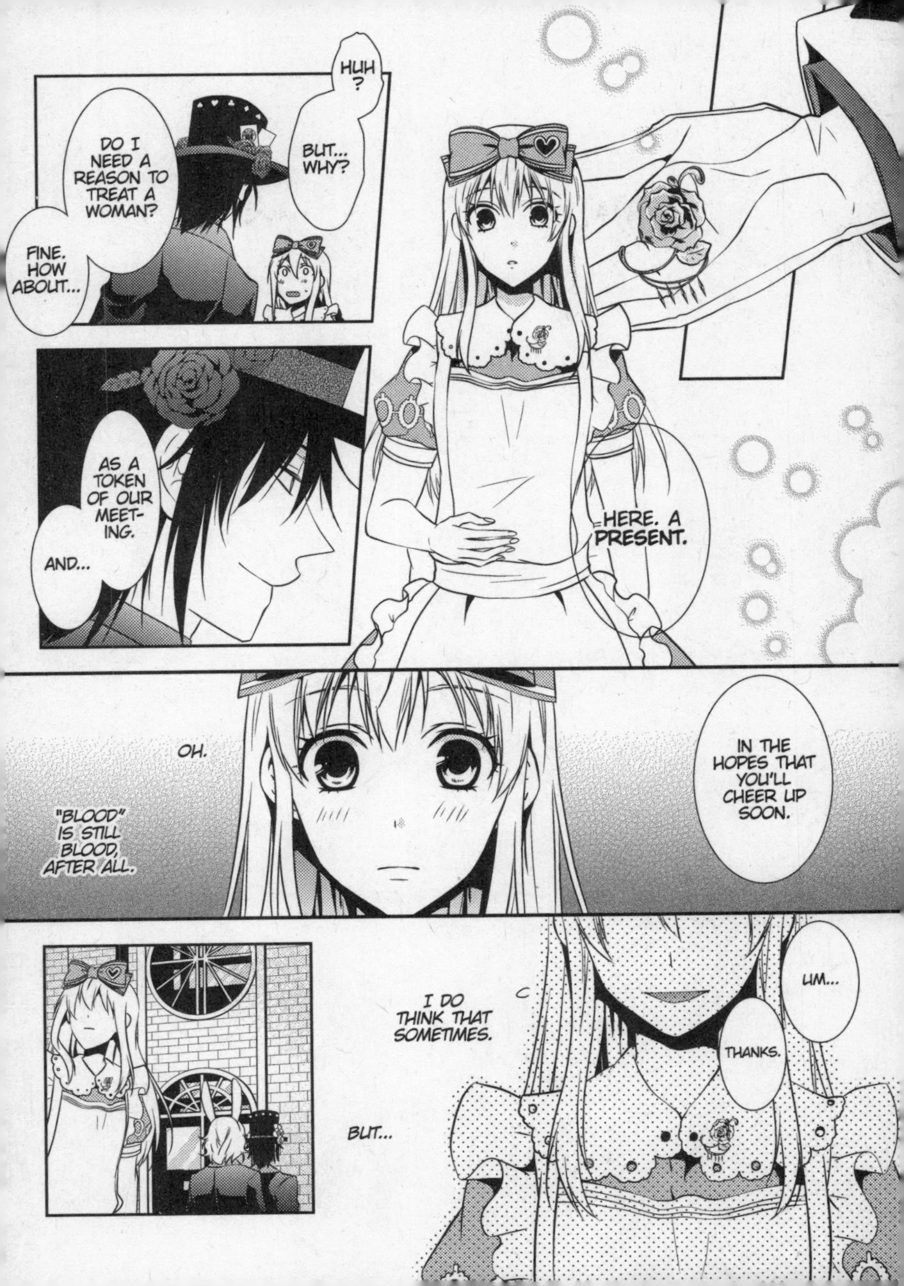
HERE. A PRESENT.
HUH?
BUT... WHY?
DO I NEED A REASON TO TREAT A WOMAN?
FINE. HOW ABOUT...
AS A TOKEN OF OUR MEET-ING.
AND...
IN THE HOPES THAT YOU'LL CHEER UP SOON.
OH.
"BLOOD" IS STILL BLOOD, AFTER ALL.
UM...
THANKS.
I DO THINK THAT SOMETIMES.
BUT...

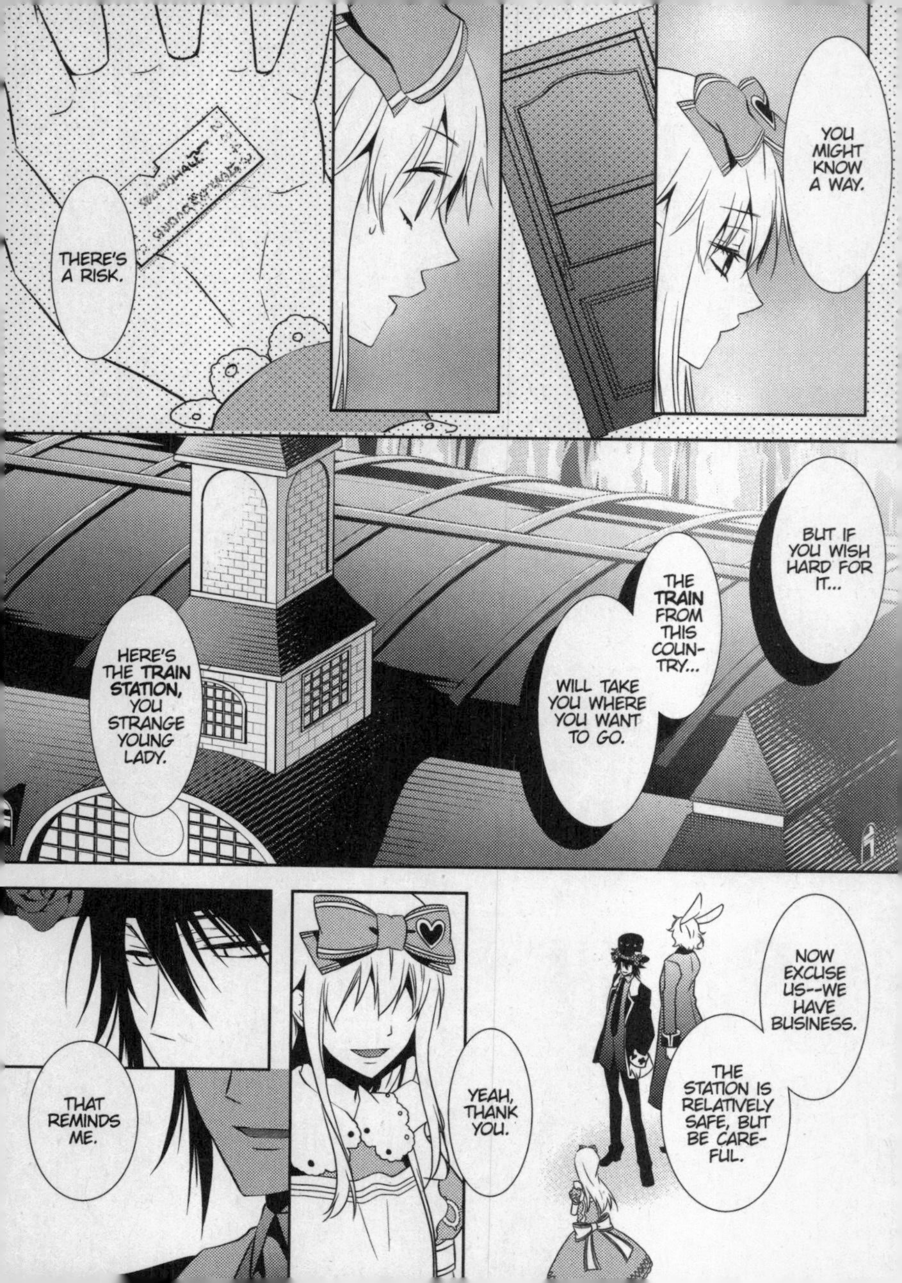
YOU MIGHT KNOW A WAY.
THERE'S A RISK.
BUT IF YOU WISH HARD FOR IT...
THE TRAIN FROM THIS COUN-TRY...
WILL TAKE YOU WHERE YOU WANT TO GO.
HERE'S THE TRAIN STATION, YOU STRANGE YOUNG LADY.
NOW EXCUSE US--WE HAVE BUSINESS.
THE STATION IS RELATIVELY SAFE, BUT BE CARE-FUL.
YEAH, THANK YOU.
THAT REMINDS ME.

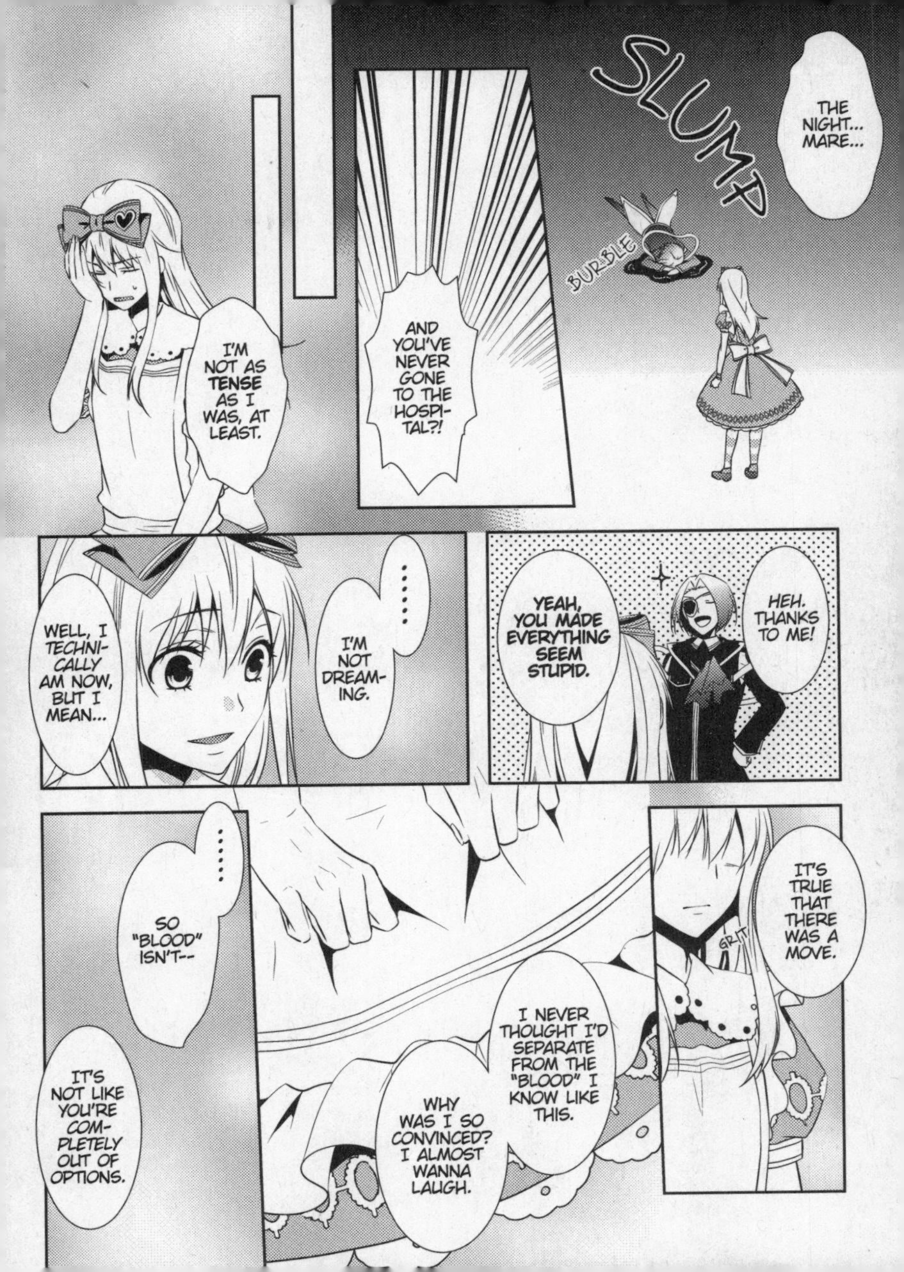
THE NIGHT... MARE...
SLUMP
BURBLE
AND YOU'VE NEVER GONE TO THE HOSPITAL?!
I'M NOT AS TENSE AS I WAS, AT LEAST.
HEH. THANKS TO ME!
YEAH, YOU MADE EVERYTHING SEEM STUPID.
......
I'M NOT DREAMING.
WELL, I TECHNICALLY AM NOW, BUT I MEAN...
IT'S TRUE THAT THERE WAS A MOVE.
GRIT
I NEVER THOUGHT I'D SEPARATE FROM THE "BLOOD" I KNOW LIKE THIS.
WHY WAS I SO CONVINCED? I ALMOST WANNA LAUGH.
......
SO "BLOOD" ISN'T--
IT'S NOT LIKE YOU'RE COMPLETELY OUT OF OPTIONS.

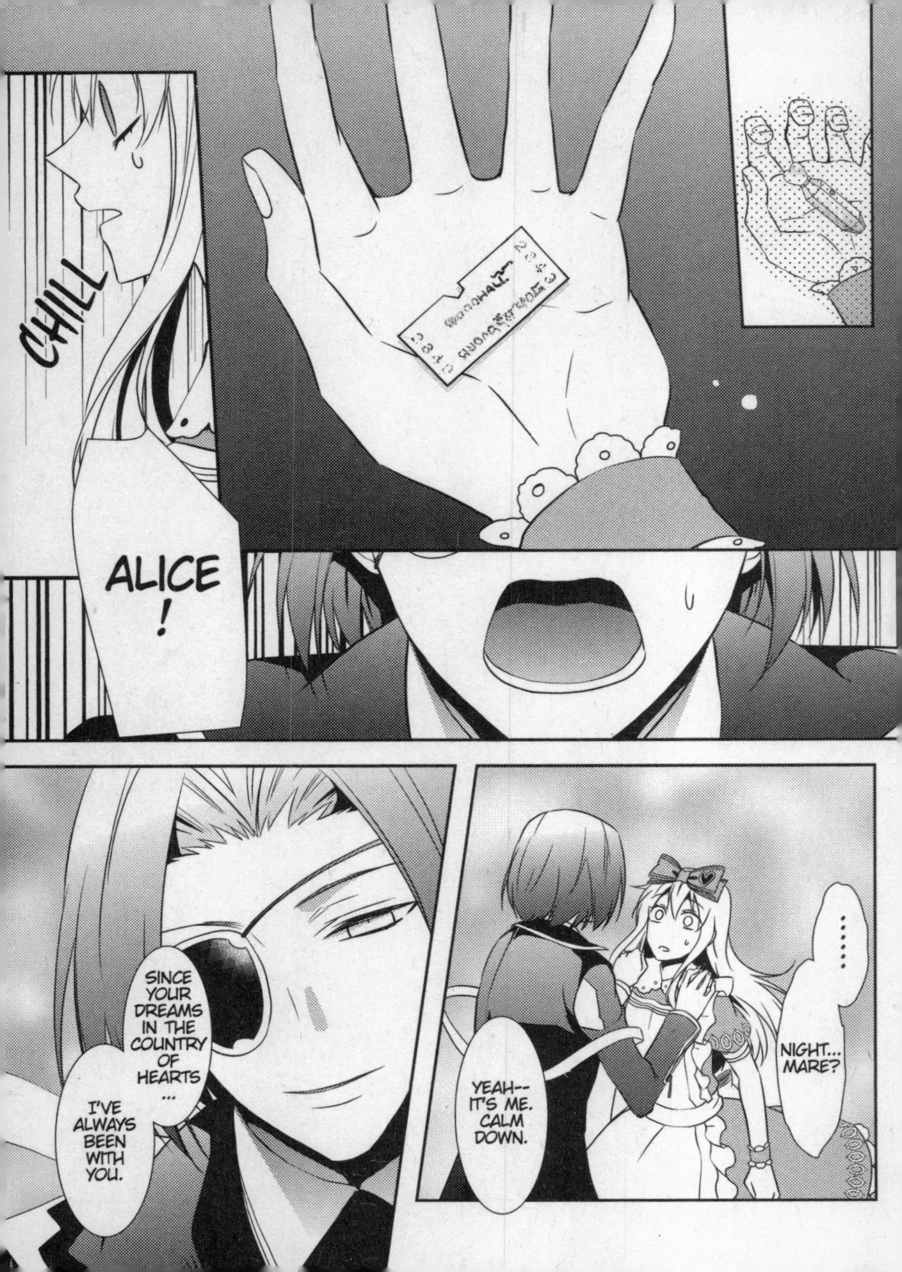
CHILL
ALICE!
......
NIGHT... MARE?
YEAH-- IT'S ME. CALM DOWN.
SINCE YOUR DREAMS IN THE COUNTRY OF HEARTS...
I'VE ALWAYS BEEN WITH YOU.

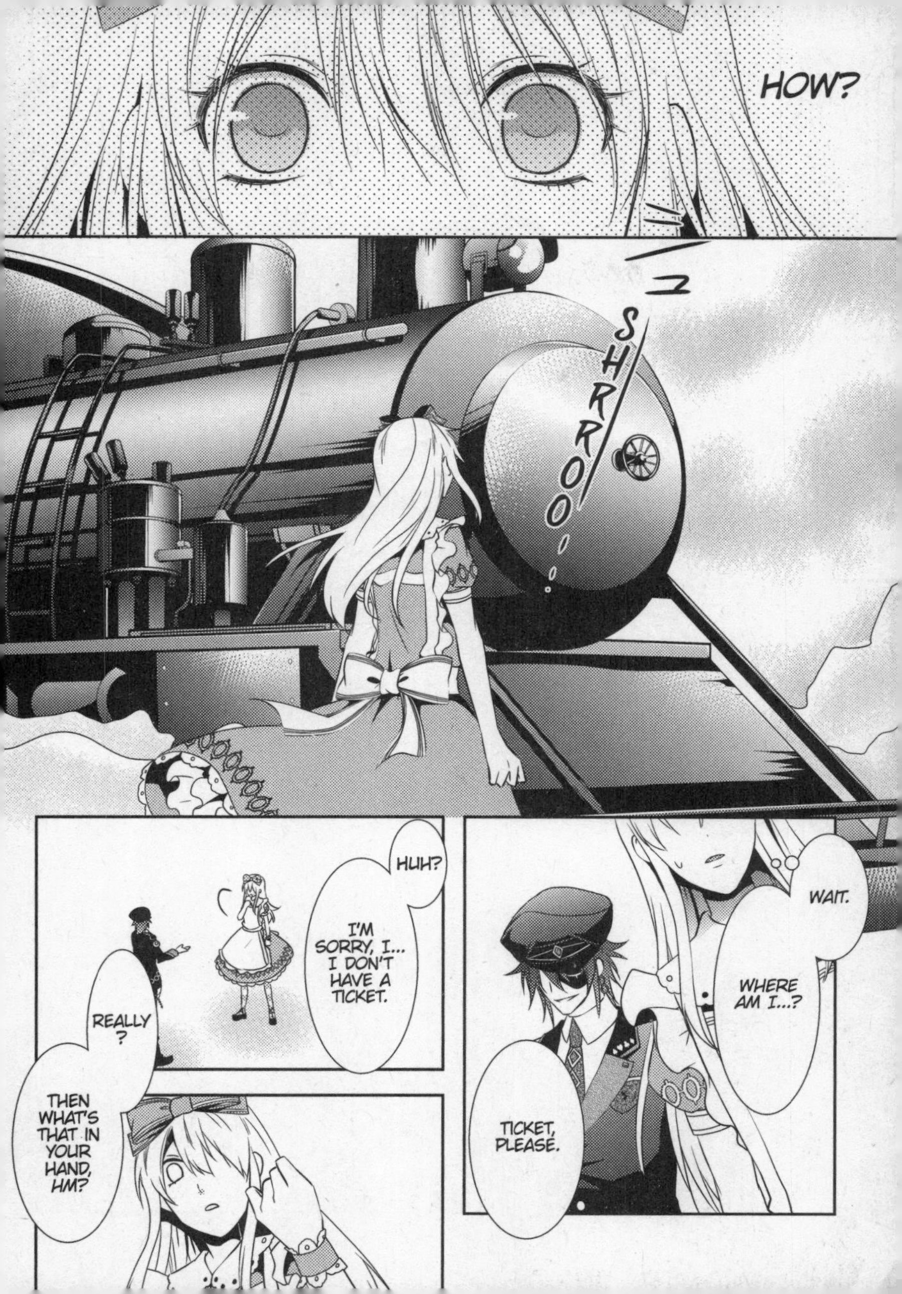
HOW?
SHRROOOOO...
WAIT.
WHERE AM I...?
TICKET, PLEASE.
HUH?
I'M SORRY, I... I DON'T HAVE A TICKET.
REALLY?
THEN WHAT'S THAT IN YOUR HAND, HM?

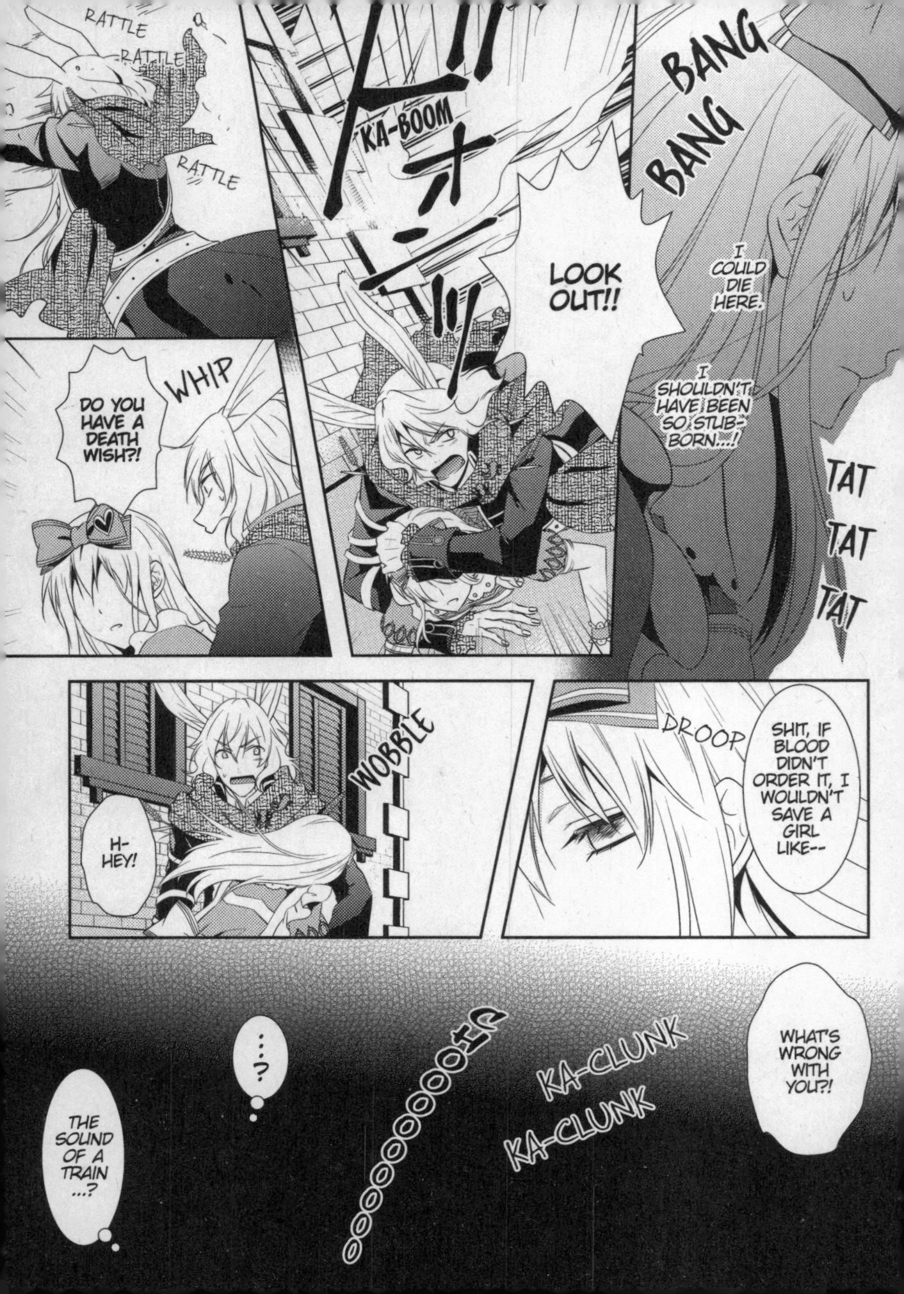
BANG
BANG
I COULD DIE HERE.
I SHOULDN'T HAVE BEEN SO STUB-BORN...!
TAT
TAT
TAT
KA-BOOM
LOOK OUT!!
RATTLE
RATTLE
RATTLE
WHIP
DO YOU HAVE A DEATH WISH?!
DROOP
SHIT, IF BLOOD DIDN'T ORDER IT, I WOULDN'T SAVE A GIRL LIKE--
WOBBLE
H-HEY!
WHAT'S WRONG WITH YOU?!
KA-CLUNK
KA-CLUNK
...?
OOOOOOOOOOOOOO
THE SOUND OF A TRAIN ...?

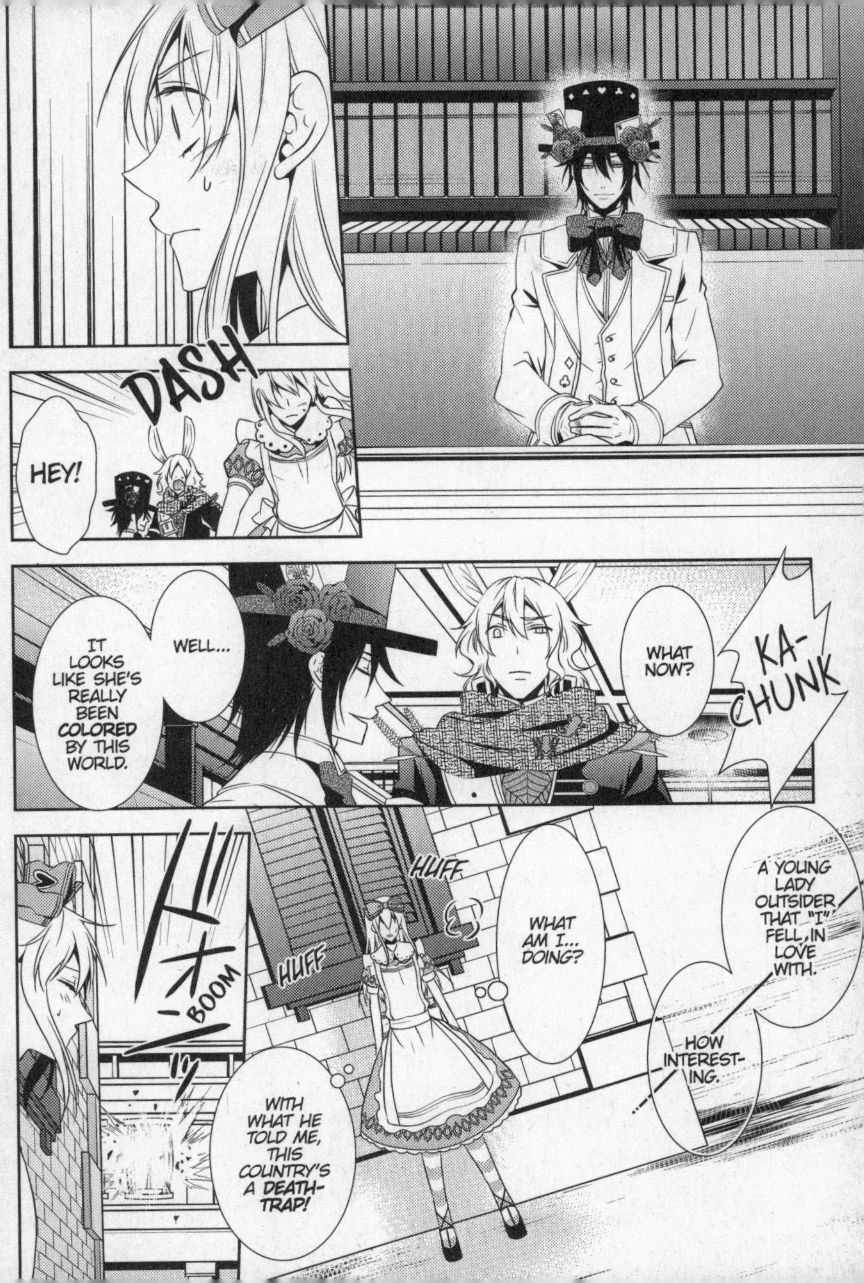
DASH
HEY!
KA-CHUNK
WHAT NOW?
WELL...
IT LOOKS LIKE SHE'S REALLY BEEN COLORED BY THIS WORLD.
A YOUNG LADY OUTSIDER THAT "I" FELL, IN LOVE WITH.
HOW INTEREST-ING.
HUFF
HUFF
WHAT AM I... DOING?
WITH WHAT HE TOLD ME, THIS COUNTRY'S A DEATH-TRAP!
BOOM

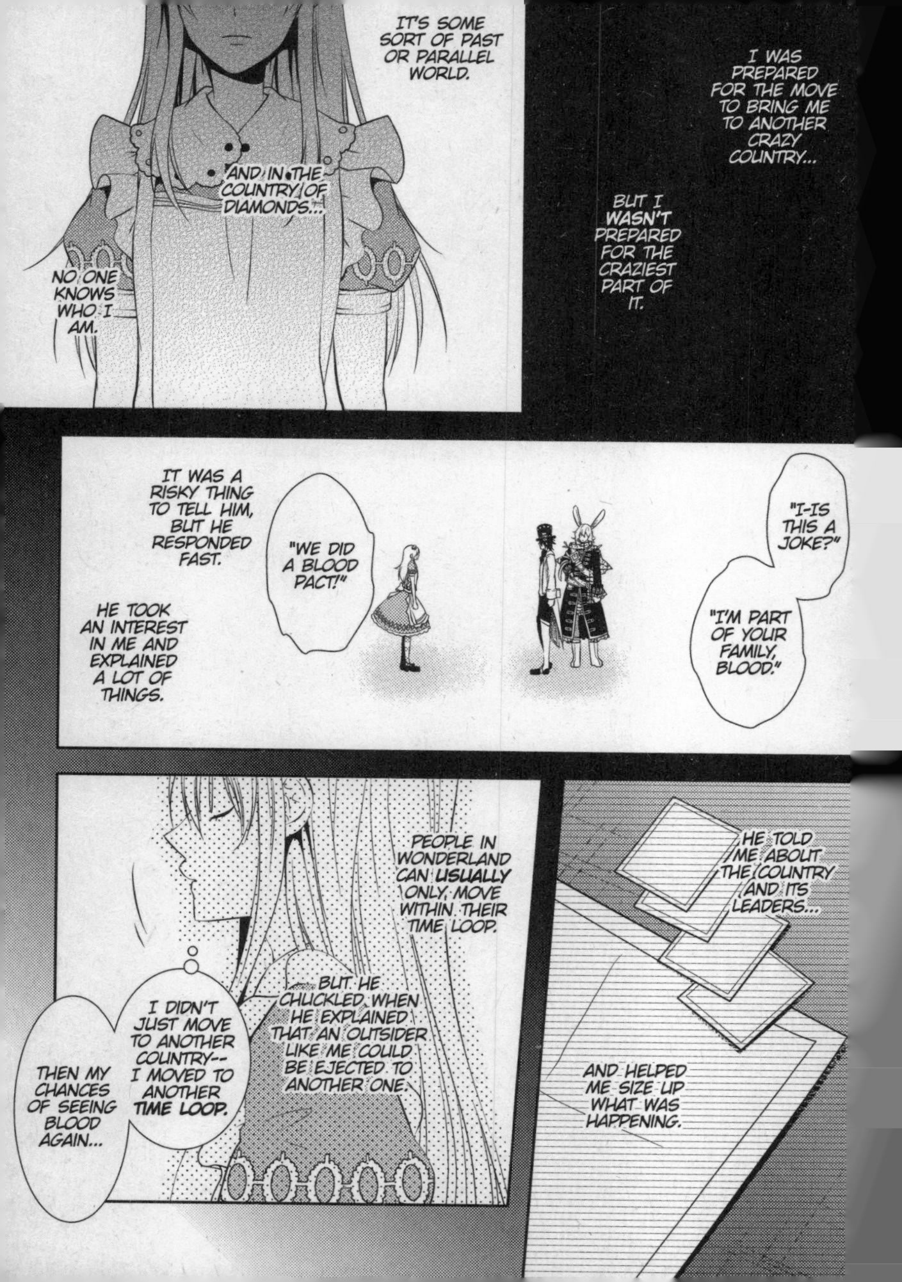
I WAS PREPARED FOR THE MOVE TO BRING ME TO ANOTHER CRAZY COUNTRY...
BUT I WASN'T PREPARED FOR THE CRAZIEST PART OF IT.
IT'S SOME SORT OF PAST OR PARALLEL WORLD.
AND IN THE COUNTRY OF DIAMONDS...
NO ONE KNOWS WHO I AM.
"I-IS THIS A JOKE?"
"I'M PART OF YOUR FAMILY, BLOOD."
"WE DID A BLOOD PACT!"
IT WAS A RISKY THING TO TELL HIM, BUT HE RESPONDED FAST.
HE TOOK AN INTEREST IN ME AND EXPLAINED A LOT OF THINGS.
HE TOLD ME ABOUT THE COUNTRY AND ITS LEADERS...
AND HELPED ME SIZE UP WHAT WAS HAPPENING.
PEOPLE IN WONDERLAND CAN USUALLY ONLY MOVE WITHIN THEIR TIME LOOP.
BUT HE CHUCKLED WHEN HE EXPLAINED THAT AN OUTSIDER LIKE ME COULD BE EJECTED TO ANOTHER ONE.
I DIDN'T JUST MOVE TO ANOTHER COUNTRY-- I MOVED TO ANOTHER TIME LOOP.
THEN MY CHANCES OF SEEING BLOOD AGAIN...

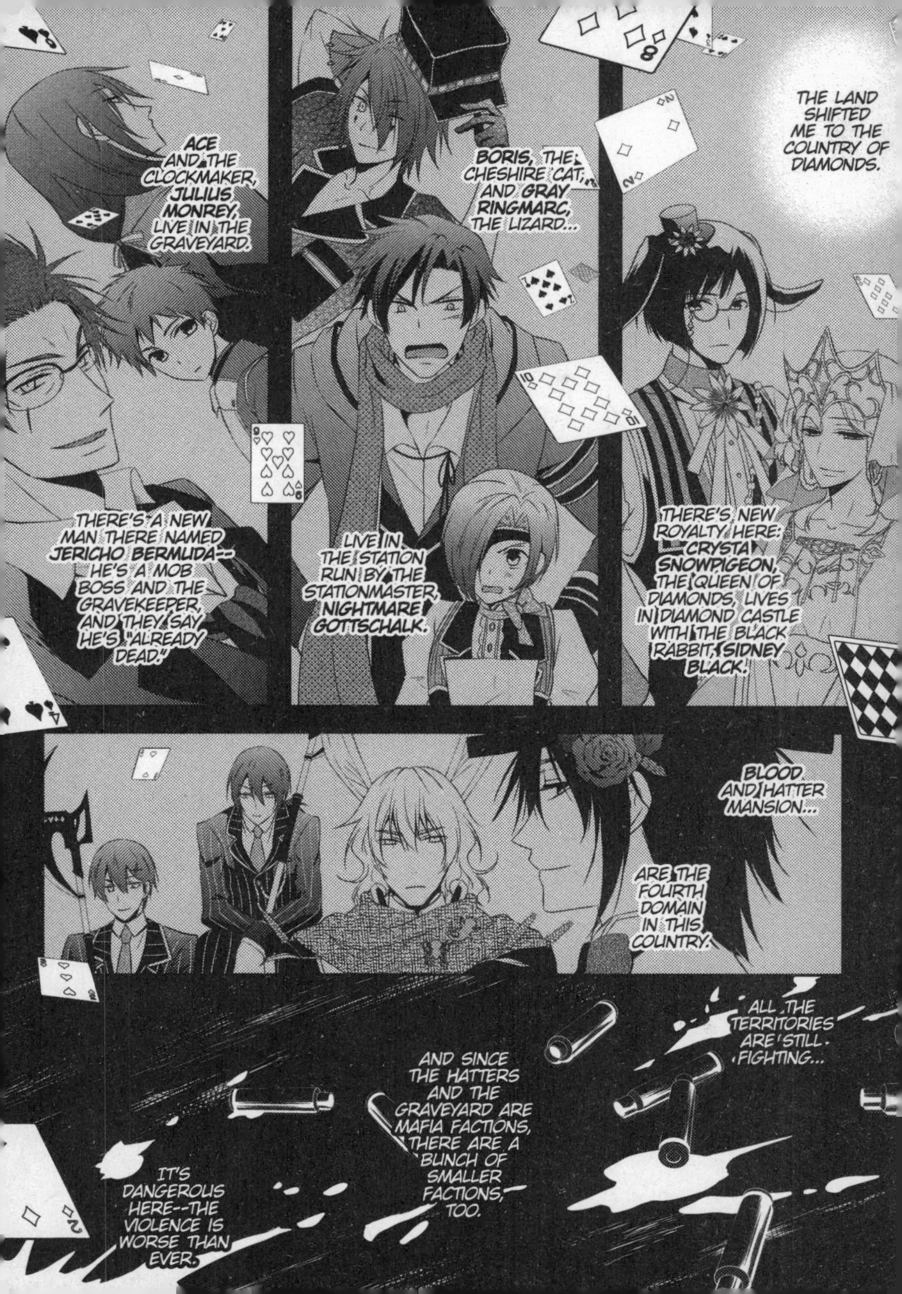
THE LAND SHIFTED ME TO THE COUNTRY OF DIAMONDS.
THERE'S NEW ROYALTY HERE: CRYSTA SNOWPIGEON, THE QUEEN OF DIAMONDS, LIVES IN DIAMOND CASTLE WITH THE BLACK RABBIT, SIDNEY BLACK.
BORIS, THE CHESHIRE CAT, AND GRAY RINGMARC, THE LIZARD...
LIVE IN THE STATION RUN BY THE STATIONMASTER, NIGHTMARE GOTTSCHALK.
ACE AND THE CLOCKMAKER, JULIUS MONREY, LIVE IN THE GRAVEYARD.
THERE'S A NEW MAN THERE NAMED JERICHO BERMUDA--HE'S A MOB BOSS AND THE GRAVEKEEPER, AND THEY SAY HE'S "ALREADY DEAD."
BLOOD AND HATTER MANSION...
ARE THE FOURTH DOMAIN IN THIS COUNTRY.
ALL THE TERRITORIES ARE STILL FIGHTING...
AND SINCE THE HATTERS AND THE GRAVEYARD ARE MAFIA FACTIONS, THERE ARE A BUNCH OF SMALLER FACTIONS, TOO.
IT'S DANGEROUS HERE--THE VIOLENCE IS WORSE THAN EVER.

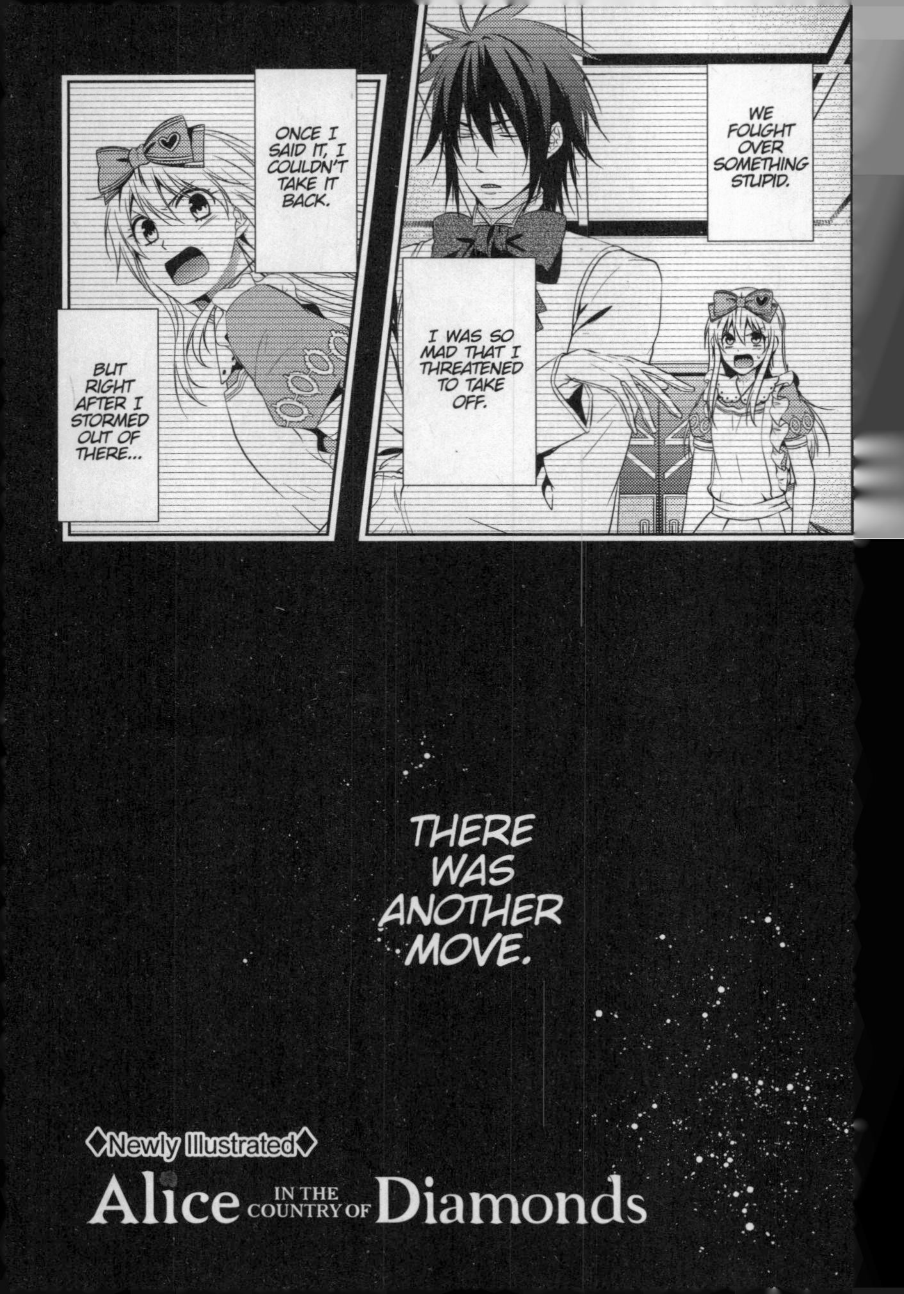
WE FOUGHT OVER SOMETHING STUPID.
I WAS SO MAD THAT I THREATENED TO TAKE OFF.
ONCE I SAID IT, I COULDN'T TAKE IT BACK.
BUT RIGHT AFTER I STORMED OUT OF THERE...
THERE WAS ANOTHER MOVE.
◆Newly Illustrated◆
Alice IN THE COUNTRY OF Diamonds

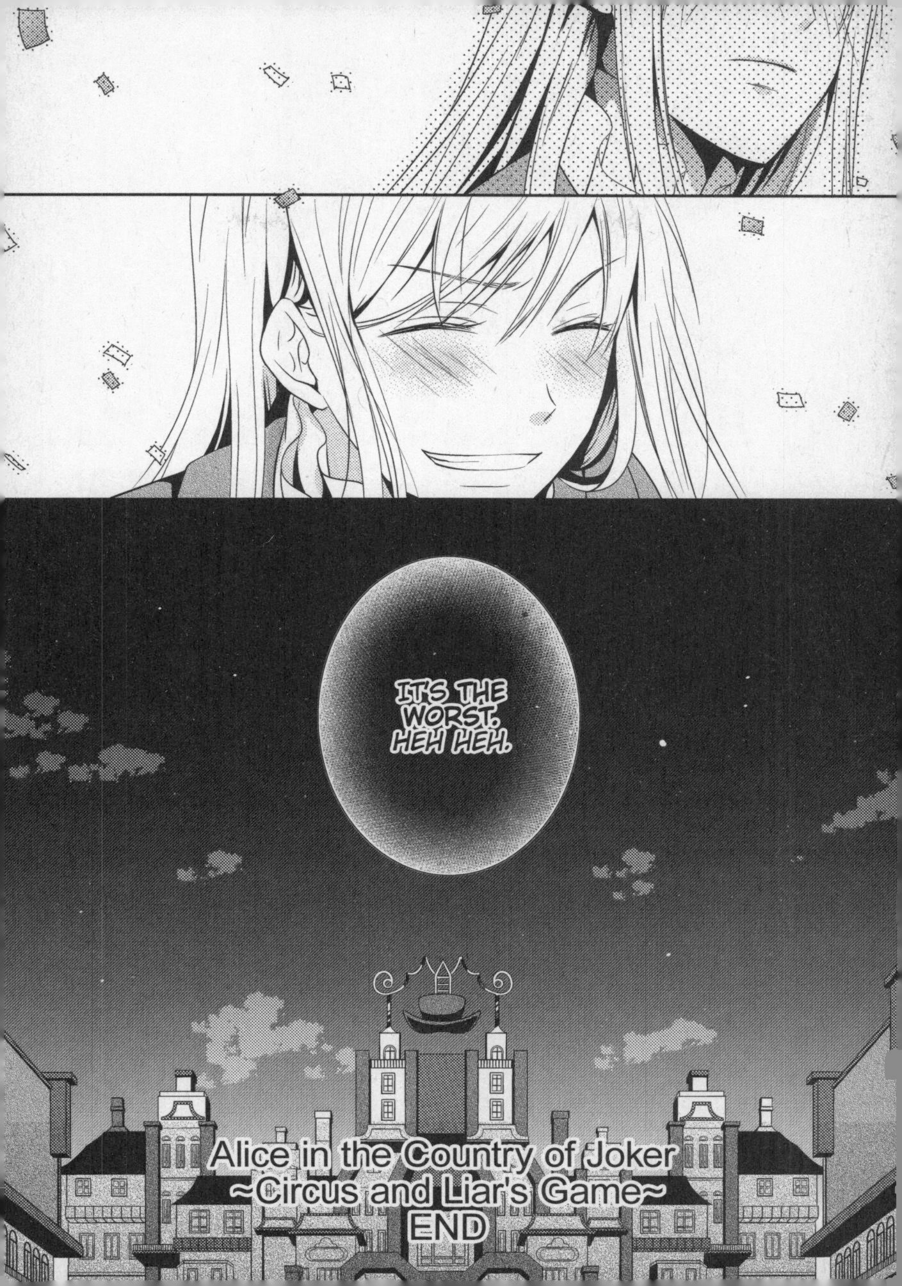
IT'S THE WORST. HEH HEH.
Alice in the Country of Joker
~Circus and Liar's Game~
END

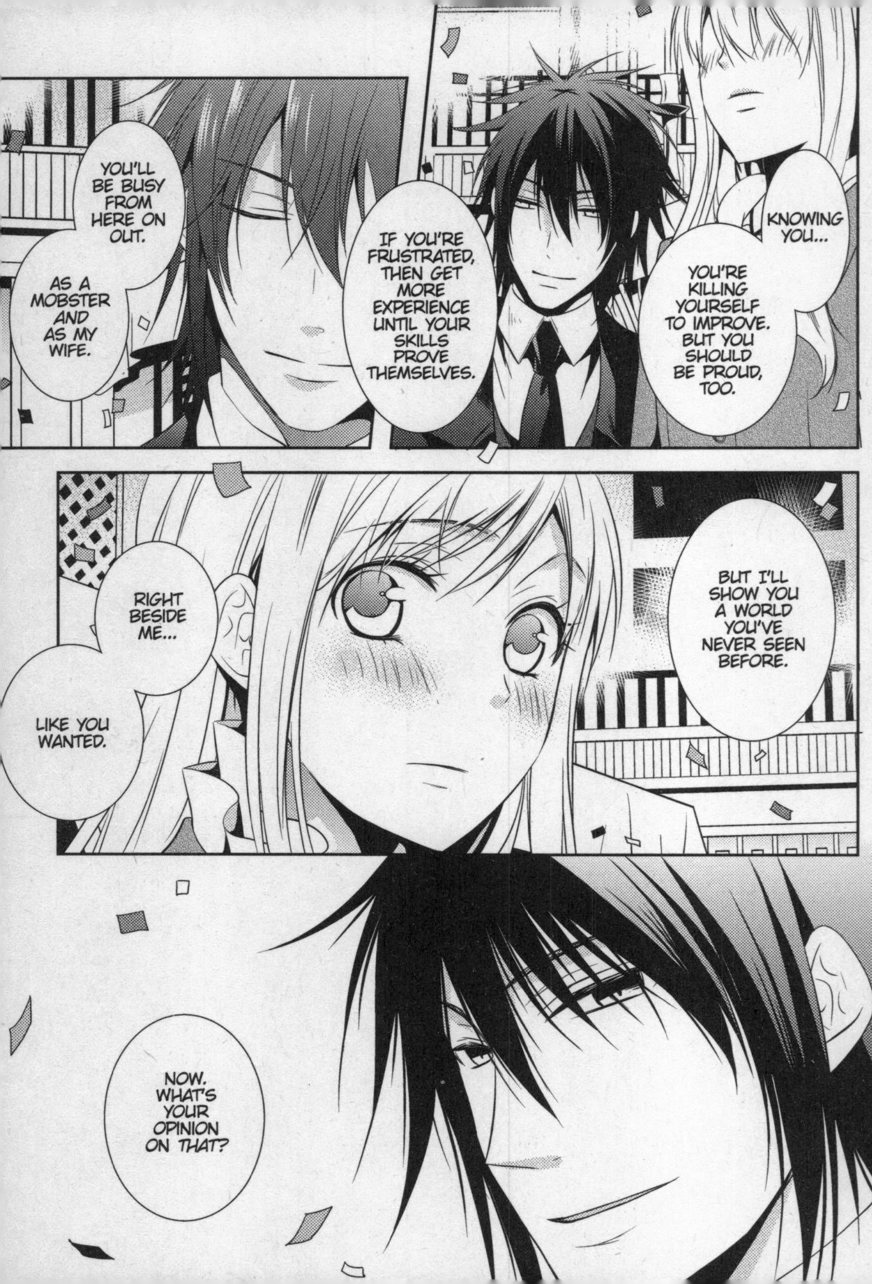
KNOWING YOU...
YOU'RE KILLING YOURSELF TO IMPROVE. BUT YOU SHOULD BE PROUD, TOO.
IF YOU'RE FRUSTRATED, THEN GET MORE EXPERIENCE UNTIL YOUR SKILLS PROVE THEMSELVES.
YOU'LL BE BUSY FROM HERE ON OUT.
AS A MOBSTER AND AS MY WIFE.
BUT I'LL SHOW YOU A WORLD YOU'VE NEVER SEEN BEFORE.
RIGHT BESIDE ME...
LIKE YOU WANTED.
NOW. WHAT'S YOUR OPINION ON THAT?

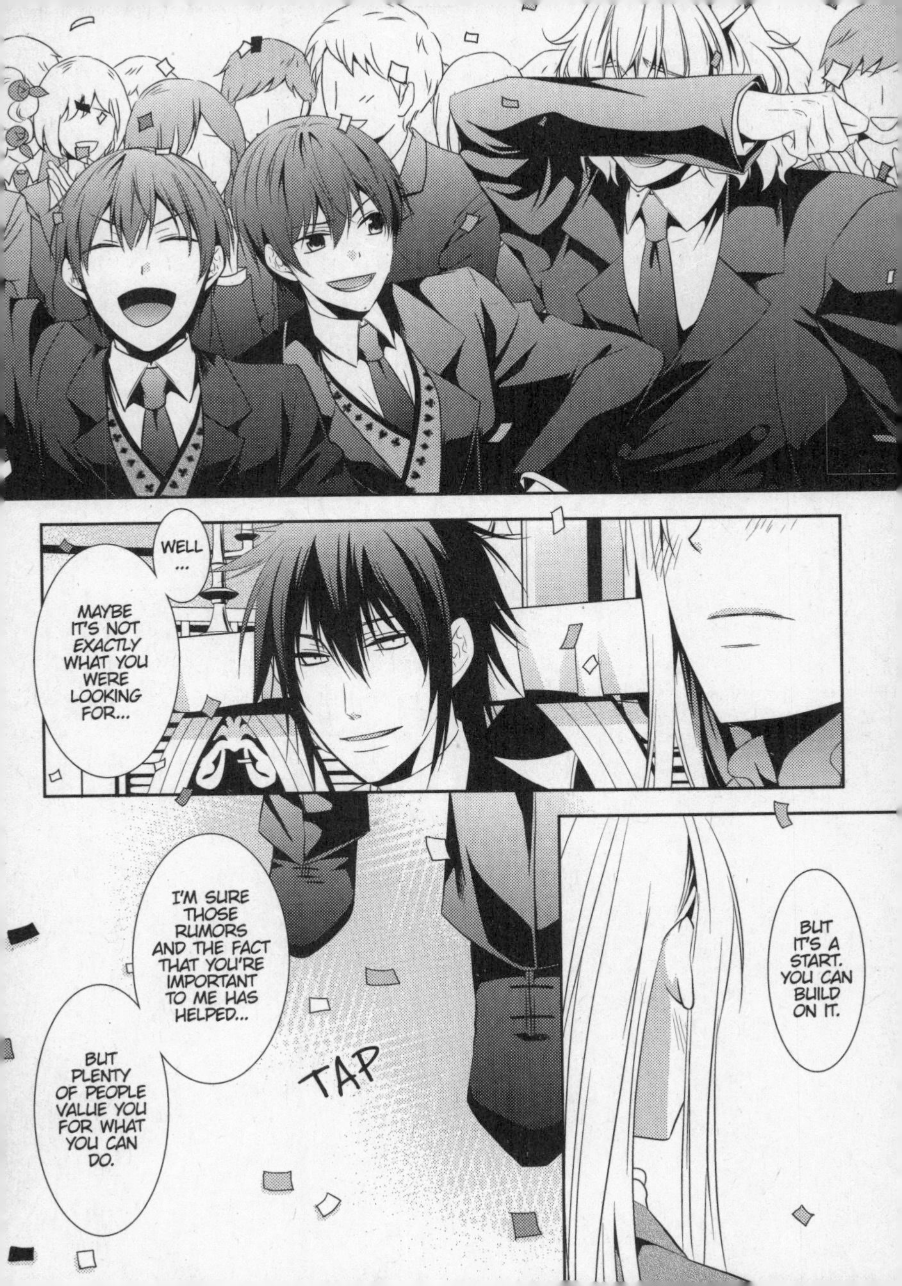
WELL ...
MAYBE IT'S NOT EXACTLY WHAT YOU WERE LOOKING FOR...
BUT IT'S A START. YOU CAN BUILD ON IT.
I'M SURE THOSE RUMORS AND THE FACT THAT YOU'RE IMPORTANT TO ME HAS HELPED...
BUT PLENTY OF PEOPLE VALUE YOU FOR WHAT YOU CAN DO.
TAP

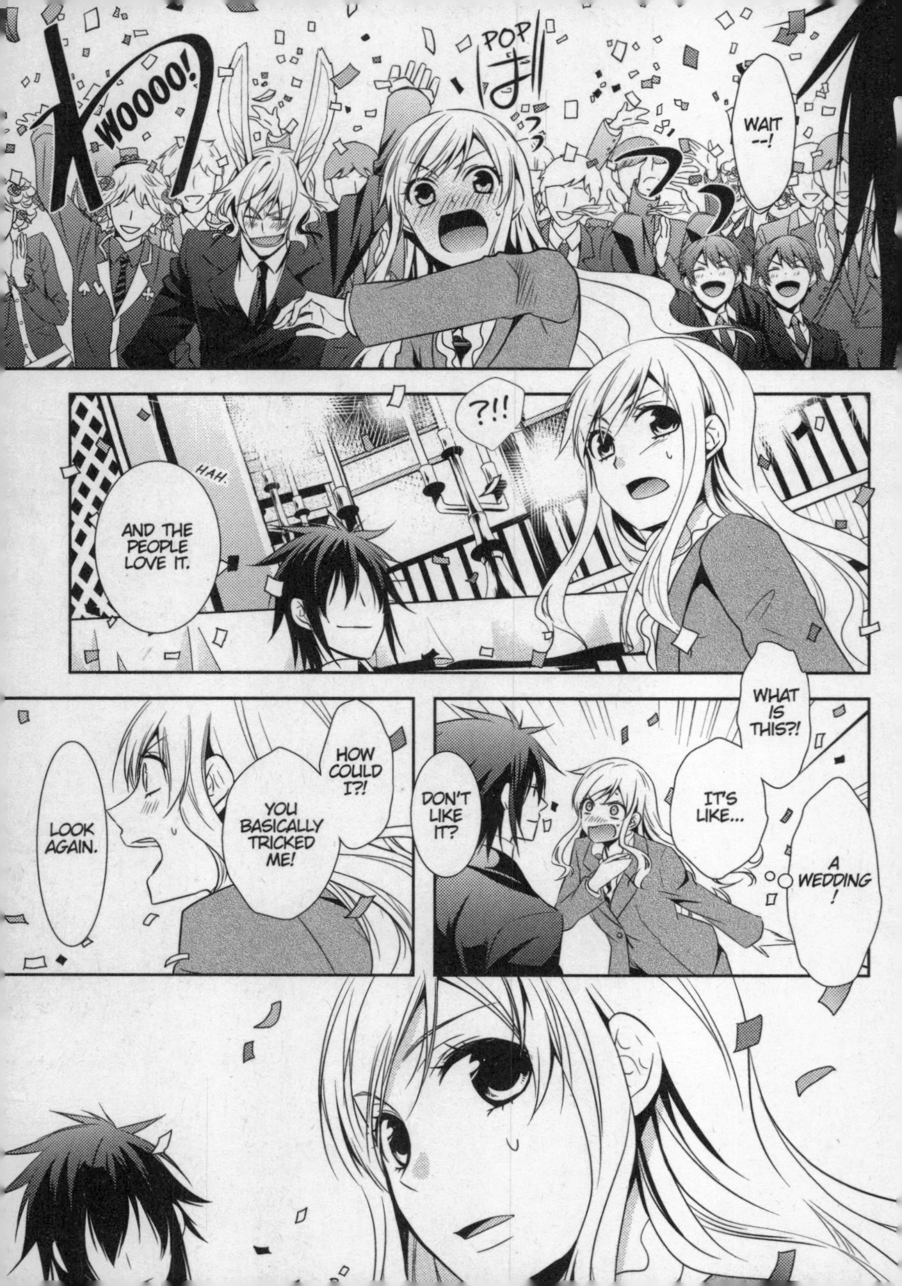
WAIT --!
POP
ぱ
WOOOO!
?!!
HAH.
AND THE PEOPLE LOVE IT.
WHAT IS THIS?!
IT'S LIKE...
A WEDDING!
DON'T LIKE IT?
HOW COULD I?!
YOU BASICALLY TRICKED ME!
LOOK AGAIN.

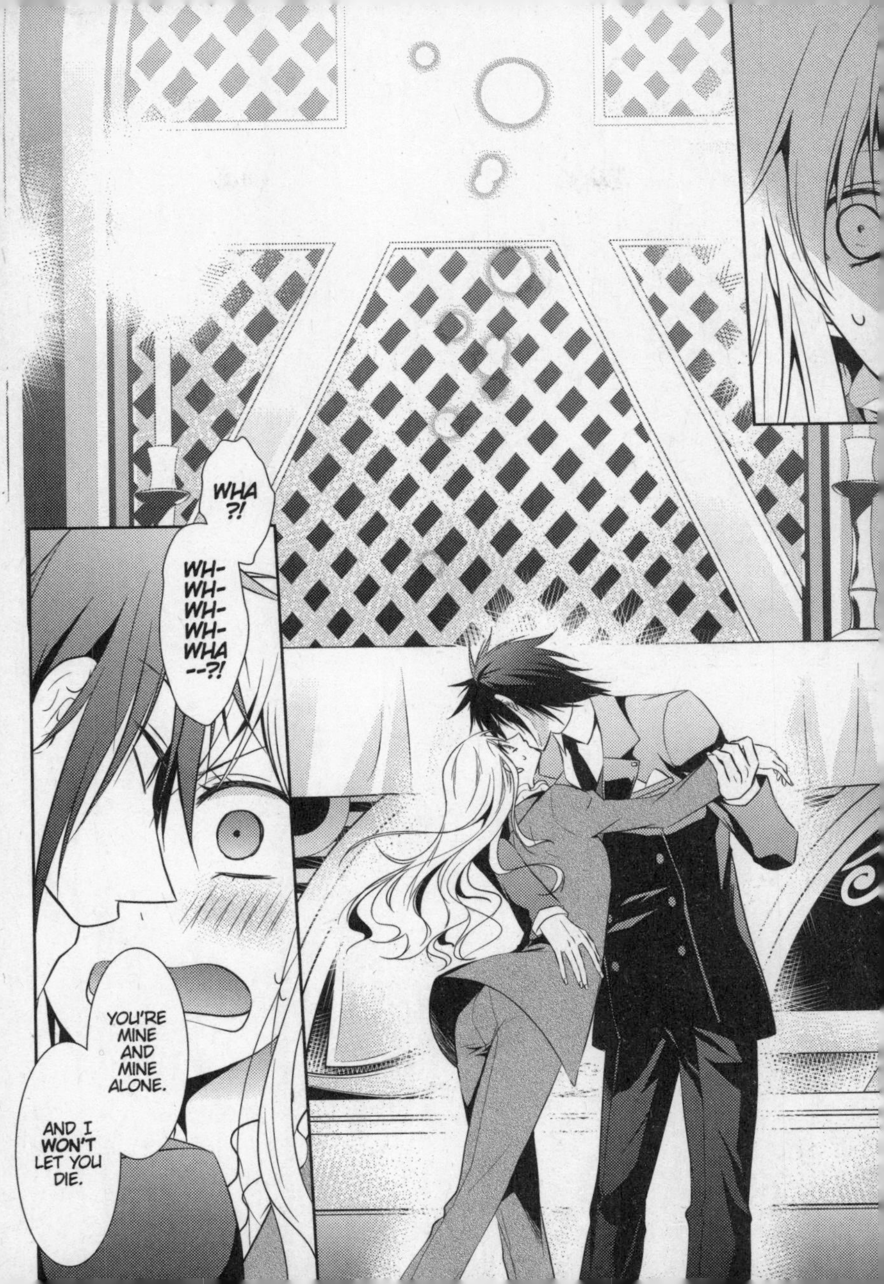
WHA ?!
WH-WH-WH-WH-WHA--?!
YOU'RE MINE AND MINE ALONE.
AND I WON'T LET YOU DIE.

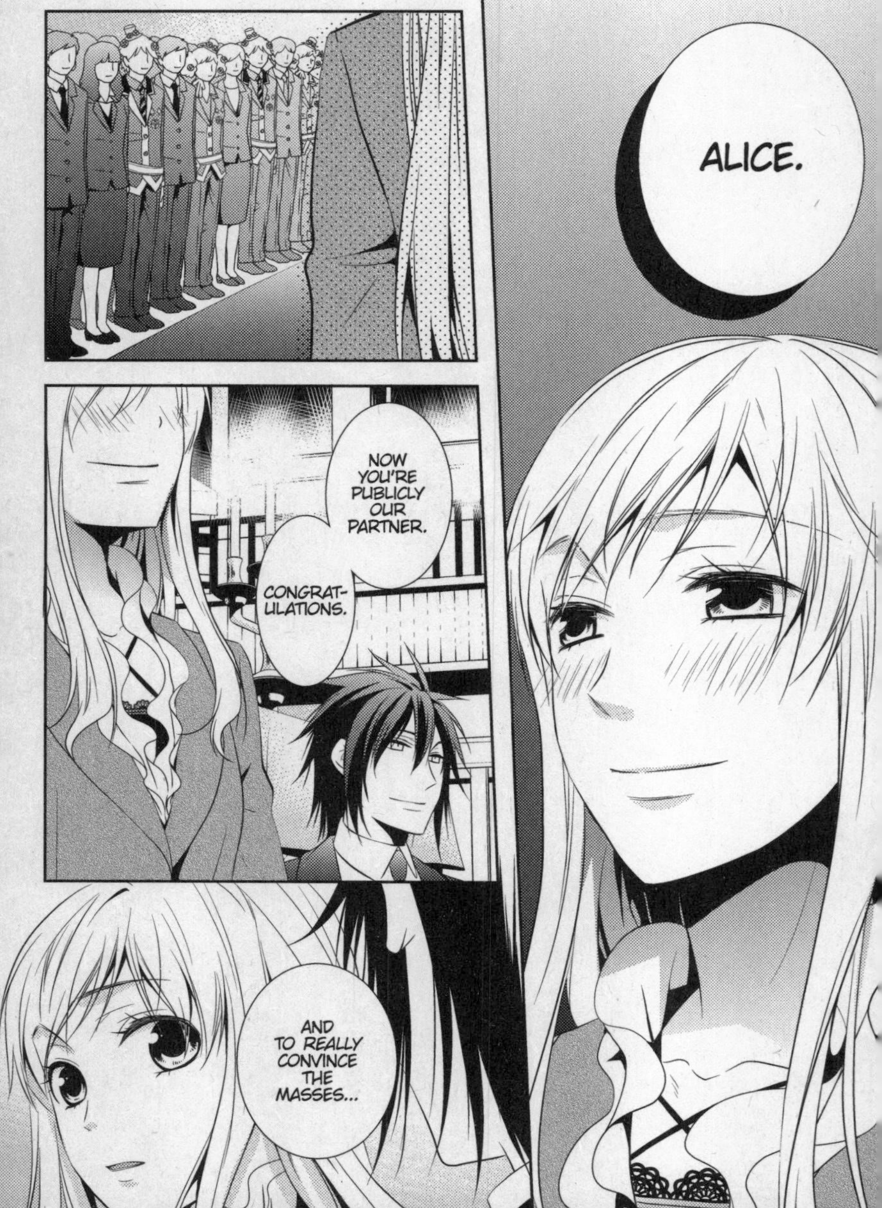
ALICE.
NOW YOU'RE PUBLICLY OUR PARTNER.
CONGRAT-ULATIONS.
AND TO REALLY CONVINCE THE MASSES...

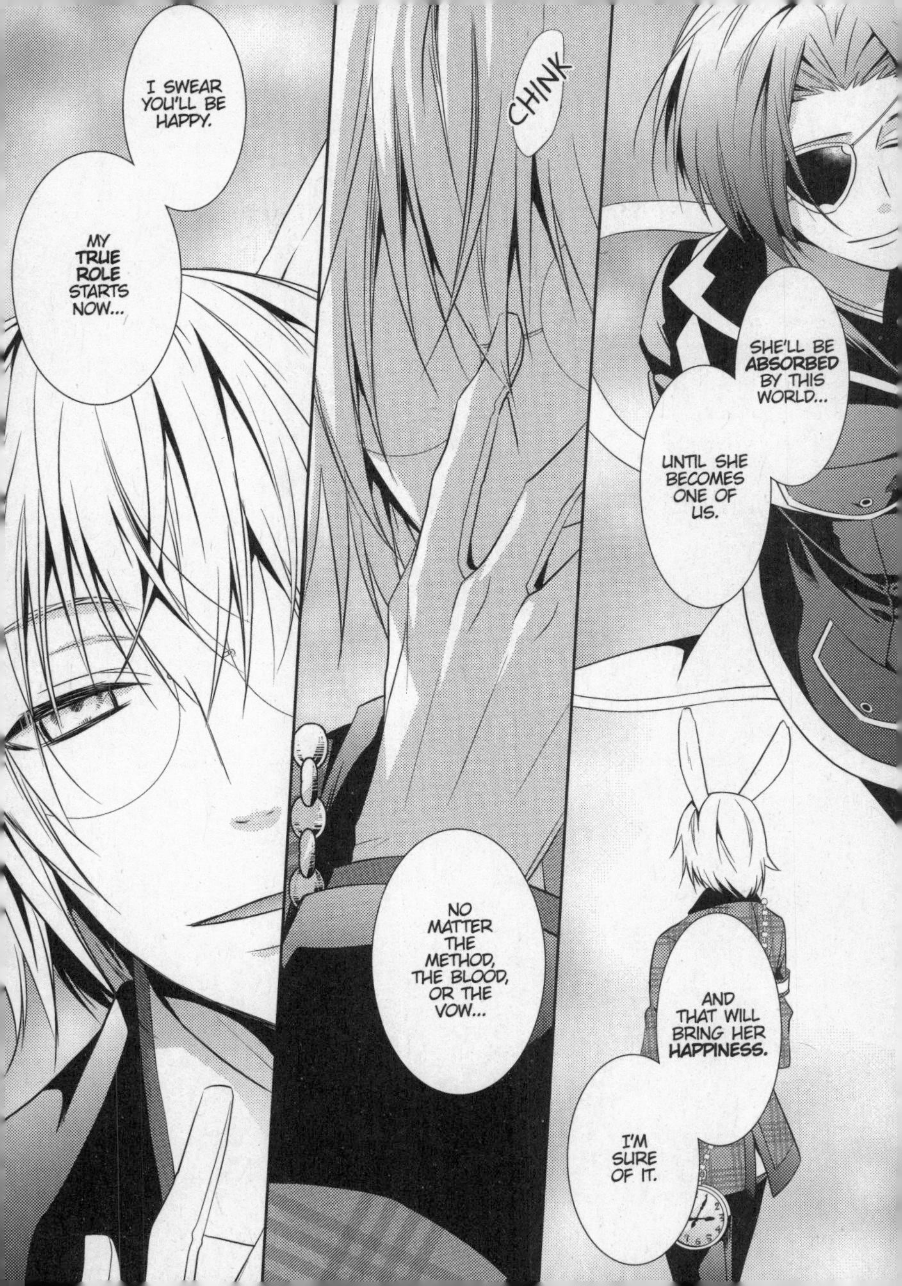
SHE'LL BE ABSORBED BY THIS WORLD...
UNTIL SHE BECOMES ONE OF US.
AND THAT WILL BRING HER HAPPINESS.
I'M SURE OF IT.
CHINK
NO MATTER THE METHOD, THE BLOOD, OR THE VOW...
I SWEAR YOU'LL BE HAPPY.
MY TRUE ROLE STARTS NOW...

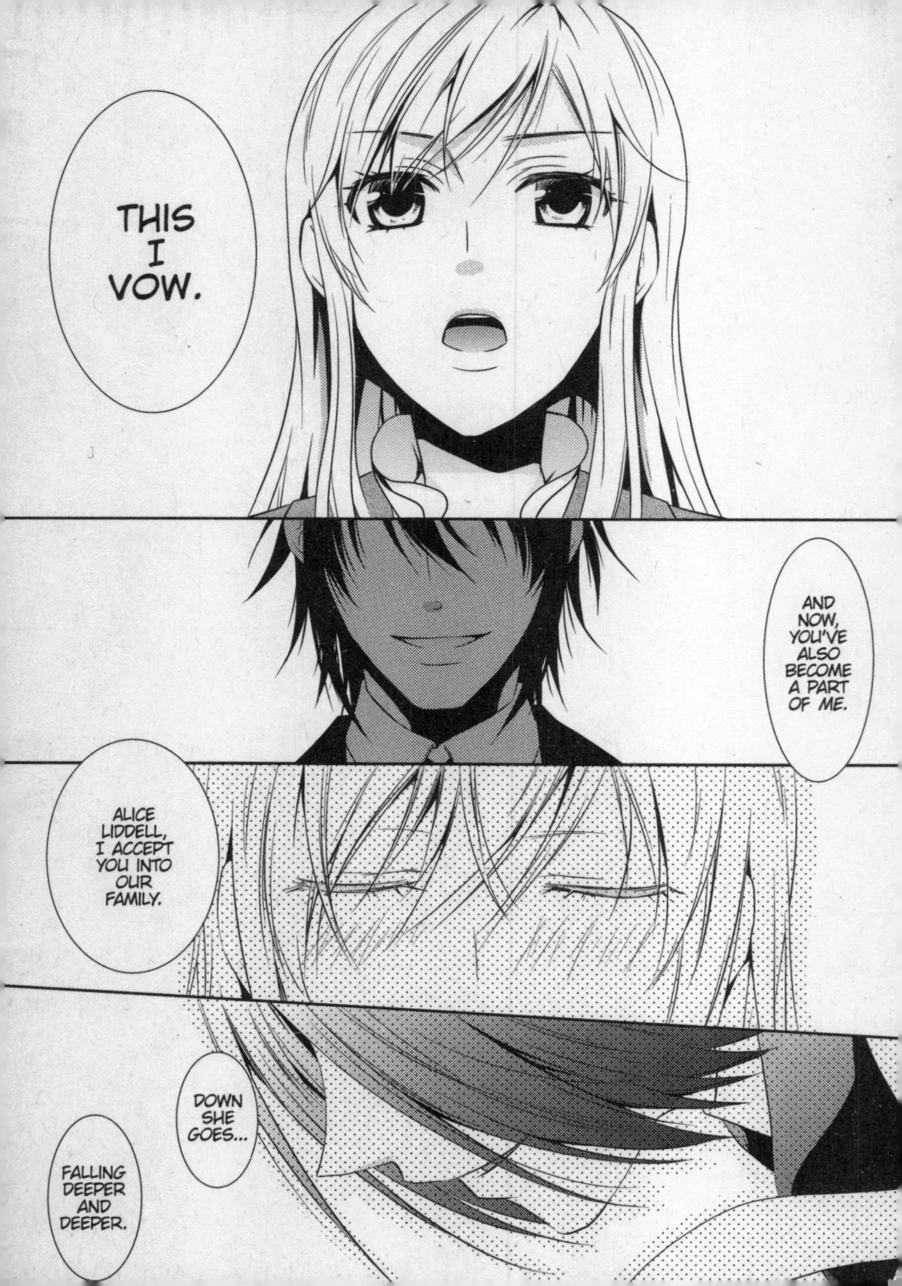
THIS I VOW.
AND NOW, YOU'VE ALSO BECOME A PART OF ME.
ALICE LIDDELL, I ACCEPT YOU INTO OUR FAMILY.
DOWN SHE GOES...
FALLING DEEPER AND DEEPER.

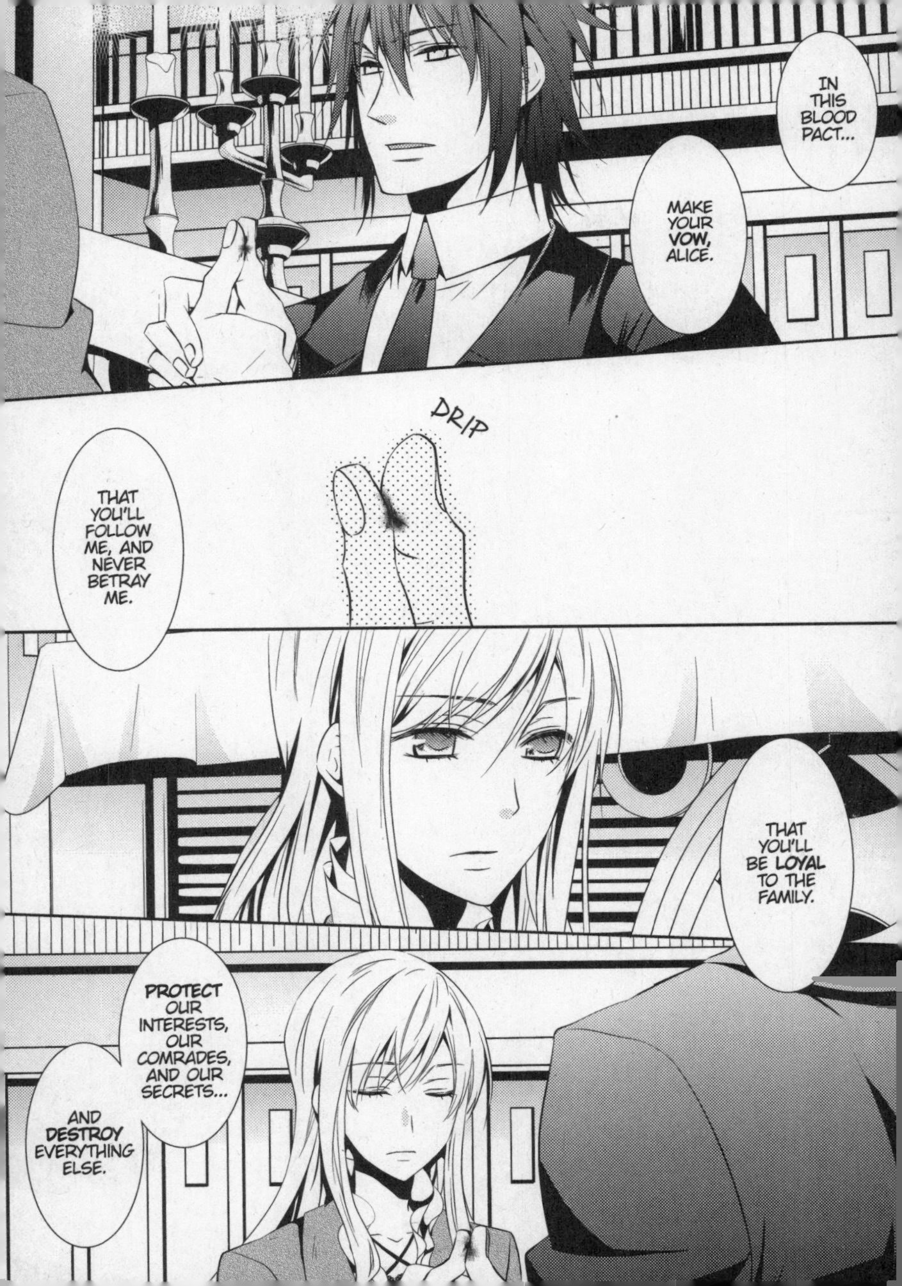
IN THIS BLOOD PACT...
MAKE YOUR VOW, ALICE.
DRIP
THAT YOU'LL FOLLOW ME, AND NEVER BETRAY ME.
THAT YOU'LL BE LOYAL TO THE FAMILY.
PROTECT OUR INTERESTS, OUR COMRADES, AND OUR SECRETS...
AND DESTROY EVERYTHING ELSE.

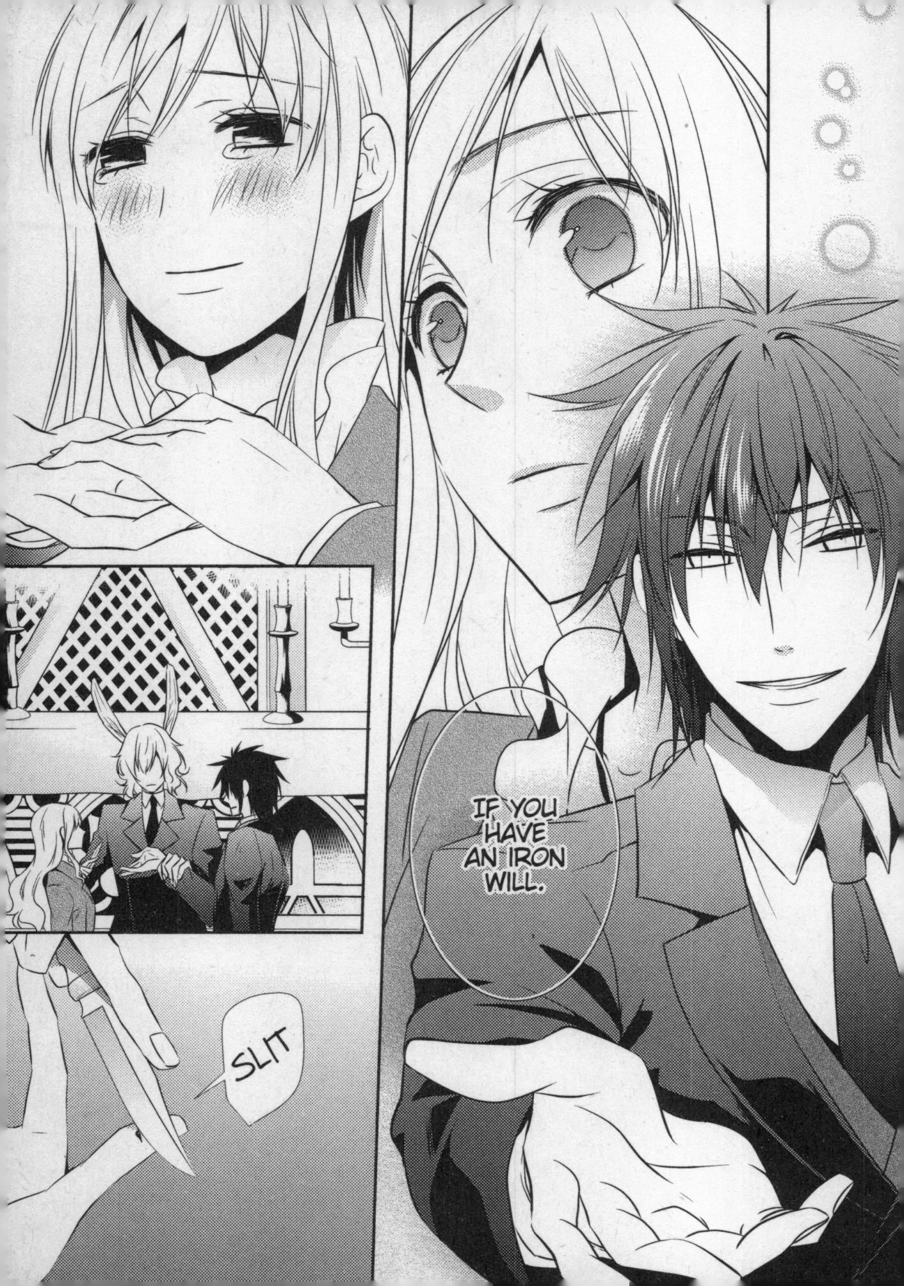
IF YOU HAVE AN IRON WILL.
SLIT

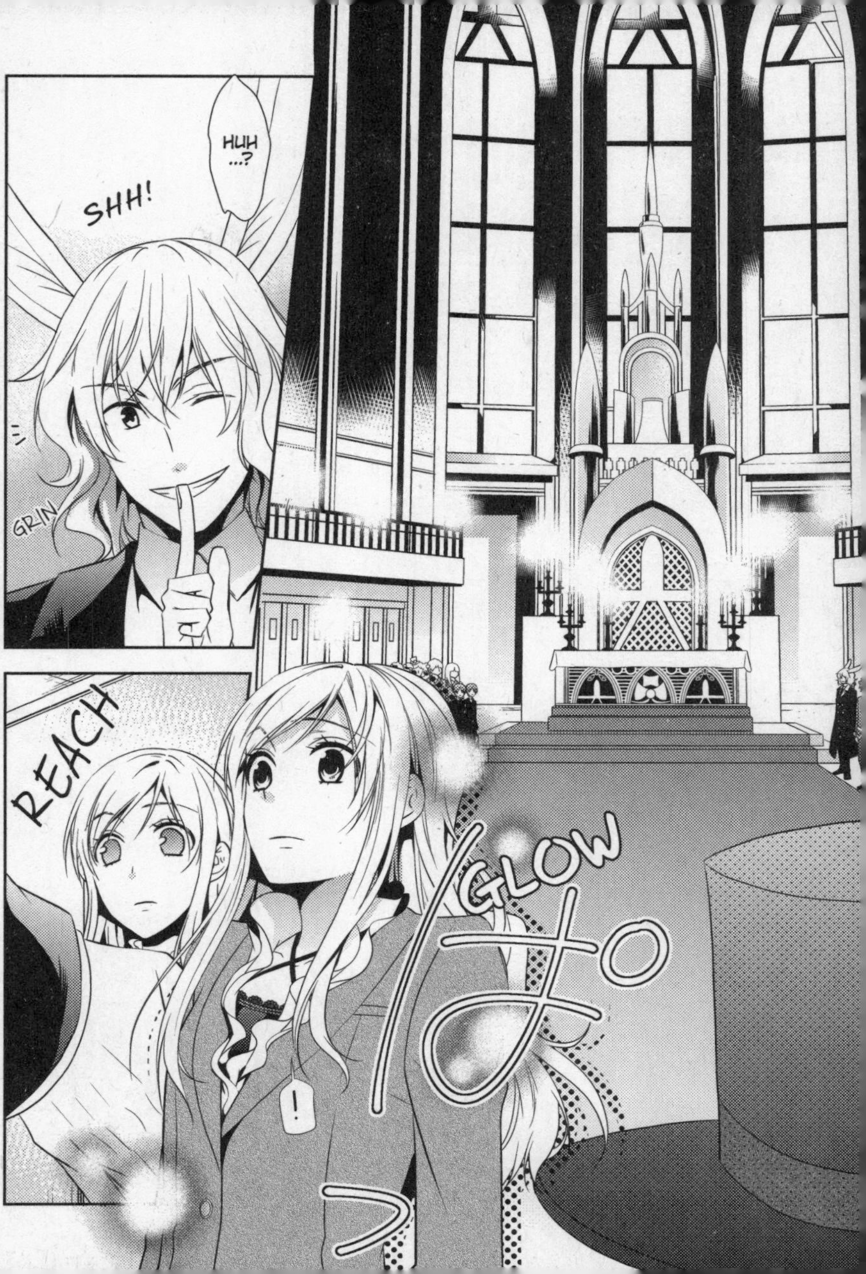
HUH ...?
SHH!
GRIN
GLOW
ぽっ
!
REACH

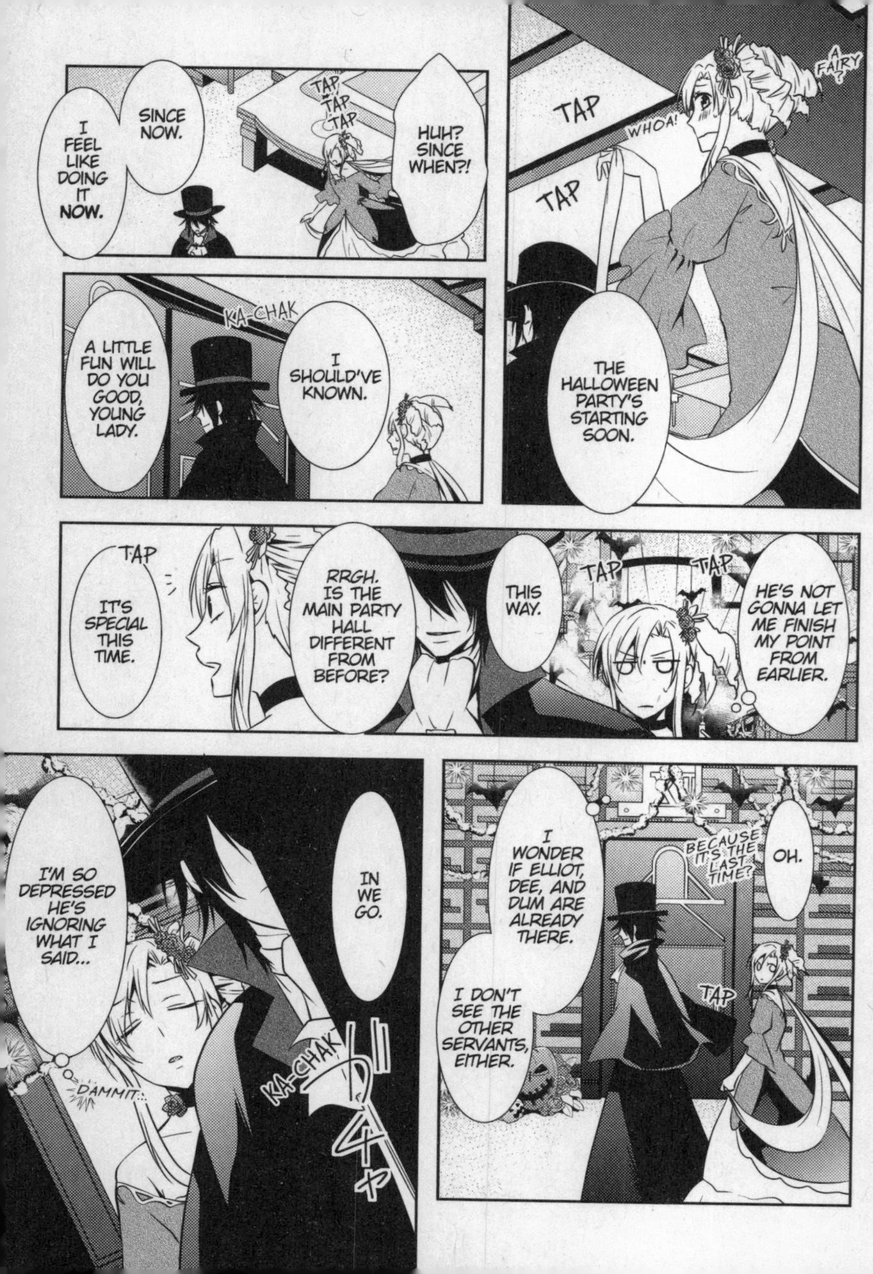
A FAIRY?
TAP
WHOA!
TAP
THE HALLOWEEN PARTY'S STARTING SOON.
HUH? SINCE WHEN?!
TAP TAP TAP
SINCE NOW.
I FEEL LIKE DOING IT NOW.
I SHOULD'VE KNOWN.
KA-CHAK
A LITTLE FUN WILL DO YOU GOOD, YOUNG LADY.
HE'S NOT GONNA LET ME FINISH MY POINT FROM EARLIER.
TAP
TAP
THIS WAY.
RRGH. IS THE MAIN PARTY HALL DIFFERENT FROM BEFORE?
TAP
IT'S SPECIAL THIS TIME.
OH.
BECAUSE IT'S THE LAST TIME?
I WONDER IF ELLIOT, DEE, AND DUM ARE ALREADY THERE.
TAP
I DON'T SEE THE OTHER SERVANTS, EITHER.
IN WE GO.
KA-CHAK
I'M SO DEPRESSED HE'S IGNORING WHAT I SAID...
DAMMIT...

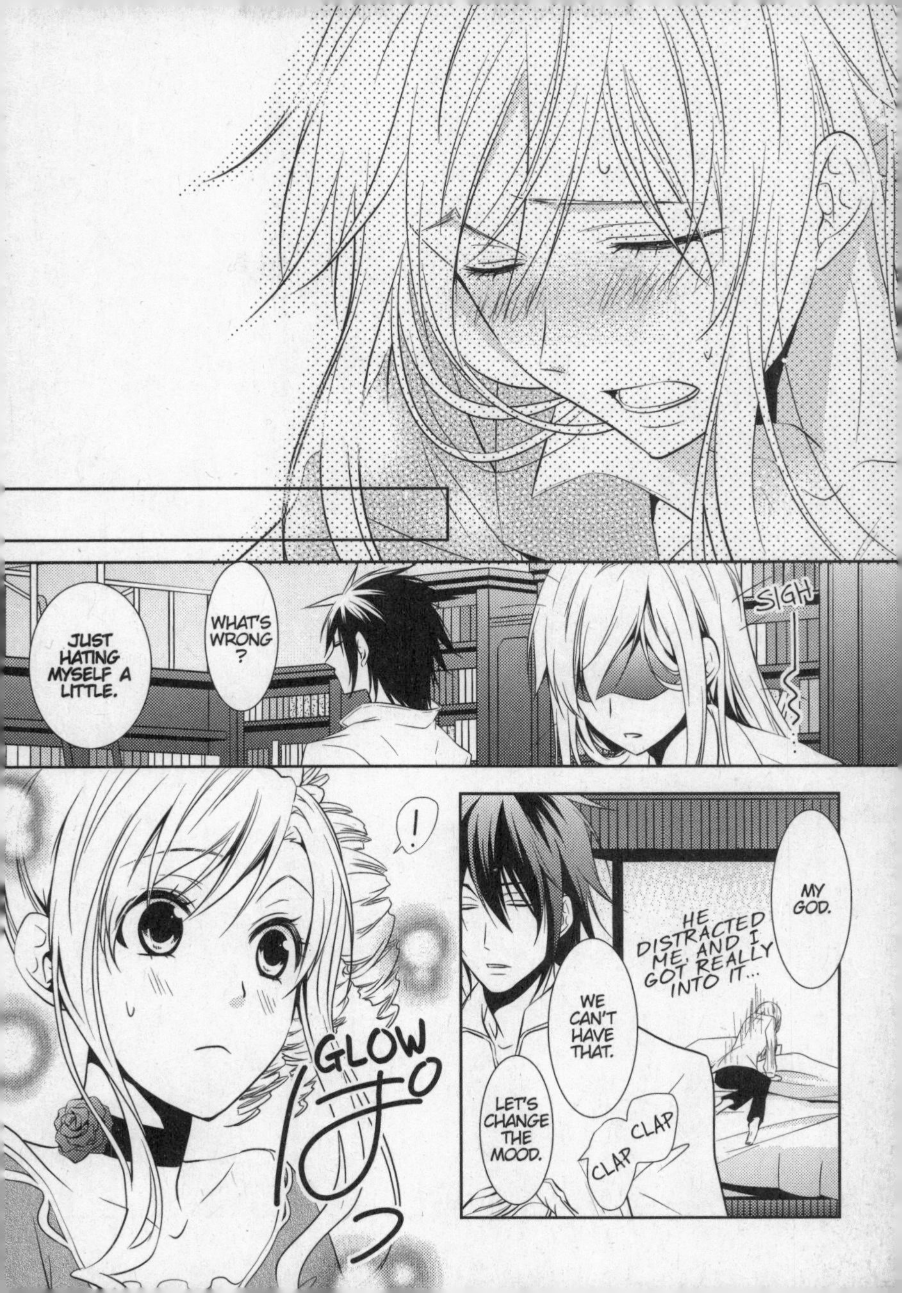

SIGH...
WHAT'S WRONG?
JUST HATING MYSELF A LITTLE.
MY GOD.
HE DISTRACTED ME, AND I GOT REALLY INTO IT...
WE CAN'T HAVE THAT.
LET'S CHANGE THE MOOD.
CLAP CLAP
!
GLOW

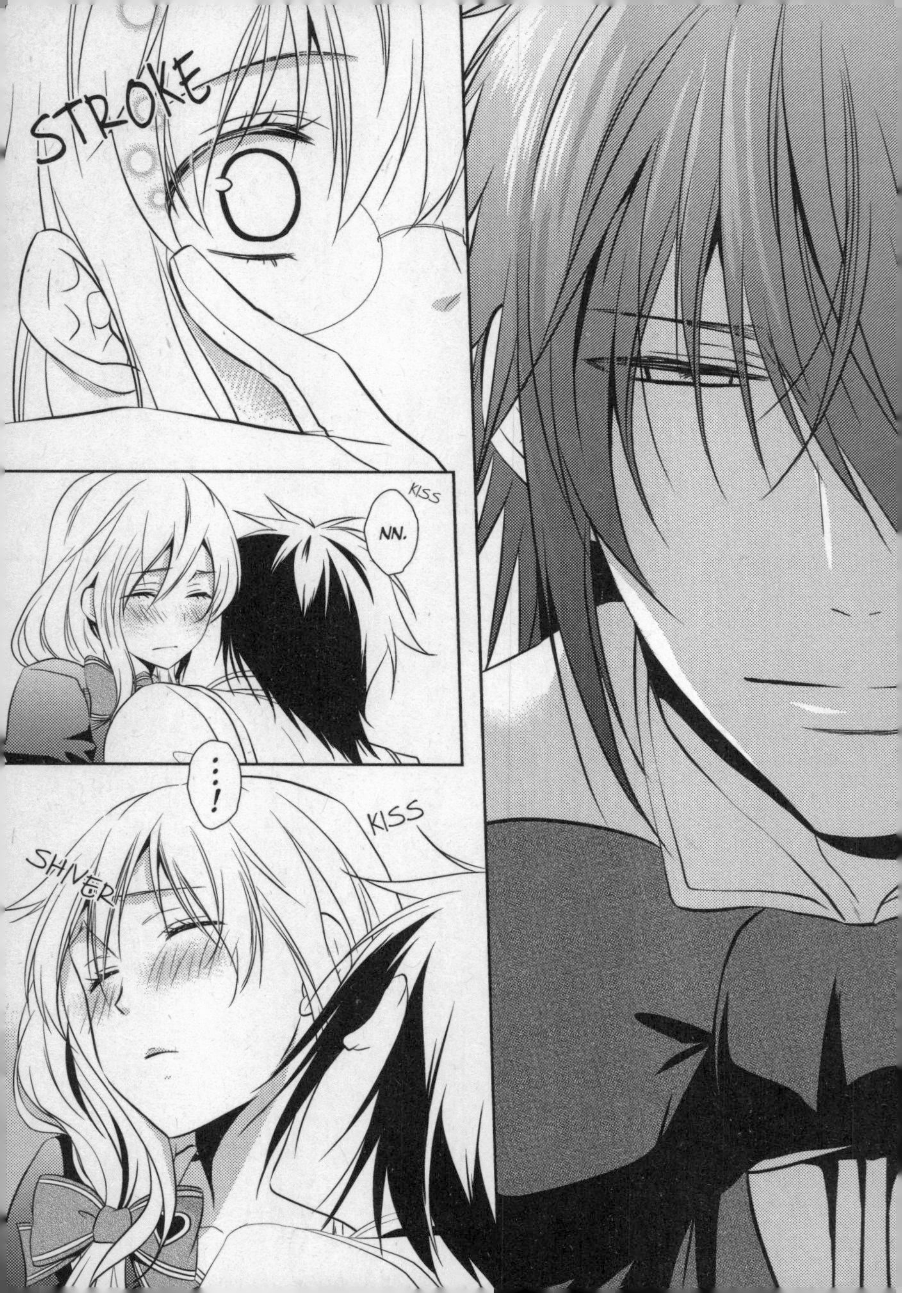
STROKE
KISS
NN.
...!
KISS
SHIVER

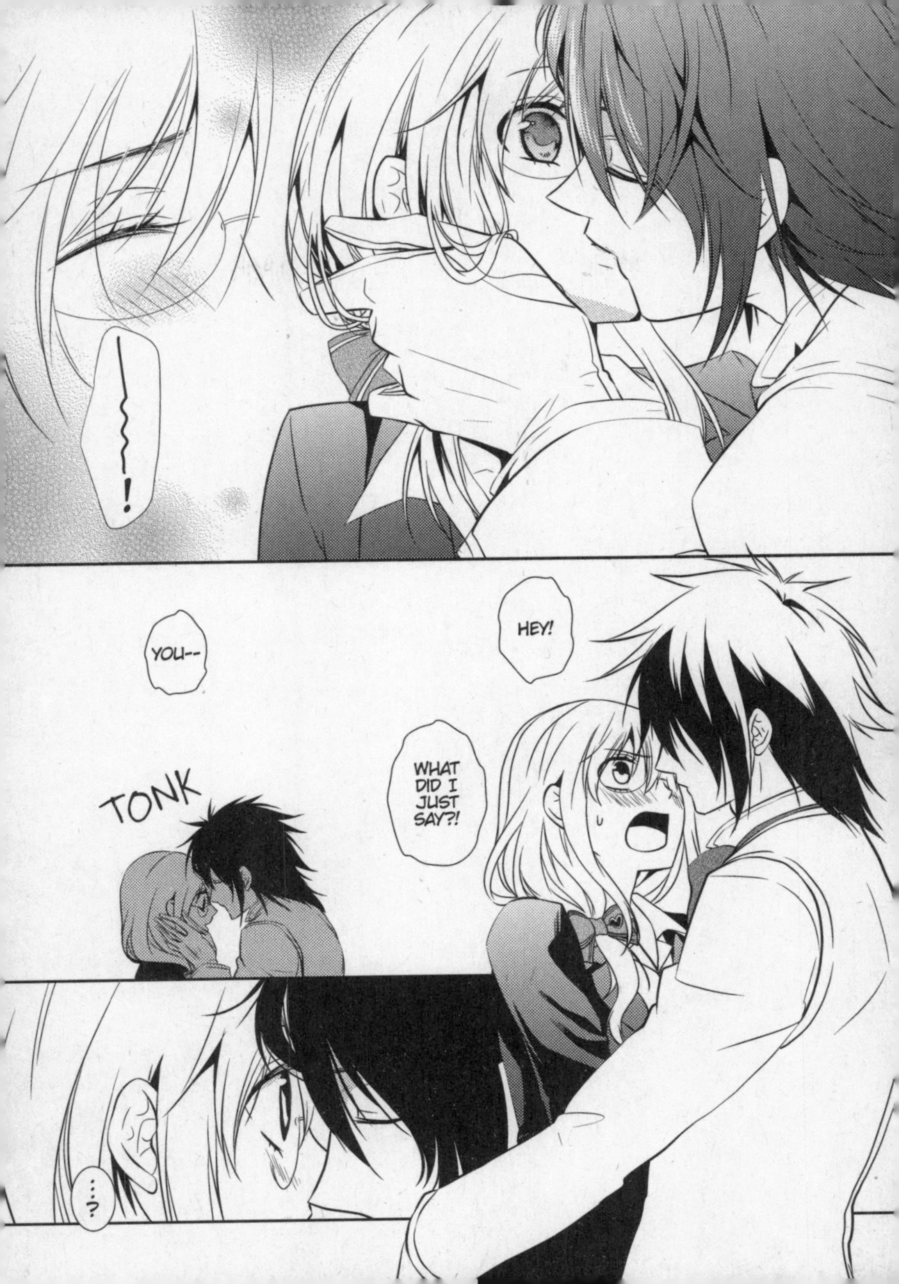

—〜〜—!
HEY!
WHAT DID I JUST SAY?!
YOU--
TONK
っ....

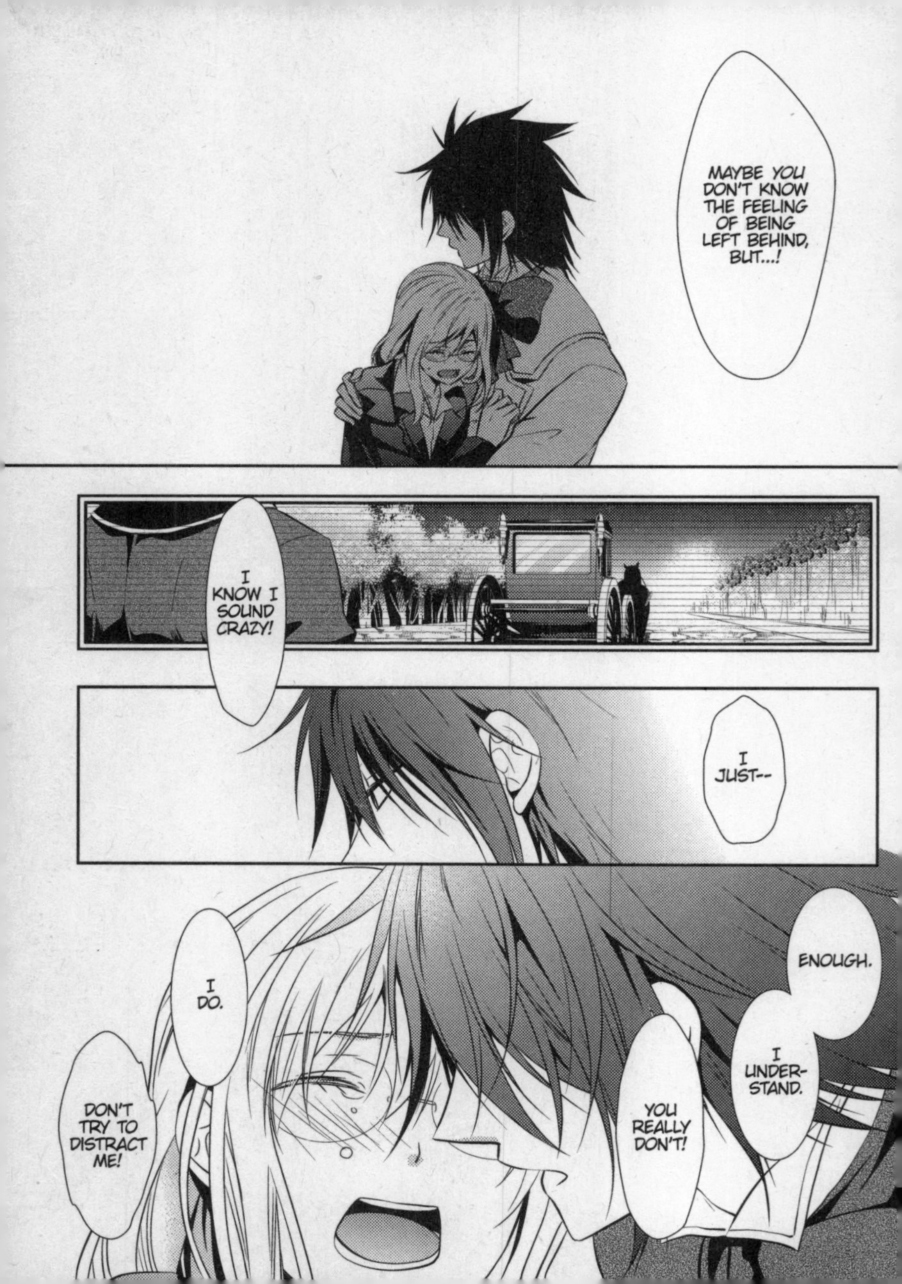
MAYBE YOU DON'T KNOW THE FEELING OF BEING LEFT BEHIND, BUT...!
I KNOW I SOUND CRAZY!
I JUST--
ENOUGH.
I UNDER-STAND.
YOU REALLY DON'T!
I DO.
DON'T TRY TO DISTRACT ME!

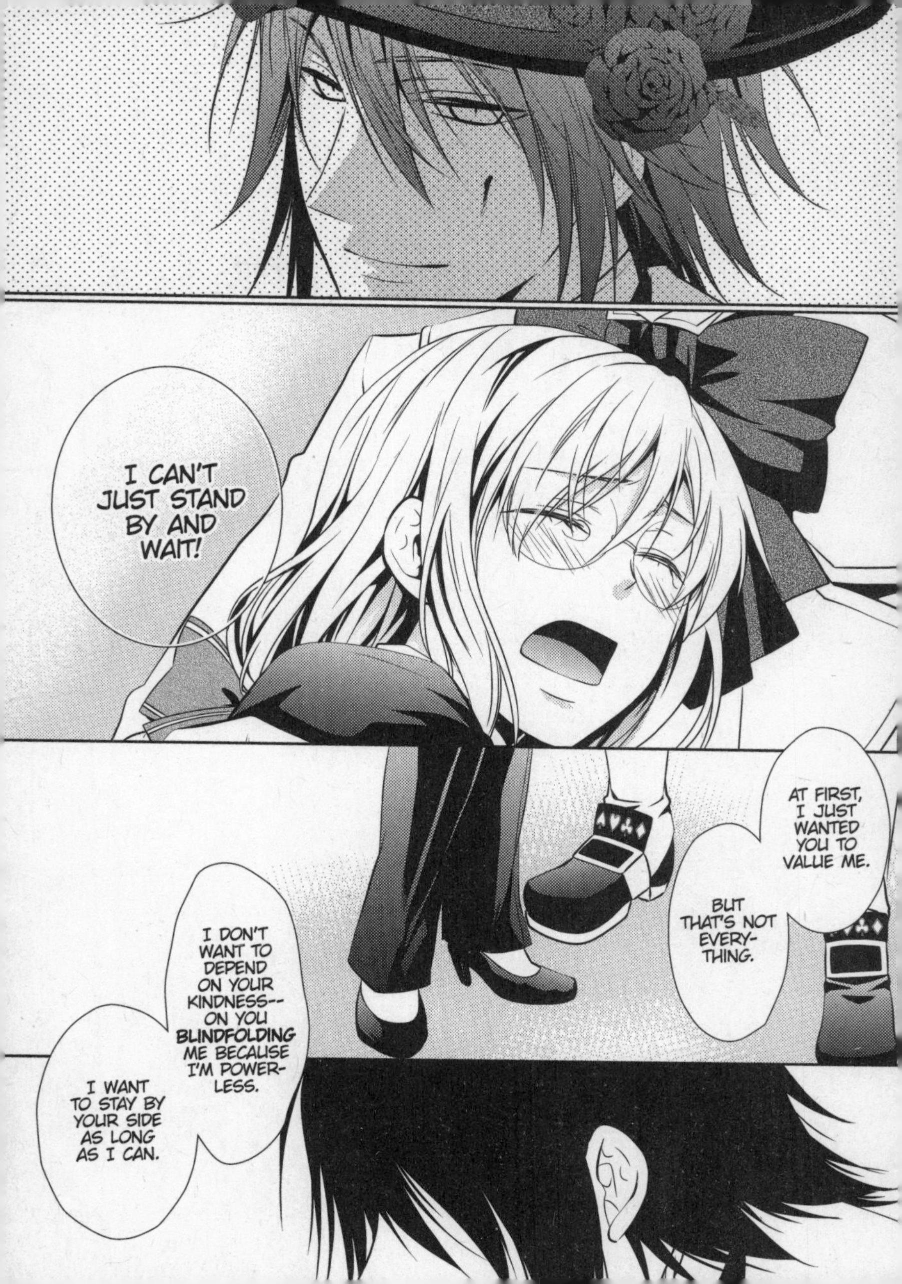
I CAN'T JUST STAND BY AND WAIT!
AT FIRST, I JUST WANTED YOU TO VALUE ME.
BUT THAT'S NOT EVERYTHING.
I DON'T WANT TO DEPEND ON YOUR KINDNESS-- ON YOU **BLINDFOLDING** ME BECAUSE I'M POWERLESS.
I WANT TO STAY BY YOUR SIDE AS LONG AS I CAN.

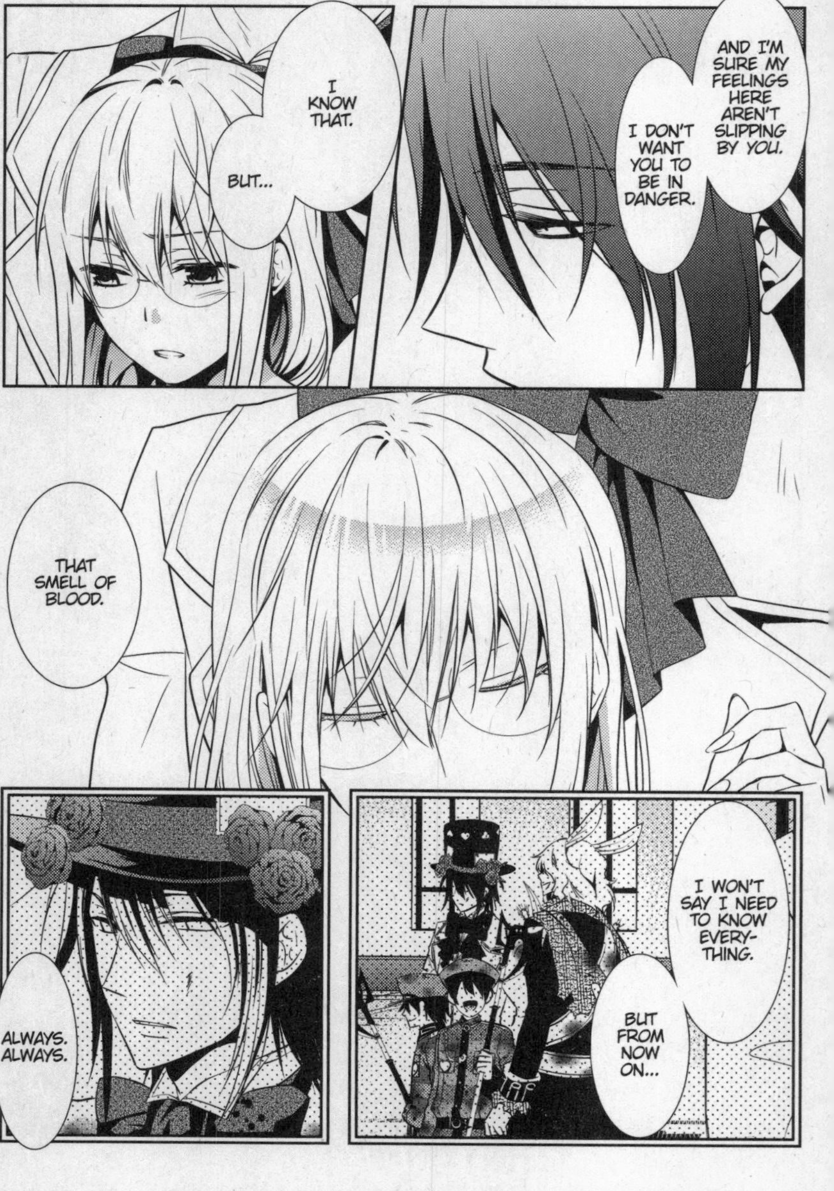
AND I'M SURE MY FEELINGS HERE AREN'T SLIPPING BY YOU.
I DON'T WANT YOU TO BE IN DANGER.
I KNOW THAT.
BUT...
THAT SMELL OF BLOOD.
I WON'T SAY I NEED TO KNOW EVERY-THING.
BUT FROM NOW ON...
ALWAYS. ALWAYS.

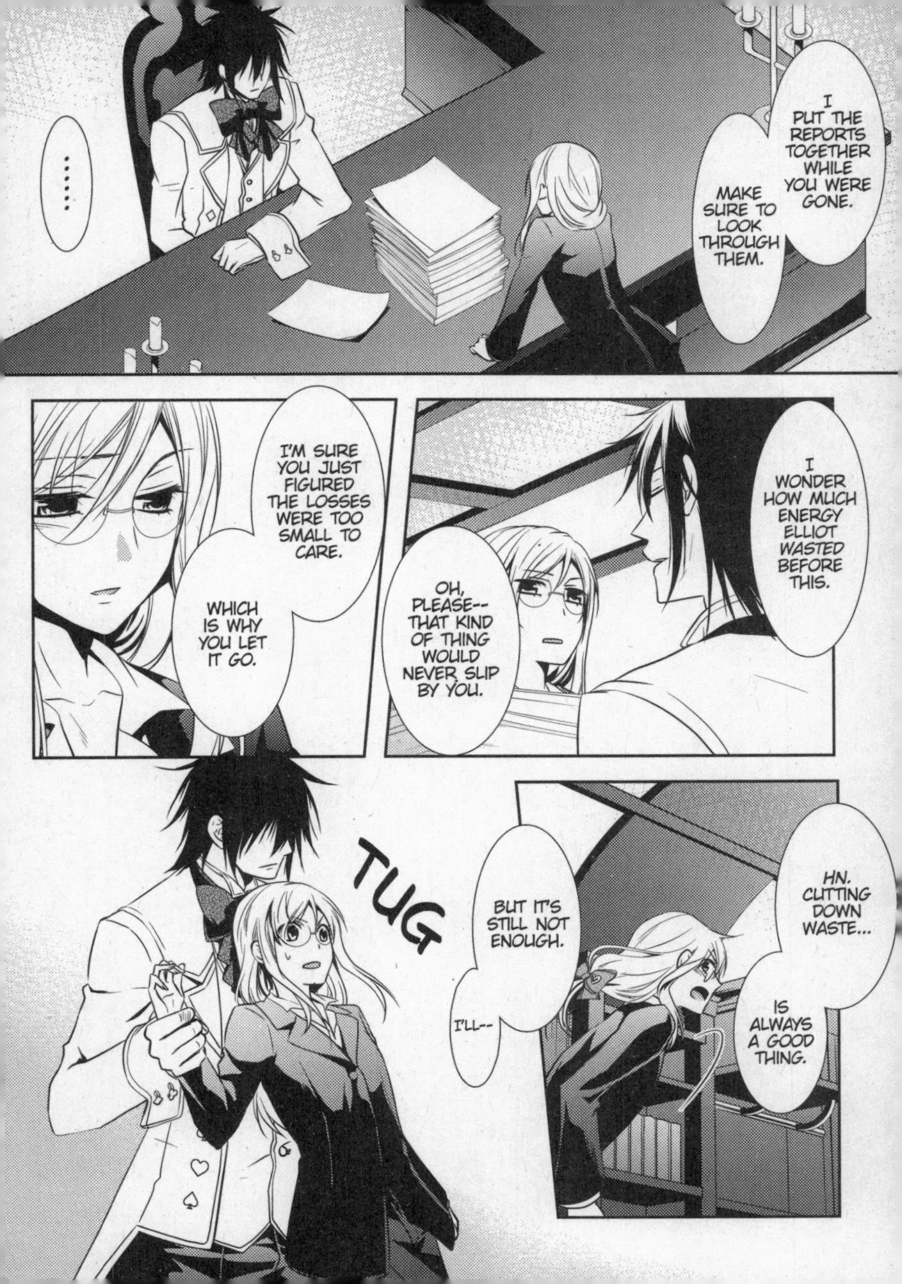
I PUT THE REPORTS TOGETHER WHILE YOU WERE GONE.
MAKE SURE TO LOOK THROUGH THEM.
......
I WONDER HOW MUCH ENERGY ELLIOT WASTED BEFORE THIS.
OH, PLEASE--THAT KIND OF THING WOULD NEVER SLIP BY YOU.
I'M SURE YOU JUST FIGURED THE LOSSES WERE TOO SMALL TO CARE.
WHICH IS WHY YOU LET IT GO.
HN. CUTTING DOWN WASTE...
IS ALWAYS A GOOD THING.
BUT IT'S STILL NOT ENOUGH.
I'LL--
TUG

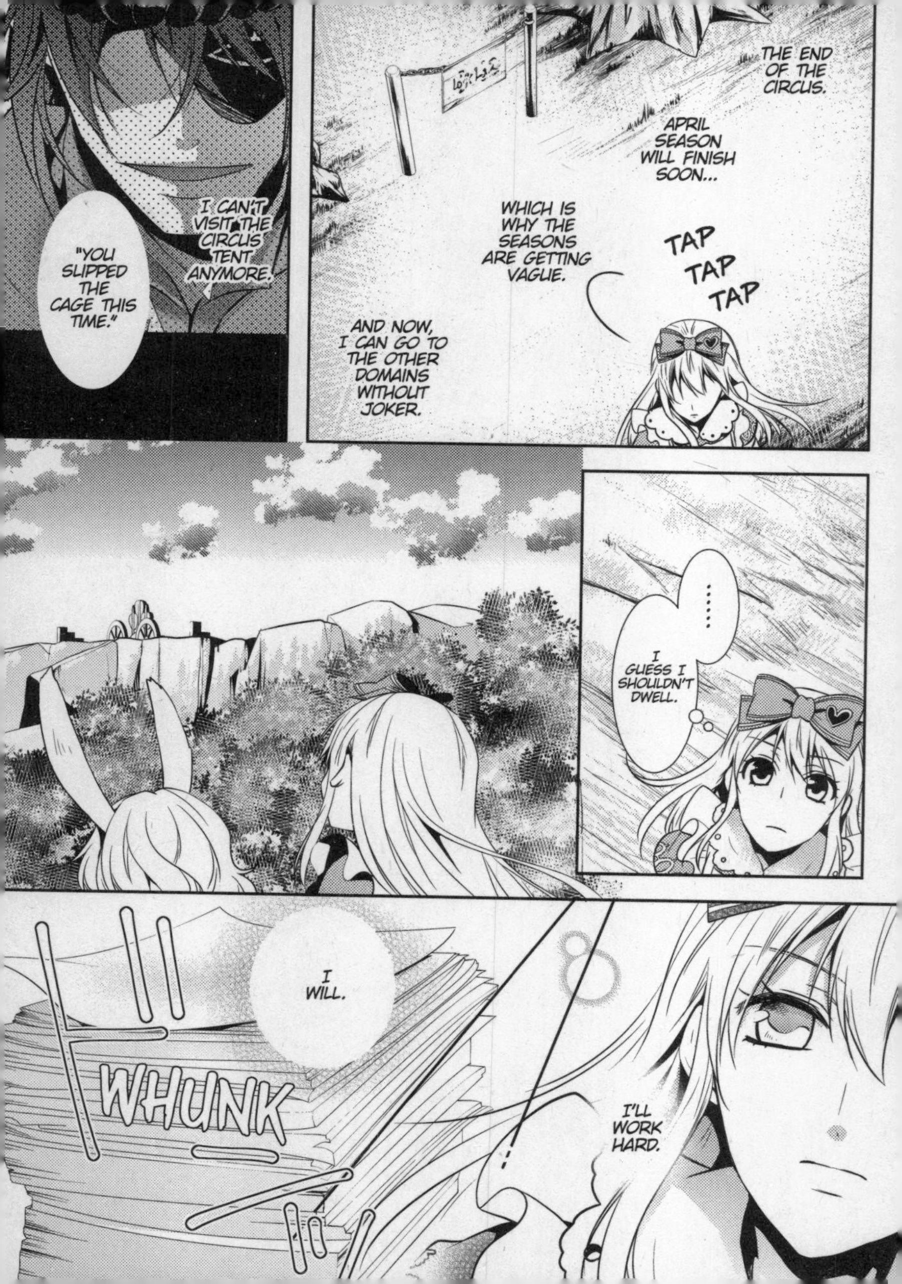
THE END OF THE CIRCUS.
APRIL SEASON WILL FINISH SOON...
WHICH IS WHY THE SEASONS ARE GETTING VAGUE.
TAP TAP TAP
AND NOW, I CAN GO TO THE OTHER DOMAINS WITHOUT JOKER.
I CAN'T VISIT THE CIRCUS TENT ANYMORE.
"YOU SLIPPED THE CAGE THIS TIME."
......
I GUESS I SHOULDN'T DWELL.
I'LL WORK HARD.
I WILL.
WHUNK

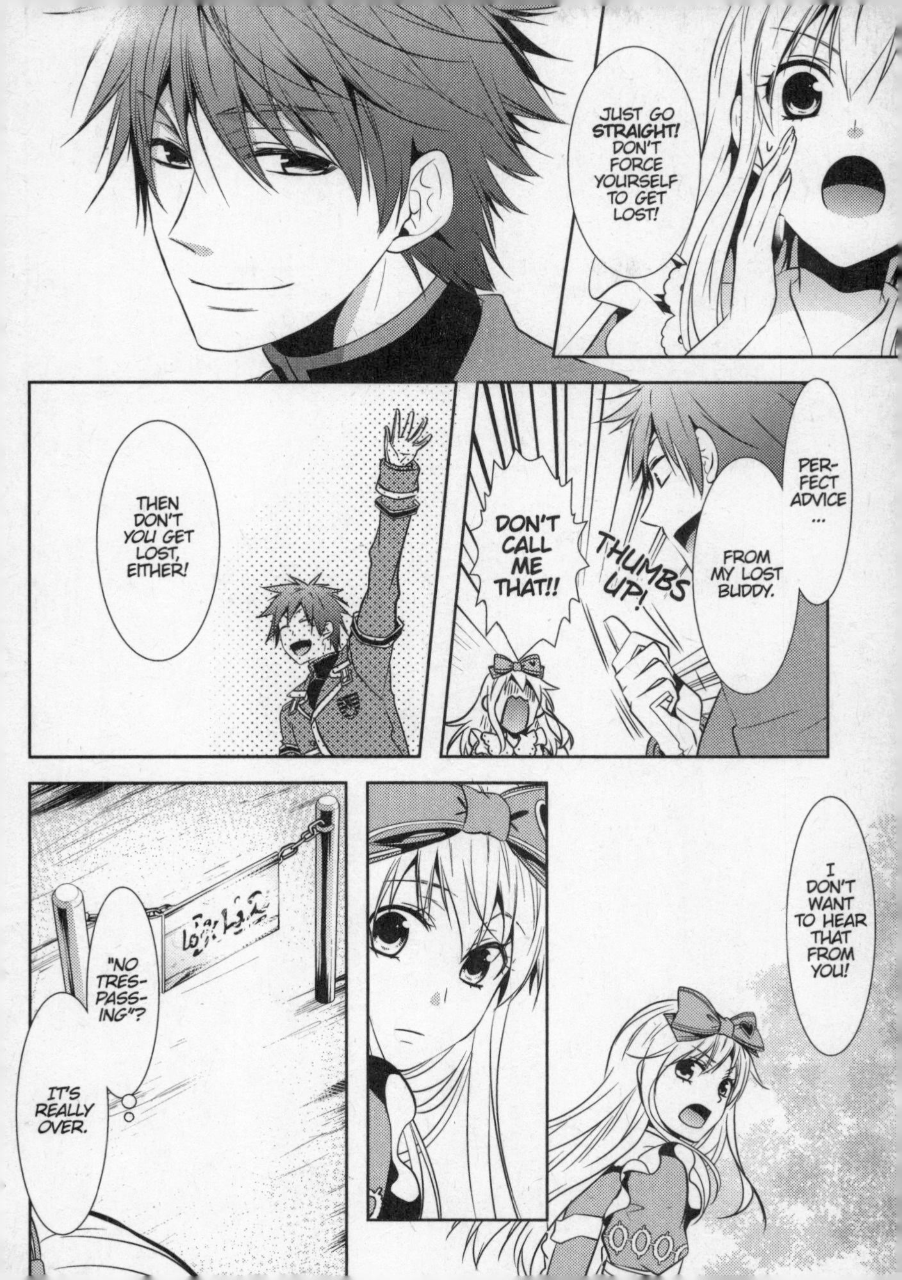
JUST GO STRAIGHT! DON'T FORCE YOURSELF TO GET LOST!
PERFECT ADVICE...
FROM MY LOST BUDDY.
THUMBS UP!
DON'T CALL ME THAT!!
THEN DON'T YOU GET LOST, EITHER!
I DON'T WANT TO HEAR THAT FROM YOU!
"NO TRES-PASS-ING"?
IT'S REALLY OVER.

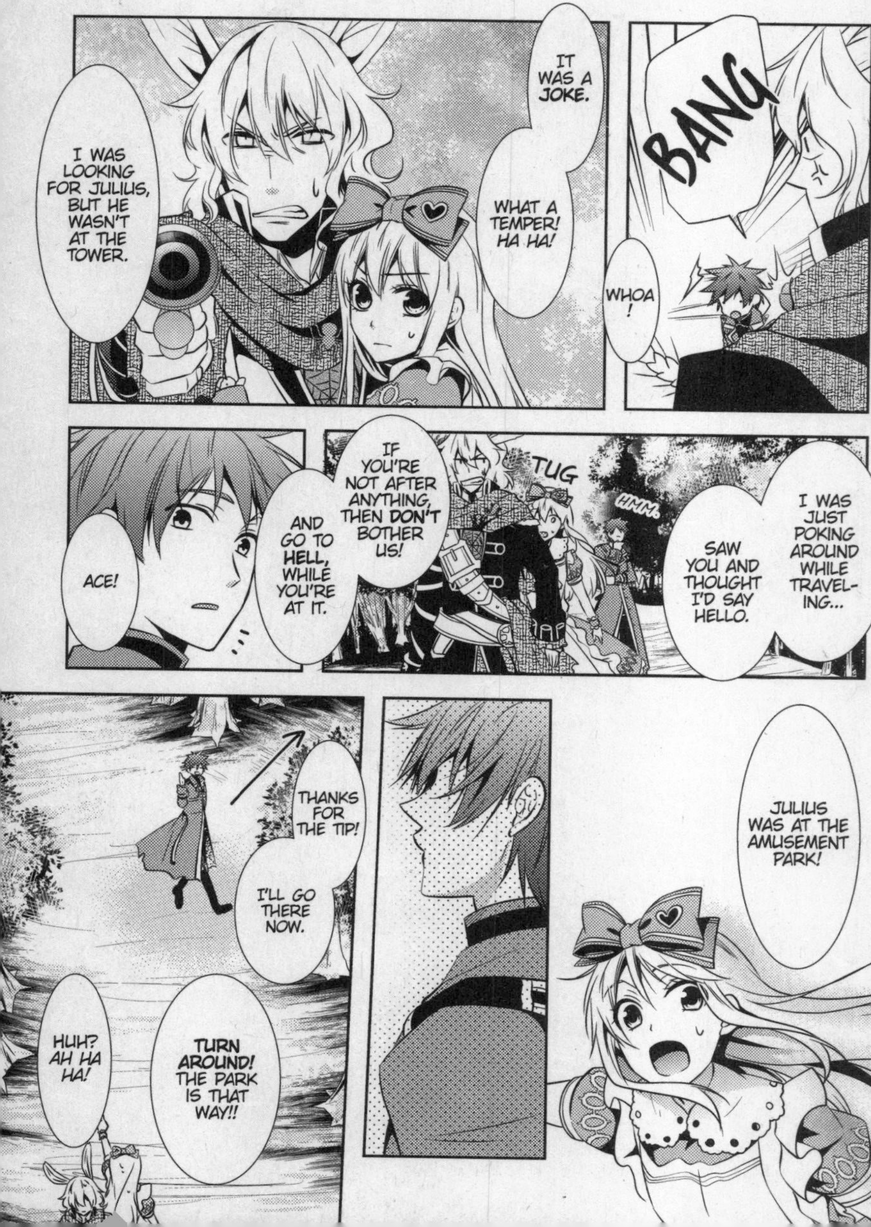
BANG
WHOA!
IT WAS A JOKE.
WHAT A TEMPER! HA HA!
I WAS LOOKING FOR JULIUS, BUT HE WASN'T AT THE TOWER.
I WAS JUST POKING AROUND WHILE TRAVELING...
SAW YOU AND THOUGHT I'D SAY HELLO.
TUG
HMM.
IF YOU'RE NOT AFTER ANYTHING, THEN DON'T BOTHER US!
AND GO TO HELL, WHILE YOU'RE AT IT.
ACE!
...
JULIUS WAS AT THE AMUSEMENT PARK!
THANKS FOR THE TIP!
I'LL GO THERE NOW.
TURN AROUND! THE PARK IS THAT WAY!!
HUH? AH HA HA!

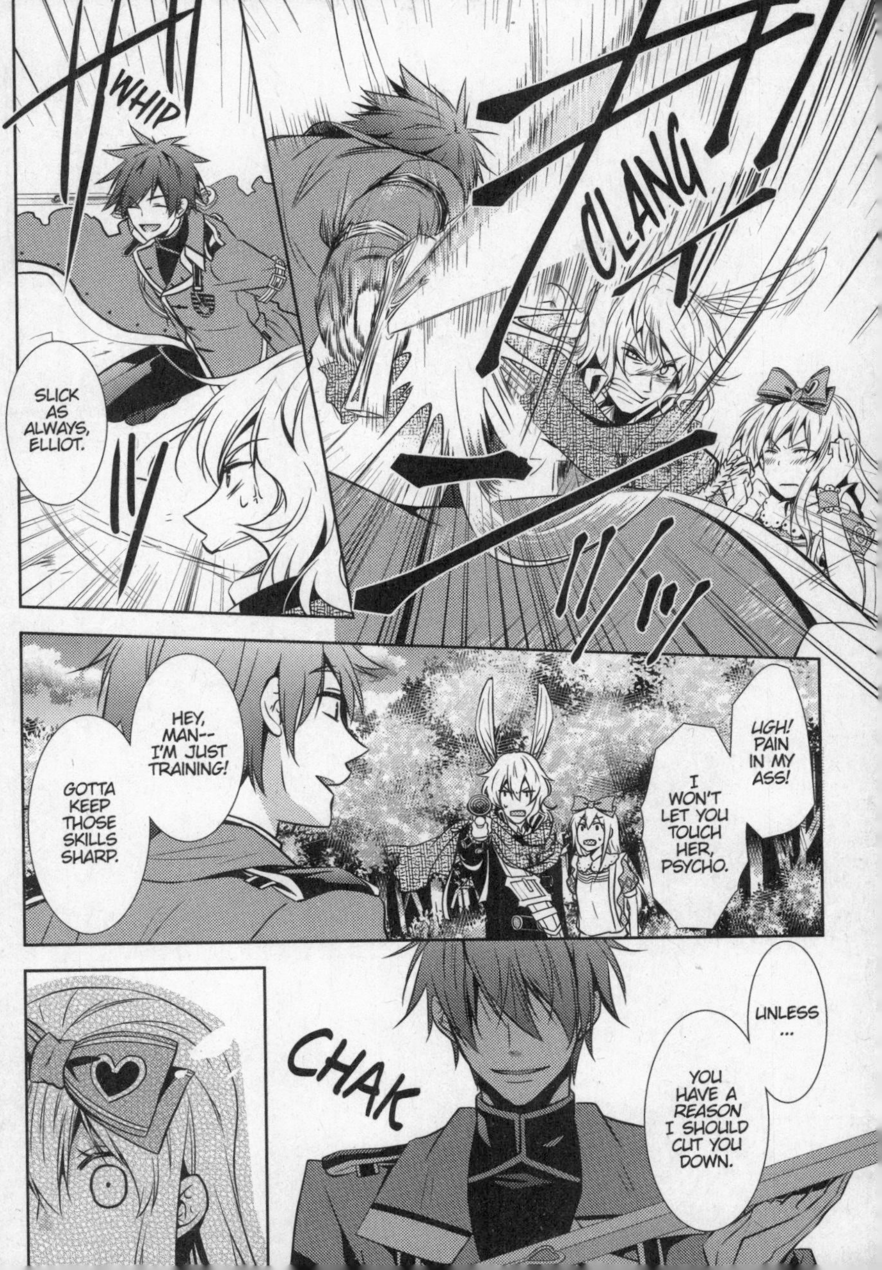
CLANG
WHIP
SLICK AS ALWAYS, ELLIOT.
UGH! PAIN IN MY ASS!
I WON'T LET YOU TOUCH HER, PSYCHO.
HEY, MAN-- I'M JUST TRAINING!
GOTTA KEEP THOSE SKILLS SHARP.
UNLESS ...
YOU HAVE A REASON I SHOULD CUT YOU DOWN.
CHAK

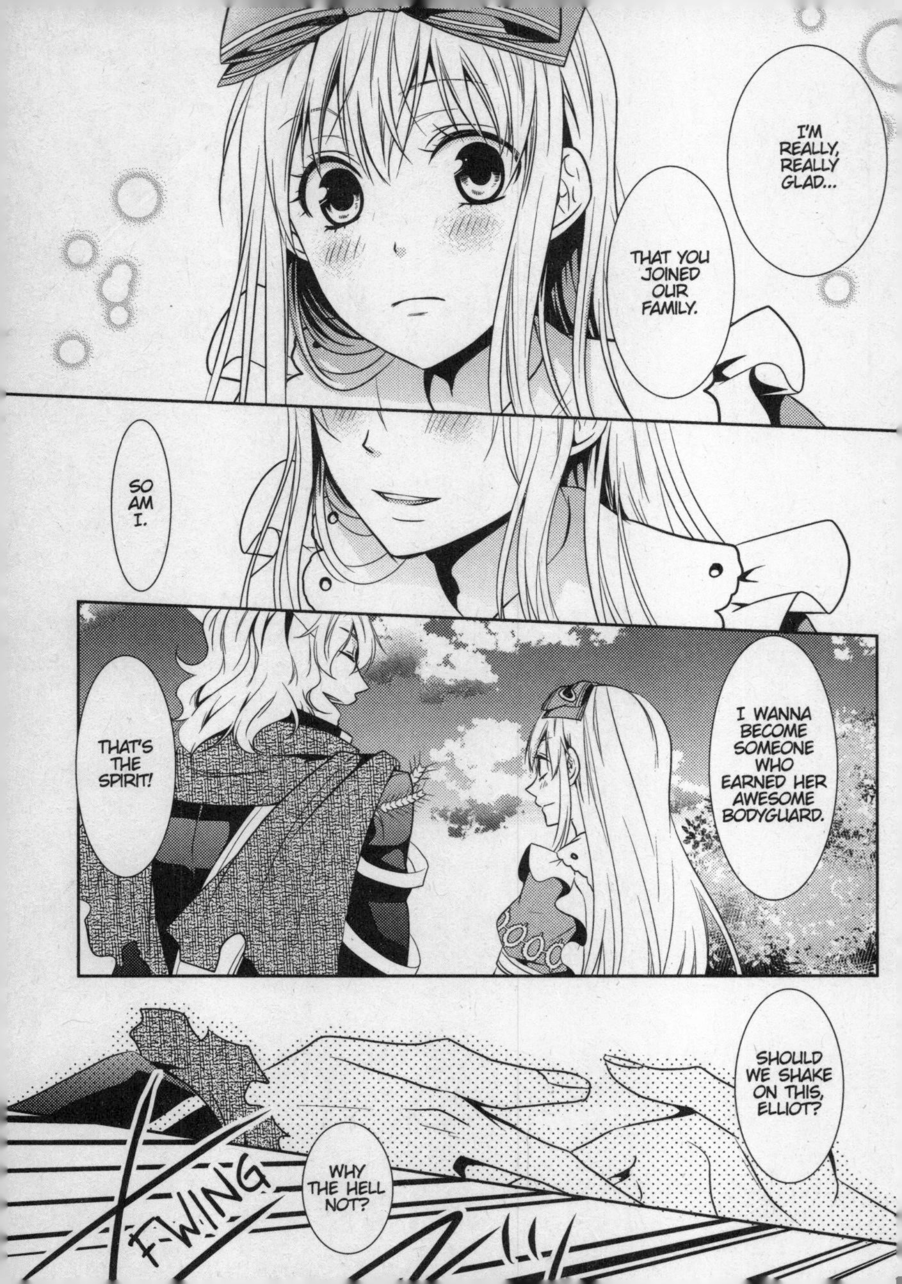
I'M REALLY, REALLY GLAD...
THAT YOU JOINED OUR FAMILY.
SO AM I.
I WANNA BECOME SOMEONE WHO EARNED HER AWESOME BODYGUARD.
THAT'S THE SPIRIT!
SHOULD WE SHAKE ON THIS, ELLIOT?
WHY THE HELL NOT?
FWING

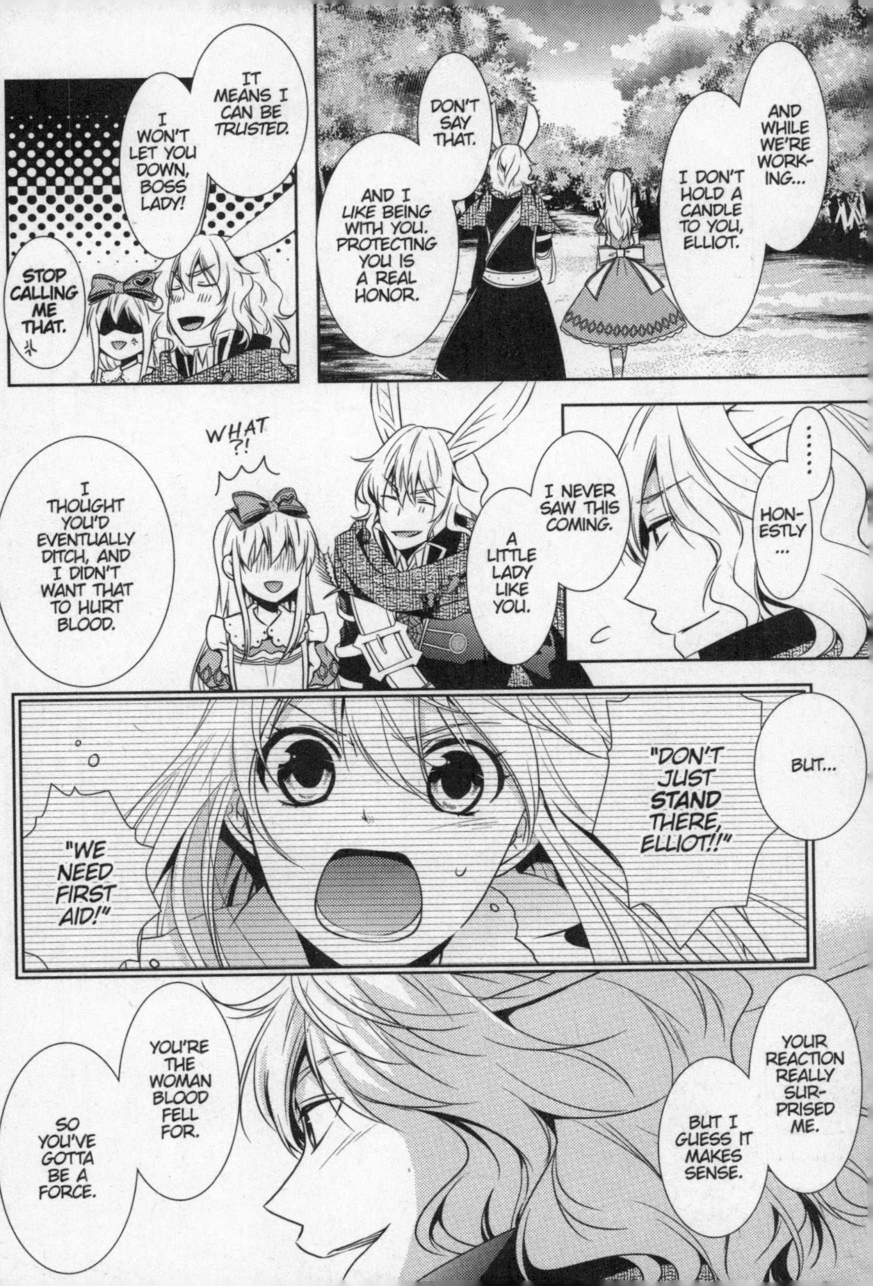
AND WHILE WE'RE WORK-ING...
I DON'T HOLD A CANDLE TO YOU, ELLIOT.
DON'T SAY THAT.
AND I LIKE BEING WITH YOU. PROTECTING YOU IS A REAL HONOR.
IT MEANS I CAN BE TRUSTED.
I WON'T LET YOU DOWN, BOSS LADY!
STOP CALLING ME THAT.
......
HON-ESTLY...
I NEVER SAW THIS COMING.
A LITTLE LADY LIKE YOU.
WHAT?!
I THOUGHT YOU'D EVENTUALLY DITCH, AND I DIDN'T WANT THAT TO HURT BLOOD.
BUT...
"DON'T JUST STAND THERE, ELLIOT!!"
"WE NEED FIRST AID!"
YOUR REACTION REALLY SUR-PRISED ME.
BUT I GUESS IT MAKES SENSE.
YOU'RE THE WOMAN BLOOD FELL FOR.
SO YOU'VE GOTTA BE A FORCE.

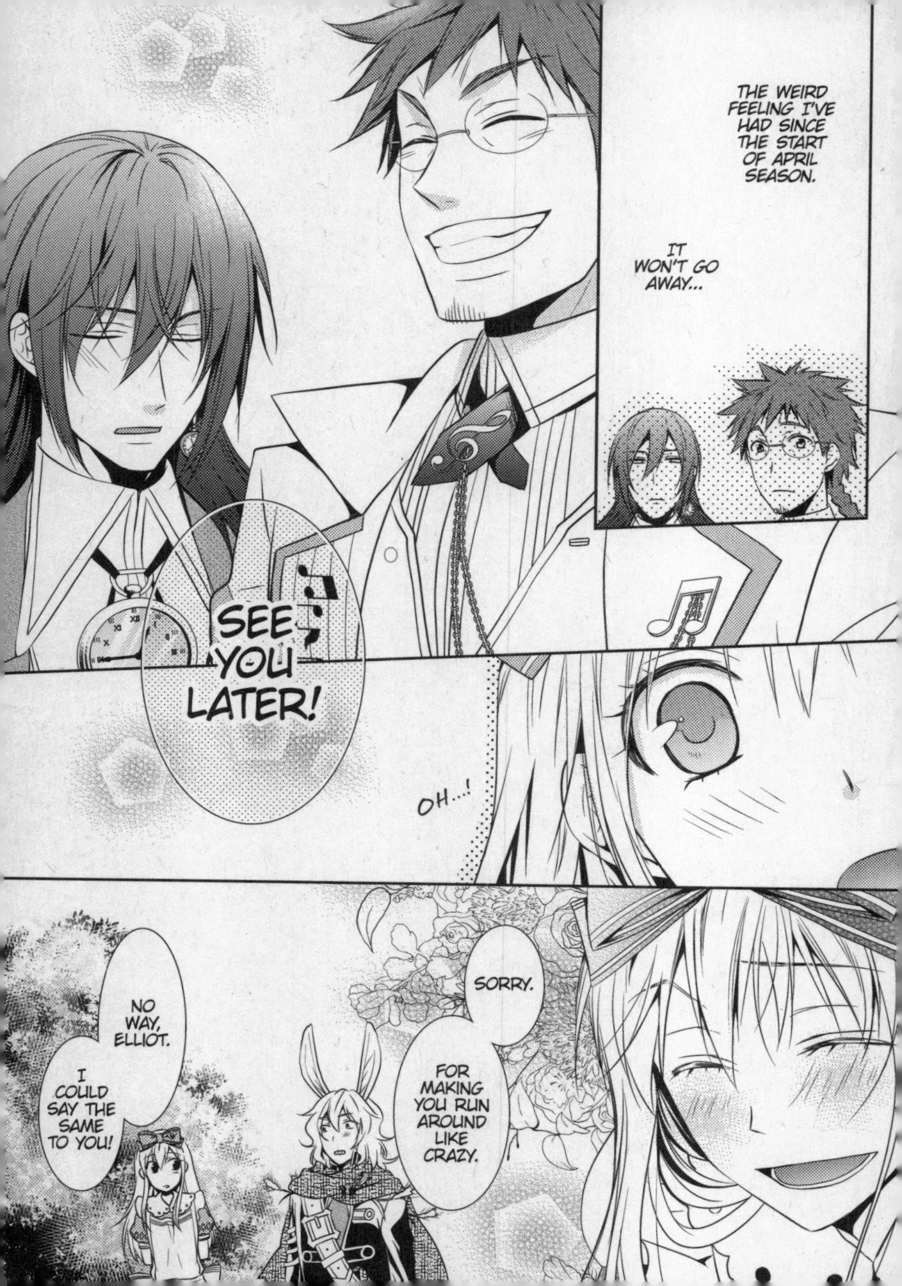
THE WEIRD FEELING I'VE HAD SINCE THE START OF APRIL SEASON.
IT WON'T GO AWAY...
SEE YOU LATER!
OH...!
SORRY.
FOR MAKING YOU RUN AROUND LIKE CRAZY.
NO WAY, ELLIOT.
I COULD SAY THE SAME TO YOU!

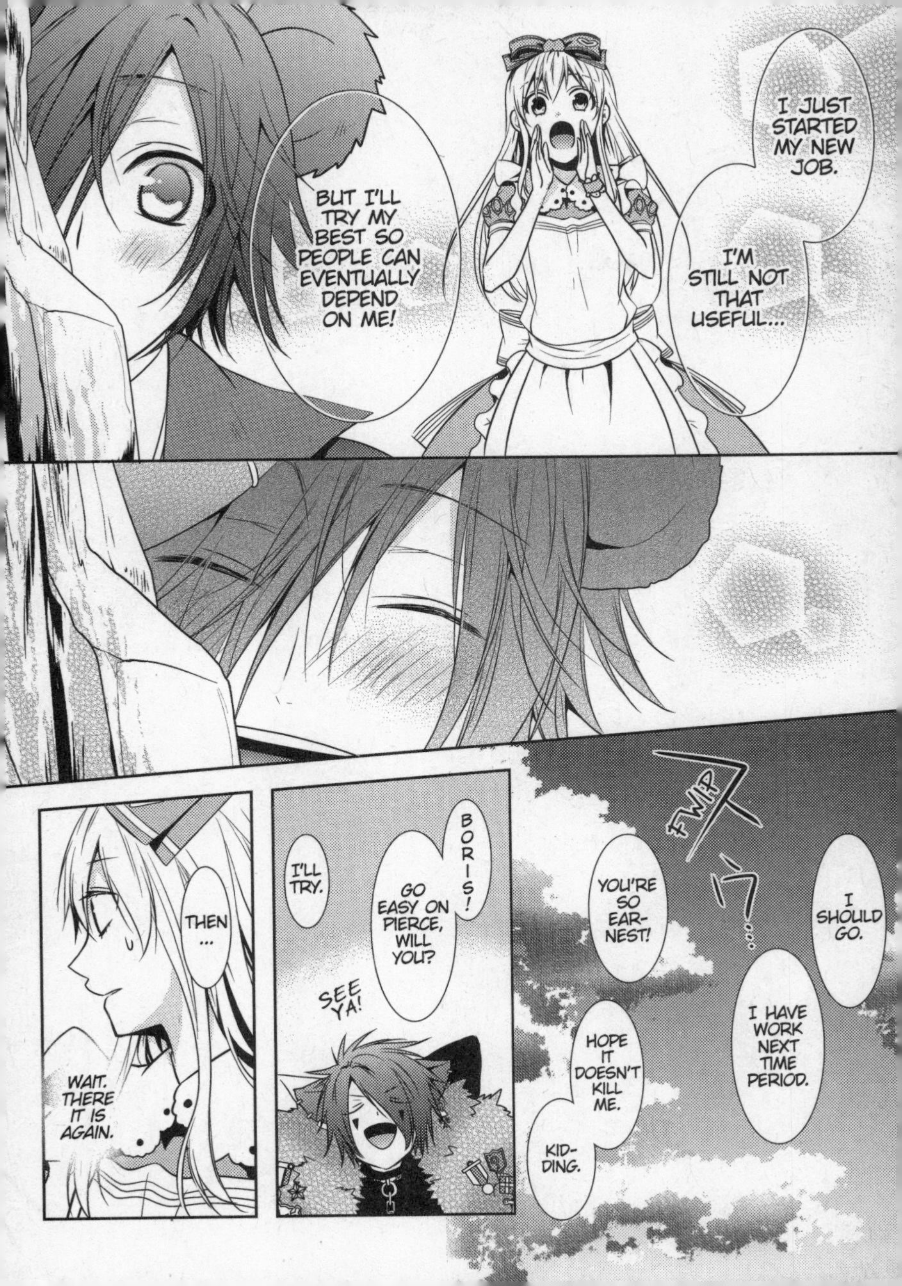
I JUST STARTED MY NEW JOB.
I'M STILL NOT THAT USEFUL...
BUT I'LL TRY MY BEST SO PEOPLE CAN EVENTUALLY DEPEND ON ME!
I SHOULD GO.
FWIP
YOU'RE SO EAR-NEST!
I HAVE WORK NEXT TIME PERIOD.
HOPE IT DOESN'T KILL ME.
KID-DING.
BORIS!
GO EASY ON PIERCE, WILL YOU?
I'LL TRY.
SEE YA!
THEN ...
WAIT. THERE IT IS AGAIN.

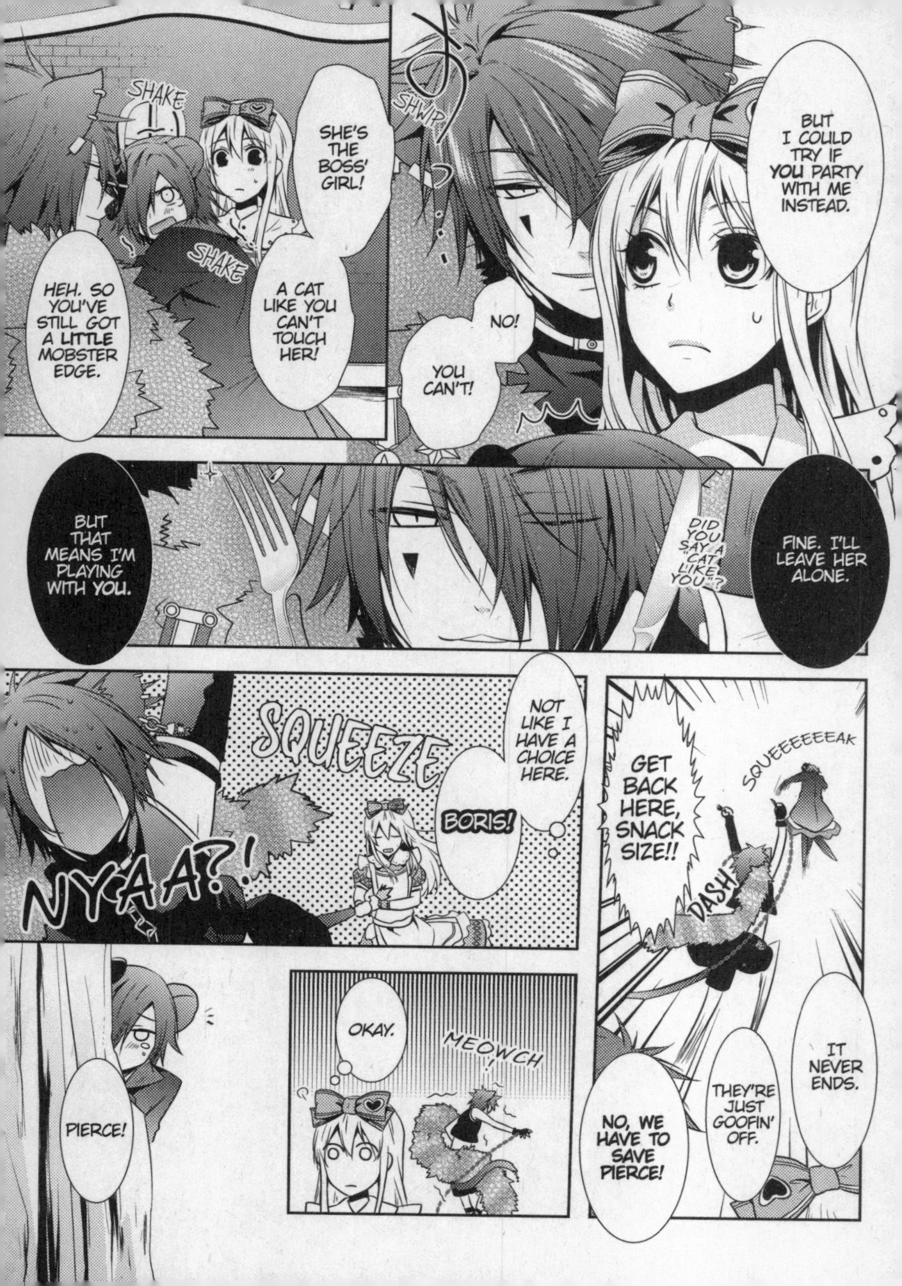
BUT I COULD TRY IF YOU PARTY WITH ME INSTEAD.
SHWIP
NO!
YOU CAN'T!
SHE'S THE BOSS' GIRL!
SHAKE
A CAT LIKE YOU CAN'T TOUCH HER!
SHAKE
HEH. SO YOU'VE STILL GOT A LITTLE MOBSTER EDGE.
FINE. I'LL LEAVE HER ALONE.
DID YOU SAY A "CAT LIKE YOU"?
BUT THAT MEANS I'M PLAYING WITH YOU.
SQUEEEEEEEAK
GET BACK HERE, SNACK SIZE!!
DASH
NOT LIKE I HAVE A CHOICE HERE.
SQUEEZE
BORIS!
NYAA?!
IT NEVER ENDS.
THEY'RE JUST GOOFIN' OFF.
NO, WE HAVE TO SAVE PIERCE!
OKAY.
MEOWCH
PIERCE!

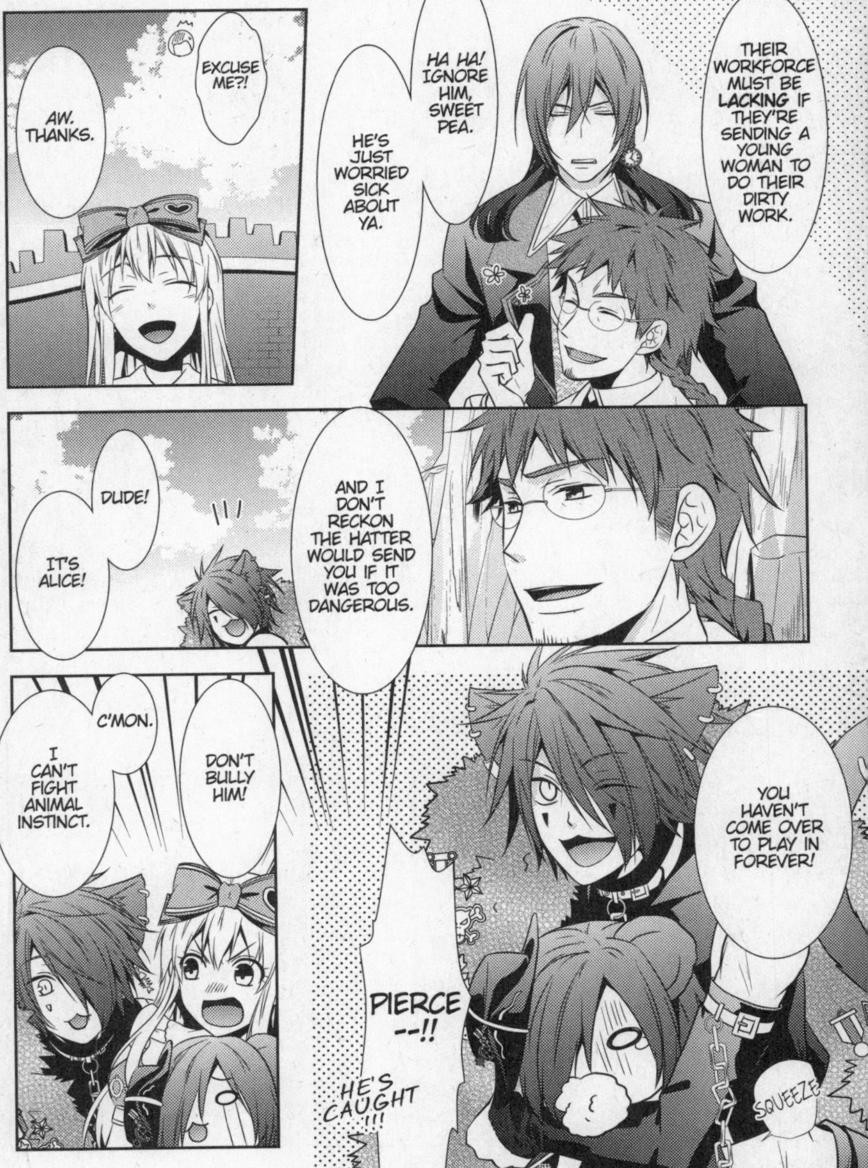
THEIR WORKFORCE MUST BE LACKING IF THEY'RE SENDING A YOUNG WOMAN TO DO THEIR DIRTY WORK.
HA HA! IGNORE HIM, SWEET PEA.
HE'S JUST WORRIED SICK ABOUT YA.
EXCUSE ME?!
AW. THANKS.
AND I DON'T RECKON THE HATTER WOULD SEND YOU IF IT WAS TOO DANGEROUS.
DUDE!
IT'S ALICE!
YOU HAVEN'T COME OVER TO PLAY IN FOREVER!
SQUEEZE
PIERCE--!!
HE'S CAUGHT!!!
DON'T BULLY HIM!
C'MON.
I CAN'T FIGHT ANIMAL INSTINCT.

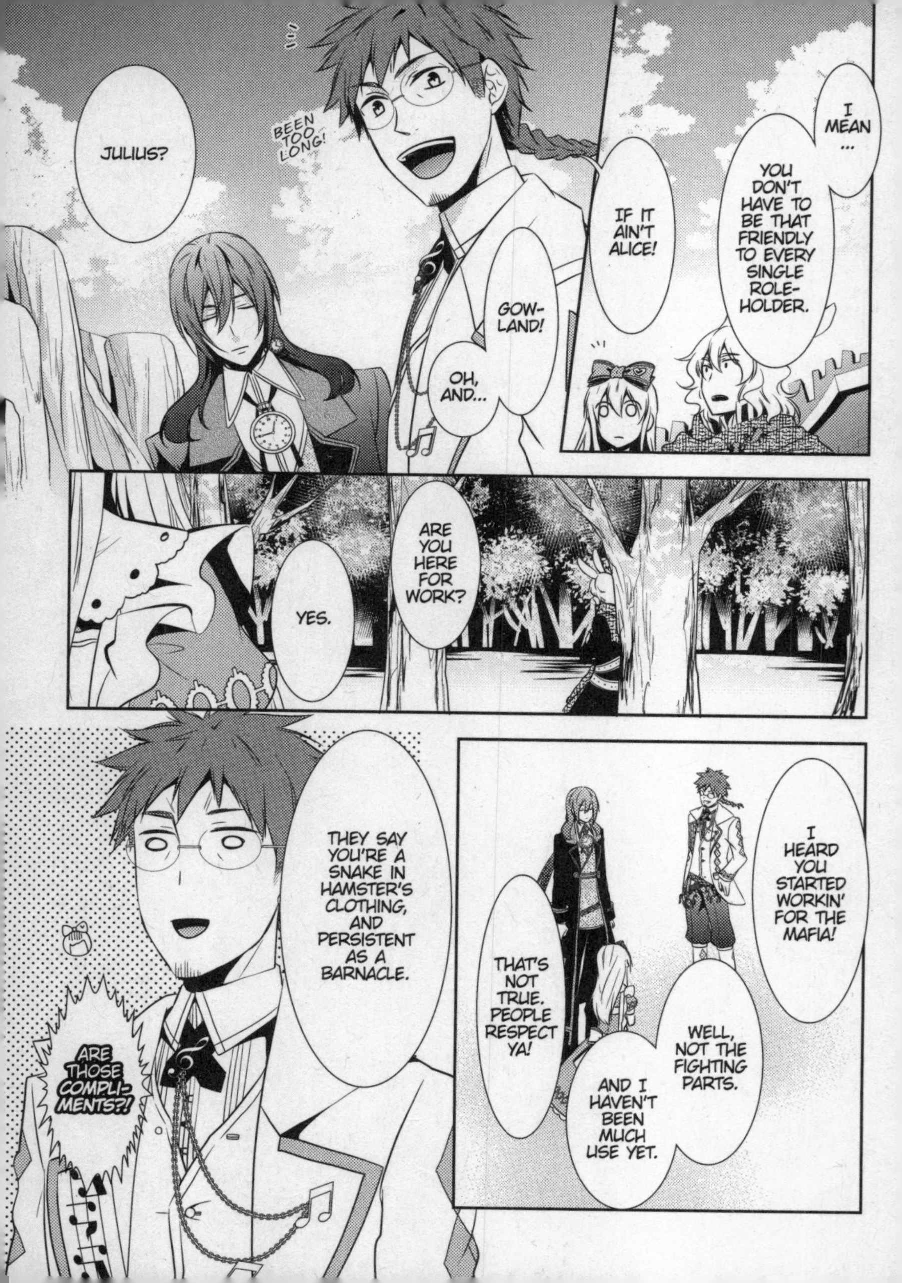
I MEAN ... YOU DON'T HAVE TO BE THAT FRIENDLY TO EVERY SINGLE ROLE-HOLDER.
IF IT AIN'T ALICE!
BEEN TOO LONG!
GOW-LAND!
OH, AND...
JULIUS?
ARE YOU HERE FOR WORK?
YES.
I HEARD YOU STARTED WORKIN' FOR THE MAFIA!
WELL, NOT THE FIGHTING PARTS.
AND I HAVEN'T BEEN MUCH USE YET.
THAT'S NOT TRUE. PEOPLE RESPECT YA!
THEY SAY YOU'RE A SNAKE IN HAMSTER'S CLOTHING, AND PERSISTENT AS A BARNACLE.
ARE THOSE COMPLI-MENTS?!

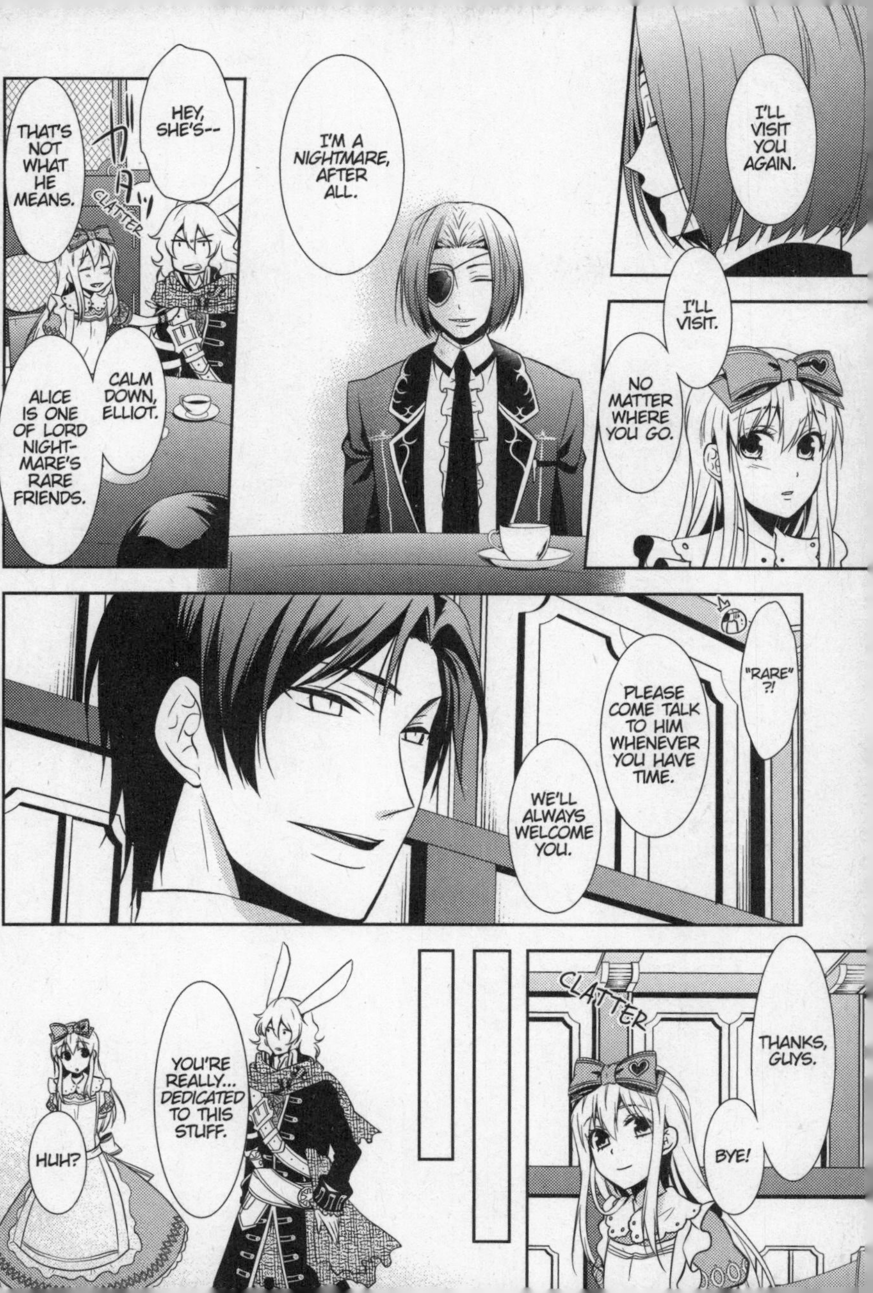
I'LL VISIT YOU AGAIN.
I'LL VISIT.
NO MATTER WHERE YOU GO.
I'M A NIGHTMARE, AFTER ALL.
HEY, SHE'S--
CLATTER
THAT'S NOT WHAT HE MEANS.
CALM DOWN, ELLIOT.
ALICE IS ONE OF LORD NIGHT-MARE'S RARE FRIENDS.
"RARE"?!
PLEASE COME TALK TO HIM WHENEVER YOU HAVE TIME.
WE'LL ALWAYS WELCOME YOU.
CLATTER
THANKS, GUYS.
BYE!
YOU'RE REALLY... DEDICATED TO THIS STUFF.
HUH?

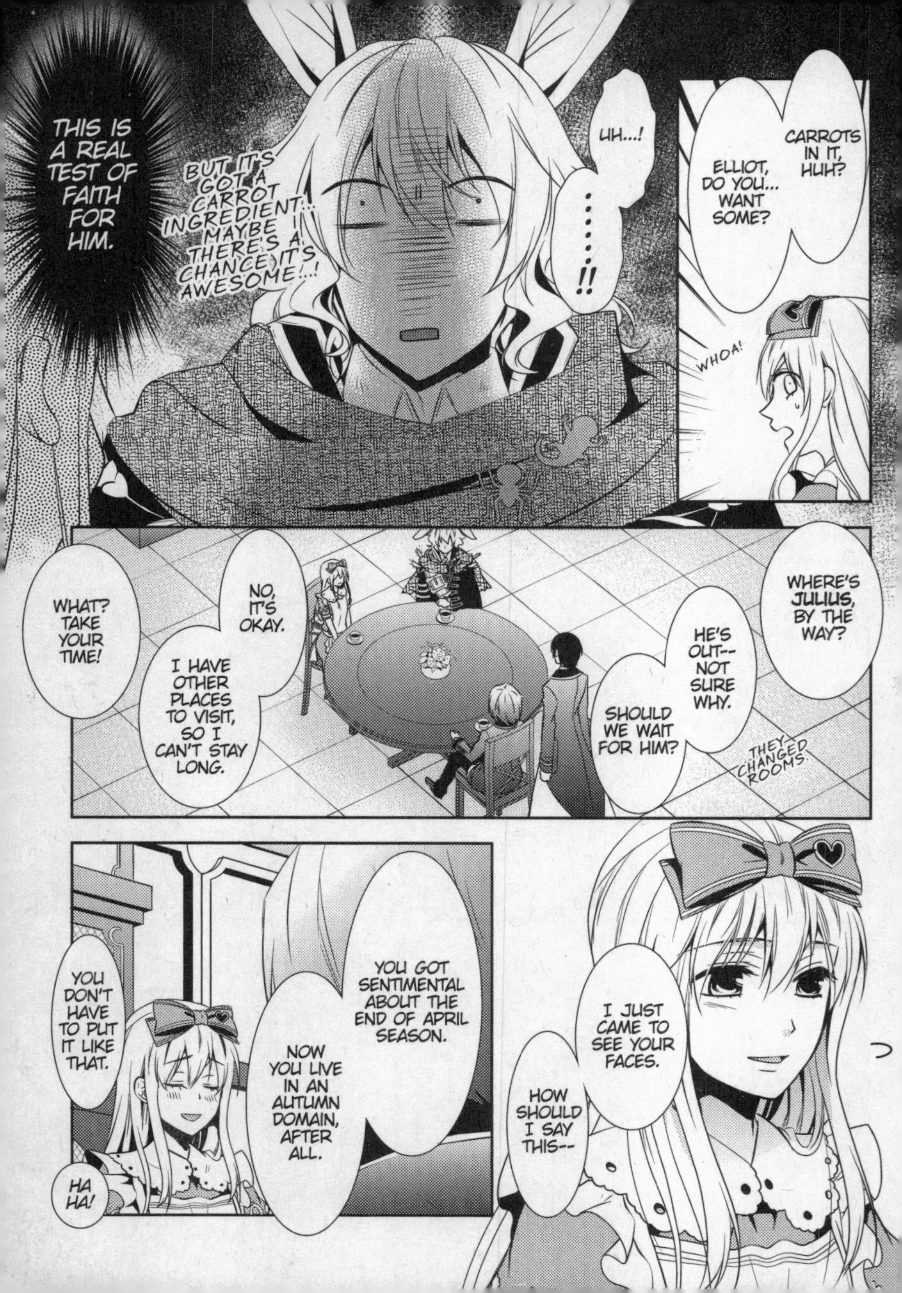
CARROTS IN IT, HUH?
ELLIOT, DO YOU... WANT SOME?
WHOA!
UH...!
......!!
BUT IT'S GOT A CARROT INGREDIENT... MAYBE THERE'S A CHANCE IT'S AWESOME...!
THIS IS A REAL TEST OF FAITH FOR HIM.
WHERE'S JULIUS, BY THE WAY?
HE'S OUT-- NOT SURE WHY.
SHOULD WE WAIT FOR HIM?
THEY CHANGED ROOMS.
NO, IT'S OKAY.
I HAVE OTHER PLACES TO VISIT, SO I CAN'T STAY LONG.
WHAT? TAKE YOUR TIME!
I JUST CAME TO SEE YOUR FACES.
HOW SHOULD I SAY THIS--
YOU GOT SENTIMENTAL ABOUT THE END OF APRIL SEASON.
NOW YOU LIVE IN AN AUTUMN DOMAIN, AFTER ALL.
YOU DON'T HAVE TO PUT IT LIKE THAT.
HA HA!

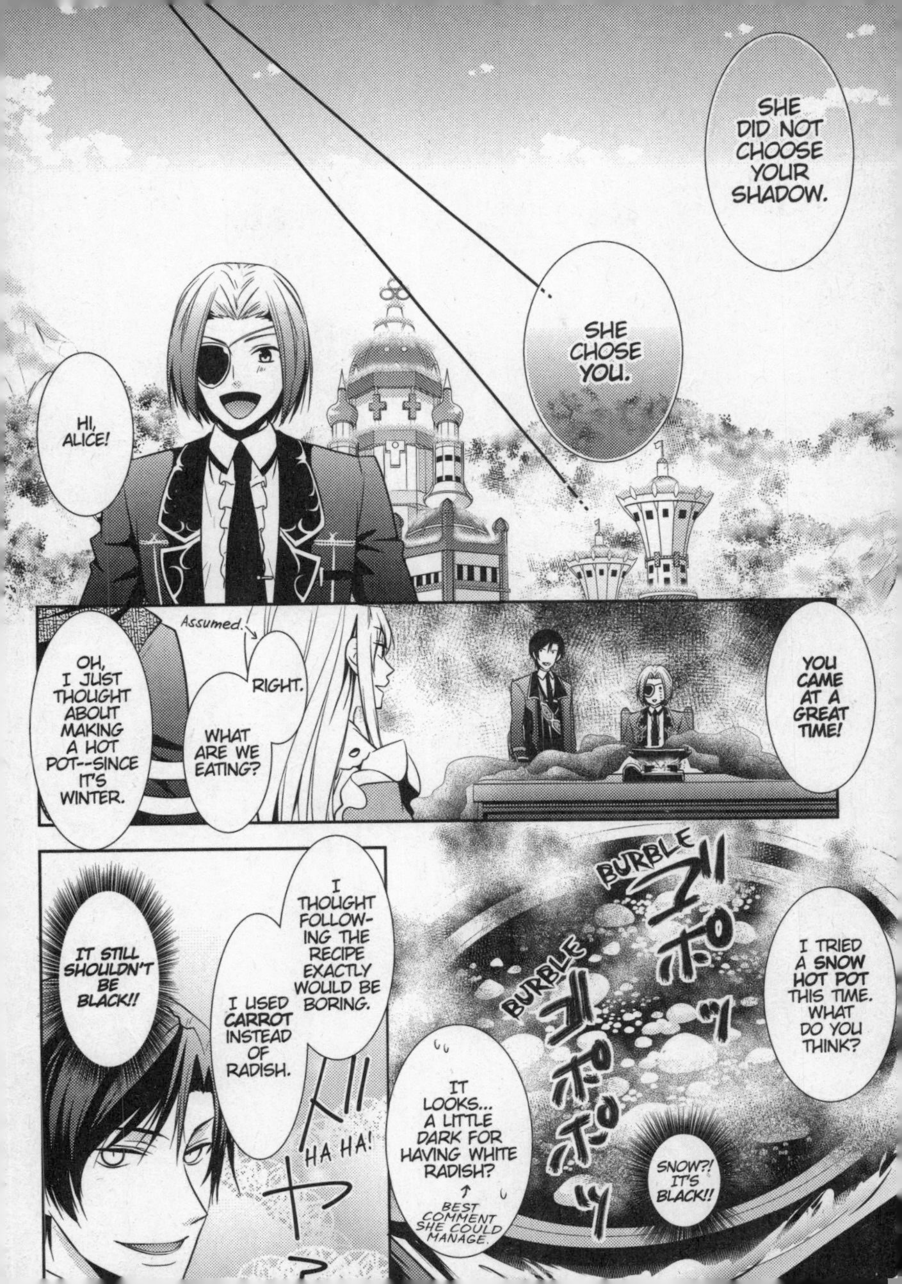
SHE DID NOT CHOOSE YOUR SHADOW.
SHE CHOSE YOU.
HI, ALICE!
YOU CAME AT A GREAT TIME!
RIGHT.
Assumed.
WHAT ARE WE EATING?
OH, I JUST THOUGHT ABOUT MAKING A HOT POT--SINCE IT'S WINTER.
I TRIED A SNOW HOT POT THIS TIME. WHAT DO YOU THINK?
BURBLE
BURBLE
SNOW?! IT'S BLACK!!
IT LOOKS... A LITTLE DARK FOR HAVING WHITE RADISH?
BEST COMMENT SHE COULD MANAGE.
I THOUGHT FOLLOW-ING THE RECIPE EXACTLY WOULD BE BORING.
I USED CARROT INSTEAD OF RADISH.
HA HA!
IT STILL SHOULDN'T BE BLACK!!

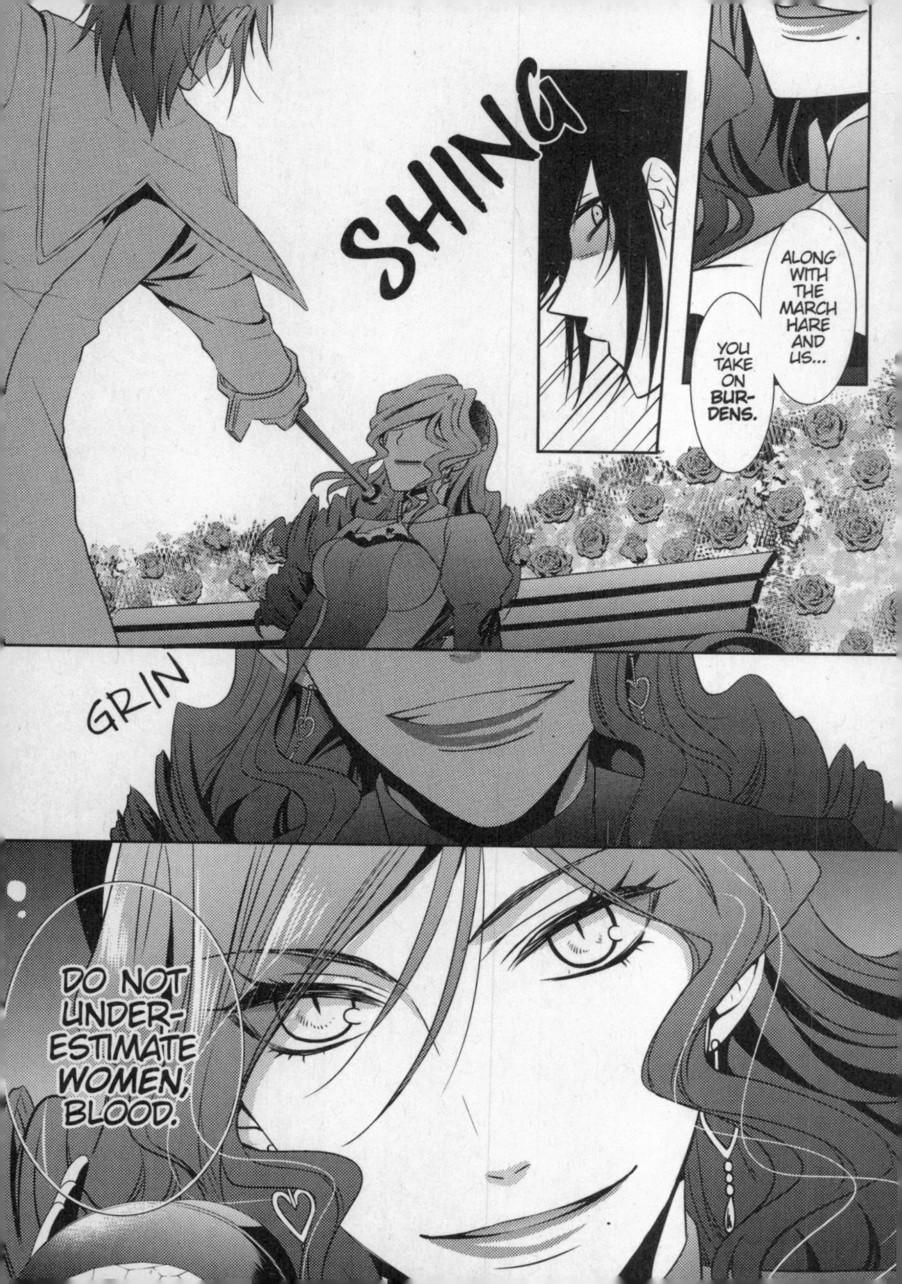
ALONG WITH THE MARCH HARE AND US...
YOU TAKE ON BURDENS.
SHING
GRIN
DO NOT UNDER-ESTIMATE WOMEN, BLOOD.

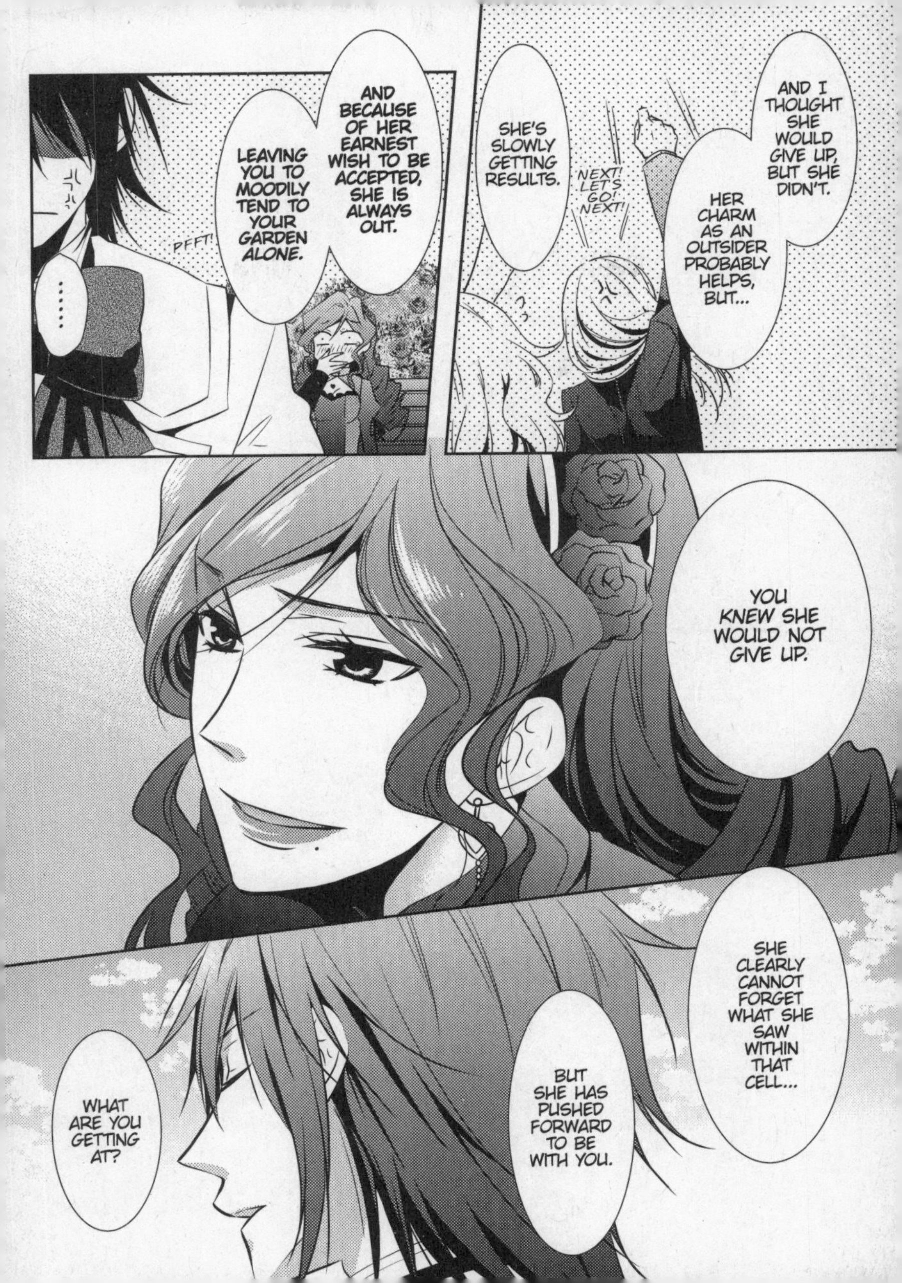
AND I THOUGHT SHE WOULD GIVE UP, BUT SHE DIDN'T.
HER CHARM AS AN OUTSIDER PROBABLY HELPS, BUT...
NEXT! LET'S GO! NEXT!
SHE'S SLOWLY GETTING RESULTS.
AND BECAUSE OF HER EARNEST WISH TO BE ACCEPTED, SHE IS ALWAYS OUT.
LEAVING YOU TO MOODILY TEND TO YOUR GARDEN ALONE.
PFFT!
......
YOU KNEW SHE WOULD NOT GIVE UP.
SHE CLEARLY CANNOT FORGET WHAT SHE SAW WITHIN THAT CELL...
BUT SHE HAS PUSHED FORWARD TO BE WITH YOU.
WHAT ARE YOU GETTING AT?

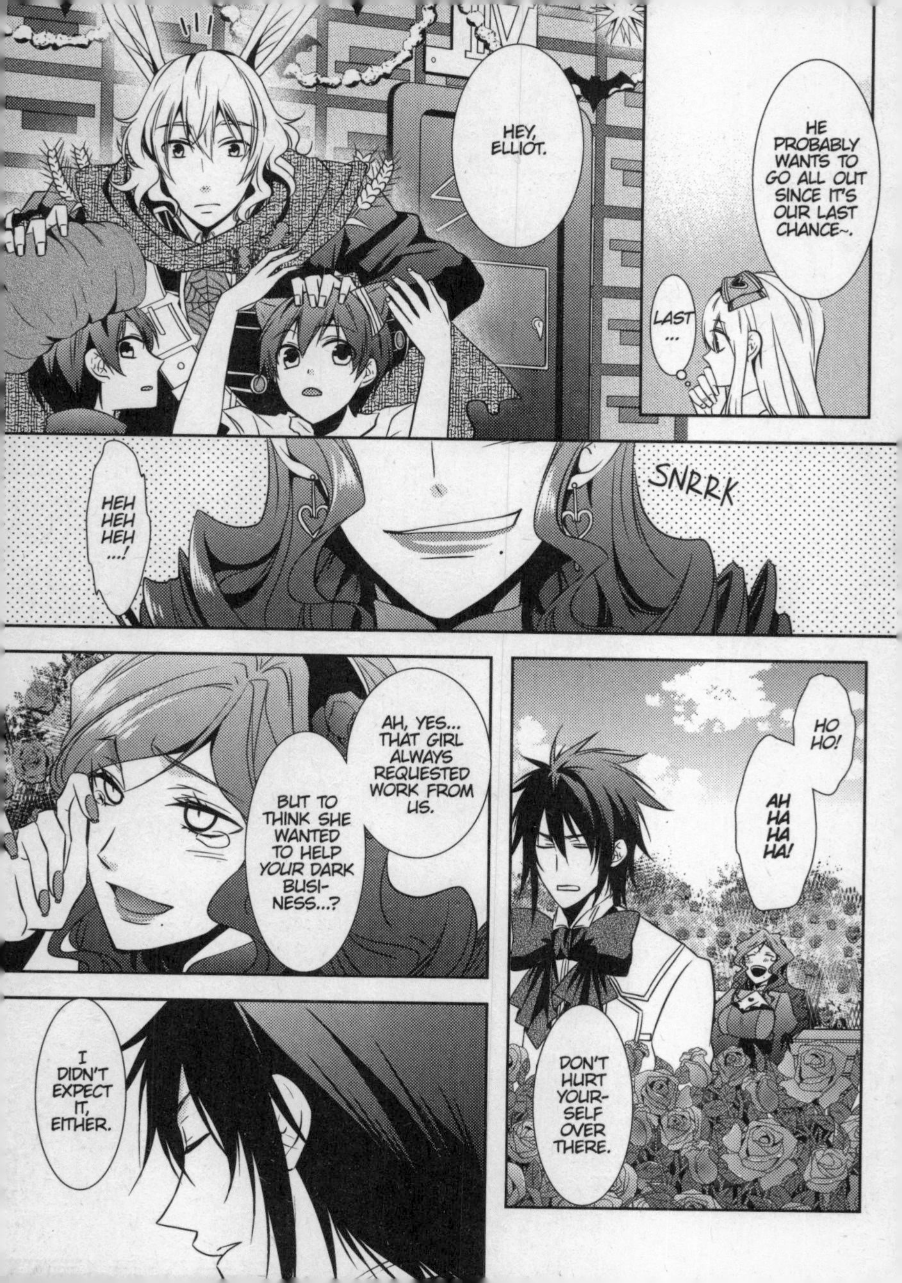
HE PROBABLY WANTS TO GO ALL OUT SINCE IT'S OUR LAST CHANCE~.
LAST ...
HEY, ELLIOT.
SNRRK
HEH HEH HEH ....!
HO HO!
AH HA HA HA!
DON'T HURT YOUR-SELF OVER THERE.
AH, YES... THAT GIRL ALWAYS REQUESTED WORK FROM US.
BUT TO THINK SHE WANTED TO HELP YOUR DARK BUSI-NESS...?
I DIDN'T EXPECT IT, EITHER.

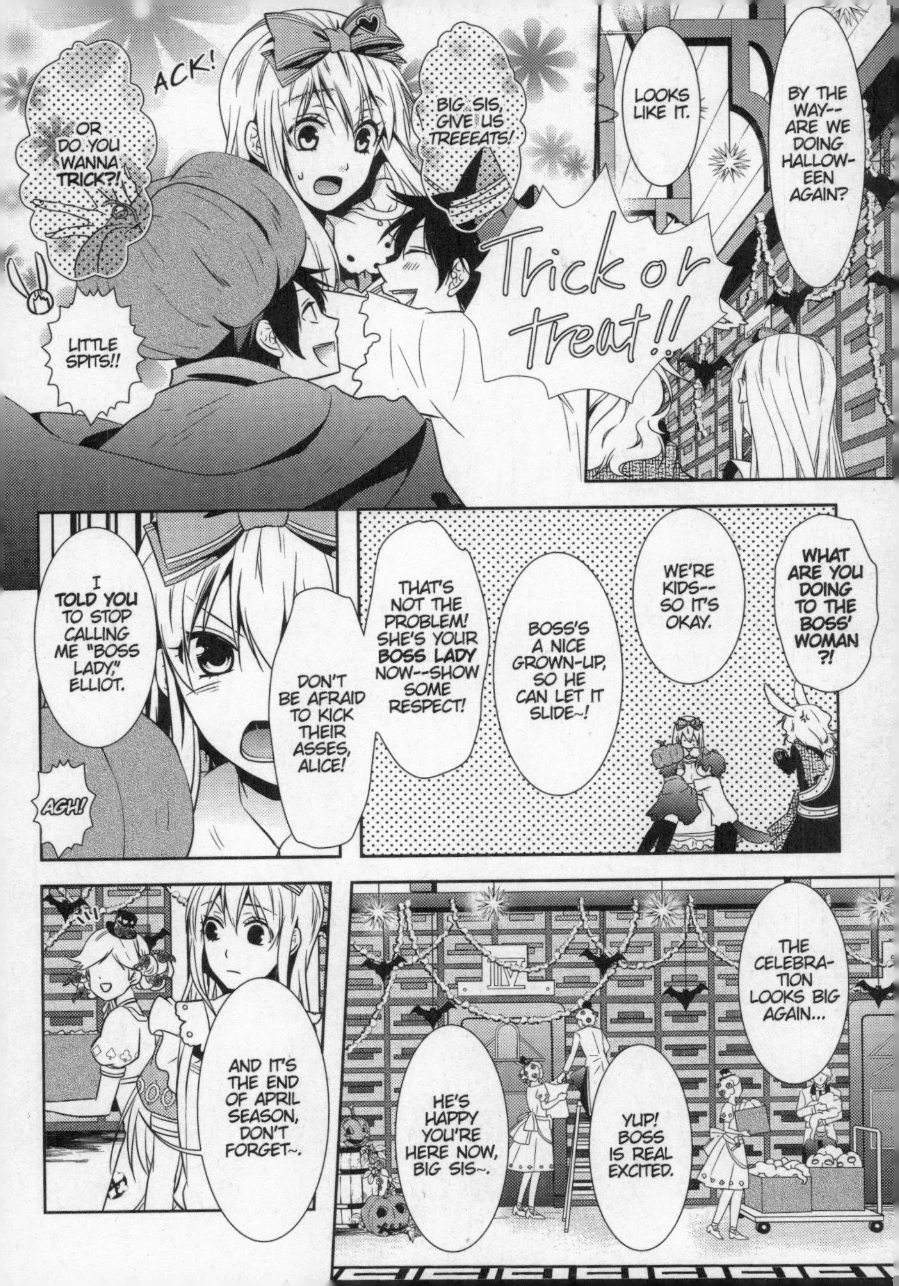
BY THE WAY--ARE WE DOING HALLOWEEN AGAIN?
LOOKS LIKE IT.
Trick or treat!!
BIG SIS, GIVE US TREEEATS!
ACK!
OR DO YOU WANNA TRICK?!
LITTLE SPITS!!
WHAT ARE YOU DOING TO THE BOSS' WOMAN?!
WE'RE KIDS--SO IT'S OKAY.
BOSS'S A NICE GROWN-UP, SO HE CAN LET IT SLIDE~!
THAT'S NOT THE PROBLEM! SHE'S YOUR BOSS LADY NOW--SHOW SOME RESPECT!
DON'T BE AFRAID TO KICK THEIR ASSES, ALICE!
I TOLD YOU TO STOP CALLING ME "BOSS LADY," ELLIOT.
AGH!
THE CELEBRATION LOOKS BIG AGAIN...
YUP! BOSS IS REAL EXCITED.
HE'S HAPPY YOU'RE HERE NOW, BIG SIS~.
AND IT'S THE END OF APRIL SEASON, DON'T FORGET~.

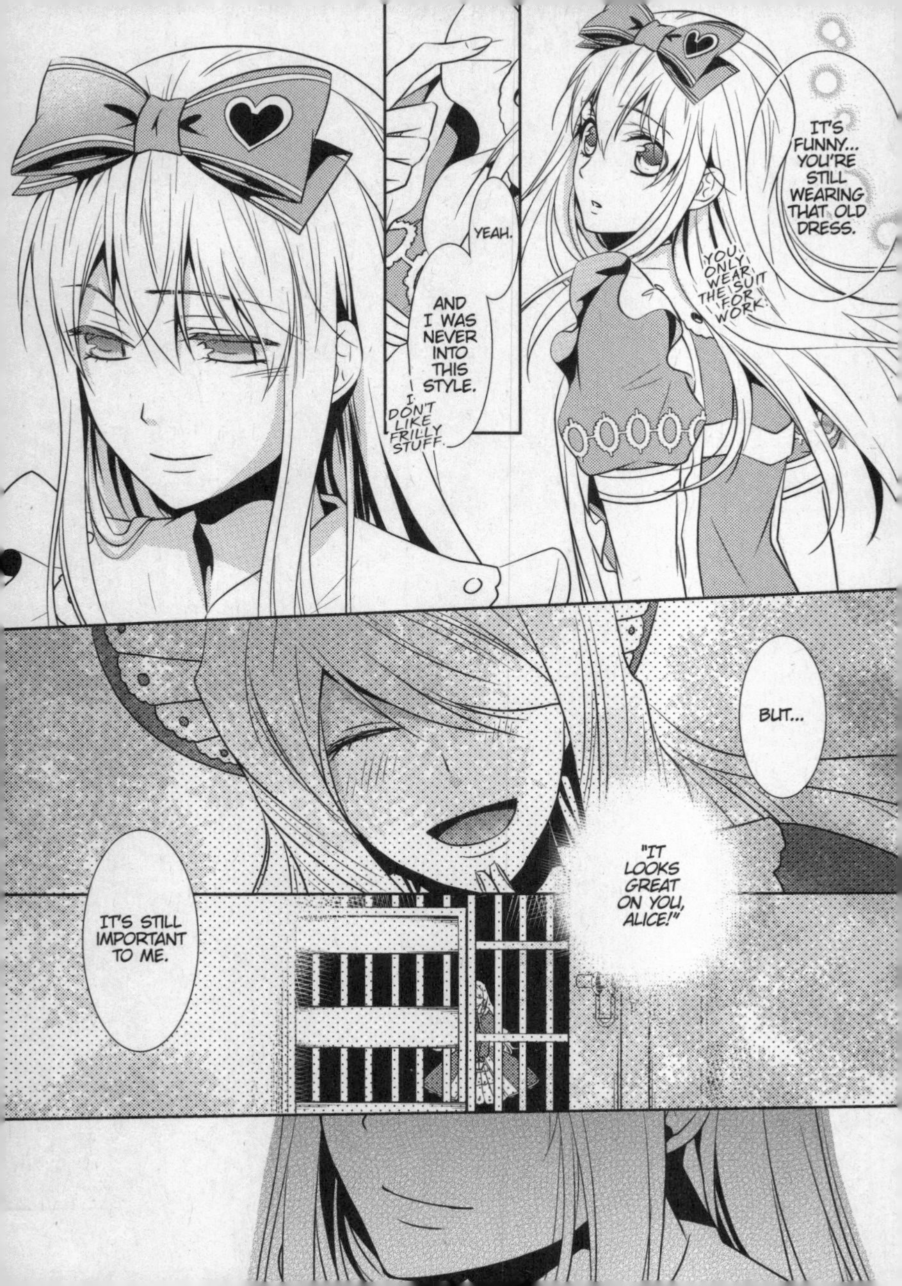
IT'S FUNNY... YOU'RE STILL WEARING THAT OLD DRESS.
YOU ONLY WEAR THE SUIT FOR WORK.
YEAH.
AND I WAS NEVER INTO THIS STYLE.
I DON'T LIKE FRILLY STUFF.
BUT...
"IT LOOKS GREAT ON YOU, ALICE!"
IT'S STILL IMPORTANT TO ME.

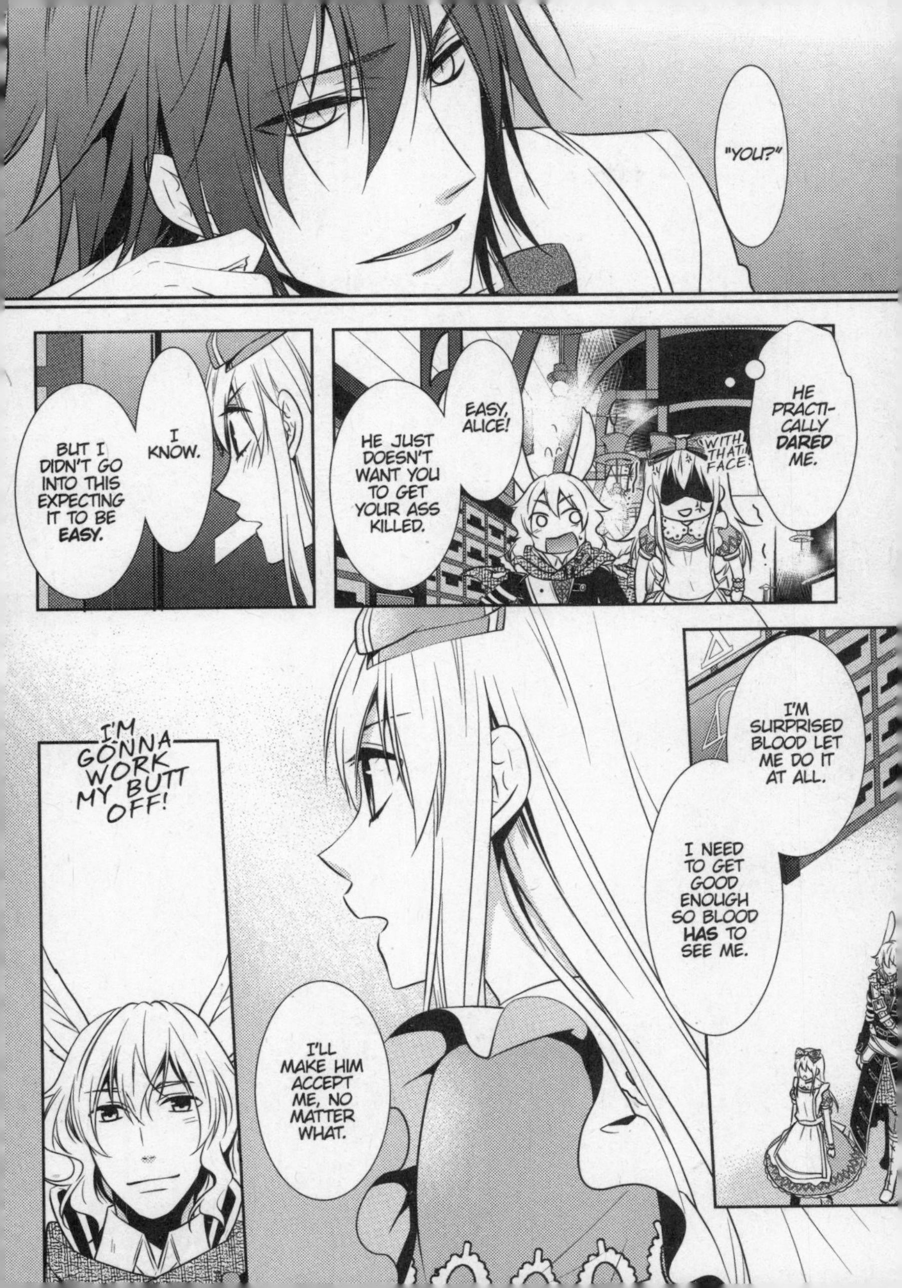
"YOU?"
HE PRACTI-CALLY DARED ME.
WITH THAT FACE.
EASY, ALICE!
HE JUST DOESN'T WANT YOU TO GET YOUR ASS KILLED.
I KNOW.
BUT I DIDN'T GO INTO THIS EXPECTING IT TO BE EASY.
I'M SURPRISED BLOOD LET ME DO IT AT ALL.
I NEED TO GET GOOD ENOUGH SO BLOOD HAS TO SEE ME.
I'LL MAKE HIM ACCEPT ME, NO MATTER WHAT.
I'M GONNA WORK MY BUTT OFF!

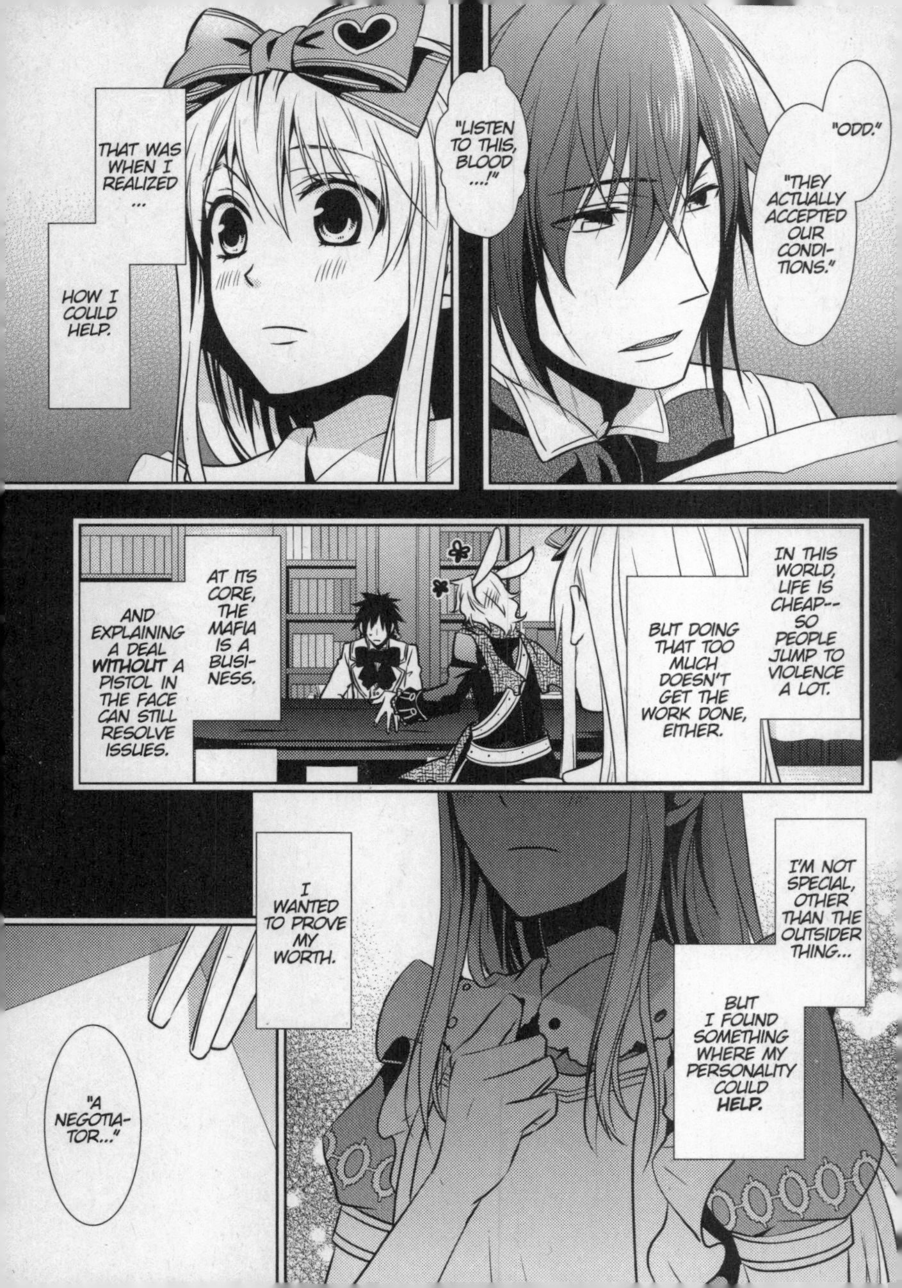
"ODD."
"THEY ACTUALLY ACCEPTED OUR CONDITIONS."
"LISTEN TO THIS, BLOOD ....!"
THAT WAS WHEN I REALIZED ...
HOW I COULD HELP.
IN THIS WORLD, LIFE IS CHEAP-- SO PEOPLE JUMP TO VIOLENCE A LOT.
BUT DOING THAT TOO MUCH DOESN'T GET THE WORK DONE, EITHER.
AT ITS CORE, THE MAFIA IS A BUSINESS.
AND EXPLAINING A DEAL **WITHOUT** A PISTOL IN THE FACE CAN STILL RESOLVE ISSUES.
I'M NOT SPECIAL, OTHER THAN THE OUTSIDER THING...
I WANTED TO PROVE MY WORTH.
BUT I FOUND SOMETHING WHERE MY PERSONALITY COULD **HELP.**
"A NEGOTIATOR..."

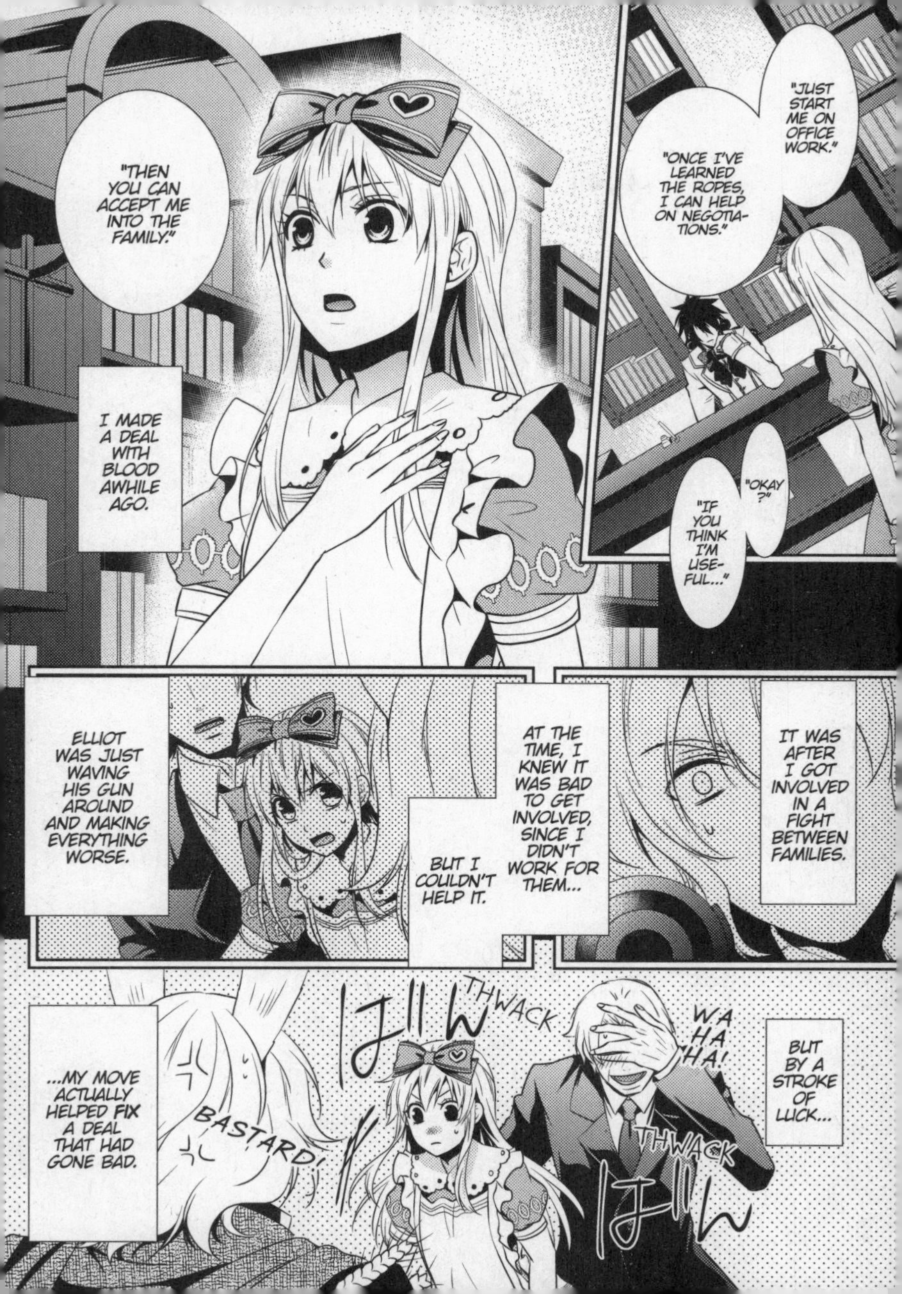
"JUST START ME ON OFFICE WORK."
"ONCE I'VE LEARNED THE ROPES, I CAN HELP ON NEGOTIATIONS."
"OKAY?"
"IF YOU THINK I'M USEFUL..."
"THEN YOU CAN ACCEPT ME INTO THE FAMILY."
I MADE A DEAL WITH BLOOD AWHILE AGO.
IT WAS AFTER I GOT INVOLVED IN A FIGHT BETWEEN FAMILIES.
AT THE TIME, I KNEW IT WAS BAD TO GET INVOLVED, SINCE I DIDN'T WORK FOR THEM...
BUT I COULDN'T HELP IT.
ELLIOT WAS JUST WAVING HIS GUN AROUND AND MAKING EVERYTHING WORSE.
BUT BY A STROKE OF LUCK...
WA HA HA!
THWACK
THWACK
BASTARD!
...MY MOVE ACTUALLY HELPED **FIX** A DEAL THAT HAD GONE BAD.

Stand: Final Chapter

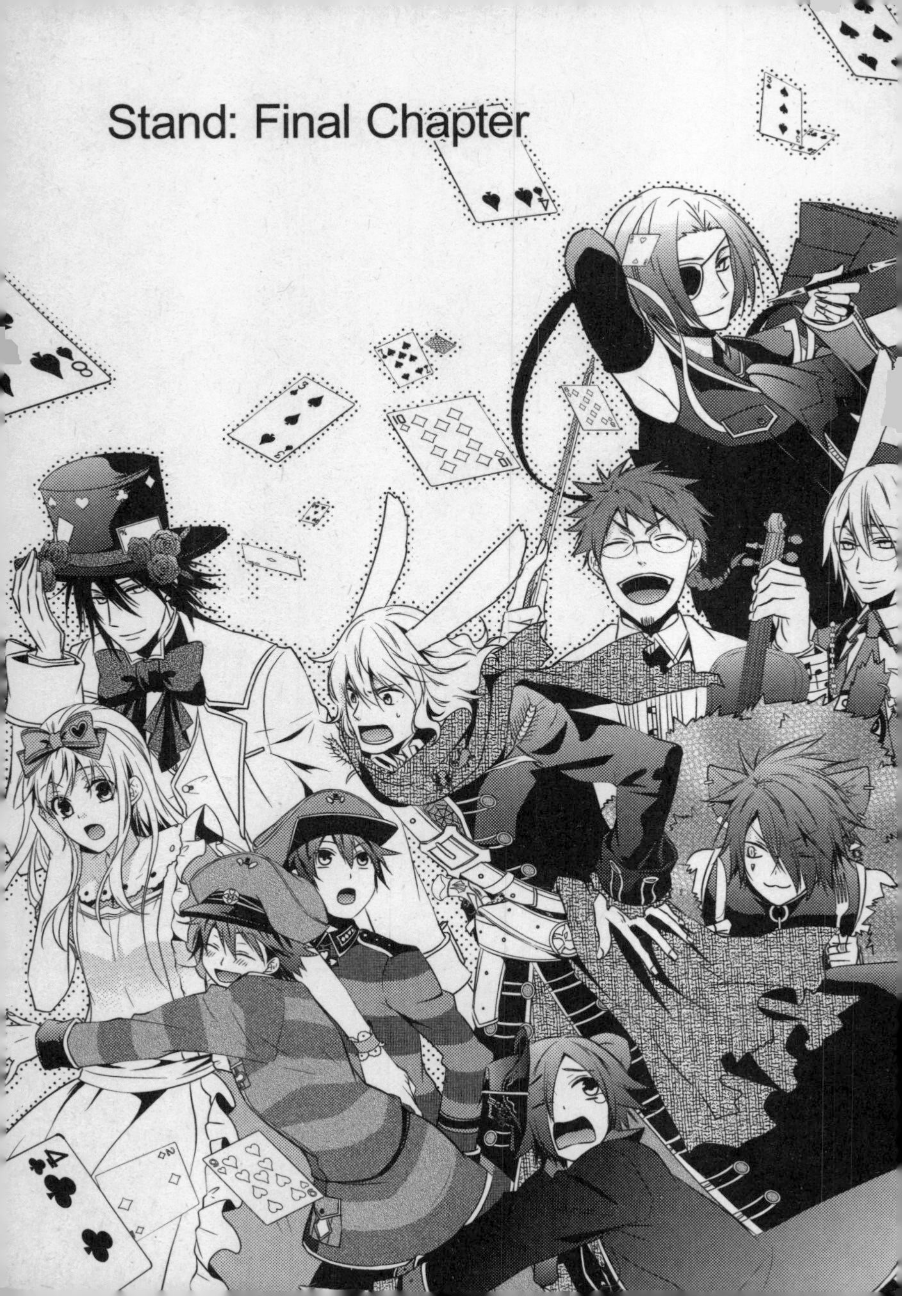

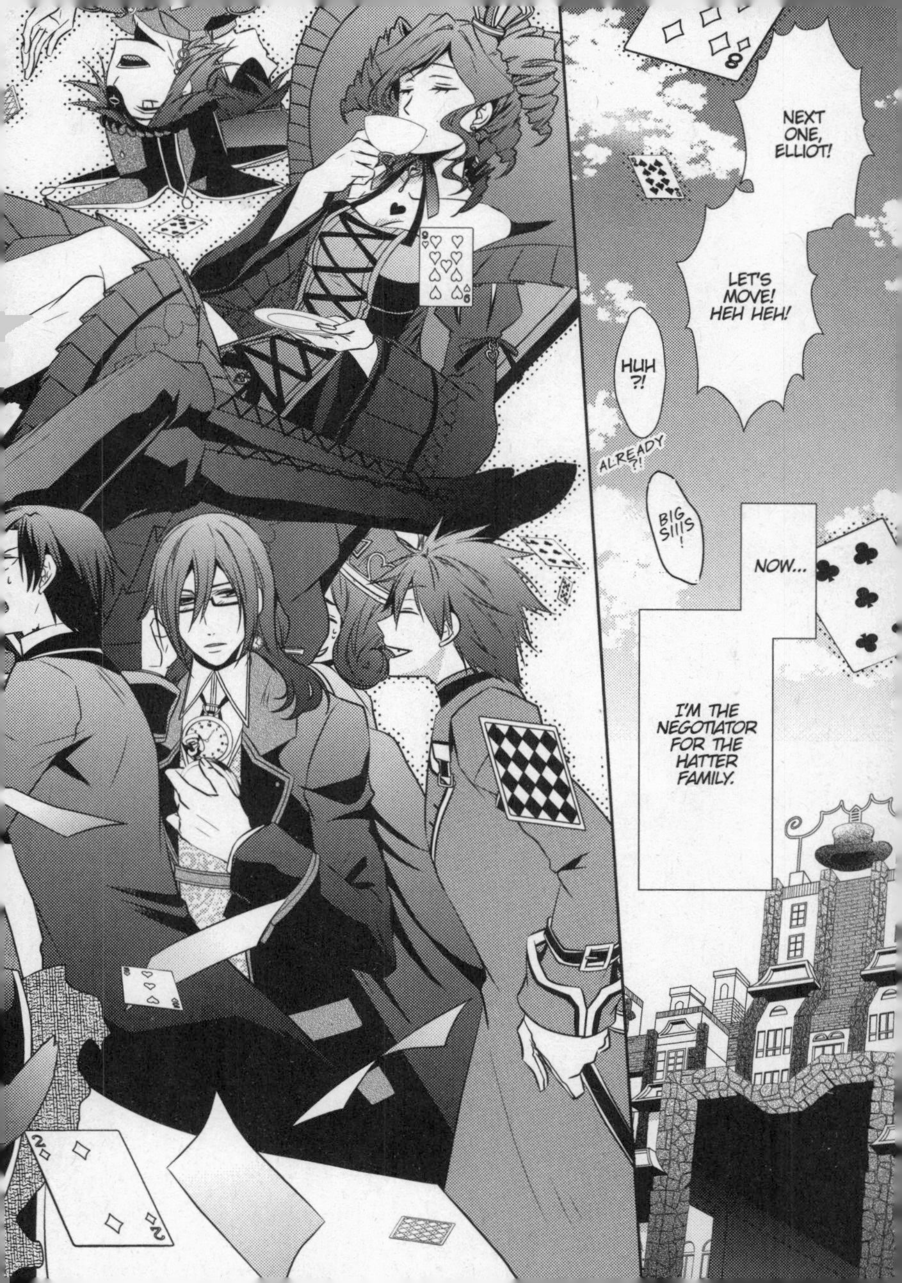
NEXT ONE, ELLIOT!
LET'S MOVE! HEH HEH!
HUH?!
ALREADY?!
BIG SIIIS!
NOW...
I'M THE NEGOTIATOR FOR THE HATTER FAMILY.

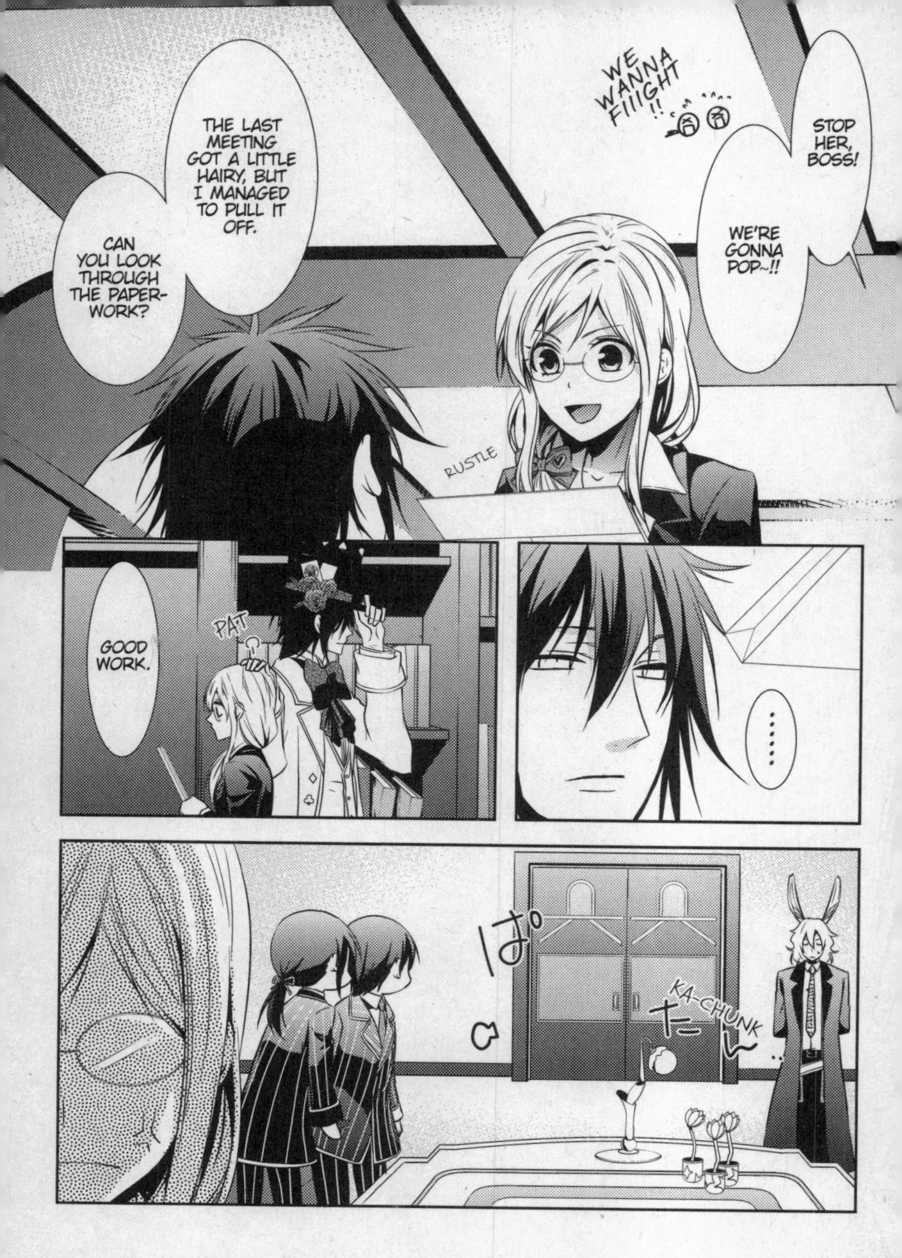
STOP HER, BOSS!
WE WANNA FIIIGHT!!
WE'RE GONNA POP~!!
THE LAST MEETING GOT A LITTLE HAIRY, BUT I MANAGED TO PULL IT OFF.
CAN YOU LOOK THROUGH THE PAPER-WORK?
RUSTLE
......
GOOD WORK.
PAT
KA-CHUNK

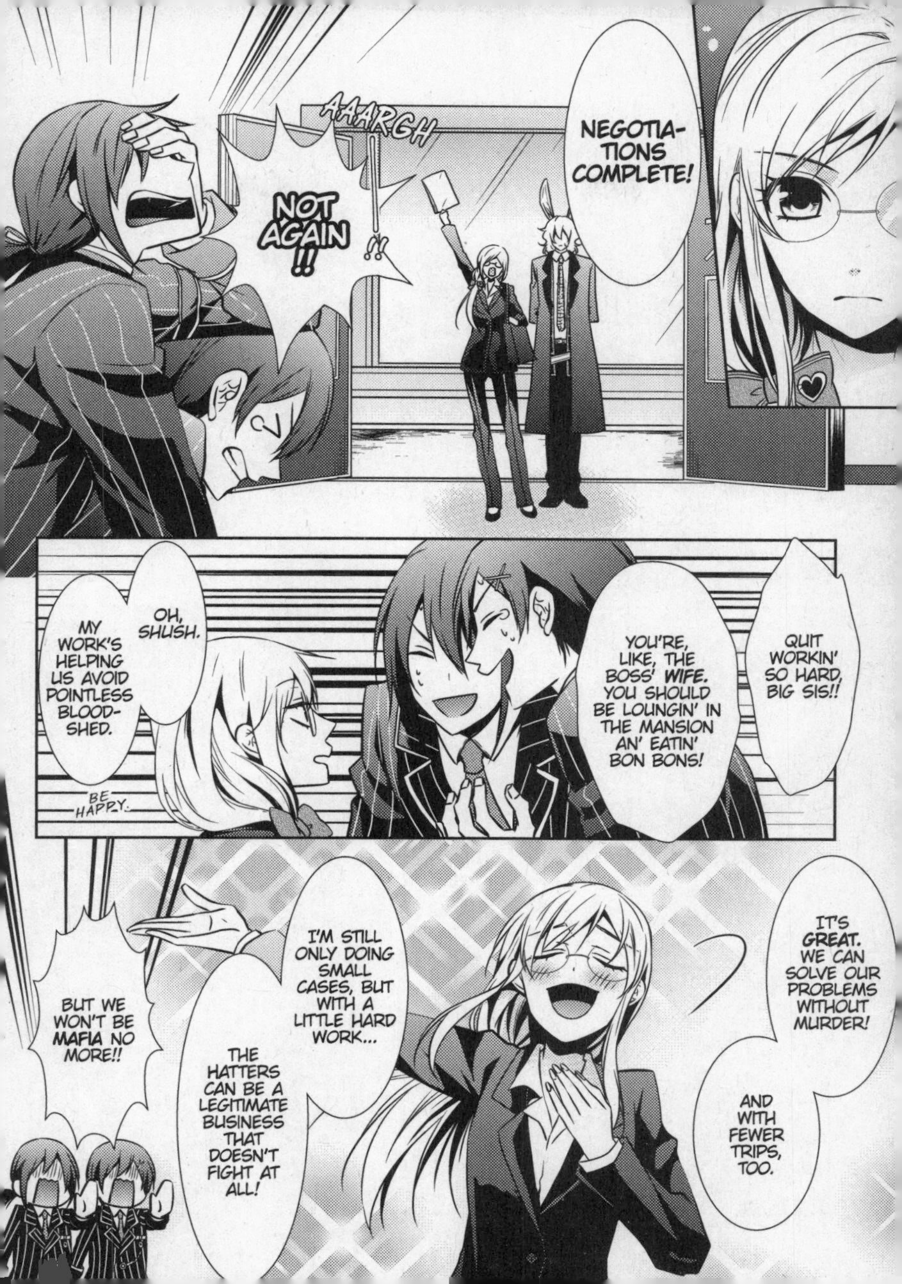
NEGOTIA-TIONS COMPLETE!
AAARGH
NOT AGAIN!!
!?!!
QUIT WORKIN' SO HARD, BIG SIS!!
YOU'RE, LIKE, THE BOSS' **WIFE.** YOU SHOULD BE LOUNGIN' IN THE MANSION AN' EATIN' BON BONS!
OH, SHUSH.
MY WORK'S HELPING US AVOID POINTLESS BLOOD-SHED.
BE HAPPY.
IT'S **GREAT.** WE CAN SOLVE OUR PROBLEMS WITHOUT MURDER!
AND WITH FEWER TRIPS, TOO.
I'M STILL ONLY DOING SMALL CASES, BUT WITH A LITTLE HARD WORK...
THE HATTERS CAN BE A LEGITIMATE BUSINESS THAT DOESN'T FIGHT AT ALL!
BUT WE WON'T BE **MAFIA** NO MORE!!

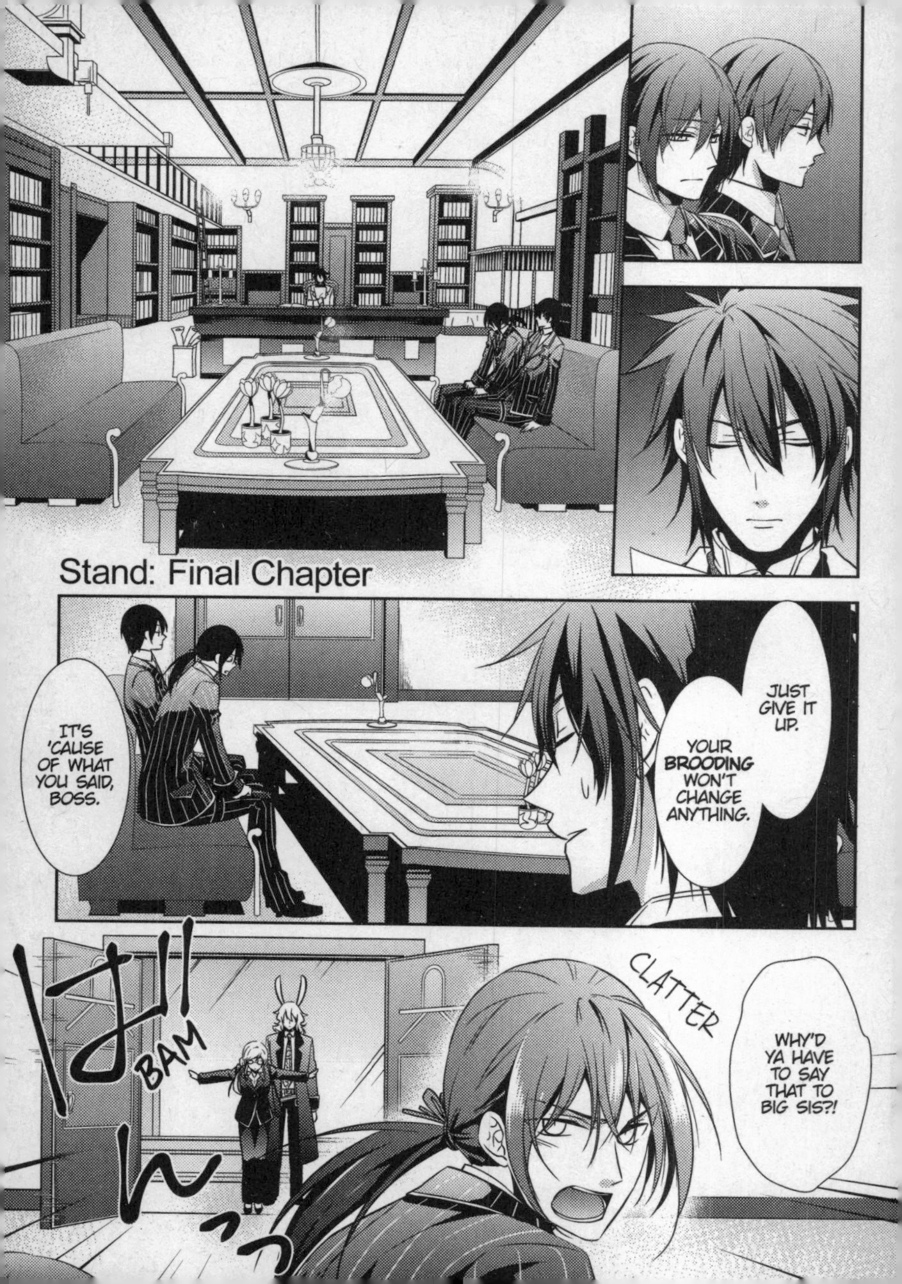
Stand: Final Chapter
JUST GIVE IT UP.
YOUR BROODING WON'T CHANGE ANYTHING.
IT'S 'CAUSE OF WHAT YOU SAID, BOSS.
WHY'D YA HAVE TO SAY THAT TO BIG SIS?!
CLATTER
BAM

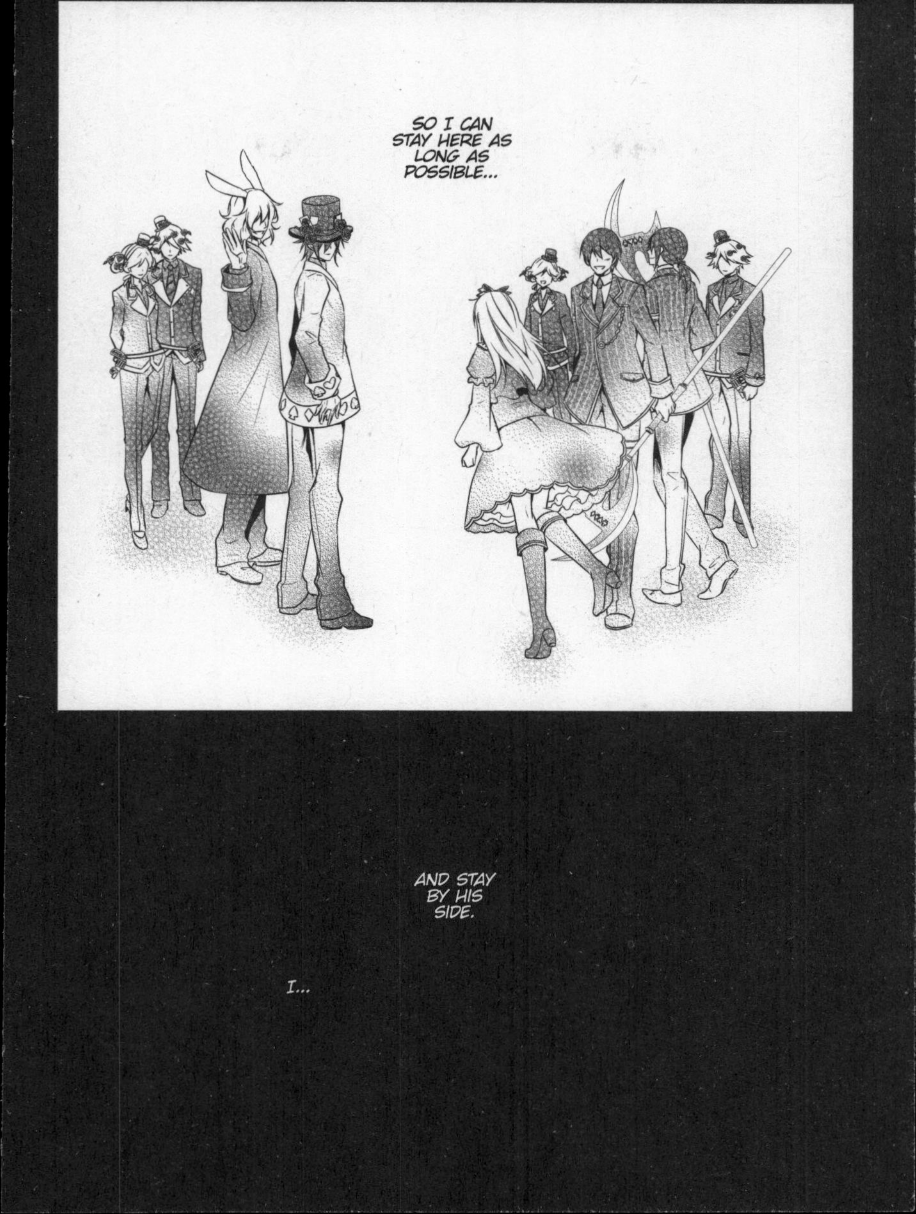
SO I CAN STAY HERE AS LONG AS POSSIBLE...
AND STAY BY HIS SIDE.
I...

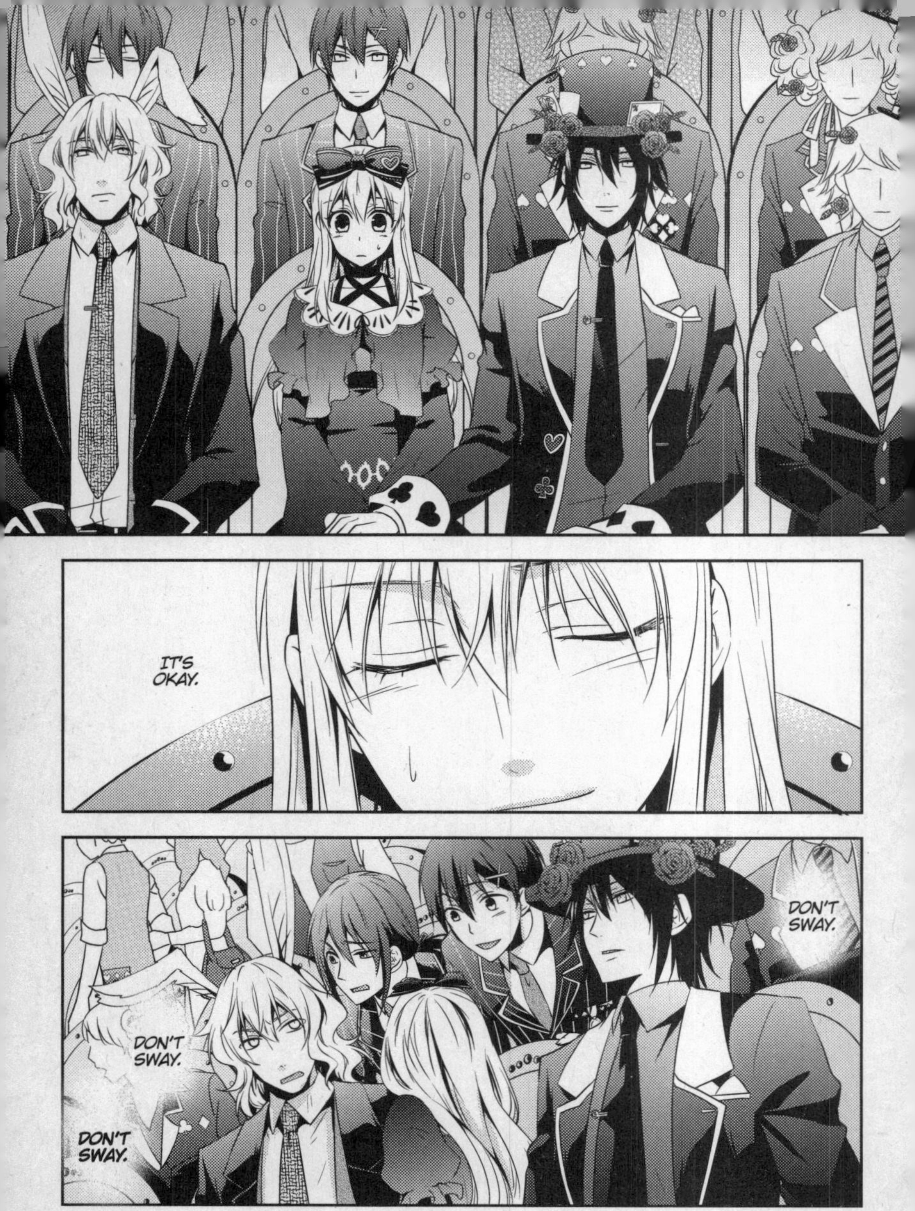
IT'S OKAY.
DON'T SWAY.
DON'T SWAY.
DON'T SWAY.

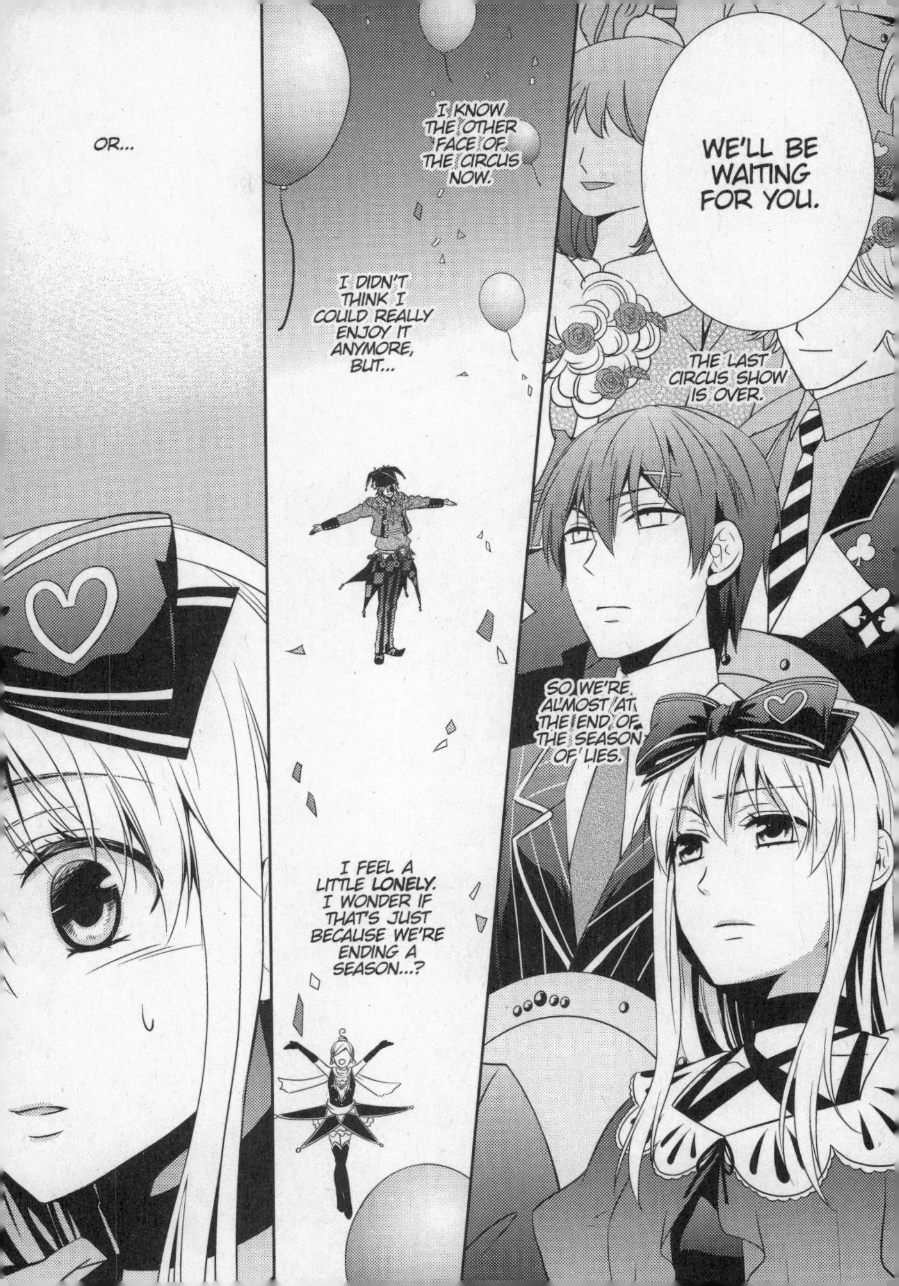
WE'LL BE WAITING FOR YOU.
THE LAST CIRCUS SHOW IS OVER.
SO WE'RE ALMOST AT THE END OF THE SEASON OF LIES.
I KNOW THE OTHER FACE OF THE CIRCUS NOW.
I DIDN'T THINK I COULD REALLY ENJOY IT ANYMORE, BUT...
I FEEL A LITTLE LONELY. I WONDER IF THAT'S JUST BECAUSE WE'RE ENDING A SEASON...?
OR...

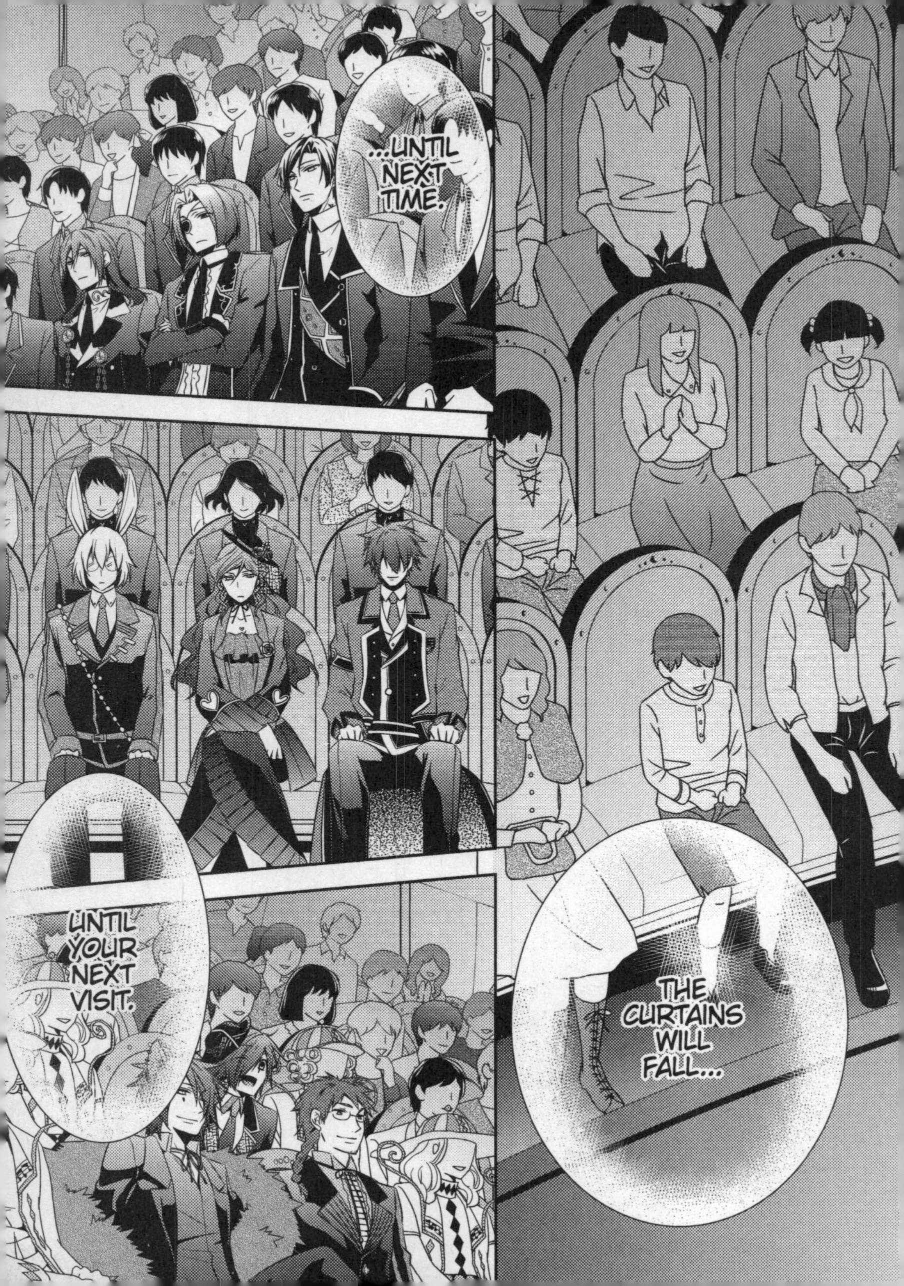
THE CURTAINS WILL FALL...
...UNTIL NEXT TIME.
UNTIL YOUR NEXT VISIT.

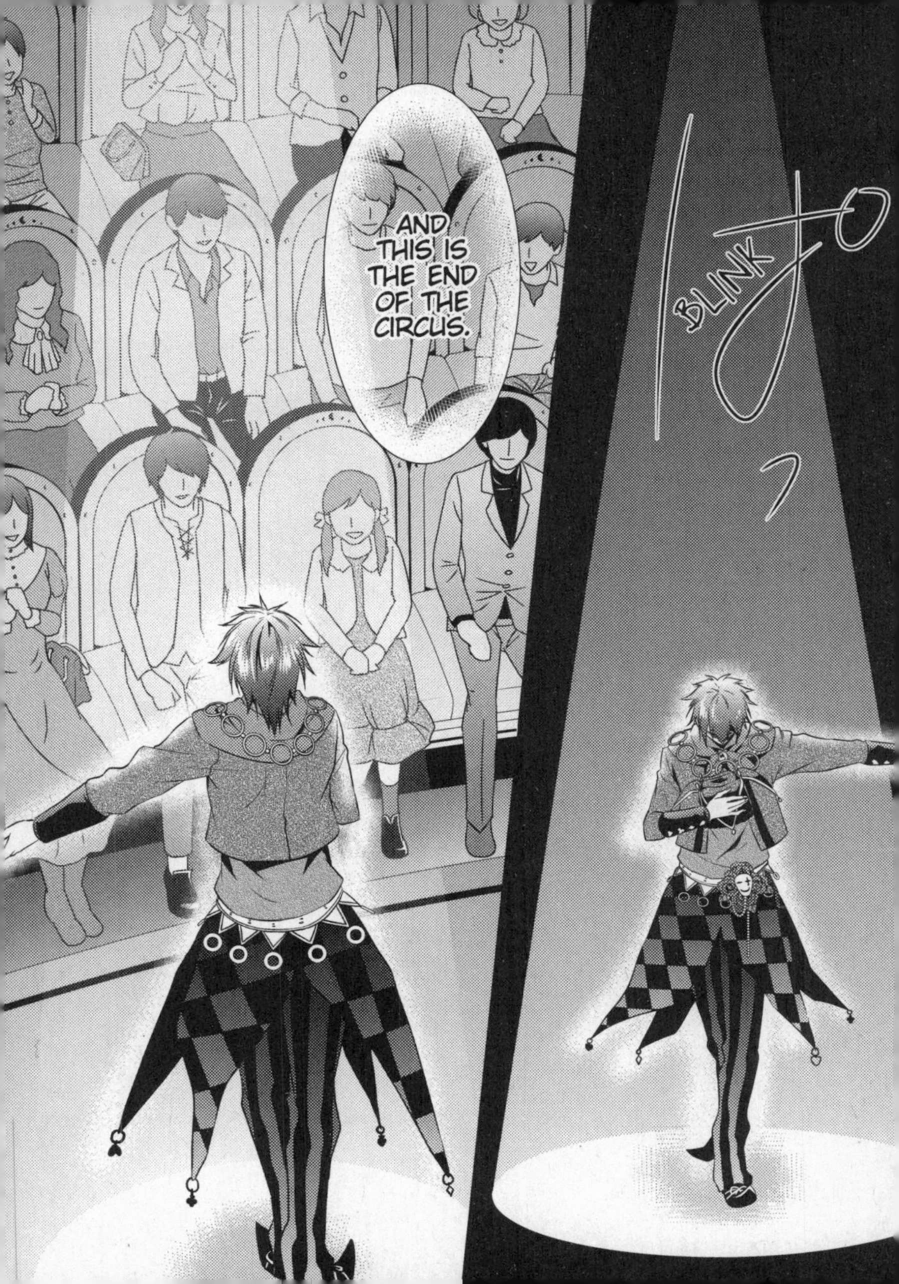
BLINK
AND THIS IS THE END OF THE CIRCUS.

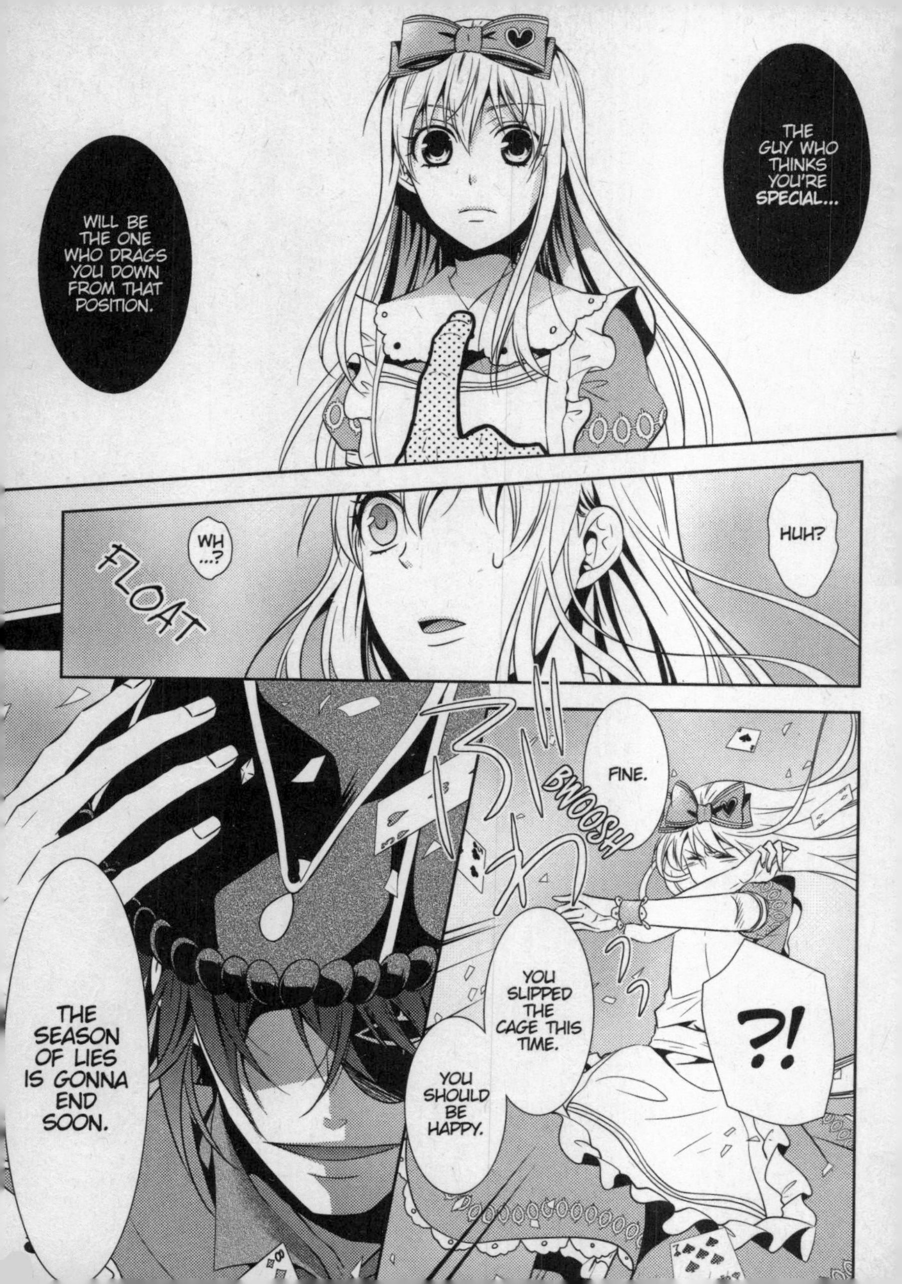
THE GUY WHO THINKS YOU'RE SPECIAL...
WILL BE THE ONE WHO DRAGS YOU DOWN FROM THAT POSITION.
HUH?
WH ...?
FLOAT
FINE.
BWOOSH
?!
YOU SLIPPED THE CAGE THIS TIME.
YOU SHOULD BE HAPPY.
THE SEASON OF LIES IS GONNA END SOON.

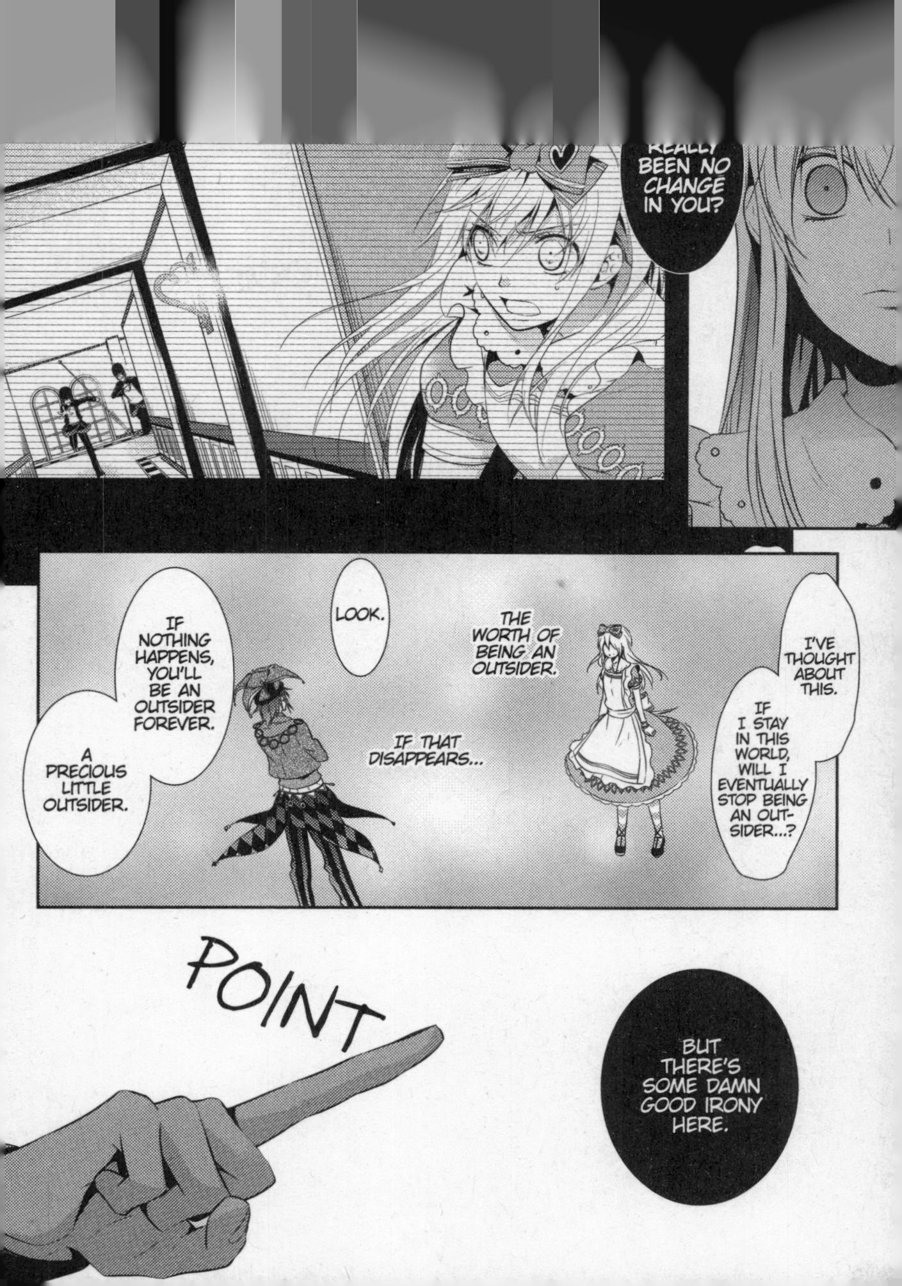
BEEN NO CHANGE IN YOU?
I'VE THOUGHT ABOUT THIS.
IF I STAY IN THIS WORLD, WILL I EVENTUALLY STOP BEING AN OUT-SIDER...?
THE WORTH OF BEING AN OUTSIDER.
IF THAT DISAPPEARS...
LOOK.
IF NOTHING HAPPENS, YOU'LL BE AN OUTSIDER FOREVER.
A PRECIOUS LITTLE OUTSIDER.
BUT THERE'S SOME DAMN GOOD IRONY HERE.
POINT

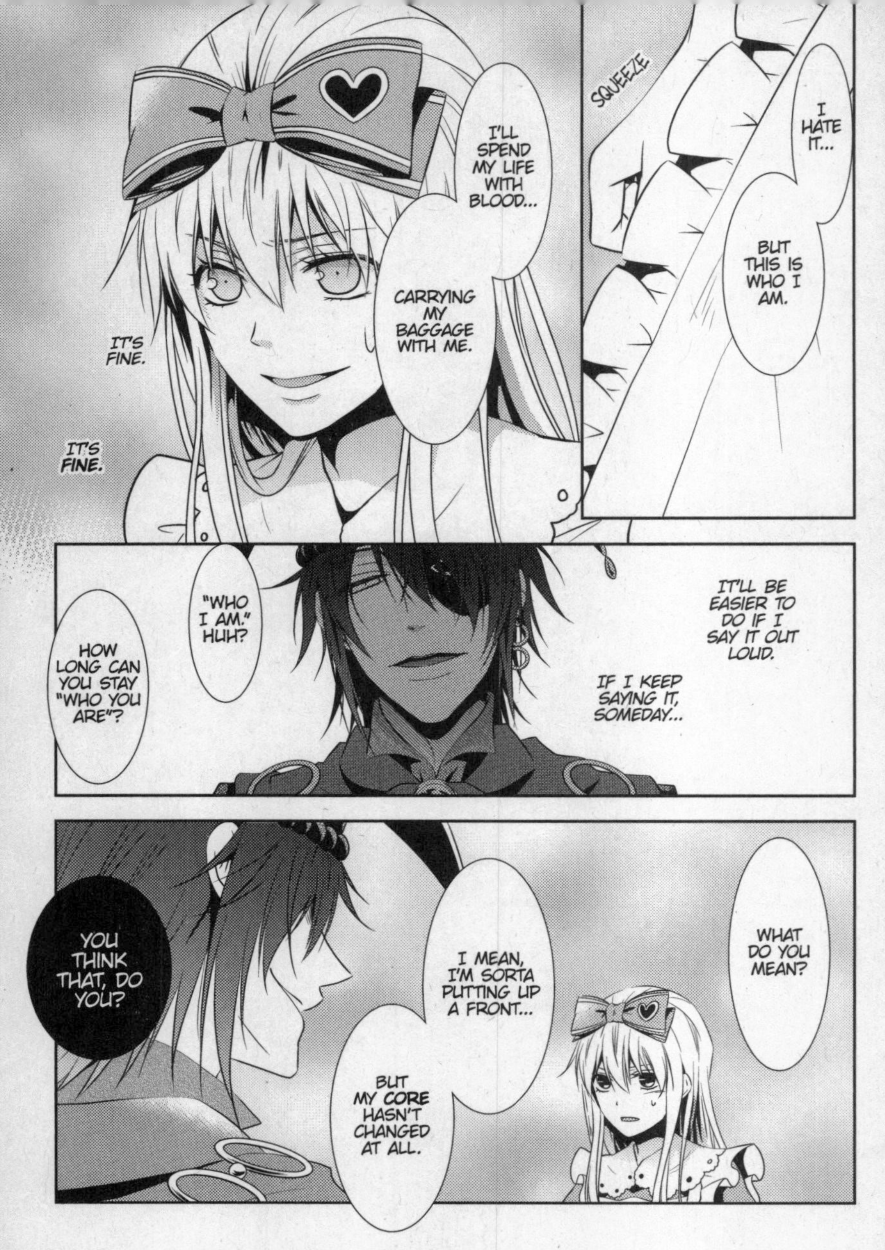
SQUEEZE
I HATE IT...
BUT THIS IS WHO I AM.
I'LL SPEND MY LIFE WITH BLOOD...
CARRYING MY BAGGAGE WITH ME.
IT'S FINE.
IT'S FINE.
IT'LL BE EASIER TO DO IF I SAY IT OUT LOUD.
IF I KEEP SAYING IT, SOMEDAY...
"WHO I AM." HUH?
HOW LONG CAN YOU STAY "WHO YOU ARE"?
WHAT DO YOU MEAN?
I MEAN, I'M SORTA PUTTING UP A FRONT...
BUT MY CORE HASN'T CHANGED AT ALL.
YOU THINK THAT, DO YOU?

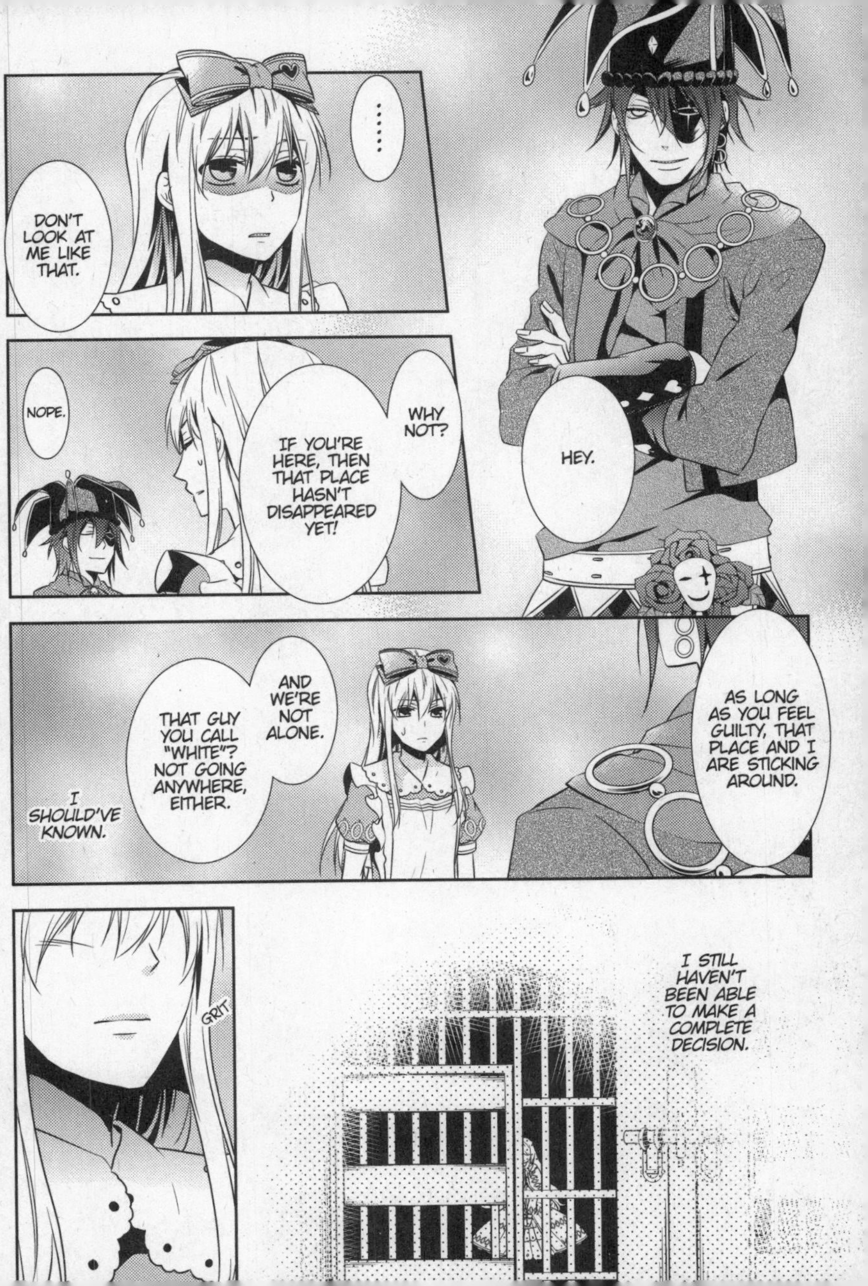
HEY.
......
DON'T LOOK AT ME LIKE THAT.
WHY NOT?
IF YOU'RE HERE, THEN THAT PLACE HASN'T DISAPPEARED YET!
NOPE.
AS LONG AS YOU FEEL GUILTY, THAT PLACE AND I ARE STICKING AROUND.
AND WE'RE NOT ALONE.
THAT GUY YOU CALL "WHITE"? NOT GOING ANYWHERE, EITHER.
I SHOULD'VE KNOWN.
I STILL HAVEN'T BEEN ABLE TO MAKE A COMPLETE DECISION.
GRIT

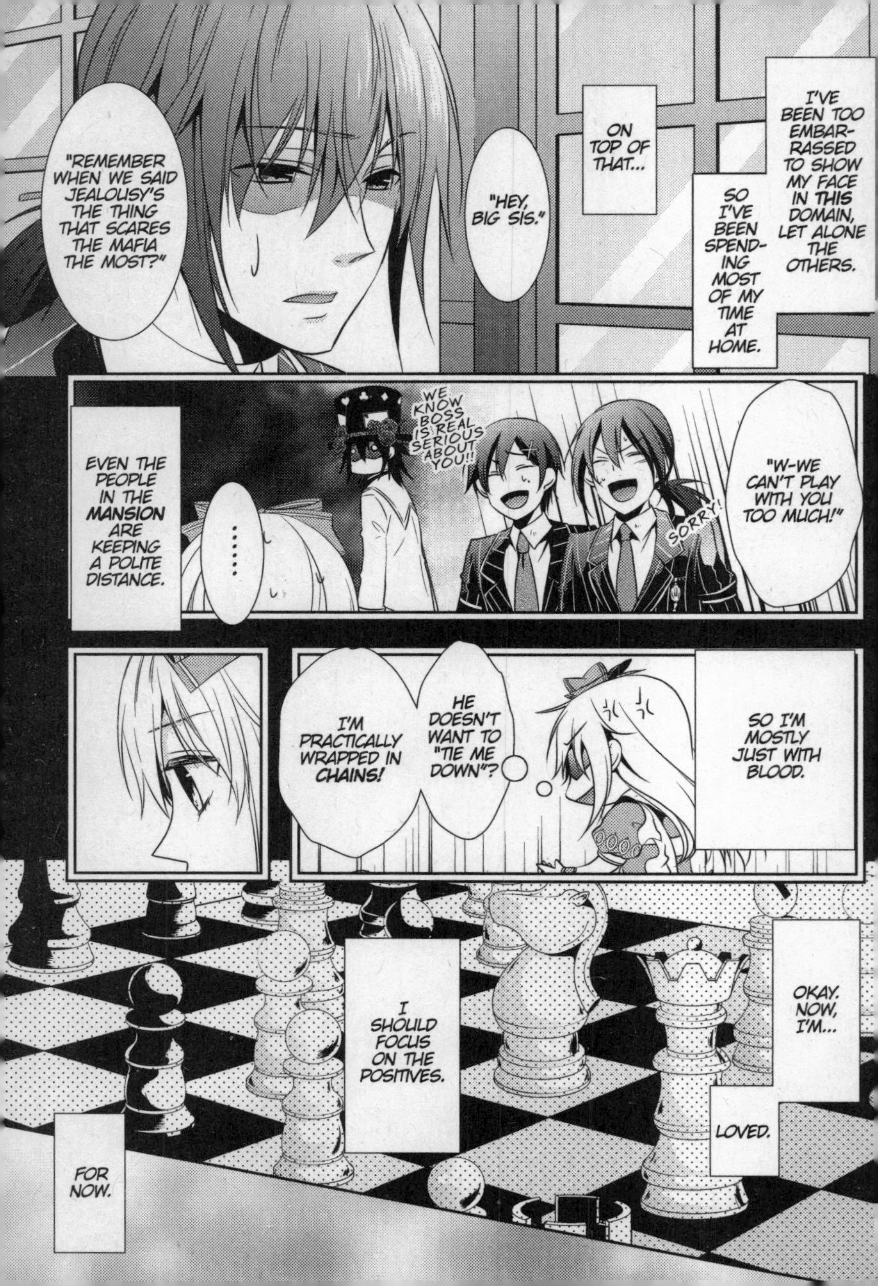
I'VE BEEN TOO EMBAR-RASSED TO SHOW MY FACE IN THIS DOMAIN, LET ALONE THE OTHERS.
SO I'VE BEEN SPEND-ING MOST OF MY TIME AT HOME.
ON TOP OF THAT...
"HEY, BIG SIS."
"REMEMBER WHEN WE SAID JEALOUSY'S THE THING THAT SCARES THE MAFIA THE MOST?"
"W-WE CAN'T PLAY WITH YOU TOO MUCH!"
SORRY!
WE KNOW BOSS IS REAL SERIOUS ABOUT YOU!!
......
EVEN THE PEOPLE IN THE MANSION ARE KEEPING A POLITE DISTANCE.
SO I'M MOSTLY JUST WITH BLOOD.
HE DOESN'T WANT TO "TIE ME DOWN"?
I'M PRACTICALLY WRAPPED IN CHAINS!
OKAY. NOW, I'M...
LOVED.
I SHOULD FOCUS ON THE POSITIVES.
FOR NOW.

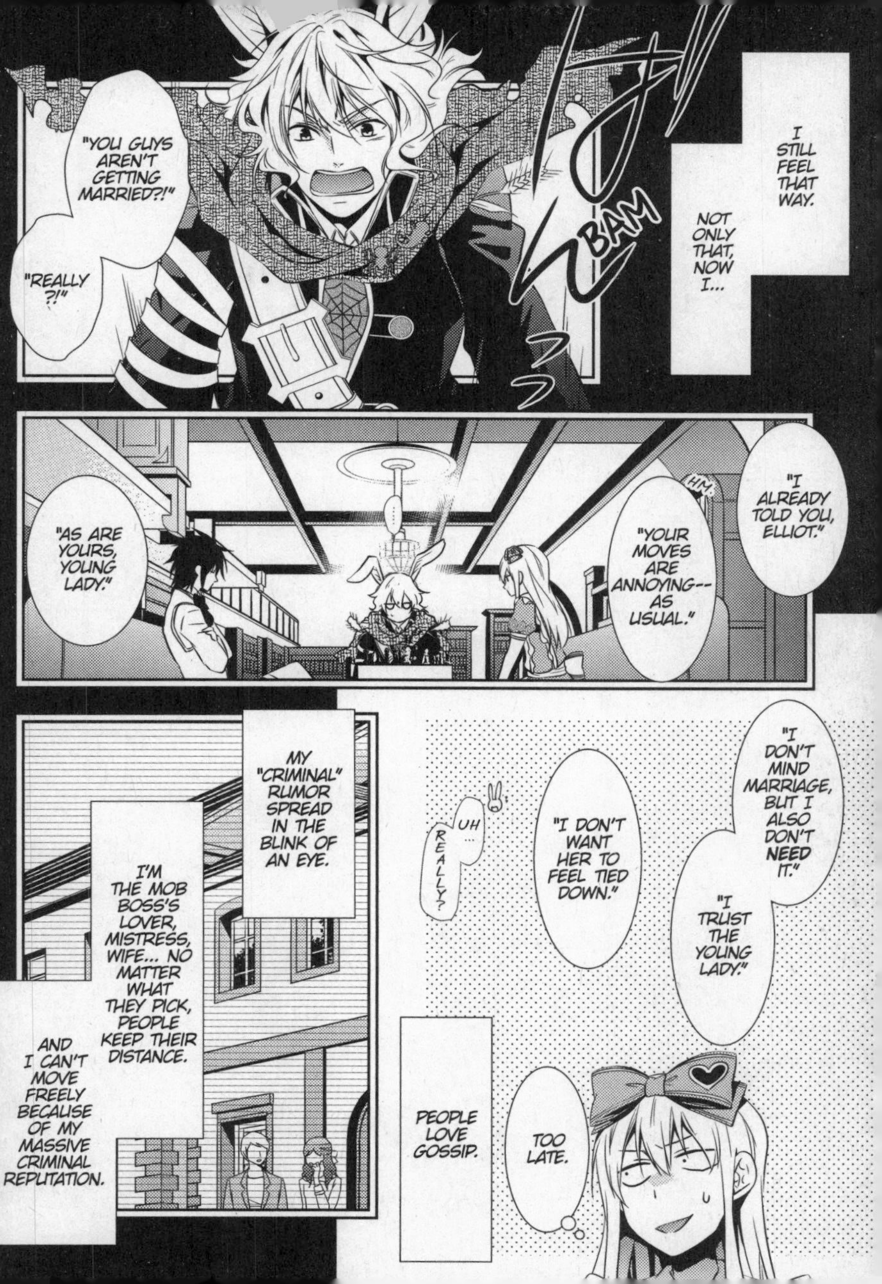
I STILL FEEL THAT WAY.
NOT ONLY THAT, NOW I...
BAM
"YOU GUYS AREN'T GETTING MARRIED?!"
"REALLY?!"
"I ALREADY TOLD YOU, ELLIOT."
HM.
"YOUR MOVES ARE ANNOYING-- AS USUAL."
"AS ARE YOURS, YOUNG LADY."
"I DON'T MIND MARRIAGE, BUT I ALSO DON'T NEED IT."
"I TRUST THE YOUNG LADY."
"I DON'T WANT HER TO FEEL TIED DOWN."
UH... REALLY?
TOO LATE.
PEOPLE LOVE GOSSIP.
MY "CRIMINAL" RUMOR SPREAD IN THE BLINK OF AN EYE.
I'M THE MOB BOSS'S LOVER, MISTRESS, WIFE... NO MATTER WHAT THEY PICK, PEOPLE KEEP THEIR DISTANCE.
AND I CAN'T MOVE FREELY BECAUSE OF MY MASSIVE CRIMINAL REPUTATION.

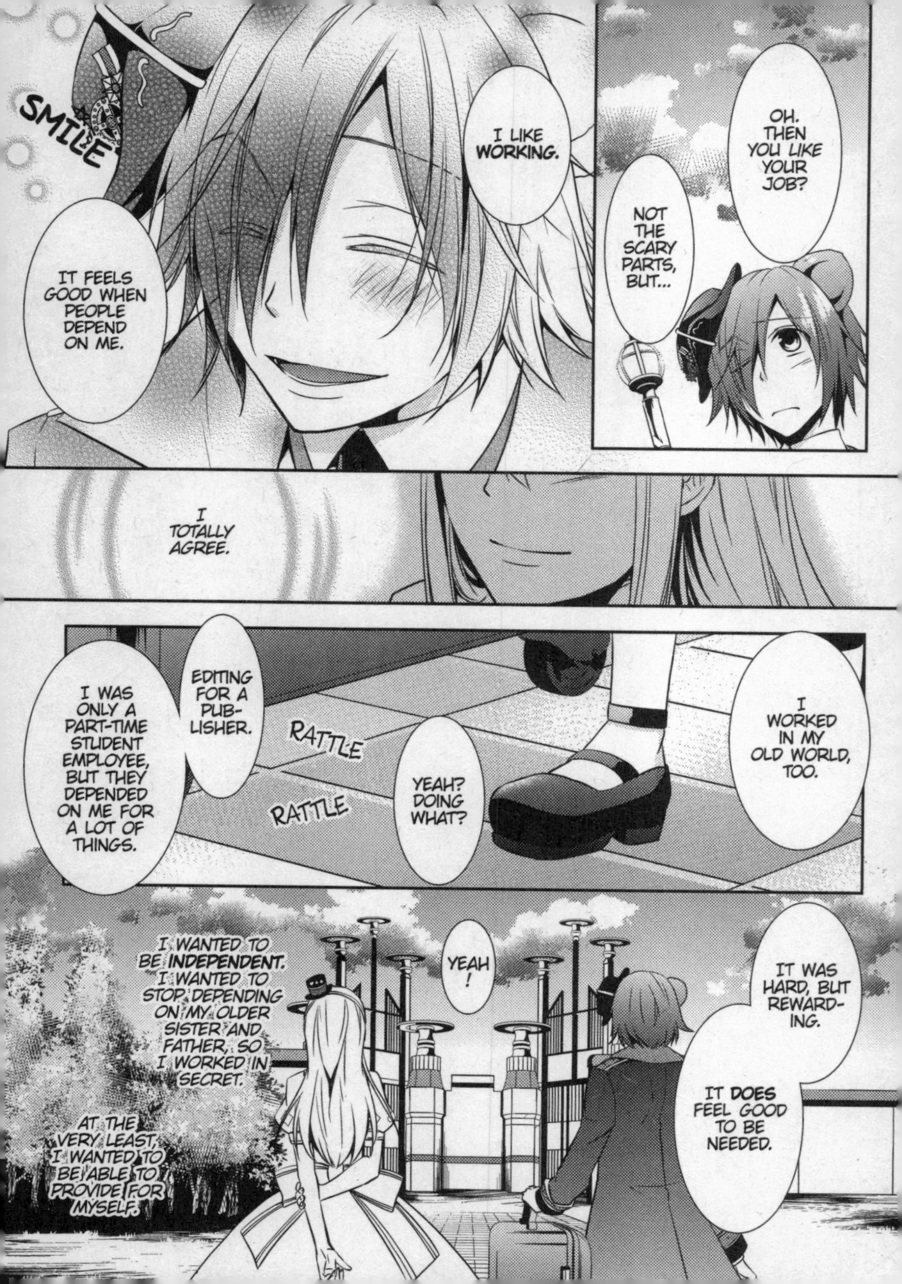
OH. THEN YOU LIKE YOUR JOB?
NOT THE SCARY PARTS, BUT...
I LIKE WORKING.
SMILE
IT FEELS GOOD WHEN PEOPLE DEPEND ON ME.
I TOTALLY AGREE.
I WORKED IN MY OLD WORLD, TOO.
YEAH? DOING WHAT?
RATTLE
RATTLE
EDITING FOR A PUBLISHER.
I WAS ONLY A PART-TIME STUDENT EMPLOYEE, BUT THEY DEPENDED ON ME FOR A LOT OF THINGS.
IT WAS HARD, BUT REWARDING.
IT DOES FEEL GOOD TO BE NEEDED.
YEAH!
I WANTED TO BE INDEPENDENT. I WANTED TO STOP DEPENDING ON MY OLDER SISTER AND FATHER, SO I WORKED IN SECRET.
AT THE VERY LEAST, I WANTED TO BE ABLE TO PROVIDE FOR MYSELF.

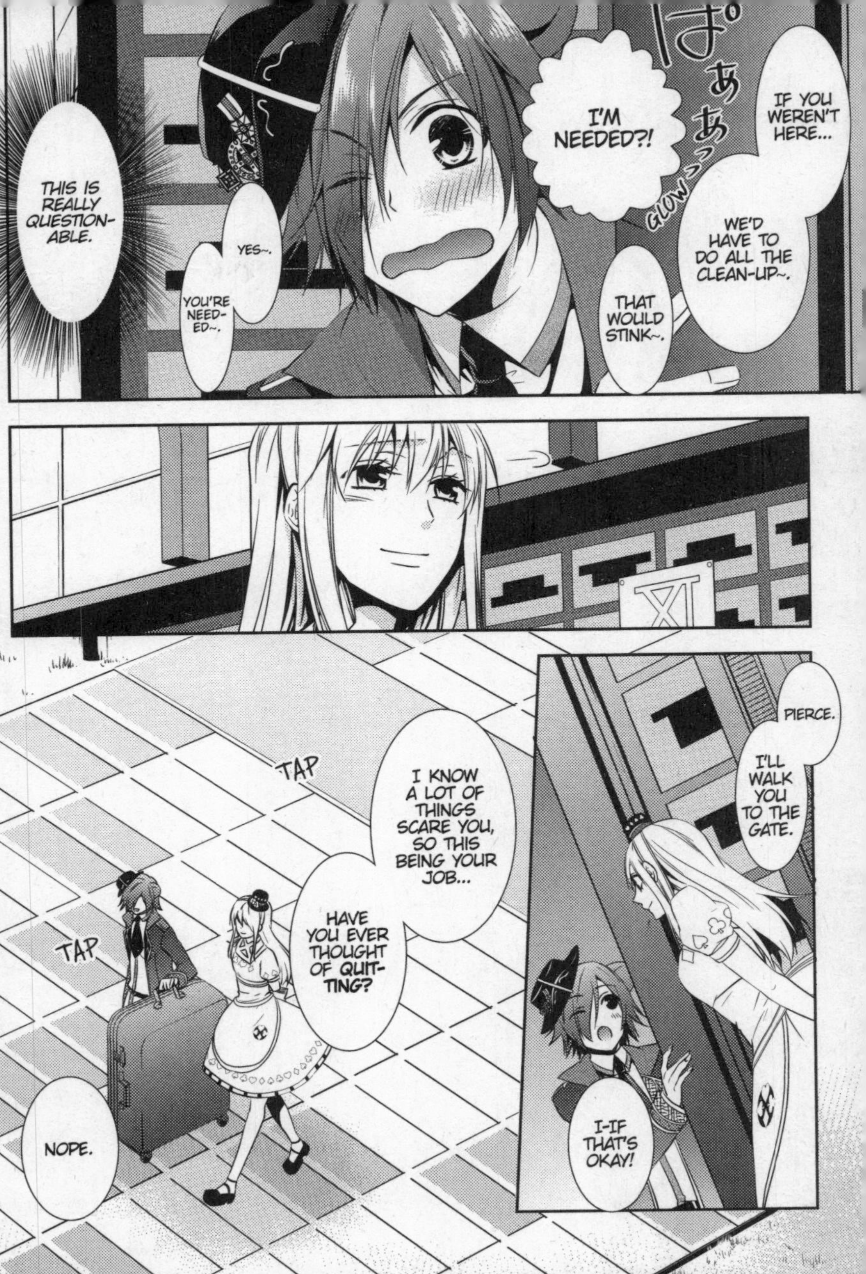
ぱぁぁっ
GLOW
IF YOU WEREN'T HERE...
I'M NEEDED?!
WE'D HAVE TO DO ALL THE CLEAN-UP~.
THAT WOULD STINK~.
YES~.
YOU'RE NEEDED-ED~.
THIS IS REALLY QUESTION-ABLE.
PIERCE.
I'LL WALK YOU TO THE GATE.
I-IF THAT'S OKAY!
TAP
I KNOW A LOT OF THINGS SCARE YOU, SO THIS BEING YOUR JOB...
HAVE YOU EVER THOUGHT OF QUIT-TING?
TAP
NOPE.

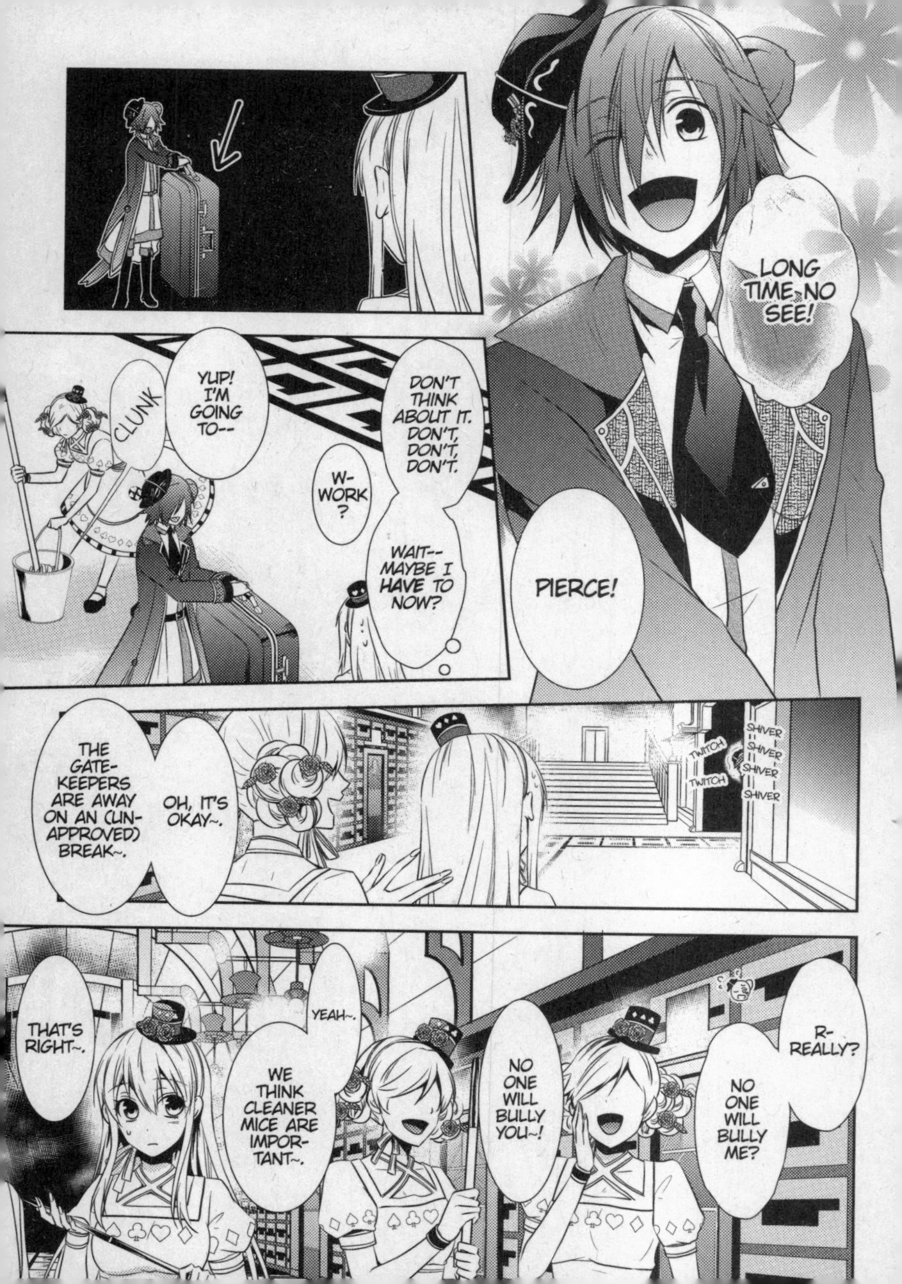
LONG TIME NO SEE!
PIERCE!
DON'T THINK ABOUT IT. DON'T, DON'T, DON'T.
WAIT-- MAYBE I HAVE TO NOW?
W-WORK?
YUP! I'M GOING TO--
CLUNK
SHIVER SHIVER SHIVER SHIVER
TWITCH TWITCH
OH, IT'S OKAY~.
THE GATE-KEEPERS ARE AWAY ON AN (UN-APPROVED) BREAK~.
R-REALLY?
NO ONE WILL BULLY ME?
NO ONE WILL BULLY YOU~!
YEAH~.
WE THINK CLEANER MICE ARE IMPOR-TANT~.
THAT'S RIGHT~.

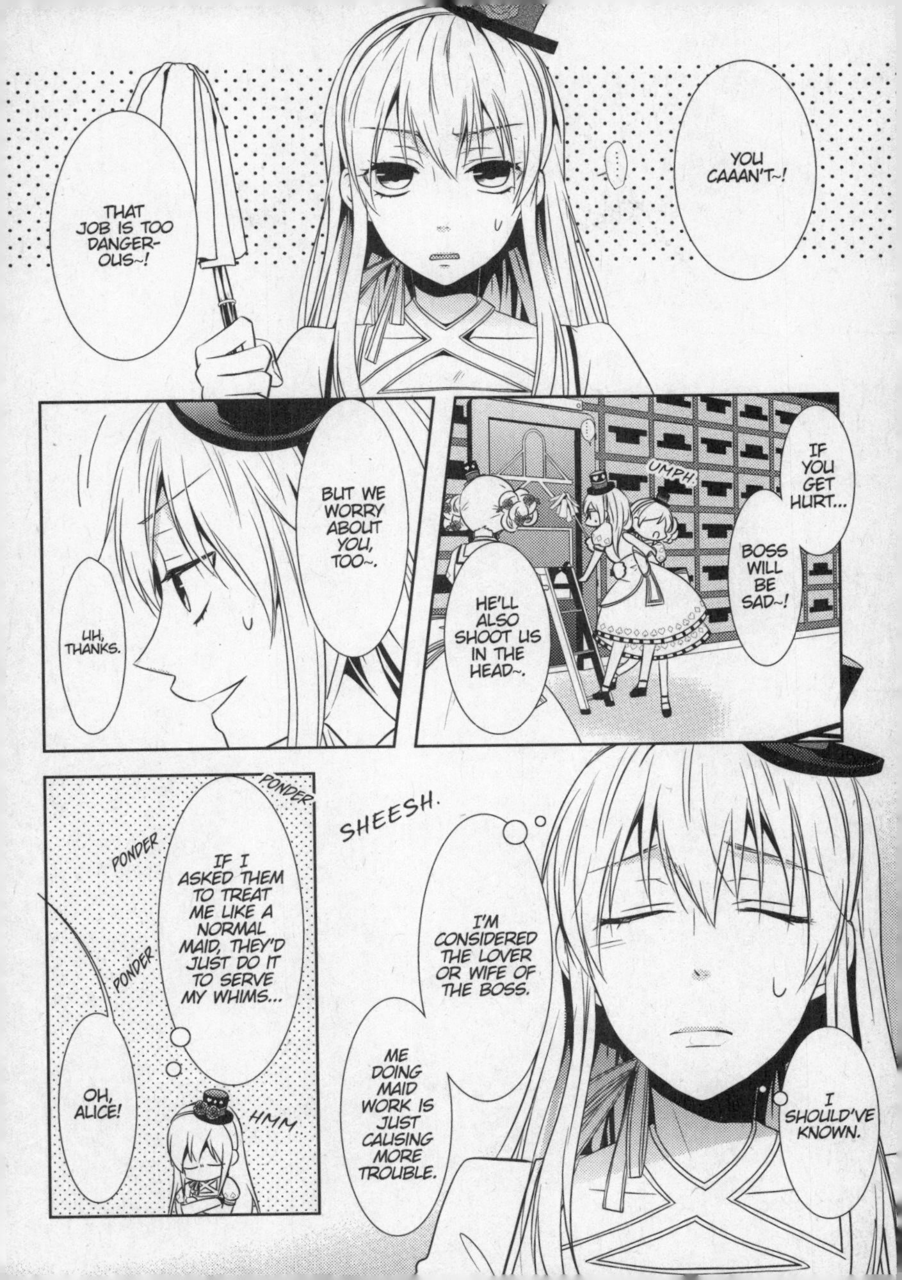
YOU CAAAN'T~!
...
THAT JOB IS TOO DANGER-OUS~!
IF YOU GET HURT...
BOSS WILL BE SAD~!
UMPH.
...
HE'LL ALSO SHOOT US IN THE HEAD~.
BUT WE WORRY ABOUT YOU, TOO~.
UH, THANKS.
SHEESH.
I'M CONSIDERED THE LOVER OR WIFE OF THE BOSS.
I SHOULD'VE KNOWN.
ME DOING MAID WORK IS JUST CAUSING MORE TROUBLE.
PONDER
PONDER
IF I ASKED THEM TO TREAT ME LIKE A NORMAL MAID, THEY'D JUST DO IT TO SERVE MY WHIMS...
PONDER
OH, ALICE!
HMM

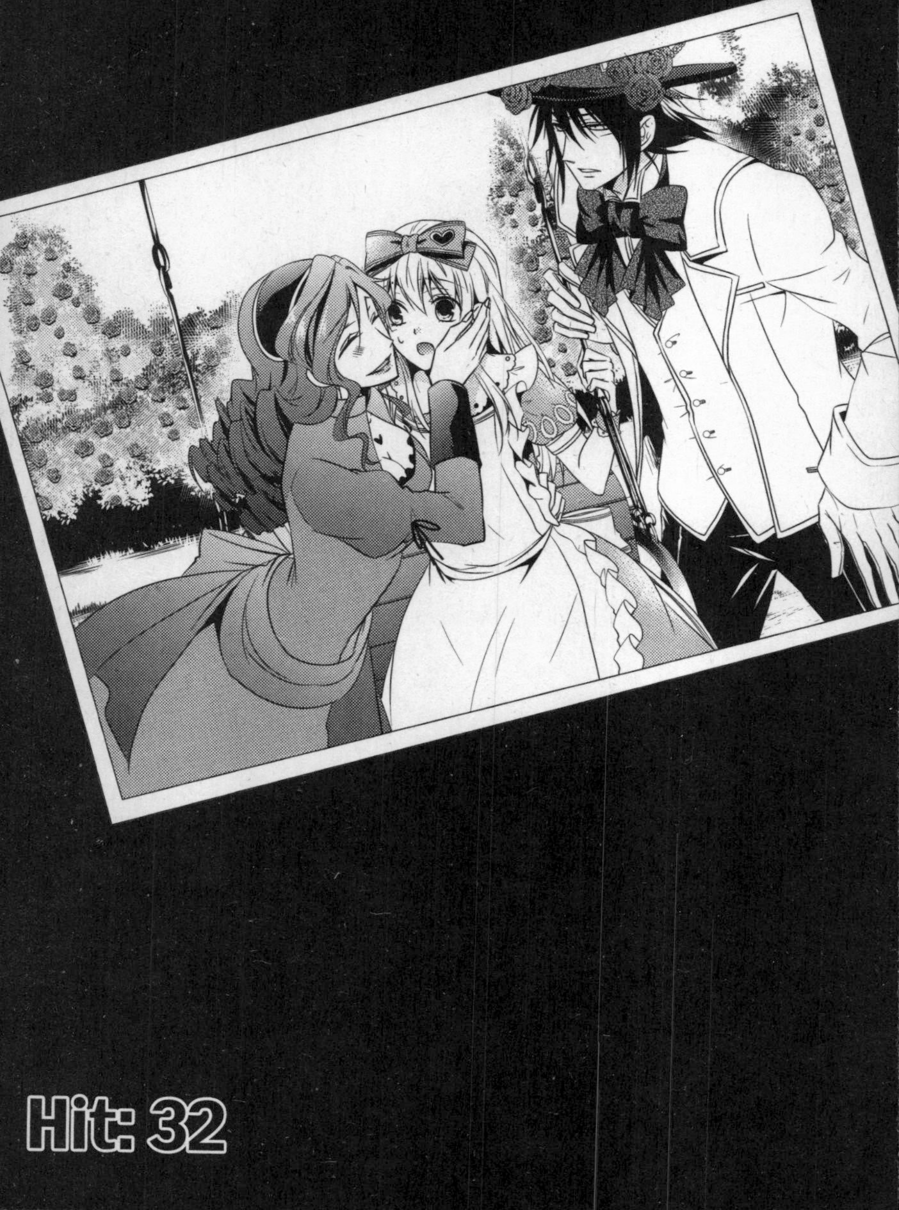

Hit: 32

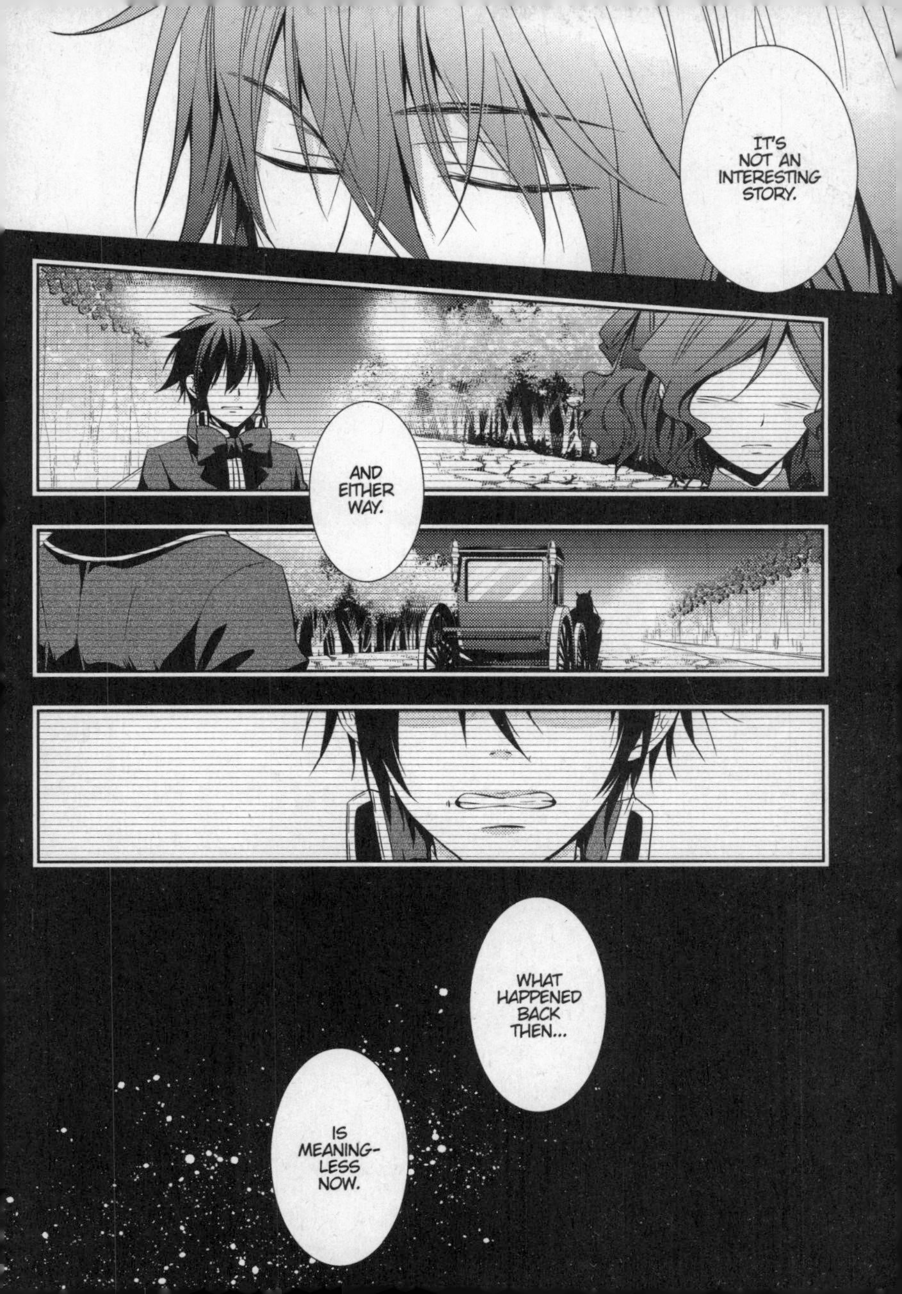
IT'S NOT AN INTERESTING STORY.
AND EITHER WAY.
WHAT HAPPENED BACK THEN...
IS MEANING-LESS NOW.

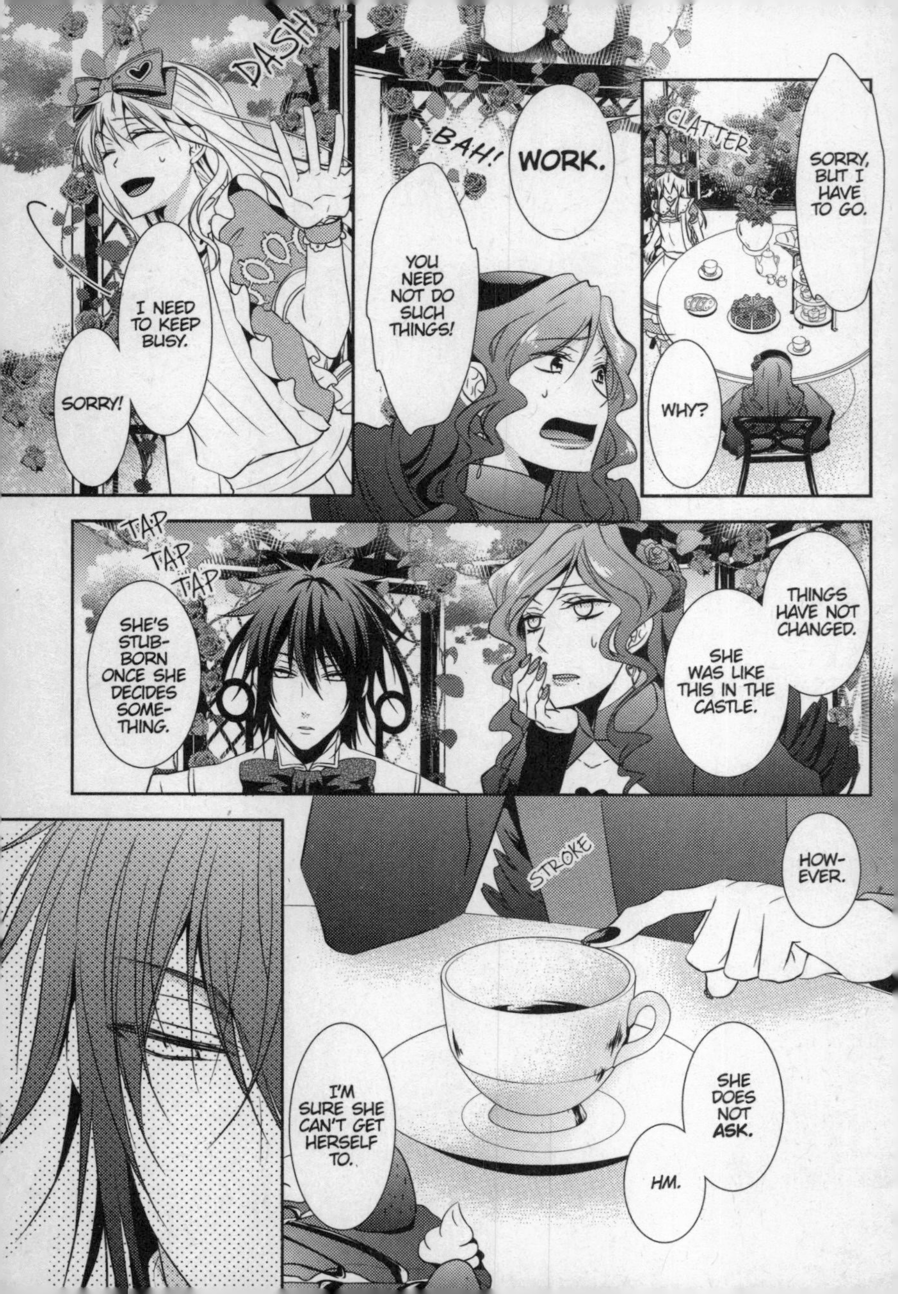
CLATTER
SORRY, BUT I HAVE TO GO.
WHY?
WORK.
BAH!
YOU NEED NOT DO SUCH THINGS!
DASH
I NEED TO KEEP BUSY.
SORRY!
THINGS HAVE NOT CHANGED.
SHE WAS LIKE THIS IN THE CASTLE.
TAP TAP TAP
SHE'S STUBBORN ONCE SHE DECIDES SOMETHING.
HOWEVER.
STROKE
SHE DOES NOT ASK.
HM.
I'M SURE SHE CAN'T GET HERSELF TO.

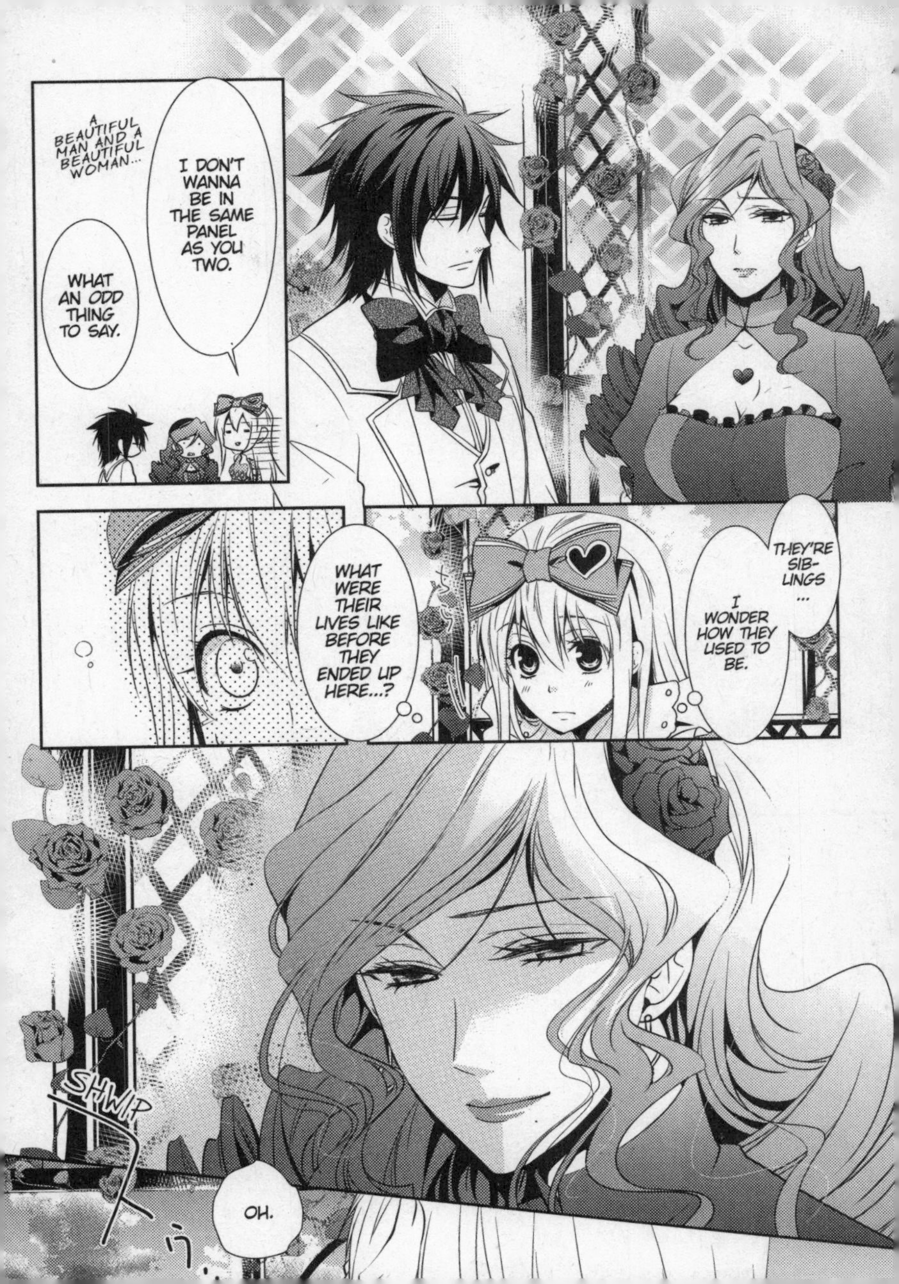
A BEAUTIFUL MAN AND A BEAUTIFUL WOMAN...
I DON'T WANNA BE IN THE SAME PANEL AS YOU TWO.
WHAT AN ODD THING TO SAY.
THEY'RE SIB-LINGS...
I WONDER HOW THEY USED TO BE.
WHAT WERE THEIR LIVES LIKE BEFORE THEY ENDED UP HERE...?
SHWIP
OH.

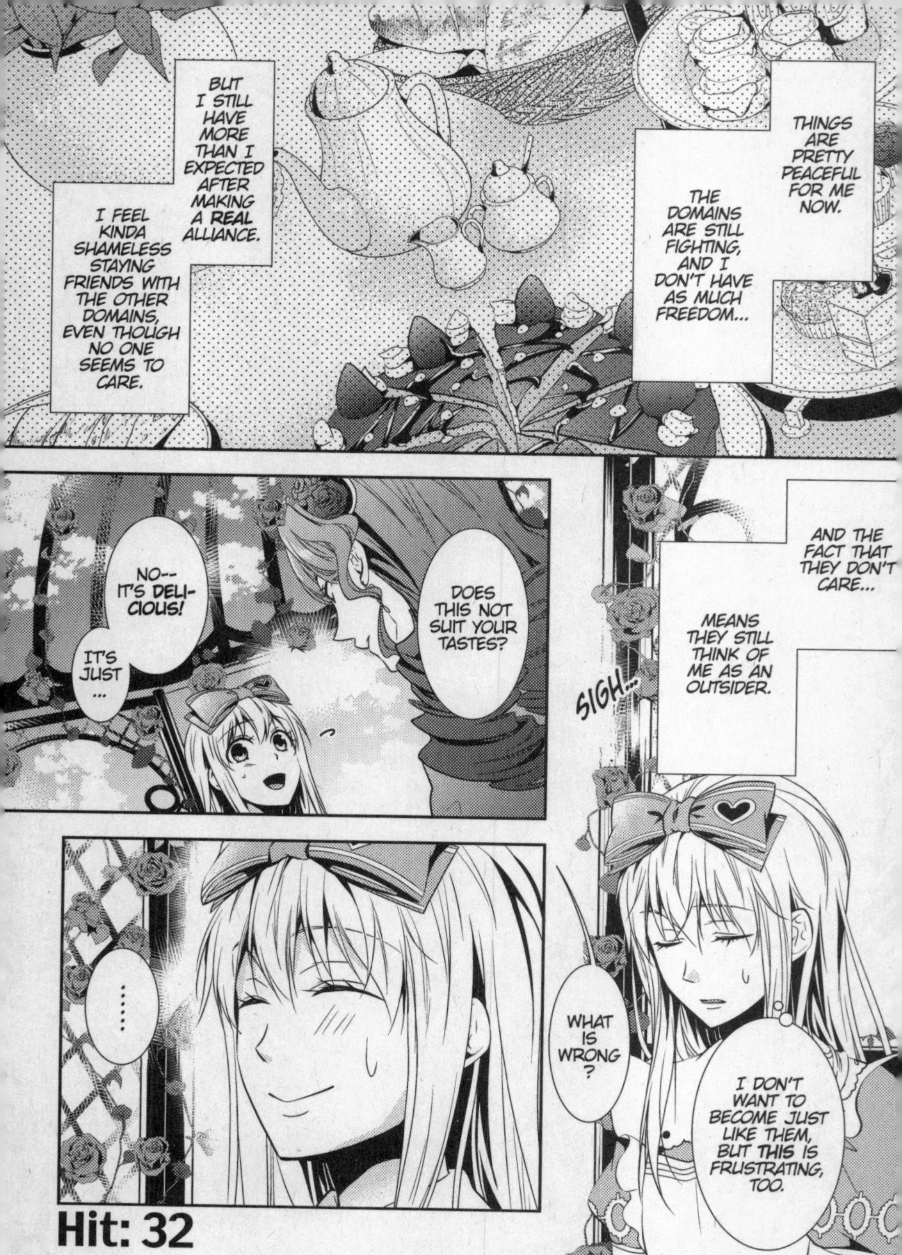
THINGS ARE PRETTY PEACEFUL FOR ME NOW.
THE DOMAINS ARE STILL FIGHTING, AND I DON'T HAVE AS MUCH FREEDOM...
BUT I STILL HAVE MORE THAN I EXPECTED AFTER MAKING A REAL ALLIANCE.
I FEEL KINDA SHAMELESS STAYING FRIENDS WITH THE OTHER DOMAINS, EVEN THOUGH NO ONE SEEMS TO CARE.
AND THE FACT THAT THEY DON'T CARE...
MEANS THEY STILL THINK OF ME AS AN OUTSIDER.
SIGH...
DOES THIS NOT SUIT YOUR TASTES?
NO-- IT'S DELI-CIOUS!
IT'S JUST ...
WHAT IS WRONG ?
I DON'T WANT TO BECOME JUST LIKE THEM, BUT THIS IS FRUSTRATING, TOO.
......

Hit: 32

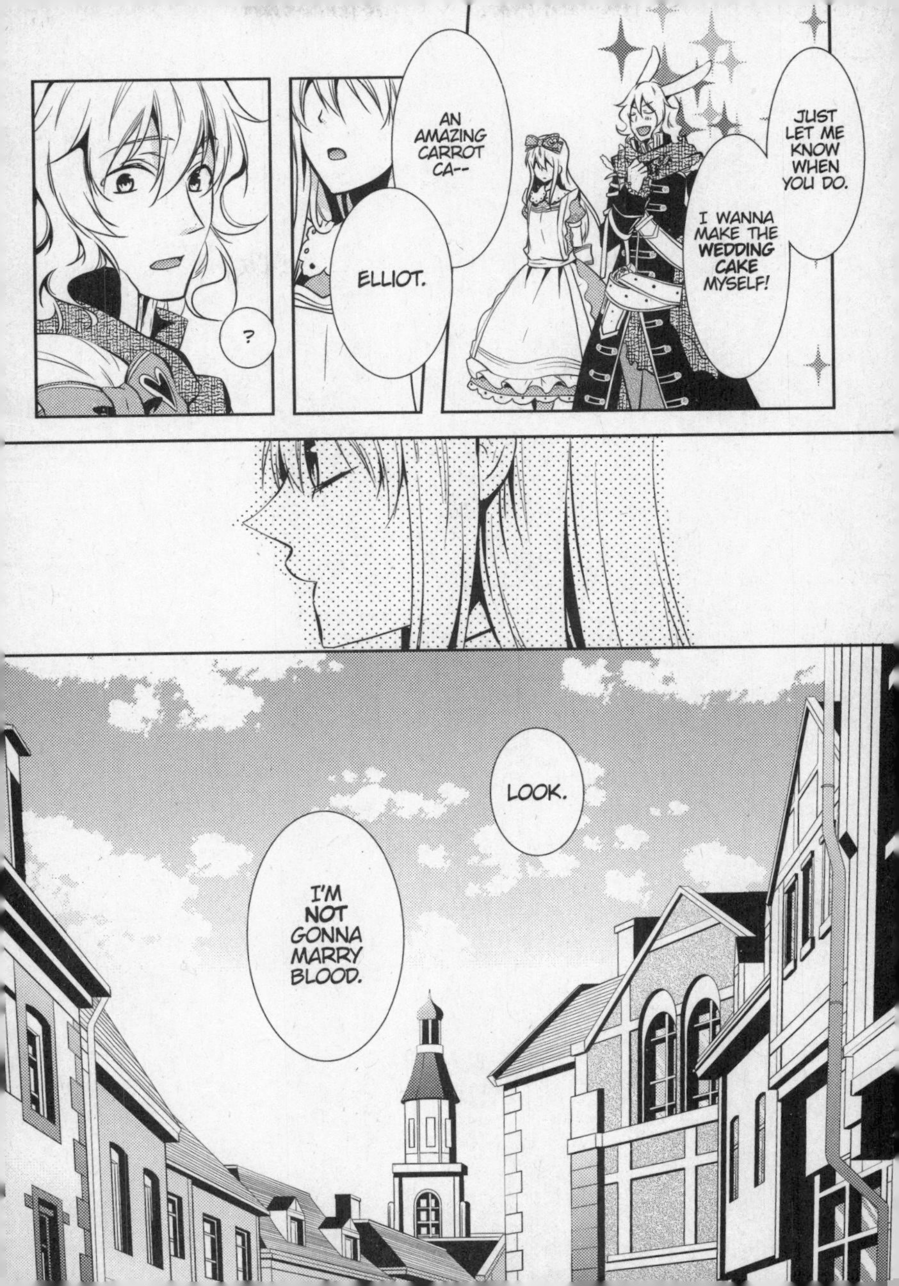
JUST LET ME KNOW WHEN YOU DO.
I WANNA MAKE THE WEDDING CAKE MYSELF!
AN AMAZING CARROT CA--
ELLIOT.
?
LOOK.
I'M NOT GONNA MARRY BLOOD.

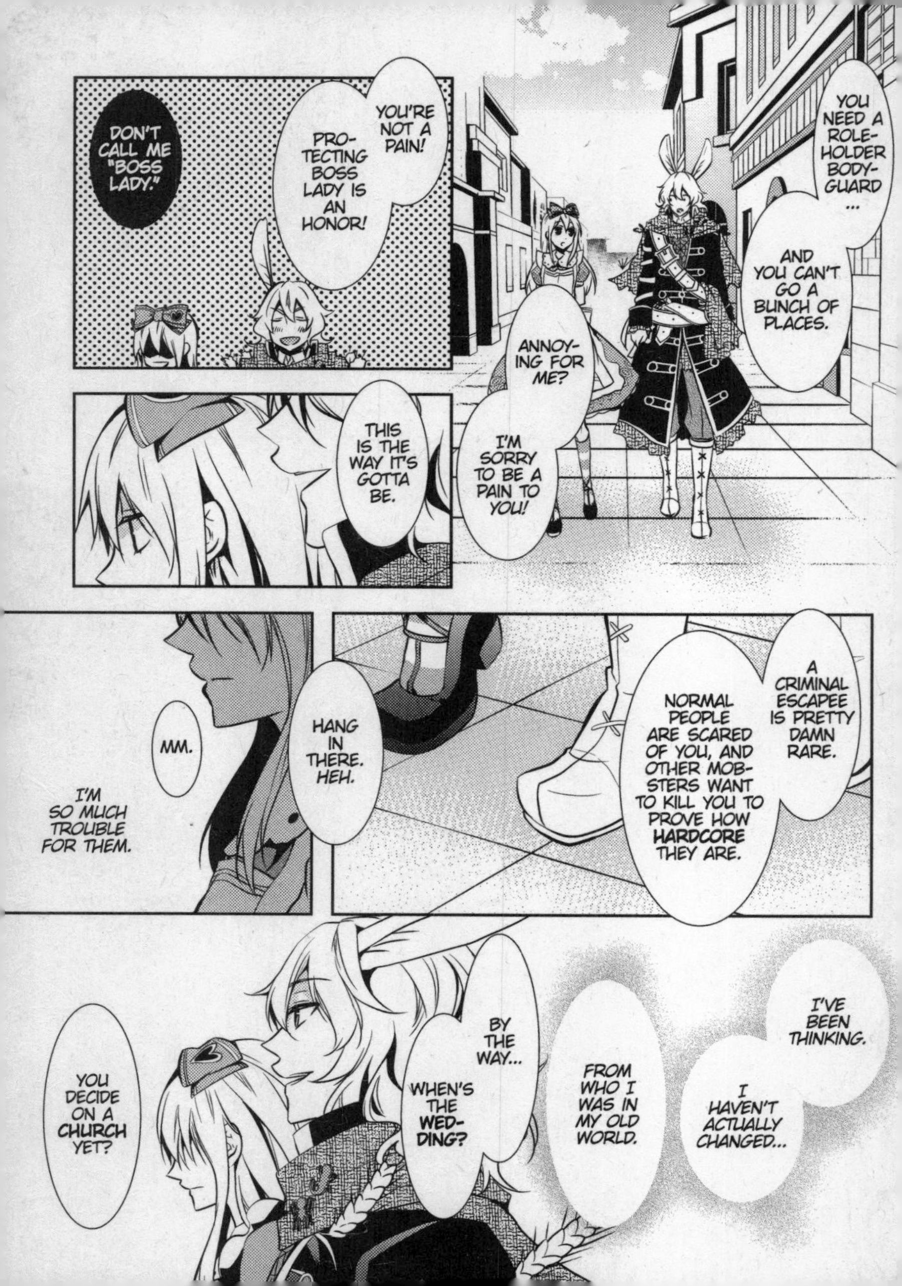
YOU NEED A ROLE-HOLDER BODY-GUARD...
AND YOU CAN'T GO A BUNCH OF PLACES.
ANNOYING FOR ME?
I'M SORRY TO BE A PAIN TO YOU!
YOU'RE NOT A PAIN!
PROTECTING BOSS LADY IS AN HONOR!
DON'T CALL ME "BOSS LADY."
THIS IS THE WAY IT'S GOTTA BE.
A CRIMINAL ESCAPEE IS PRETTY DAMN RARE.
NORMAL PEOPLE ARE SCARED OF YOU, AND OTHER MOB-STERS WANT TO KILL YOU TO PROVE HOW **HARDCORE** THEY ARE.
HANG IN THERE. HEH.
MM.
I'M SO MUCH TROUBLE FOR THEM.
I'VE BEEN THINKING.
I HAVEN'T ACTUALLY CHANGED...
FROM WHO I WAS IN MY OLD WORLD.
BY THE WAY...
WHEN'S THE WED-DING?
YOU DECIDE ON A **CHURCH** YET?

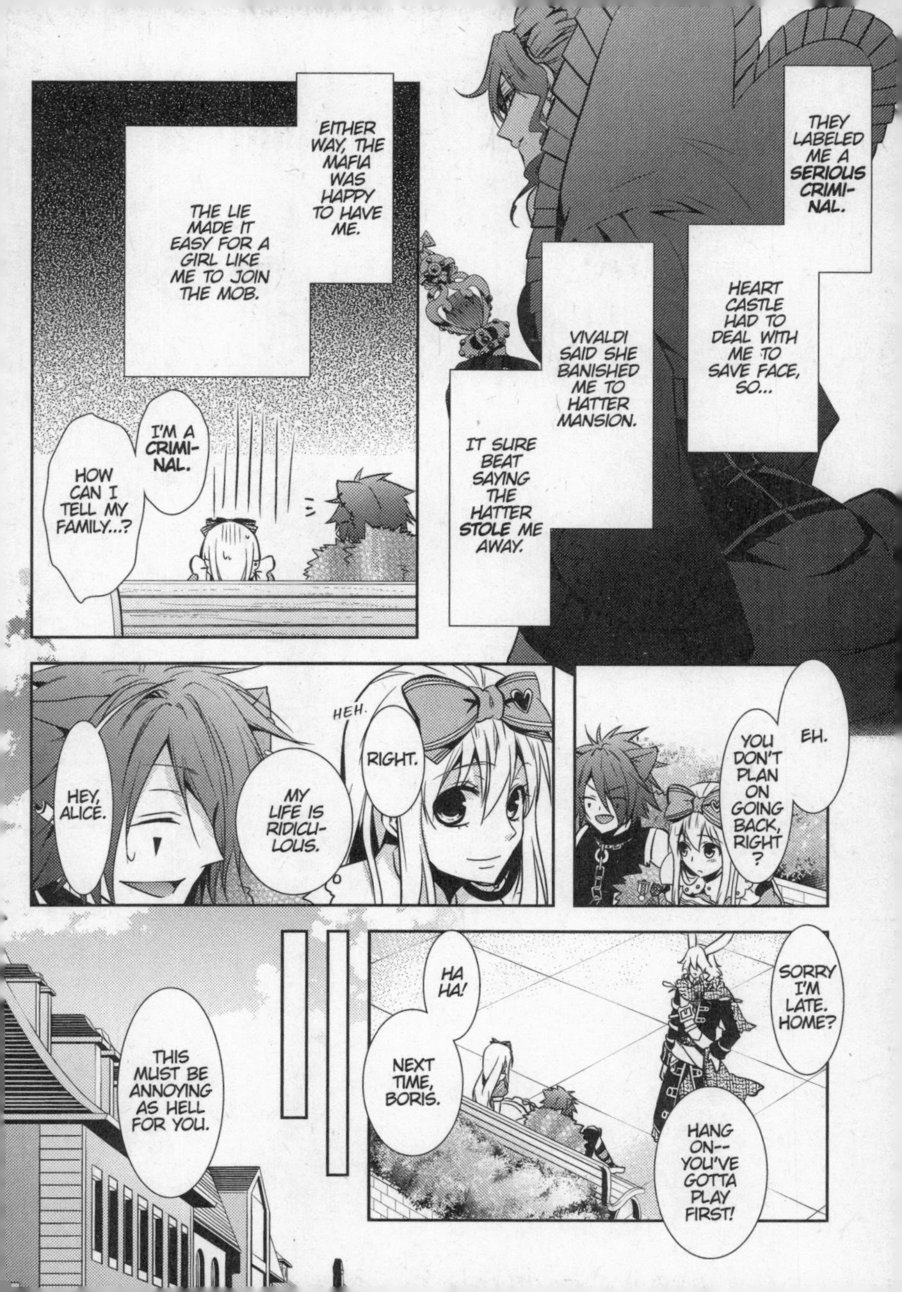
THEY LABELED ME A SERIOUS CRIMINAL.
HEART CASTLE HAD TO DEAL WITH ME TO SAVE FACE, SO...
VIVALDI SAID SHE BANISHED ME TO HATTER MANSION.
IT SURE BEAT SAYING THE HATTER STOLE ME AWAY.
EITHER WAY, THE MAFIA WAS HAPPY TO HAVE ME.
THE LIE MADE IT EASY FOR A GIRL LIKE ME TO JOIN THE MOB.
I'M A CRIMINAL.
HOW CAN I TELL MY FAMILY...?
EH.
YOU DON'T PLAN ON GOING BACK, RIGHT?
RIGHT.
HEH.
MY LIFE IS RIDICULOUS.
HEY, ALICE.
SORRY I'M LATE. HOME?
HANG ON--YOU'VE GOTTA PLAY FIRST!
HA HA!
NEXT TIME, BORIS.
THIS MUST BE ANNOYING AS HELL FOR YOU.

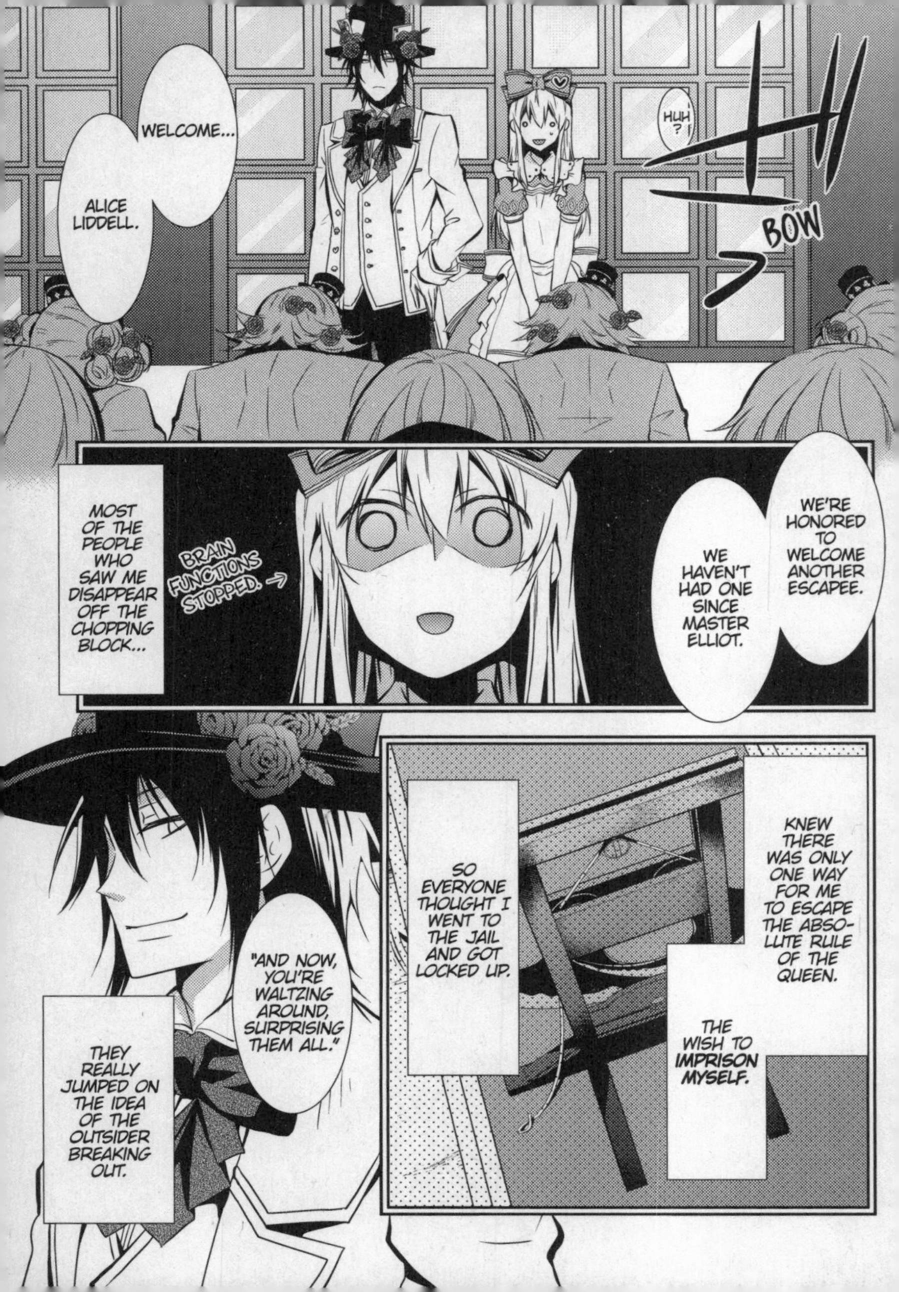
HUH ?!
BOW
WELCOME...
ALICE LIDDELL.
WE'RE HONORED TO WELCOME ANOTHER ESCAPEE.
WE HAVEN'T HAD ONE SINCE MASTER ELLIOT.
BRAIN FUNCTIONS STOPPED.
MOST OF THE PEOPLE WHO SAW ME DISAPPEAR OFF THE CHOPPING BLOCK...
KNEW THERE WAS ONLY ONE WAY FOR ME TO ESCAPE THE ABSO-LUTE RULE OF THE QUEEN.
THE WISH TO IMPRISON MYSELF.
SO EVERYONE THOUGHT I WENT TO THE JAIL AND GOT LOCKED UP.
"AND NOW, YOU'RE WALTZING AROUND, SURPRISING THEM ALL."
THEY REALLY JUMPED ON THE IDEA OF THE OUTSIDER BREAKING OUT.

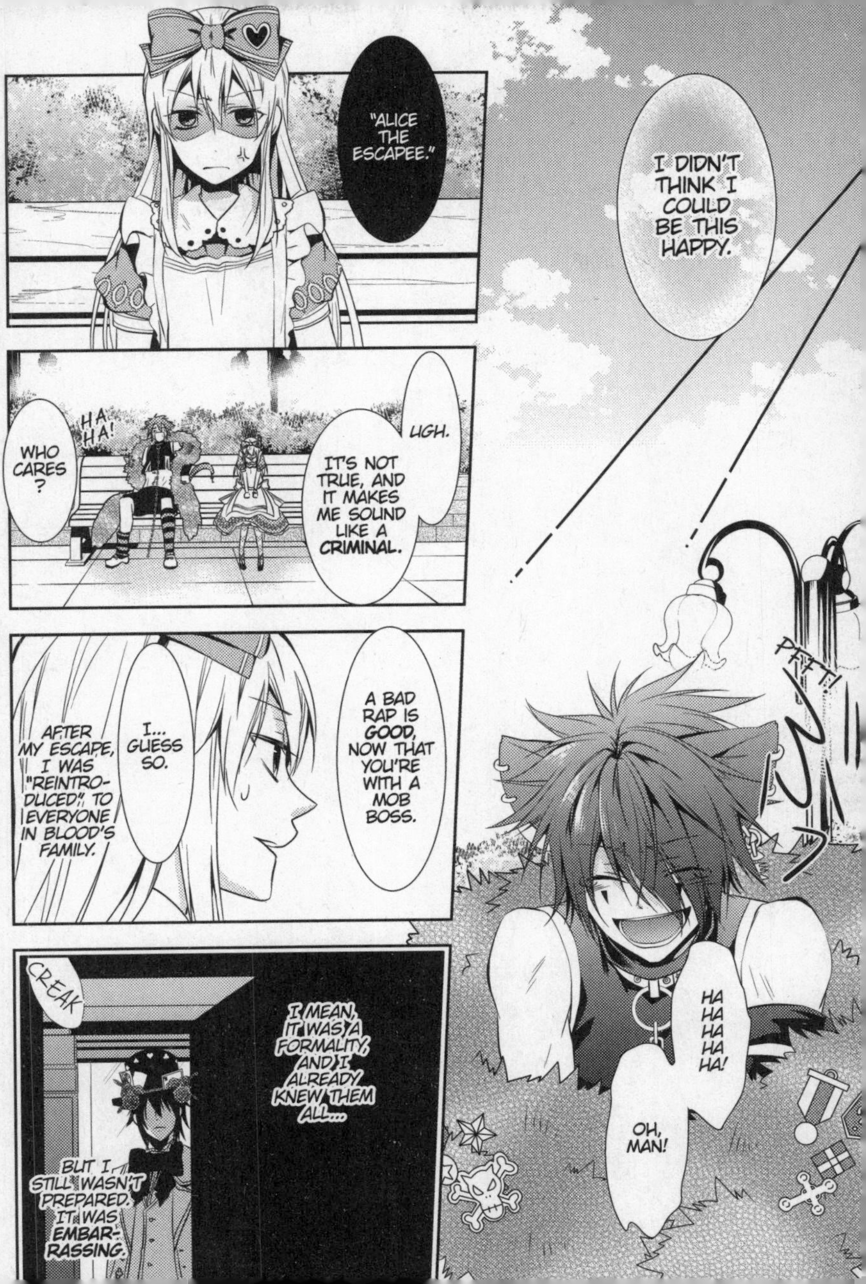
I DIDN'T THINK I COULD BE THIS HAPPY.
PFFT!
HA HA HA HA HA!
OH, MAN!
"ALICE THE ESCAPEE."
UGH.
IT'S NOT TRUE, AND IT MAKES ME SOUND LIKE A CRIMINAL.
HA HA!
WHO CARES?
A BAD RAP IS GOOD, NOW THAT YOU'RE WITH A MOB BOSS.
I... GUESS SO.
AFTER MY ESCAPE, I WAS "REINTRODUCED" TO EVERYONE IN BLOOD'S FAMILY.
I MEAN, IT WAS A FORMALITY, AND I ALREADY KNEW THEM ALL...
CREAK
BUT I STILL WASN'T PREPARED. IT WAS EMBARRASSING.

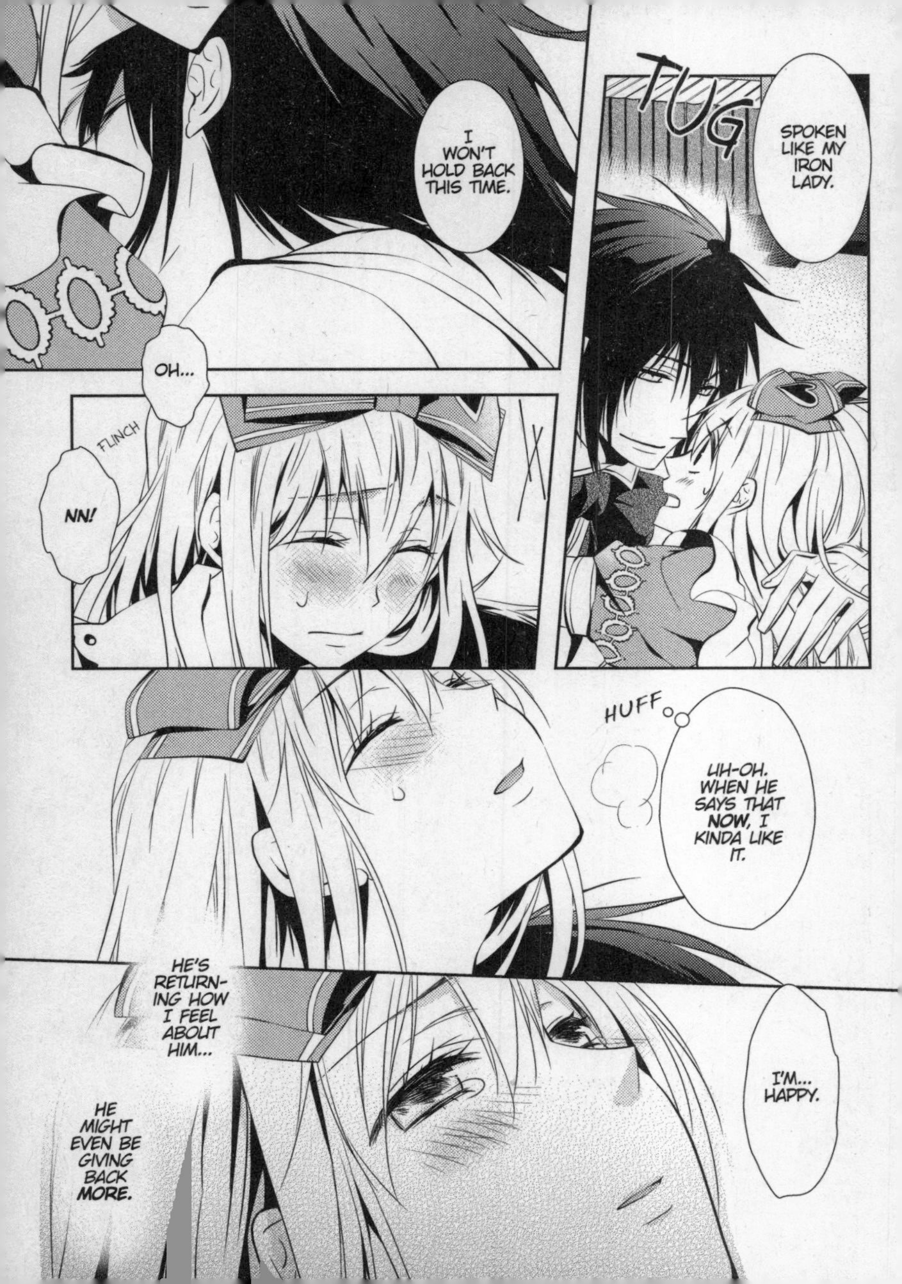
TUG
SPOKEN LIKE MY IRON LADY.
I WON'T HOLD BACK THIS TIME.
OH...
FLINCH
NN!
HUFF
UH-OH. WHEN HE SAYS THAT NOW, I KINDA LIKE IT.
I'M... HAPPY.
HE'S RETURNING HOW I FEEL ABOUT HIM...
HE MIGHT EVEN BE GIVING BACK MORE.

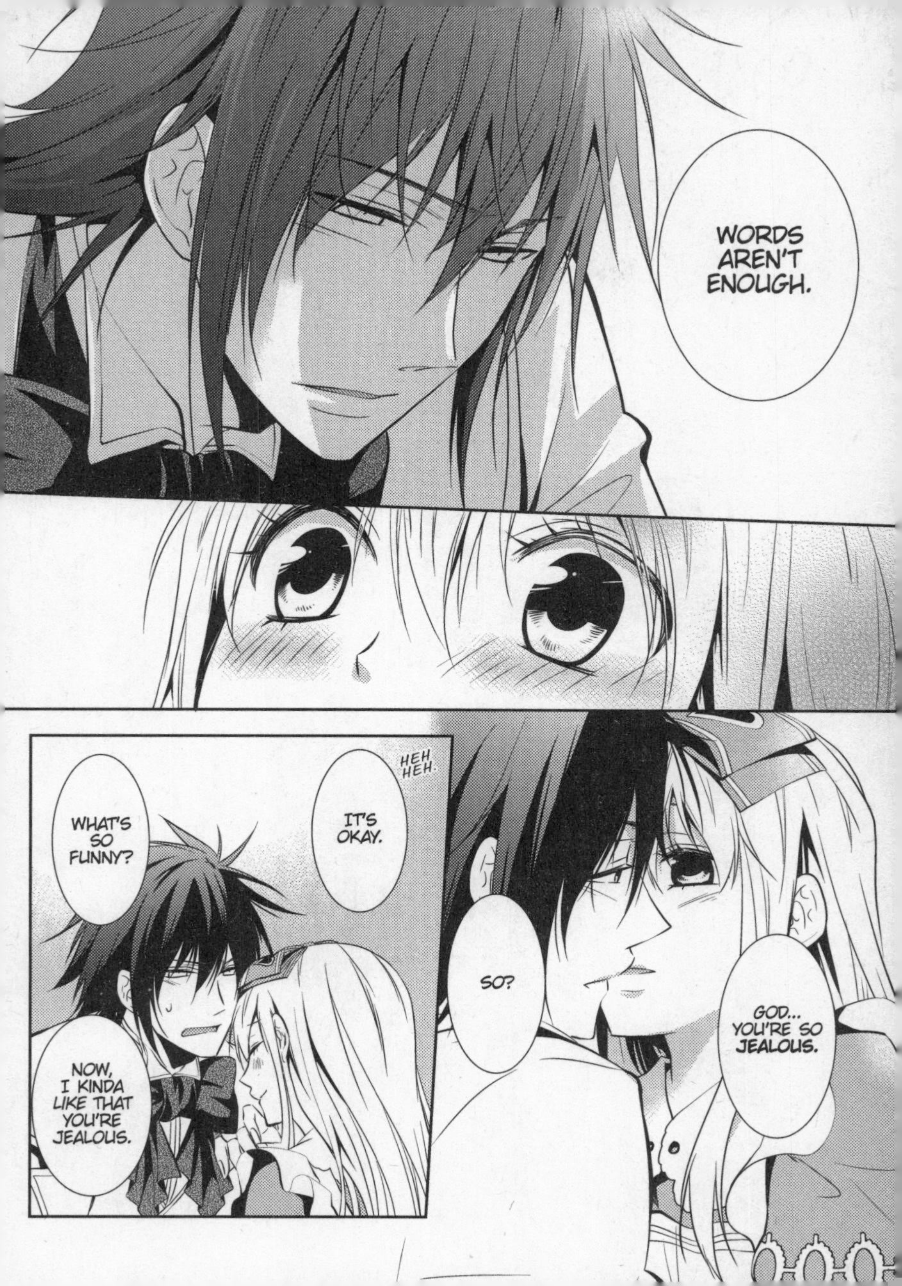
WORDS AREN'T ENOUGH.
GOD... YOU'RE SO JEALOUS.
SO?
HEH HEH.
IT'S OKAY.
WHAT'S SO FUNNY?
NOW, I KINDA LIKE THAT YOU'RE JEALOUS.

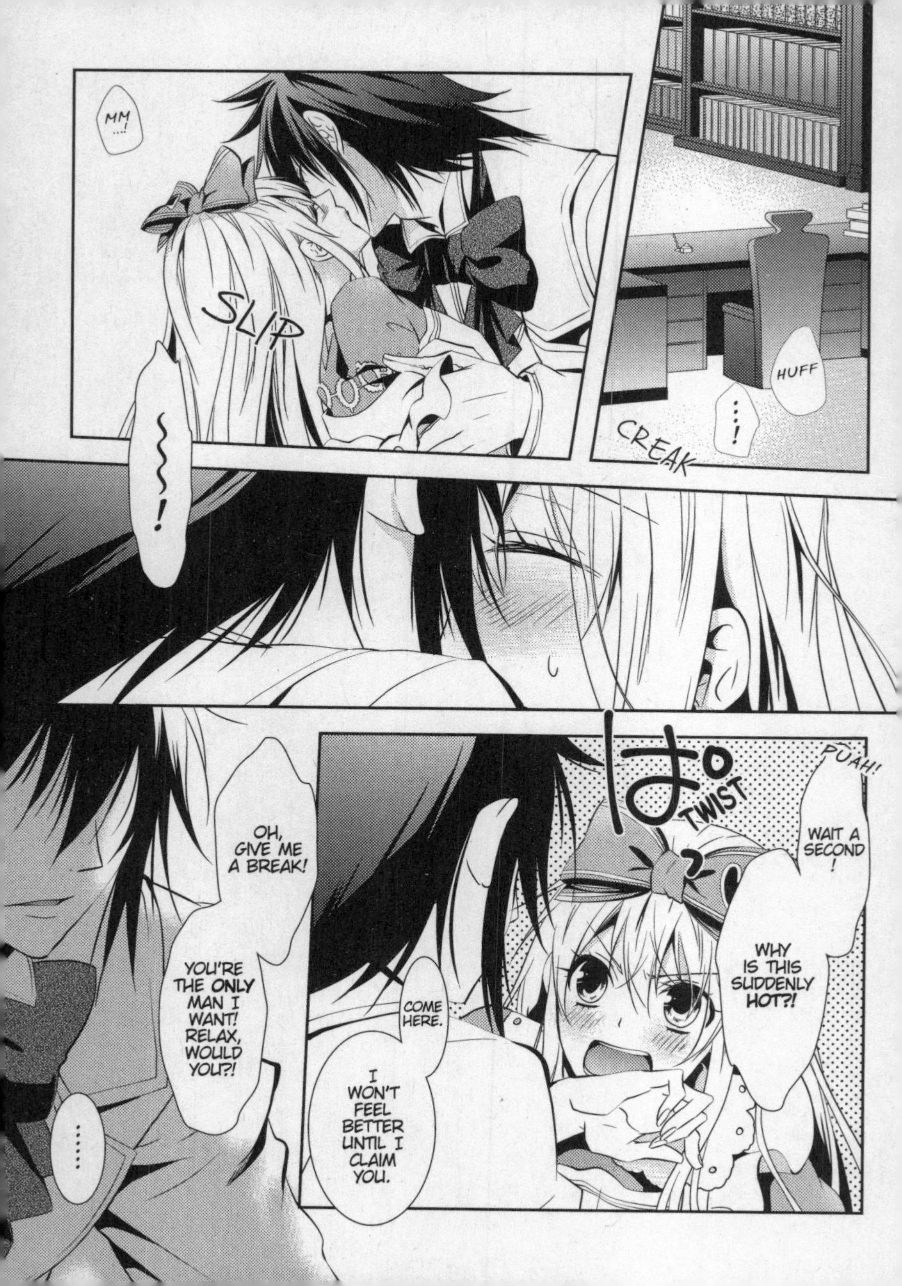
HUFF
...!
CREAK
MM ...!
SLIP
~!
は
TWIST
PUAH!
WAIT A SECOND!
WHY IS THIS SUDDENLY HOT?!
COME HERE.
I WON'T FEEL BETTER UNTIL I CLAIM YOU.
OH, GIVE ME A BREAK!
YOU'RE THE ONLY MAN I WANT! RELAX, WOULD YOU?!
......

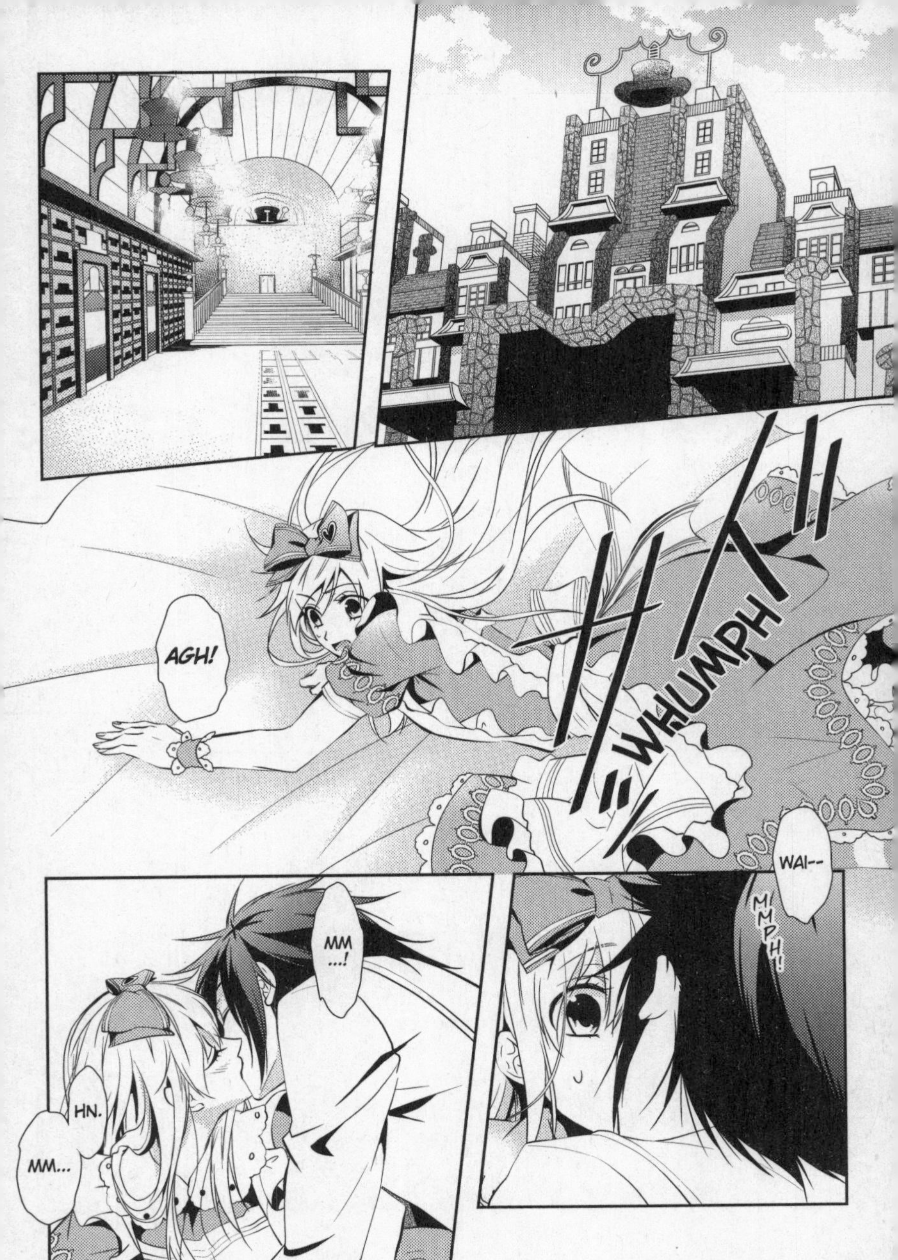
WHUMPH
AGH!
WAI--
MMPH!
MM...!
HN.
MM...

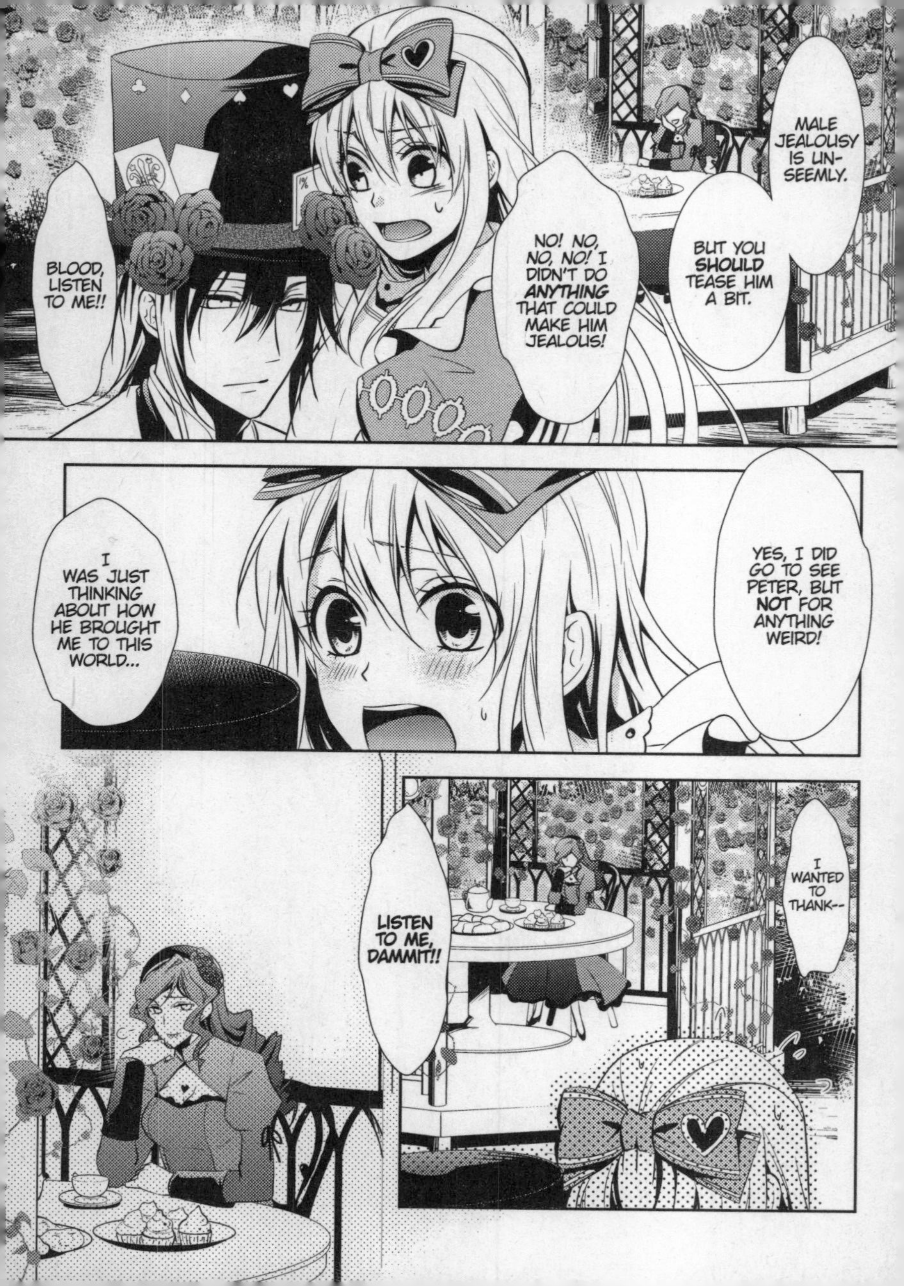
MALE JEALOUSY IS UN-SEEMLY.
BUT YOU **SHOULD** TEASE HIM A BIT.
NO! NO, NO, NO! I DIDN'T DO **ANYTHING** THAT COULD MAKE HIM JEALOUS!
BLOOD, LISTEN TO ME!!
YES, I DID GO TO SEE PETER, BUT **NOT** FOR ANYTHING WEIRD!
I WAS JUST THINKING ABOUT HOW HE BROUGHT ME TO THIS WORLD...
I WANTED TO THANK--
LISTEN TO ME, DAMMIT!!

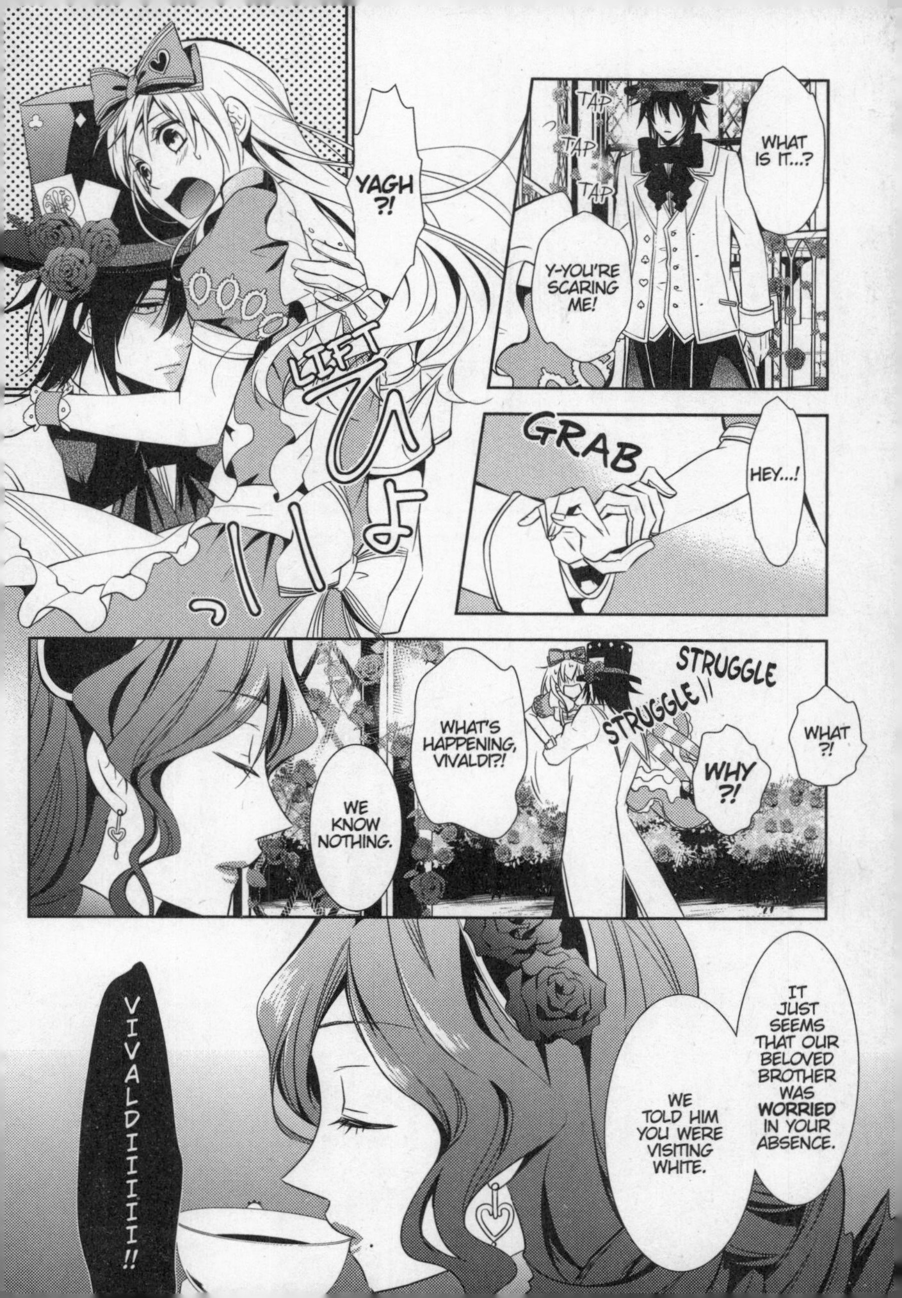
WHAT IS IT...?
TAP
TAP
TAP
Y-YOU'RE SCARING ME!
HEY...!
GRAB
YAGH ?!
LIFT
ひょいっ
WHAT ?!
STRUGGLE
STRUGGLE
WHY ?!
WHAT'S HAPPENING, VIVALDI?!
WE KNOW NOTHING.
IT JUST SEEMS THAT OUR BELOVED BROTHER WAS WORRIED IN YOUR ABSENCE.
WE TOLD HIM YOU WERE VISITING WHITE.
VIVALDIIIIII!!

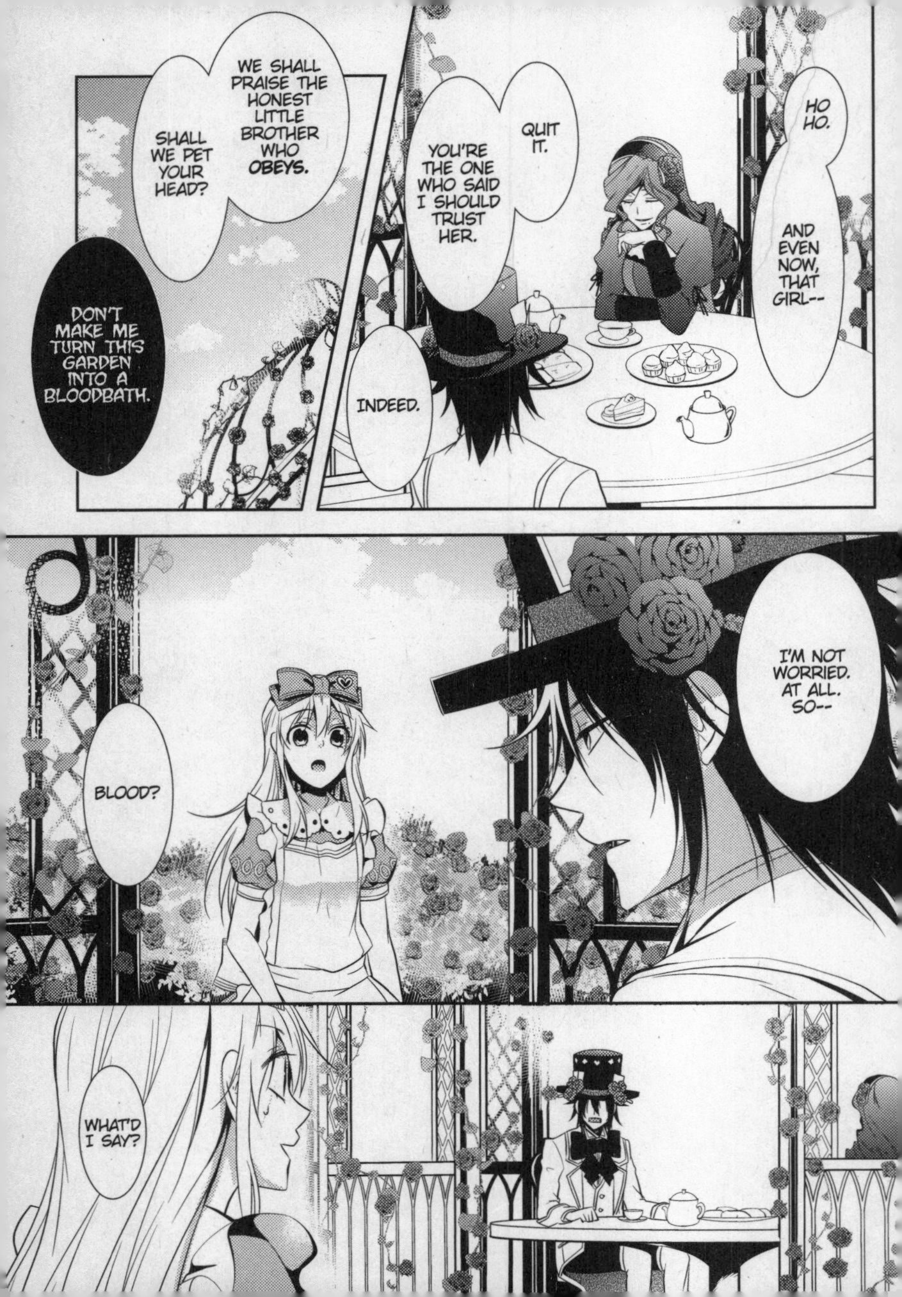
HO HO.
AND EVEN NOW, THAT GIRL--
QUIT IT.
YOU'RE THE ONE WHO SAID I SHOULD TRUST HER.
INDEED.
WE SHALL PRAISE THE HONEST LITTLE BROTHER WHO OBEYS.
SHALL WE PET YOUR HEAD?
DON'T MAKE ME TURN THIS GARDEN INTO A BLOODBATH.
I'M NOT WORRIED. AT ALL. SO--
BLOOD?
WHAT'D I SAY?

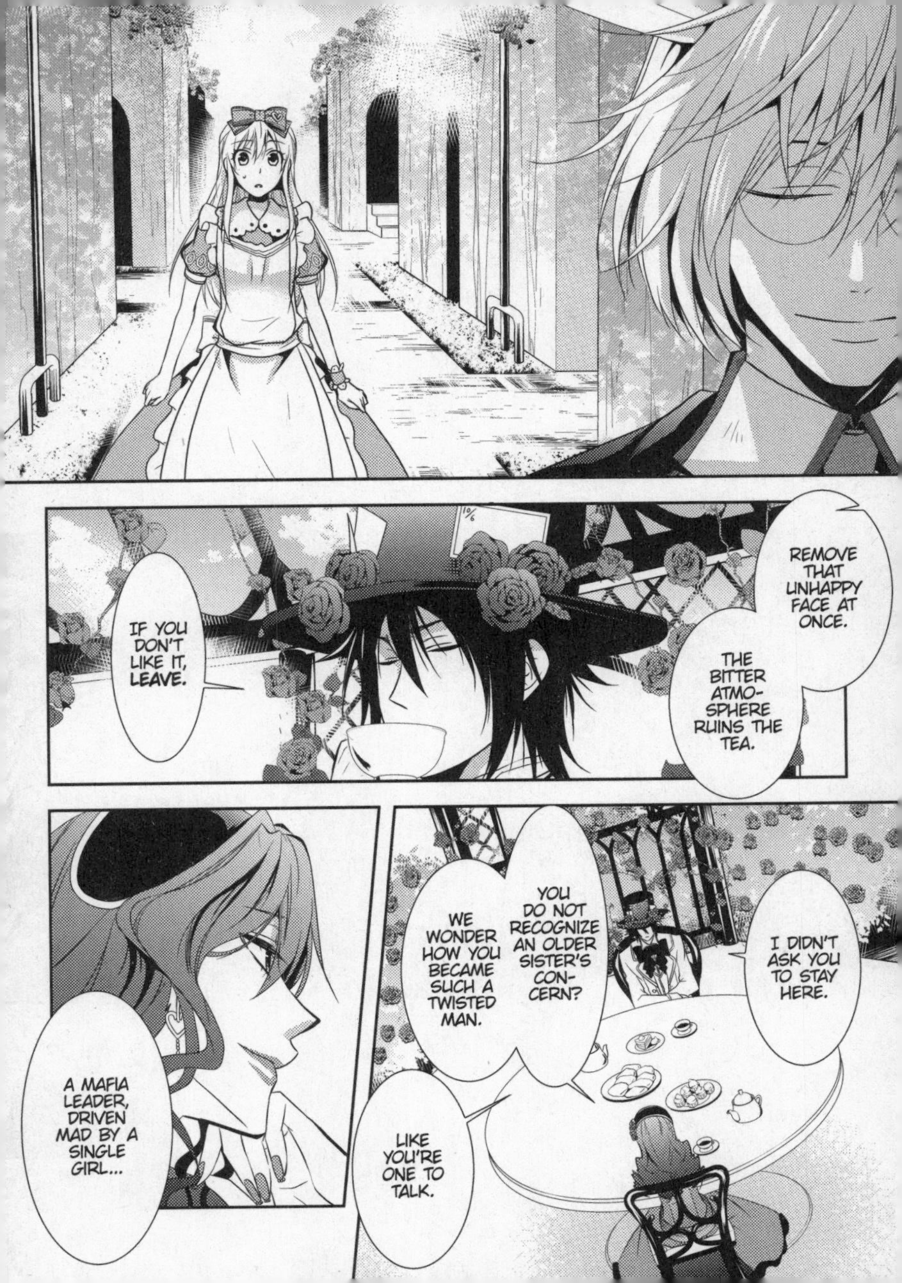
REMOVE THAT UNHAPPY FACE AT ONCE.
THE BITTER ATMOSPHERE RUINS THE TEA.
IF YOU DON'T LIKE IT, LEAVE.
I DIDN'T ASK YOU TO STAY HERE.
YOU DO NOT RECOGNIZE AN OLDER SISTER'S CONCERN?
WE WONDER HOW YOU BECAME SUCH A TWISTED MAN.
LIKE YOU'RE ONE TO TALK.
A MAFIA LEADER, DRIVEN MAD BY A SINGLE GIRL...

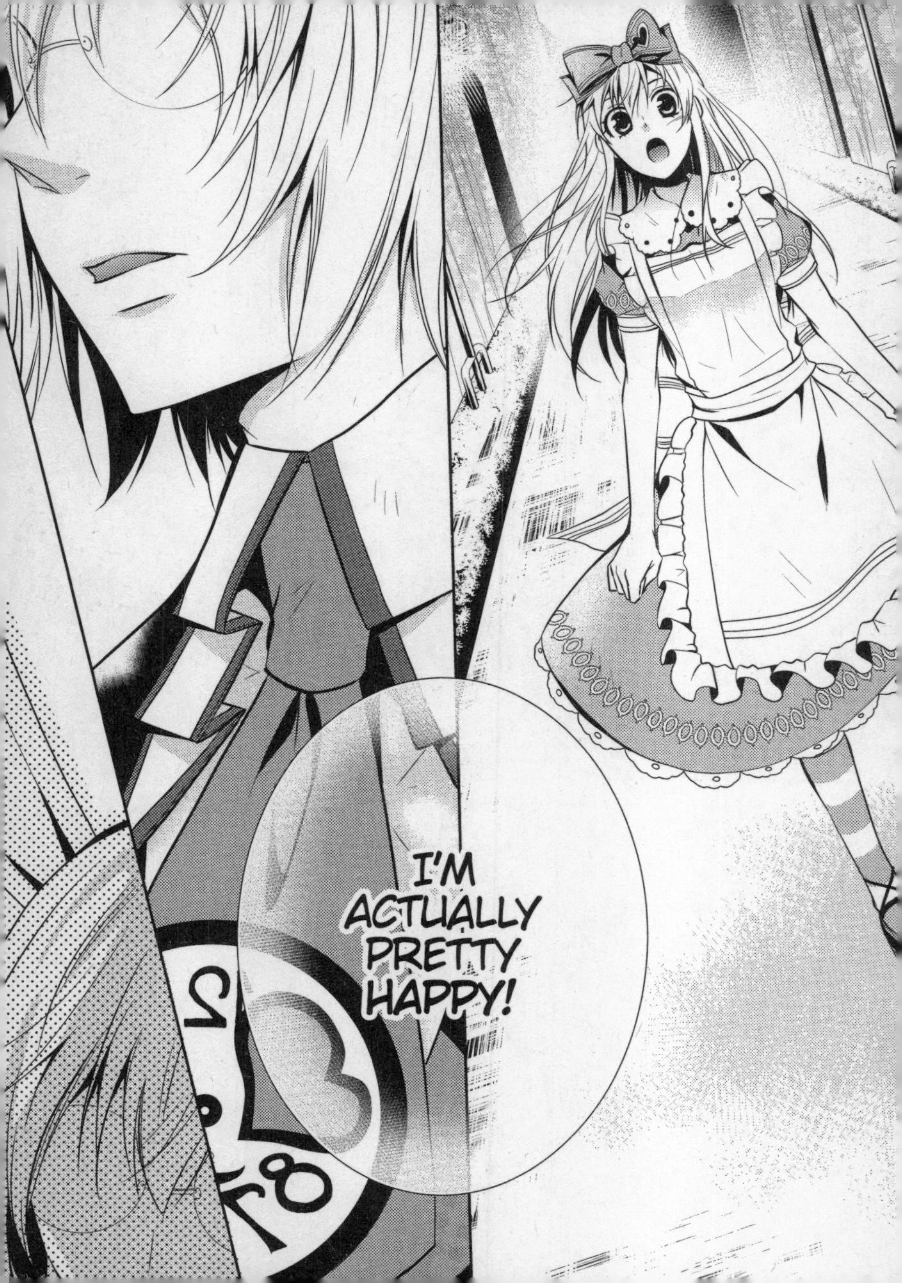
I'M ACTUALLY PRETTY HAPPY!

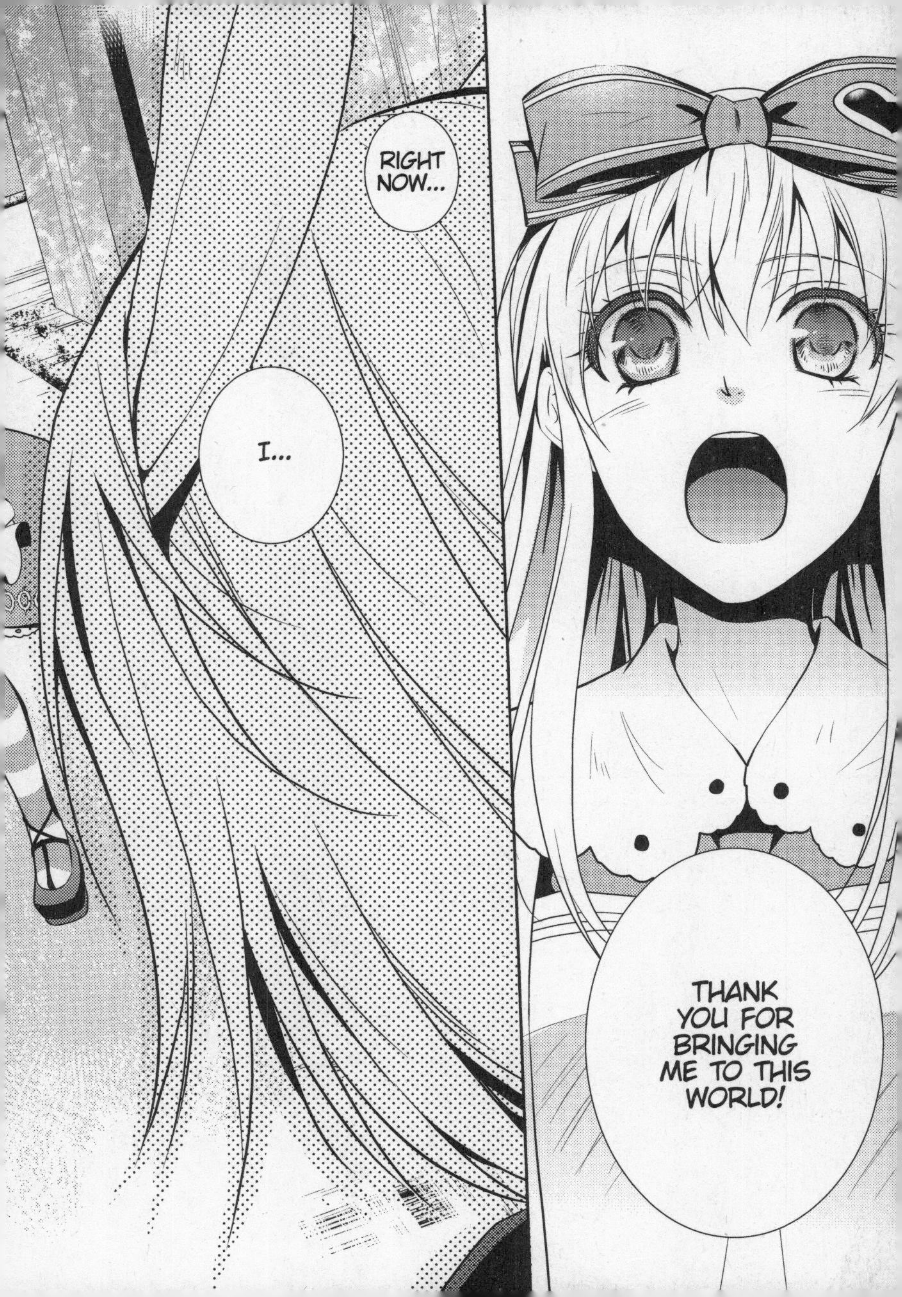
THANK YOU FOR BRINGING ME TO THIS WORLD!
RIGHT NOW...
I...

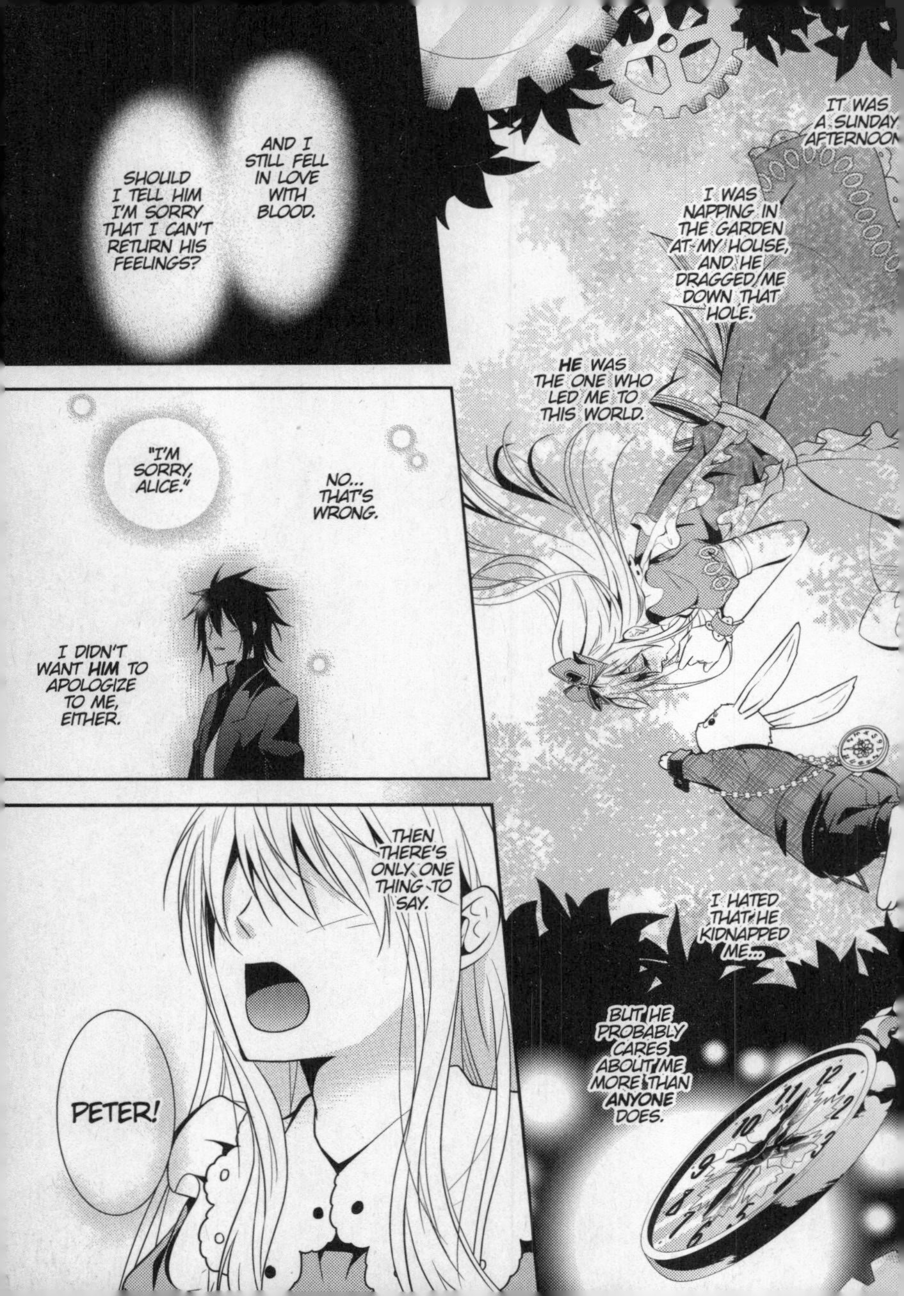
IT WAS A SUNDAY AFTERNOON.
I WAS NAPPING IN THE GARDEN AT MY HOUSE, AND HE DRAGGED ME DOWN THAT HOLE.
HE WAS THE ONE WHO LED ME TO THIS WORLD.
I HATED THAT HE KIDNAPPED ME...
BUT HE PROBABLY CARES ABOUT ME MORE THAN ANYONE DOES.
AND I STILL FELL IN LOVE WITH BLOOD.
SHOULD I TELL HIM I'M SORRY THAT I CAN'T RETURN HIS FEELINGS?
NO... THAT'S WRONG.
"I'M SORRY, ALICE."
I DIDN'T WANT HIM TO APOLOGIZE TO ME, EITHER.
THEN THERE'S ONLY ONE THING TO SAY.
PETER!

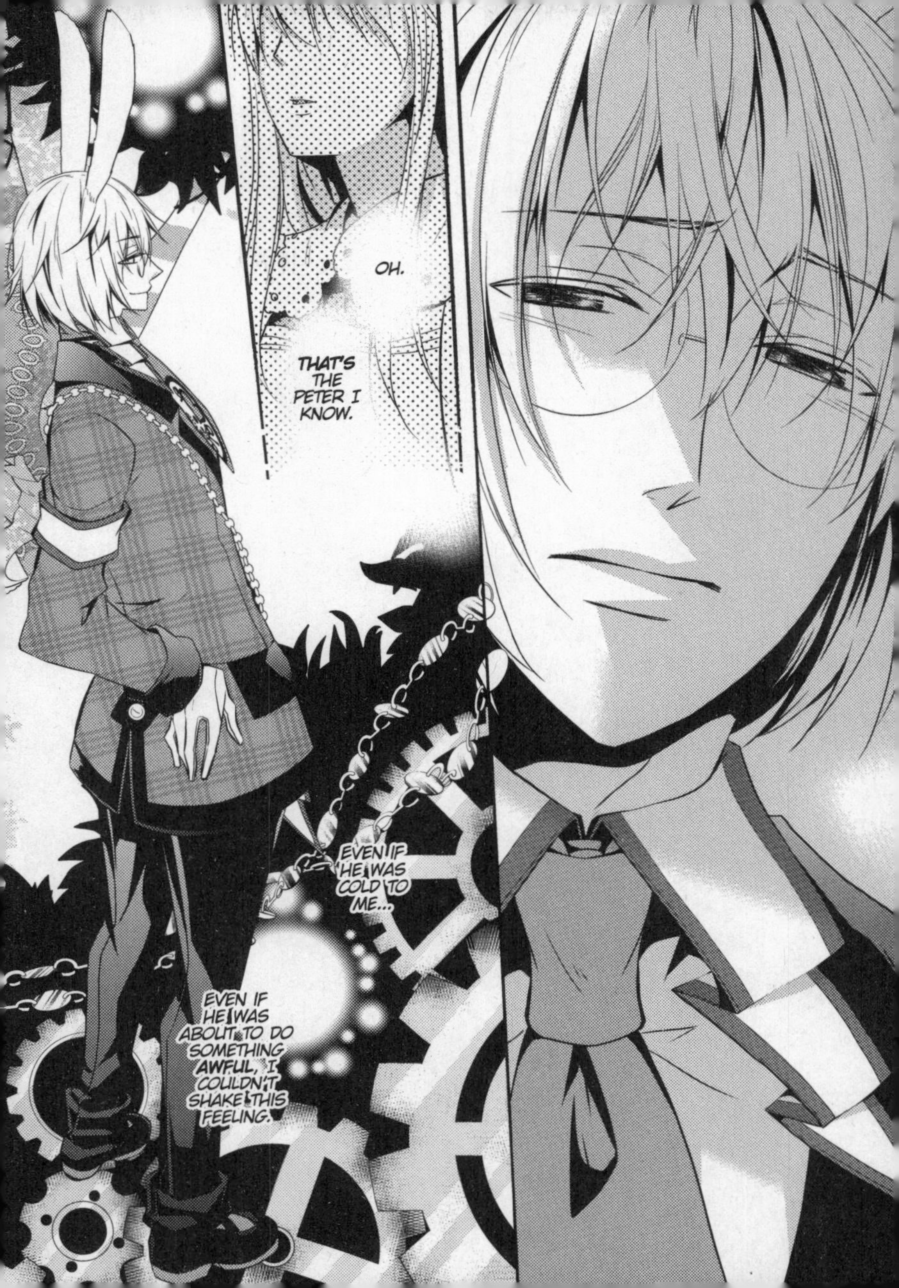
OH.
THAT'S THE PETER I KNOW.
EVEN IF HE WAS COLD TO ME...
EVEN IF HE WAS ABOUT TO DO SOMETHING AWFUL, I COULDN'T SHAKE THIS FEELING.

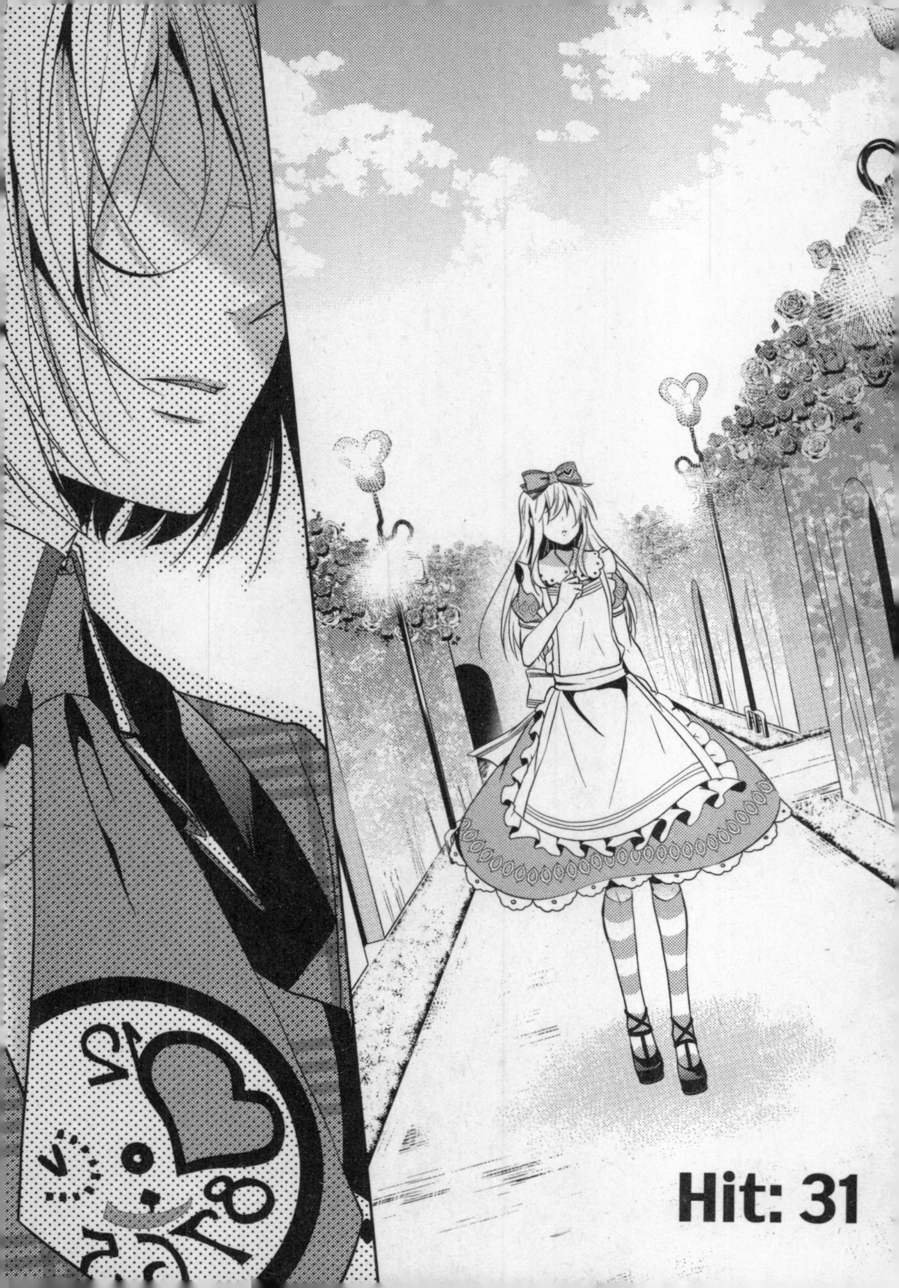
Hit: 31

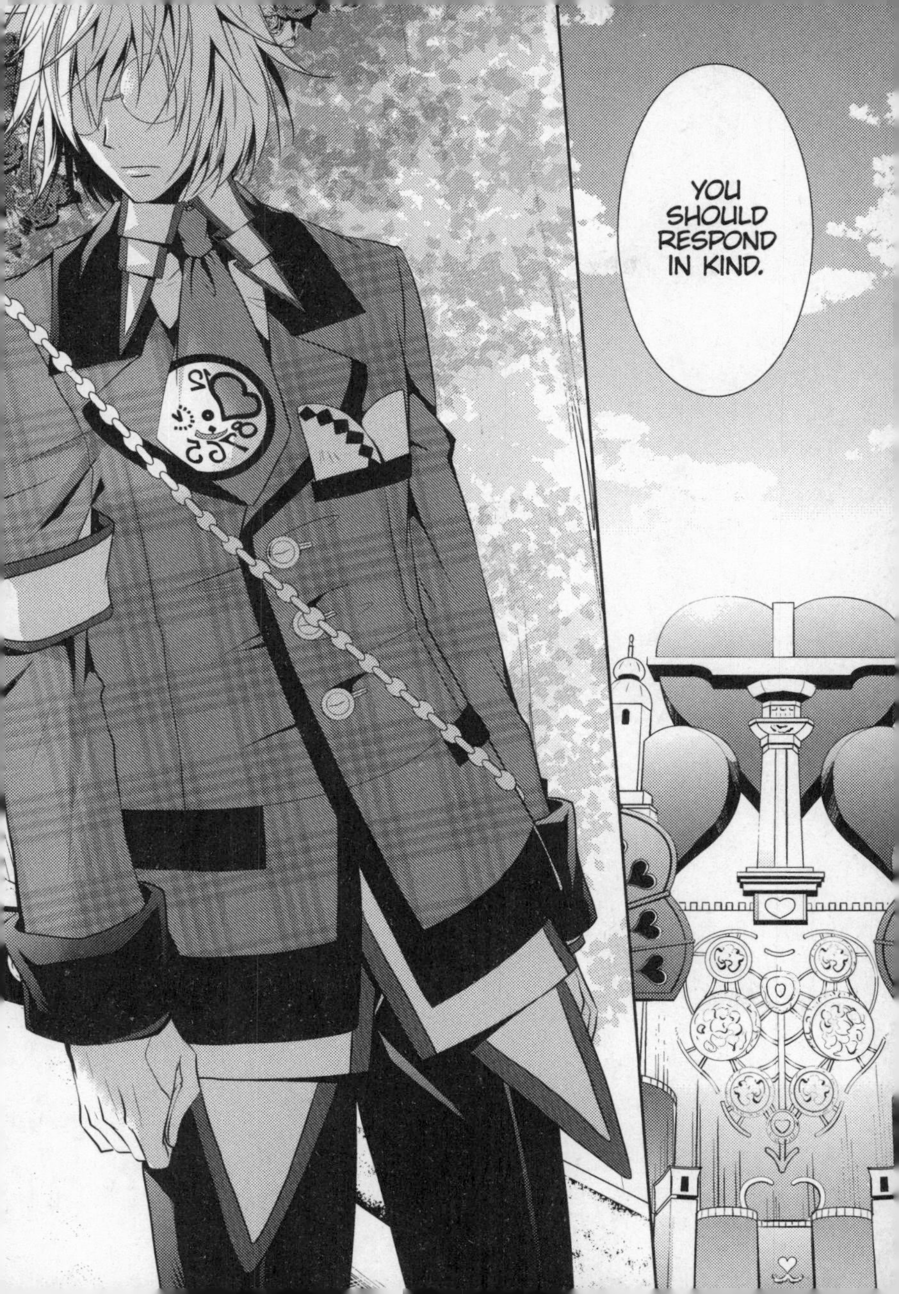
YOU SHOULD RESPOND IN KIND.

Hit: 31

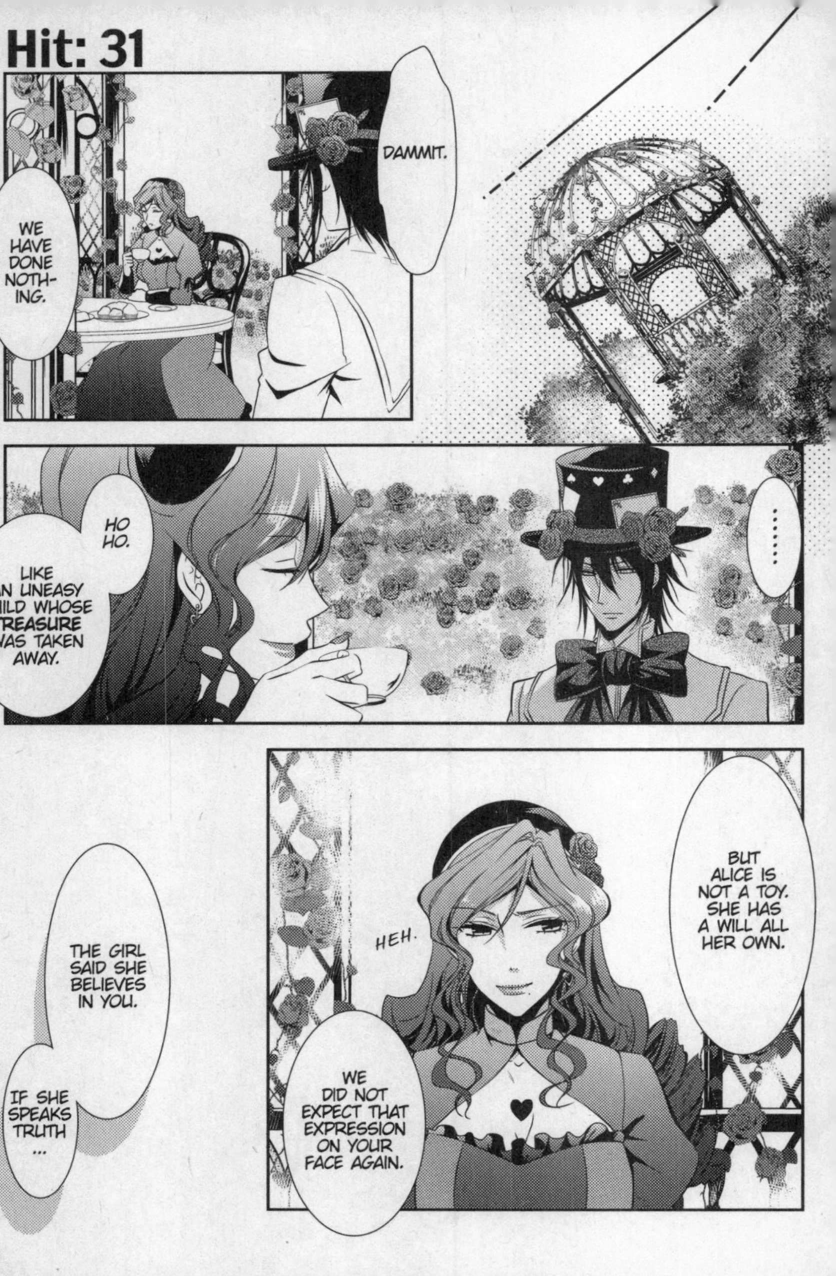
DAMMIT.
WE HAVE DONE NOTHING.
......
HO HO.
LIKE AN UNEASY CHILD WHOSE TREASURE WAS TAKEN AWAY.
BUT ALICE IS NOT A TOY. SHE HAS A WILL ALL HER OWN.
HEH.
WE DID NOT EXPECT THAT EXPRESSION ON YOUR FACE AGAIN.
THE GIRL SAID SHE BELIEVES IN YOU.
IF SHE SPEAKS TRUTH ...

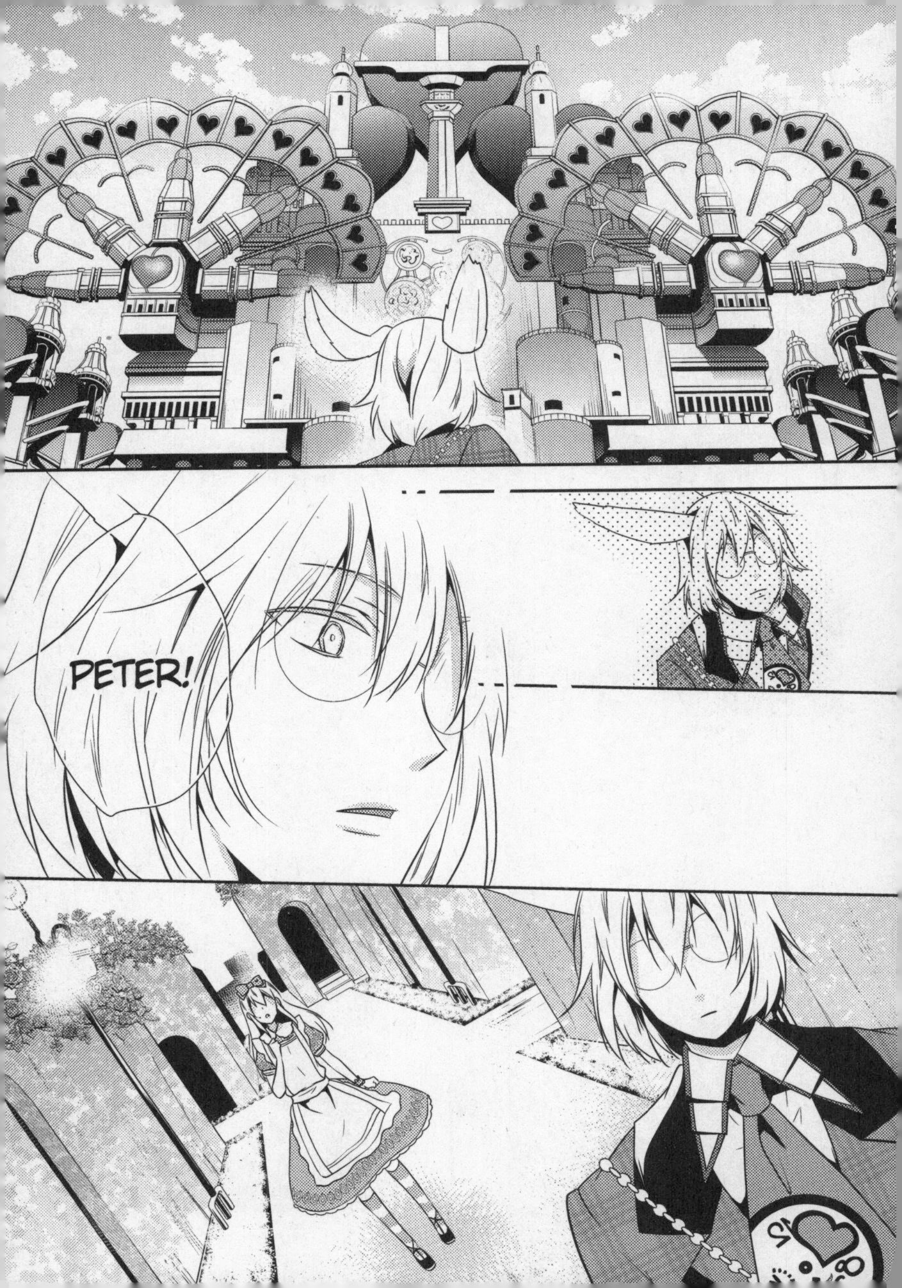
PETER!

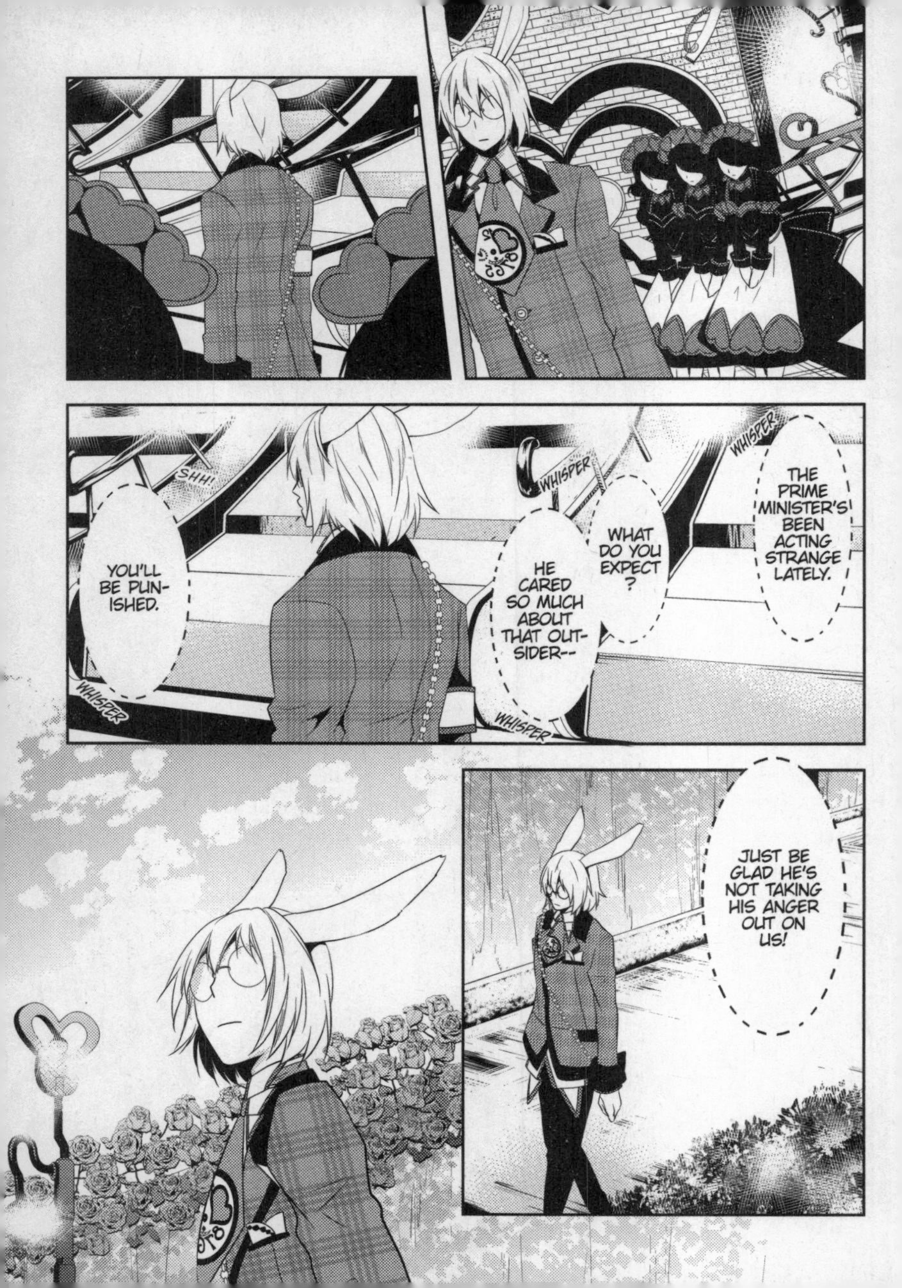
WHISPER
THE PRIME MINISTER'S BEEN ACTING STRANGE LATELY.
WHISPER
WHAT DO YOU EXPECT?
HE CARED SO MUCH ABOUT THAT OUT-SIDER--
WHISPER
SHH!
YOU'LL BE PUN-ISHED.
WHISPER
JUST BE GLAD HE'S NOT TAKING HIS ANGER OUT ON US!

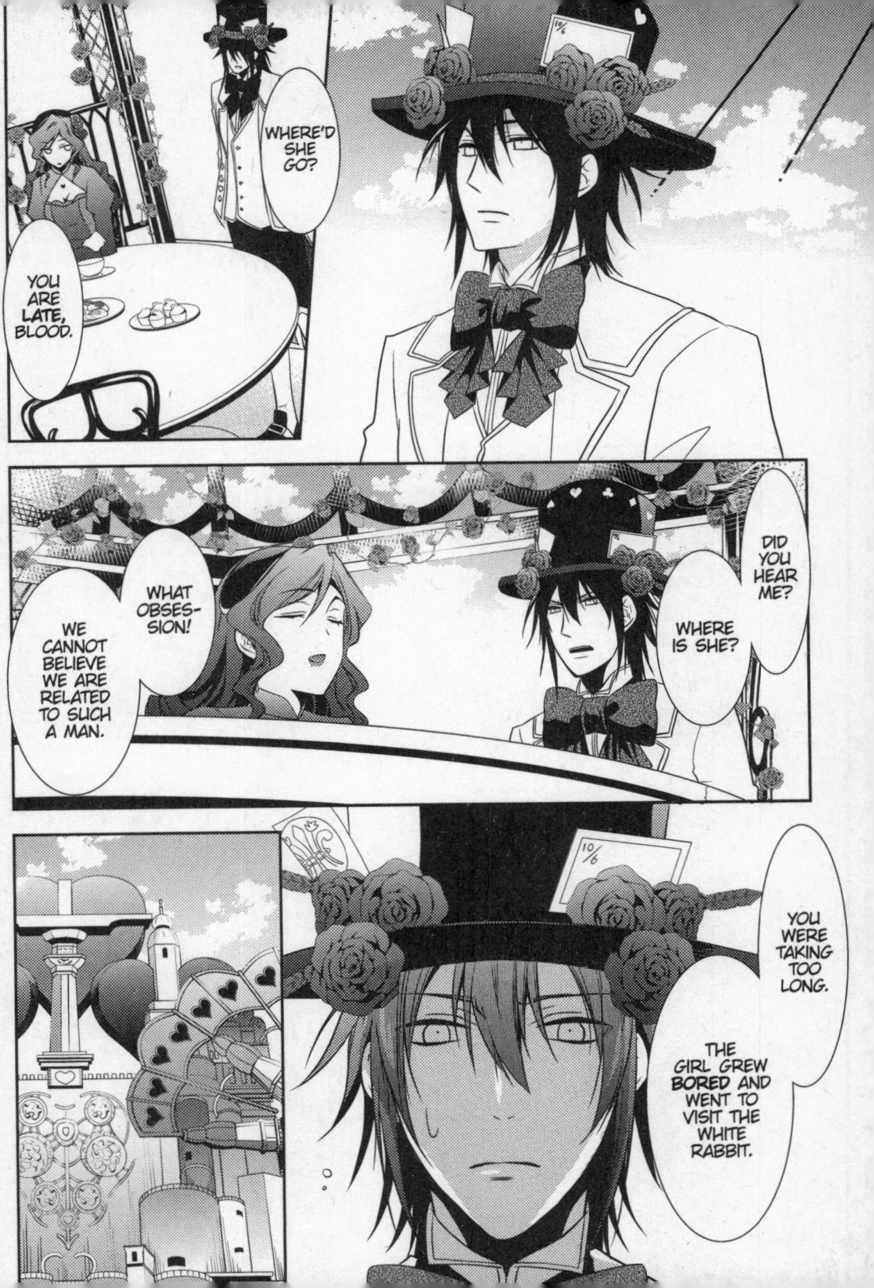
WHERE'D SHE GO?
YOU ARE LATE, BLOOD.
DID YOU HEAR ME?
WHERE IS SHE?
WHAT OBSESSION!
WE CANNOT BELIEVE WE ARE RELATED TO SUCH A MAN.
YOU WERE TAKING TOO LONG.
THE GIRL GREW BORED AND WENT TO VISIT THE WHITE RABBIT.

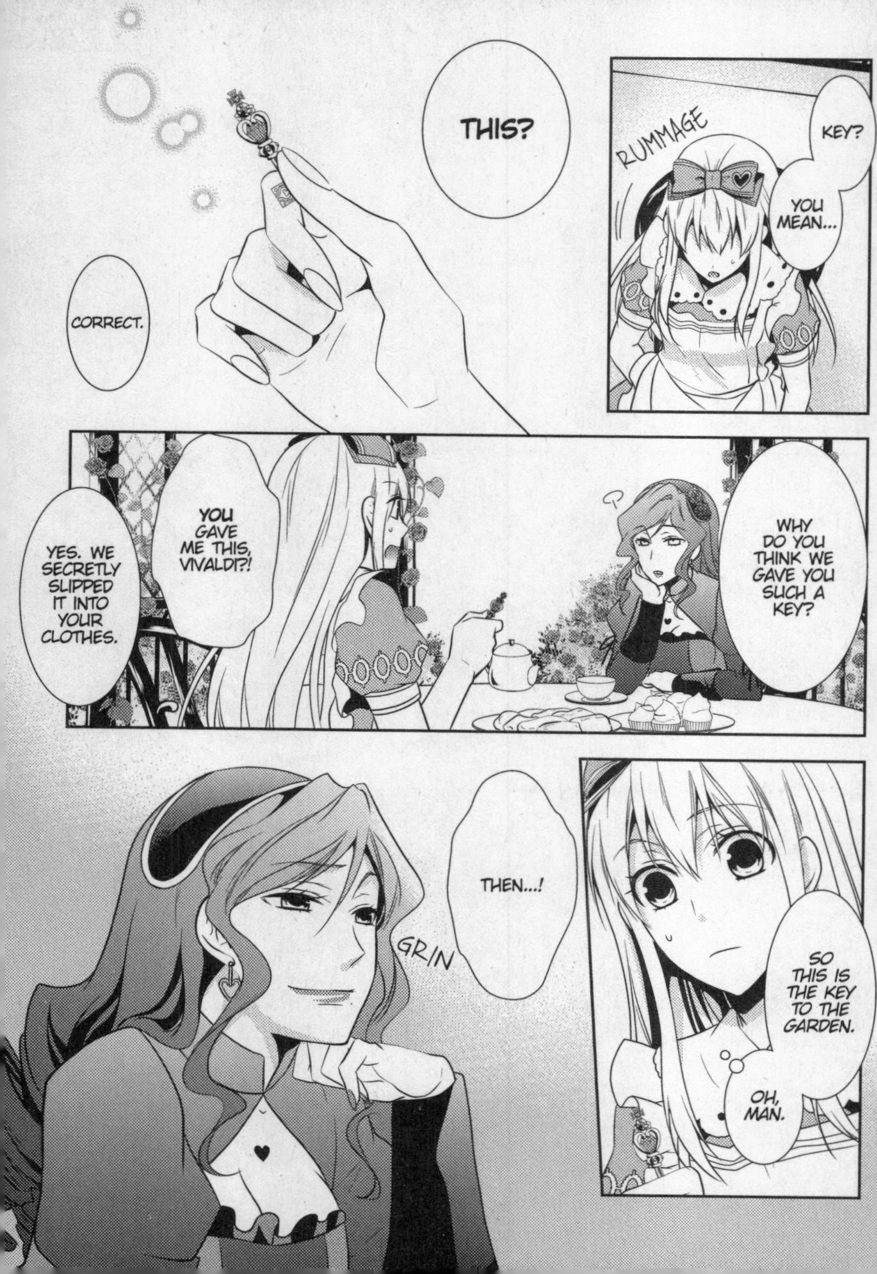
KEY?
YOU MEAN...
RUMMAGE
THIS?
CORRECT.
WHY DO YOU THINK WE GAVE YOU SUCH A KEY?
YOU GAVE ME THIS, VIVALDI?!
YES. WE SECRETLY SLIPPED IT INTO YOUR CLOTHES.
SO THIS IS THE KEY TO THE GARDEN.
OH, MAN.
THEN...!
GRIN

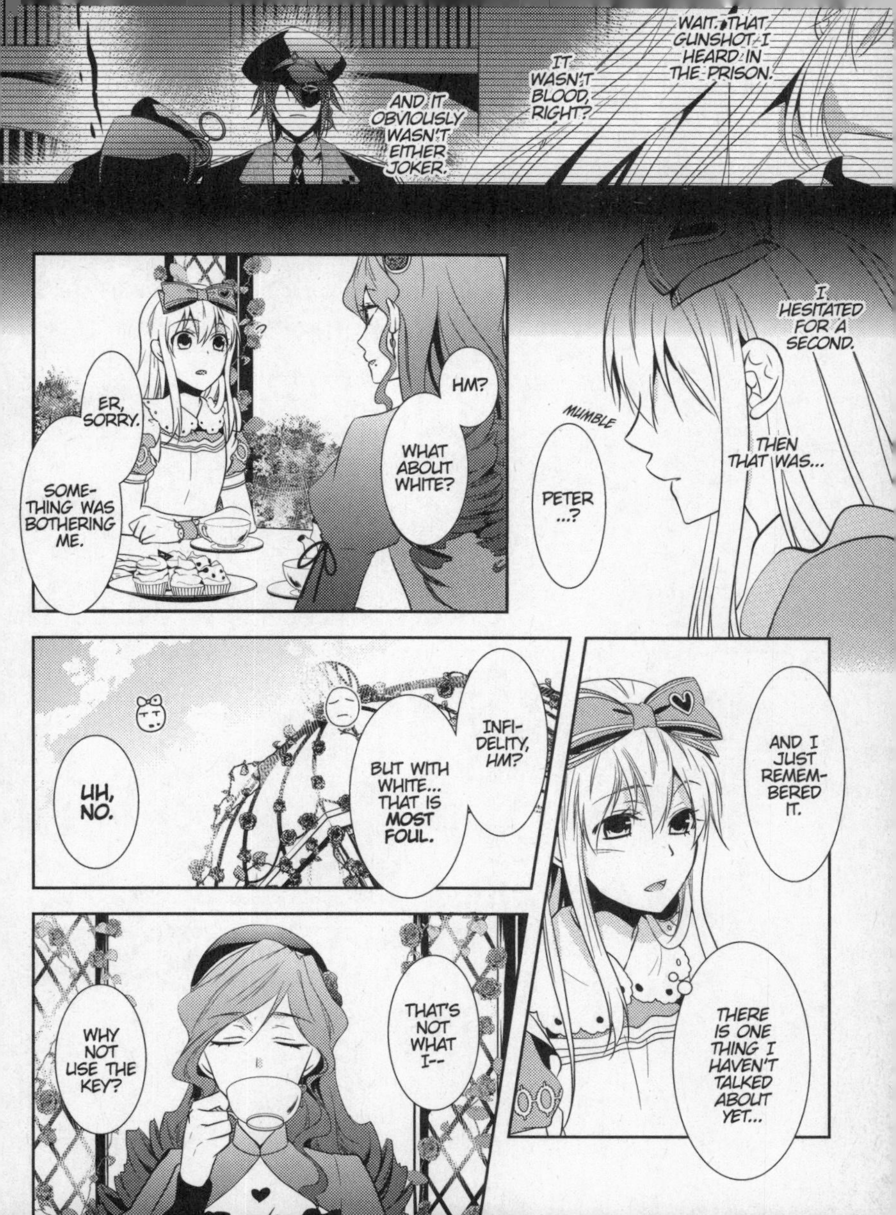
WAIT. THAT GUNSHOT I HEARD IN THE PRISON.
IT WASN'T BLOOD, RIGHT?
AND IT OBVIOUSLY WASN'T EITHER JOKER.
I HESITATED FOR A SECOND.
THEN THAT WAS...
MUMBLE
PETER ...?
HM?
WHAT ABOUT WHITE?
ER, SORRY.
SOME-THING WAS BOTHERING ME.
AND I JUST REMEM-BERED IT.
THERE IS ONE THING I HAVEN'T TALKED ABOUT YET...
INFI-DELITY, HM?
BUT WITH WHITE... THAT IS MOST FOUL.
UH, NO.
THAT'S NOT WHAT I--
WHY NOT USE THE KEY?

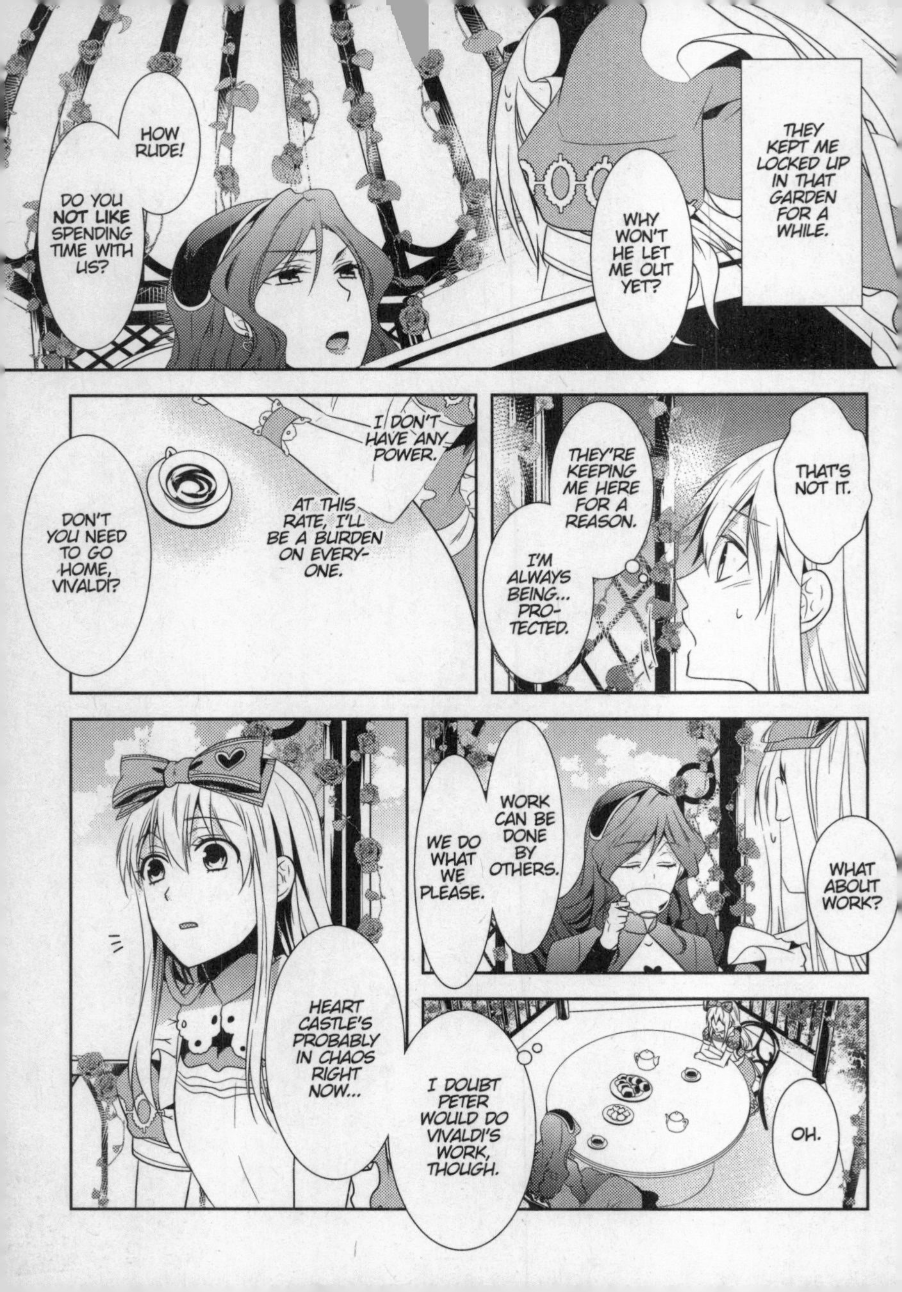
THEY KEPT ME LOCKED UP IN THAT GARDEN FOR A WHILE.
WHY WON'T HE LET ME OUT YET?
HOW RUDE!
DO YOU NOT LIKE SPENDING TIME WITH US?
THAT'S NOT IT.
THEY'RE KEEPING ME HERE FOR A REASON.
I'M ALWAYS BEING... PRO-TECTED.
I DON'T HAVE ANY POWER.
AT THIS RATE, I'LL BE A BURDEN ON EVERY-ONE.
DON'T YOU NEED TO GO HOME, VIVALDI?
WHAT ABOUT WORK?
WORK CAN BE DONE BY OTHERS.
WE DO WHAT WE PLEASE.
OH.
HEART CASTLE'S PROBABLY IN CHAOS RIGHT NOW...
I DOUBT PETER WOULD DO VIVALDI'S WORK, THOUGH.

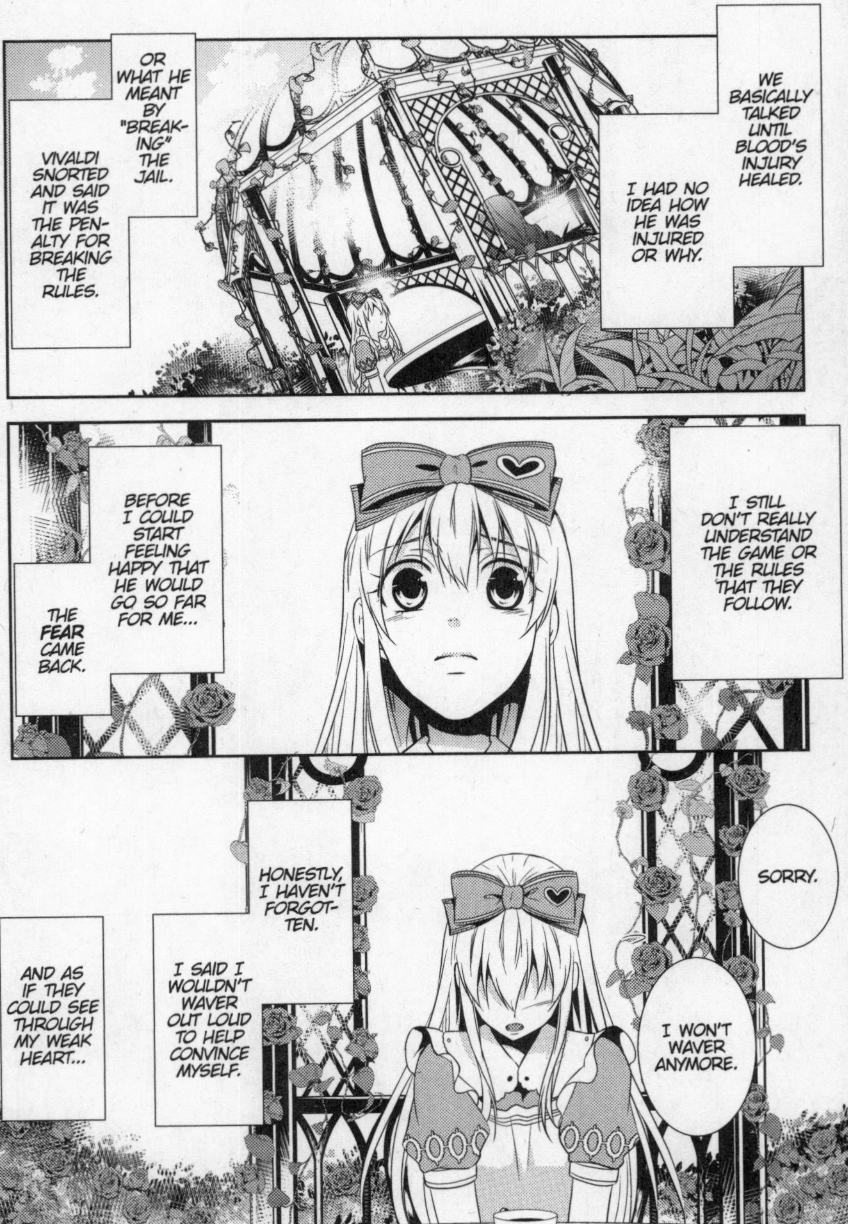
WE BASICALLY TALKED UNTIL BLOOD'S INJURY HEALED.
I HAD NO IDEA HOW HE WAS INJURED OR WHY.
OR WHAT HE MEANT BY "BREAKING" THE JAIL.
VIVALDI SNORTED AND SAID IT WAS THE PENALTY FOR BREAKING THE RULES.
I STILL DON'T REALLY UNDERSTAND THE GAME OR THE RULES THAT THEY FOLLOW.
BEFORE I COULD START FEELING HAPPY THAT HE WOULD GO SO FAR FOR ME...
THE **FEAR** CAME BACK.
SORRY.
I WON'T WAVER ANYMORE.
HONESTLY, I HAVEN'T FORGOTTEN.
I SAID I WOULDN'T WAVER OUT LOUD TO HELP CONVINCE MYSELF.
AND AS IF THEY COULD SEE THROUGH MY WEAK HEART...

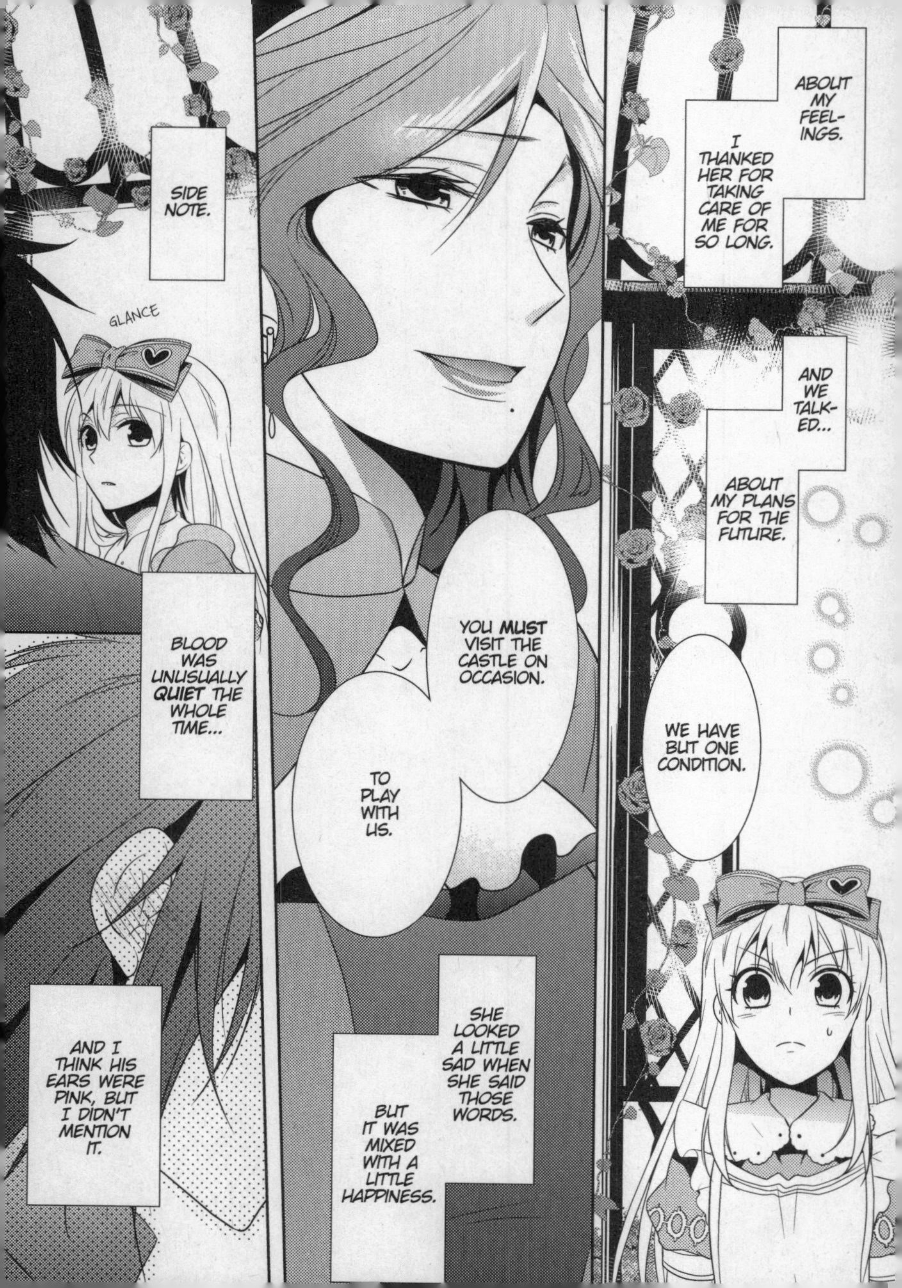
ABOUT MY FEELINGS.
I THANKED HER FOR TAKING CARE OF ME FOR SO LONG.
AND WE TALKED...
ABOUT MY PLANS FOR THE FUTURE.
WE HAVE BUT ONE CONDITION.
YOU MUST VISIT THE CASTLE ON OCCASION.
TO PLAY WITH US.
SHE LOOKED A LITTLE SAD WHEN SHE SAID THOSE WORDS.
BUT IT WAS MIXED WITH A LITTLE HAPPINESS.
SIDE NOTE.
GLANCE
BLOOD WAS UNUSUALLY QUIET THE WHOLE TIME...
AND I THINK HIS EARS WERE PINK, BUT I DIDN'T MENTION IT.

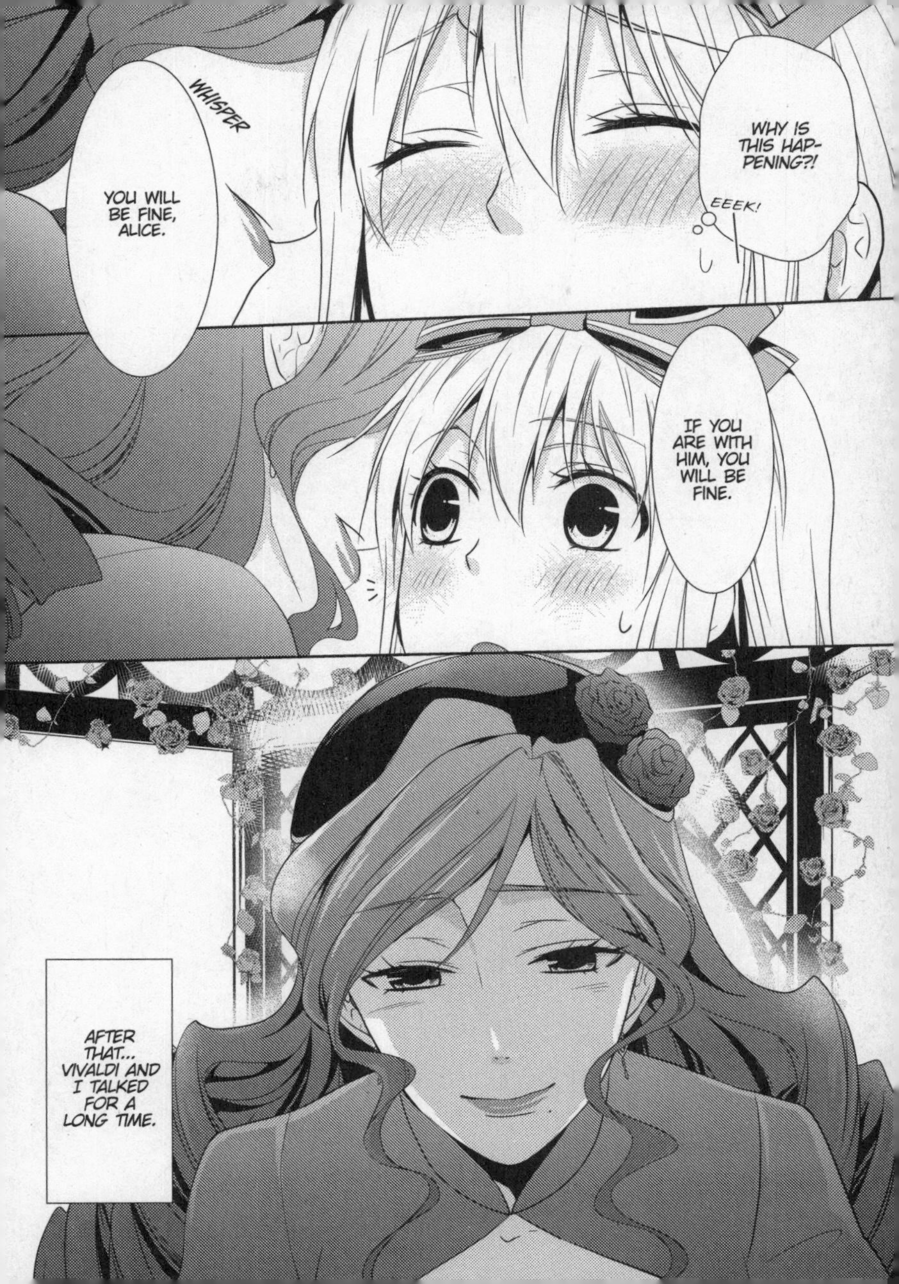
WHY IS THIS HAP-PENING?!
EEEK!
WHISPER
YOU WILL BE FINE, ALICE.
IF YOU ARE WITH HIM, YOU WILL BE FINE.
AFTER THAT... VIVALDI AND I TALKED FOR A LONG TIME.

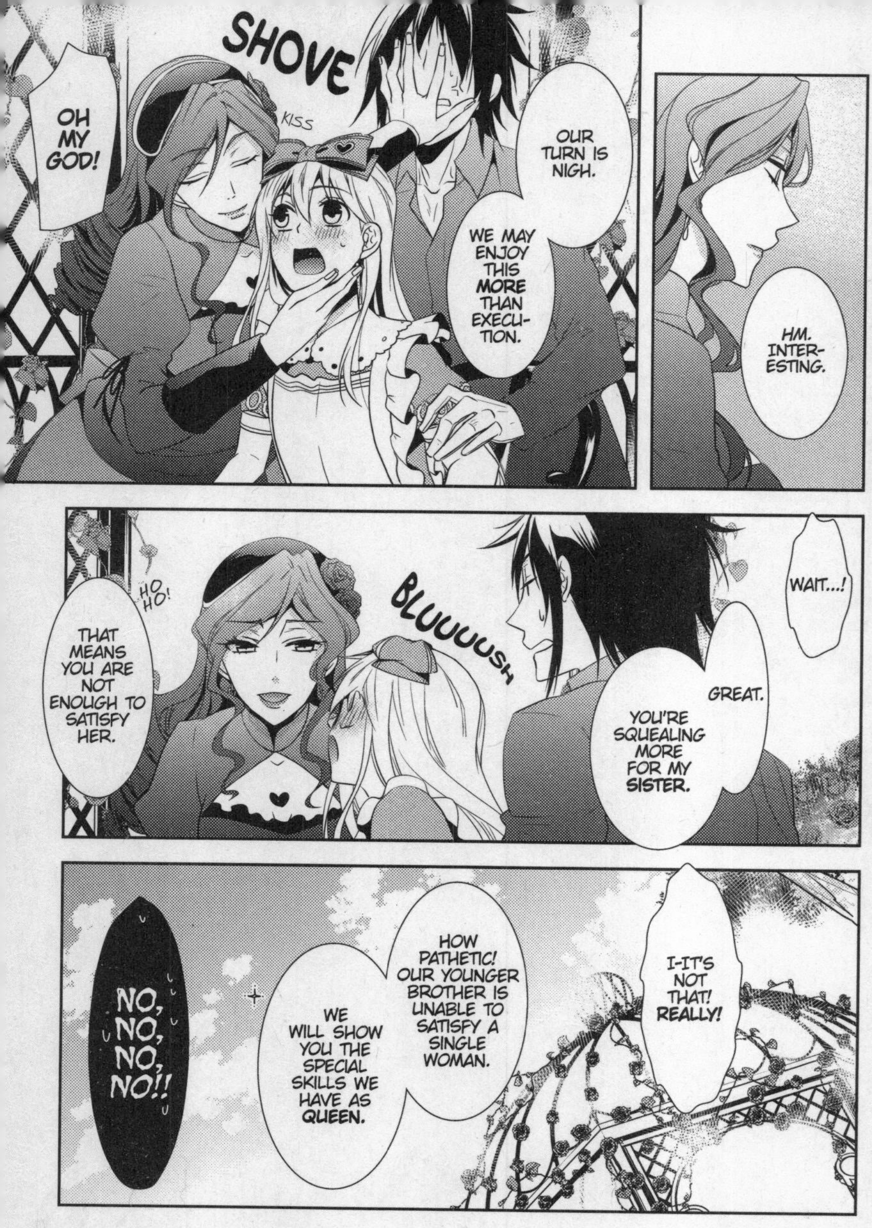
HM. INTERESTING.
OUR TURN IS NIGH.
WE MAY ENJOY THIS MORE THAN EXECUTION.
SHOVE
KISS
OH MY GOD!
WAIT...!
GREAT.
YOU'RE SQUEALING MORE FOR MY SISTER.
BLUUUUSH
HO HO!
THAT MEANS YOU ARE NOT ENOUGH TO SATISFY HER.
I-IT'S NOT THAT! REALLY!
HOW PATHETIC! OUR YOUNGER BROTHER IS UNABLE TO SATISFY A SINGLE WOMAN.
WE WILL SHOW YOU THE SPECIAL SKILLS WE HAVE AS QUEEN.
NO, NO, NO, NO!!

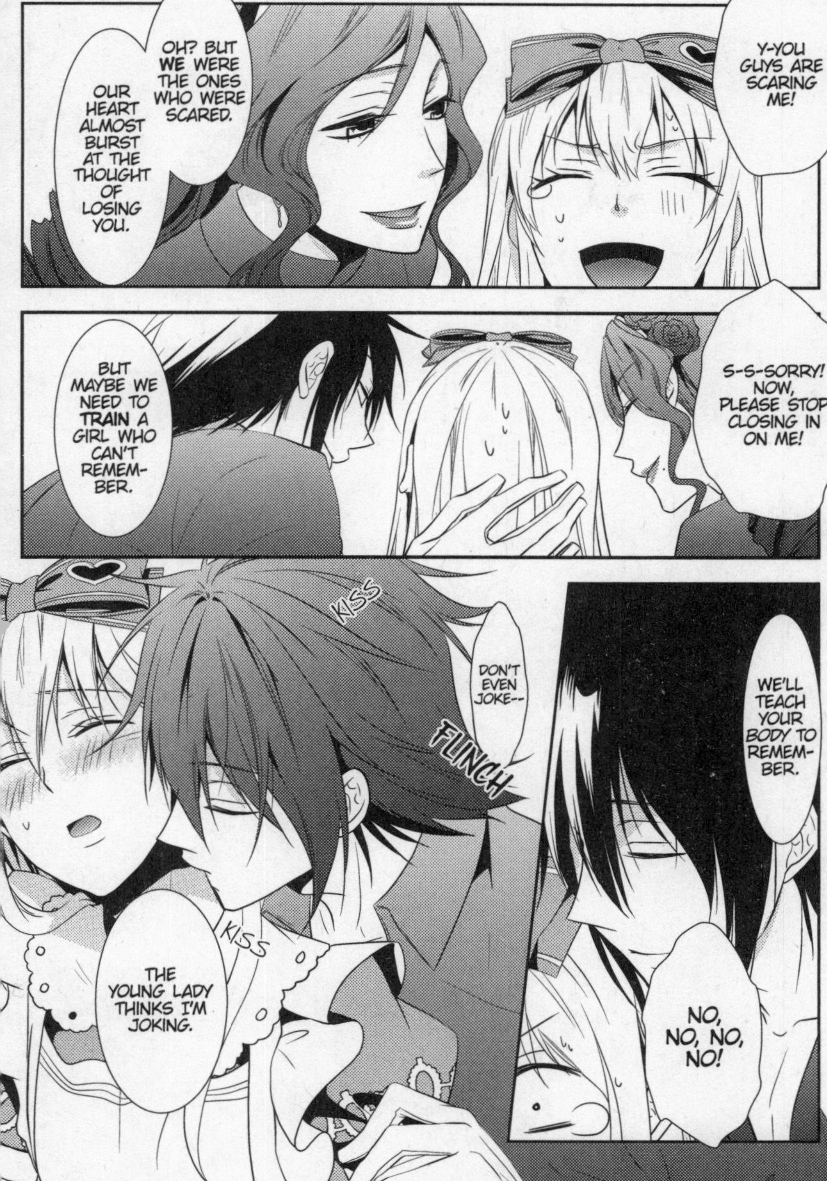
Y-YOU GUYS ARE SCARING ME!
OH? BUT WE WERE THE ONES WHO WERE SCARED.
OUR HEART ALMOST BURST AT THE THOUGHT OF LOSING YOU.
S-S-SORRY! NOW, PLEASE STOP CLOSING IN ON ME!
BUT MAYBE WE NEED TO TRAIN A GIRL WHO CAN'T REMEMBER.
WE'LL TEACH YOUR BODY TO REMEMBER.
NO, NO, NO, NO!
KISS
DON'T EVEN JOKE--
FLINCH
KISS
THE YOUNG LADY THINKS I'M JOKING.

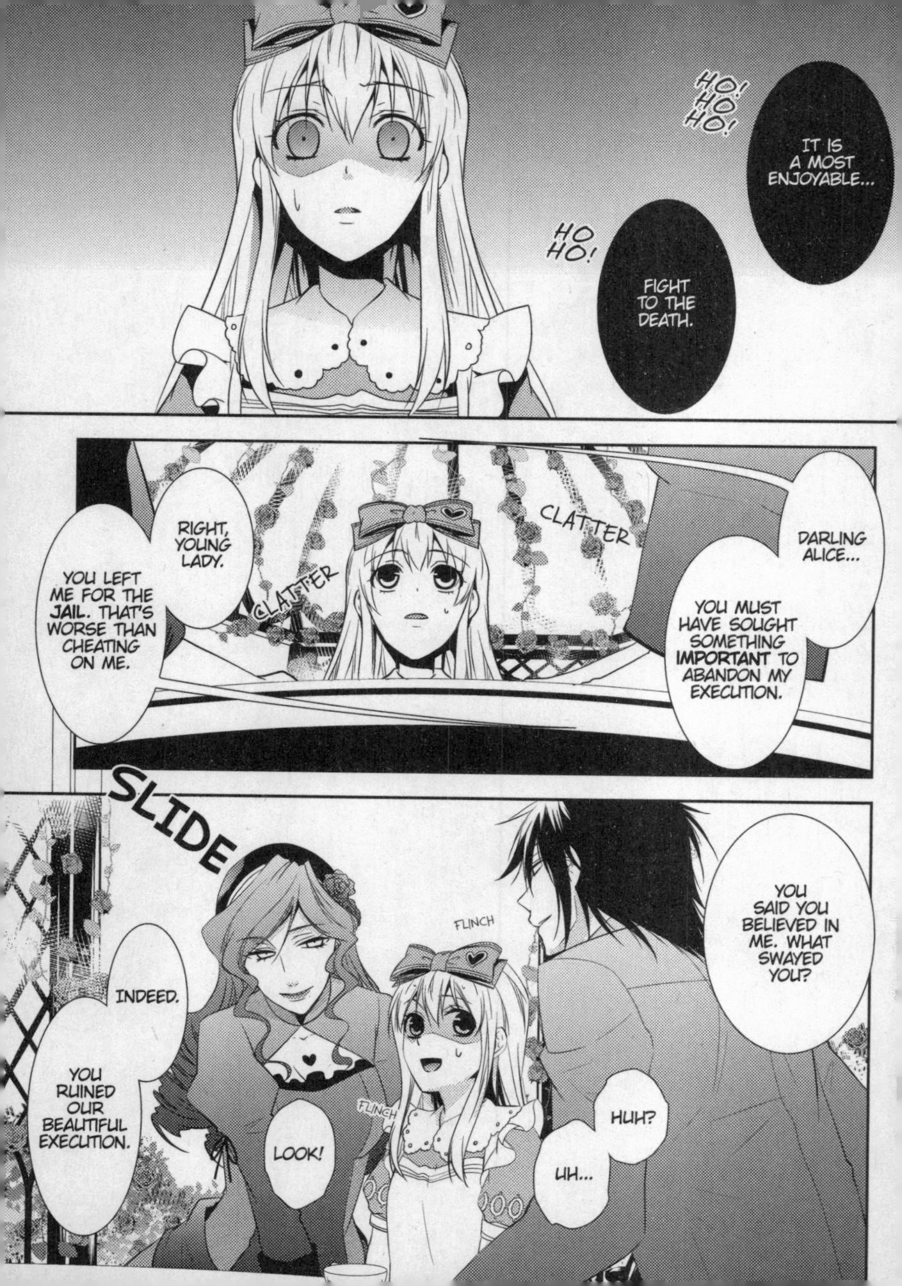
HO! HO! HO!
IT IS A MOST ENJOYABLE...
HO HO!
FIGHT TO THE DEATH.
DARLING ALICE...
YOU MUST HAVE SOUGHT SOMETHING IMPORTANT TO ABANDON MY EXECUTION.
CLATTER
CLATTER
RIGHT, YOUNG LADY.
YOU LEFT ME FOR THE JAIL. THAT'S WORSE THAN CHEATING ON ME.
SLIDE
YOU SAID YOU BELIEVED IN ME. WHAT SWAYED YOU?
FLINCH
HUH?
UH...
FLINCH
INDEED.
YOU RUINED OUR BEAUTIFUL EXECUTION.
LOOK!

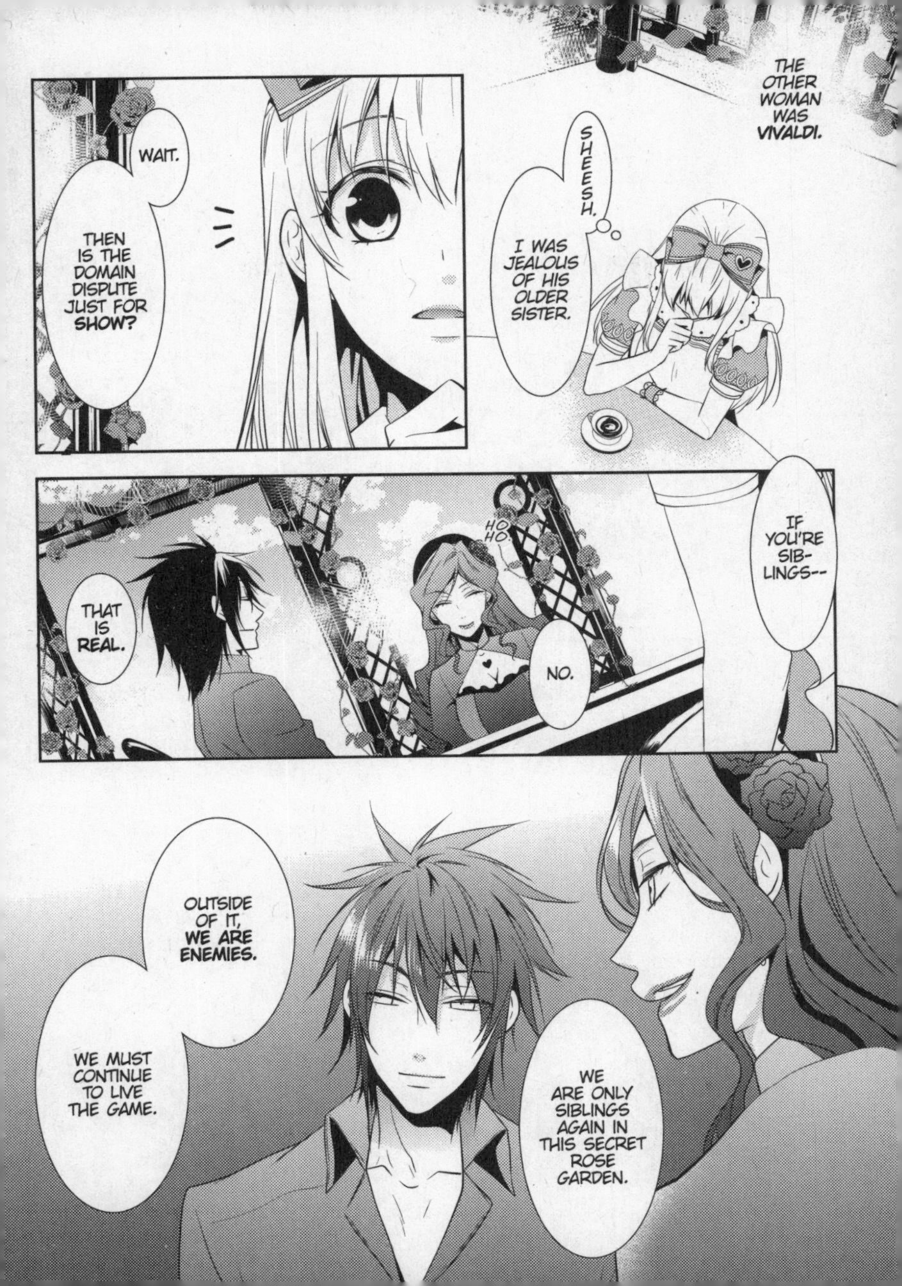
THE OTHER WOMAN WAS VIVALDI.
SHEESH.
I WAS JEALOUS OF HIS OLDER SISTER.
WAIT.
THEN IS THE DOMAIN DISPUTE JUST FOR SHOW?
IF YOU'RE SIB-LINGS--
HO HO.
NO.
THAT IS REAL.
WE ARE ONLY SIBLINGS AGAIN IN THIS SECRET ROSE GARDEN.
OUTSIDE OF IT, WE ARE ENEMIES.
WE MUST CONTINUE TO LIVE THE GAME.

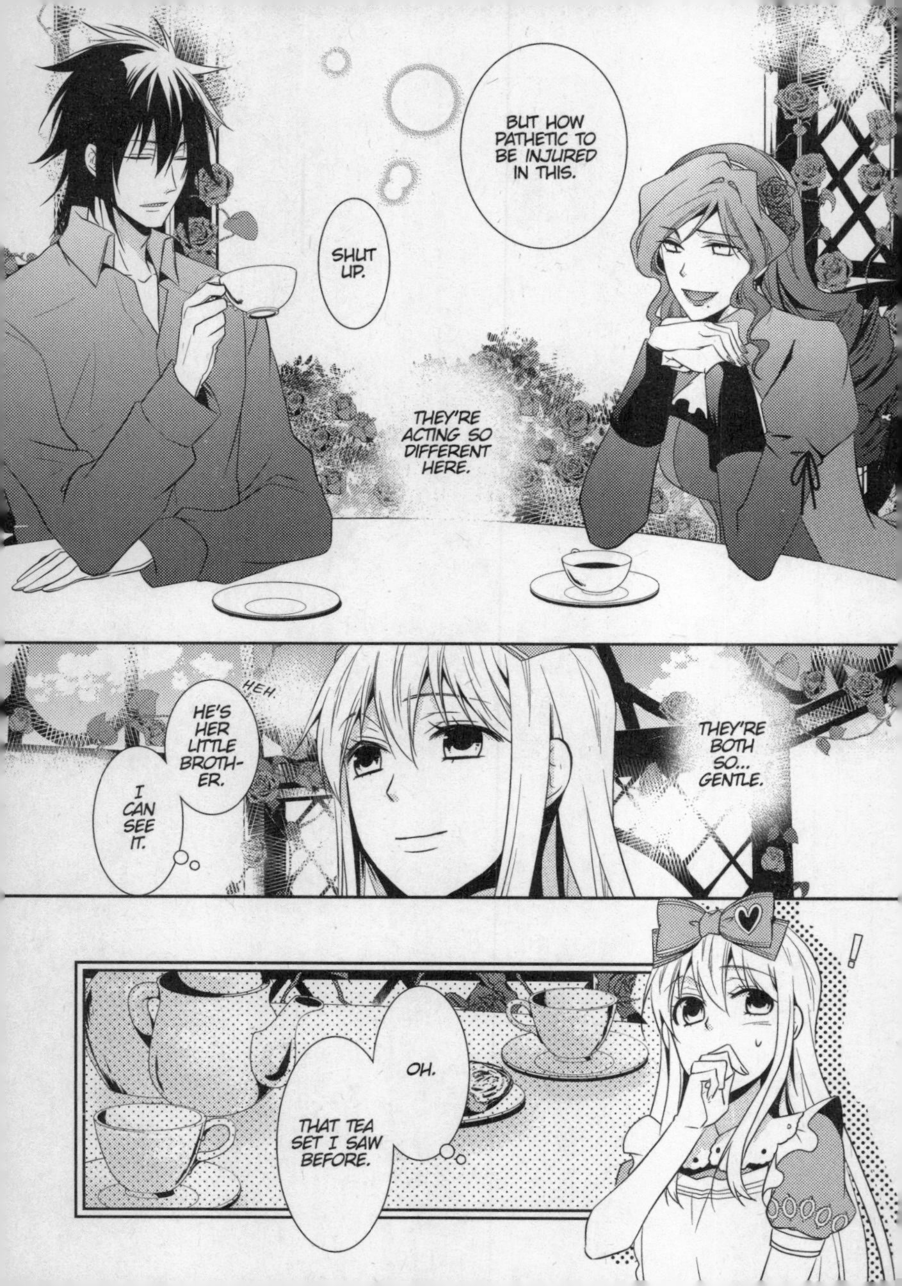

BUT HOW PATHETIC TO BE INJURED IN THIS.
SHUT UP.
THEY'RE ACTING SO DIFFERENT HERE.
THEY'RE BOTH SO... GENTLE.
HEH.
HE'S HER LITTLE BROTH-ER.
I CAN SEE IT.
!
OH.
THAT TEA SET I SAW BEFORE.

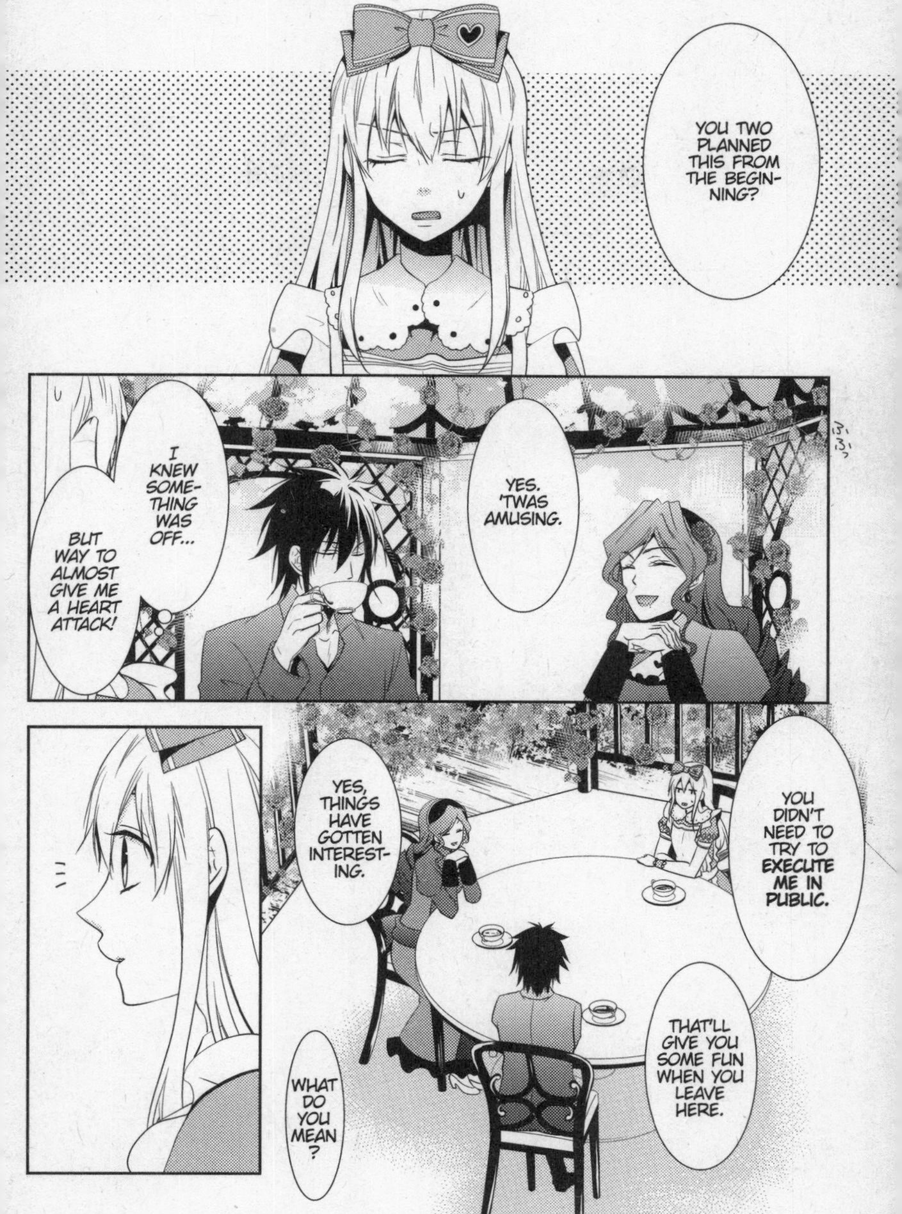
YOU TWO PLANNED THIS FROM THE BEGIN-NING?
YES. 'TWAS AMUSING.
I KNEW SOME-THING WAS OFF...
BUT WAY TO ALMOST GIVE ME A HEART ATTACK!
YOU DIDN'T NEED TO TRY TO EXECUTE ME IN PUBLIC.
YES, THINGS HAVE GOTTEN INTEREST-ING.
THAT'LL GIVE YOU SOME FUN WHEN YOU LEAVE HERE.
WHAT DO YOU MEAN?

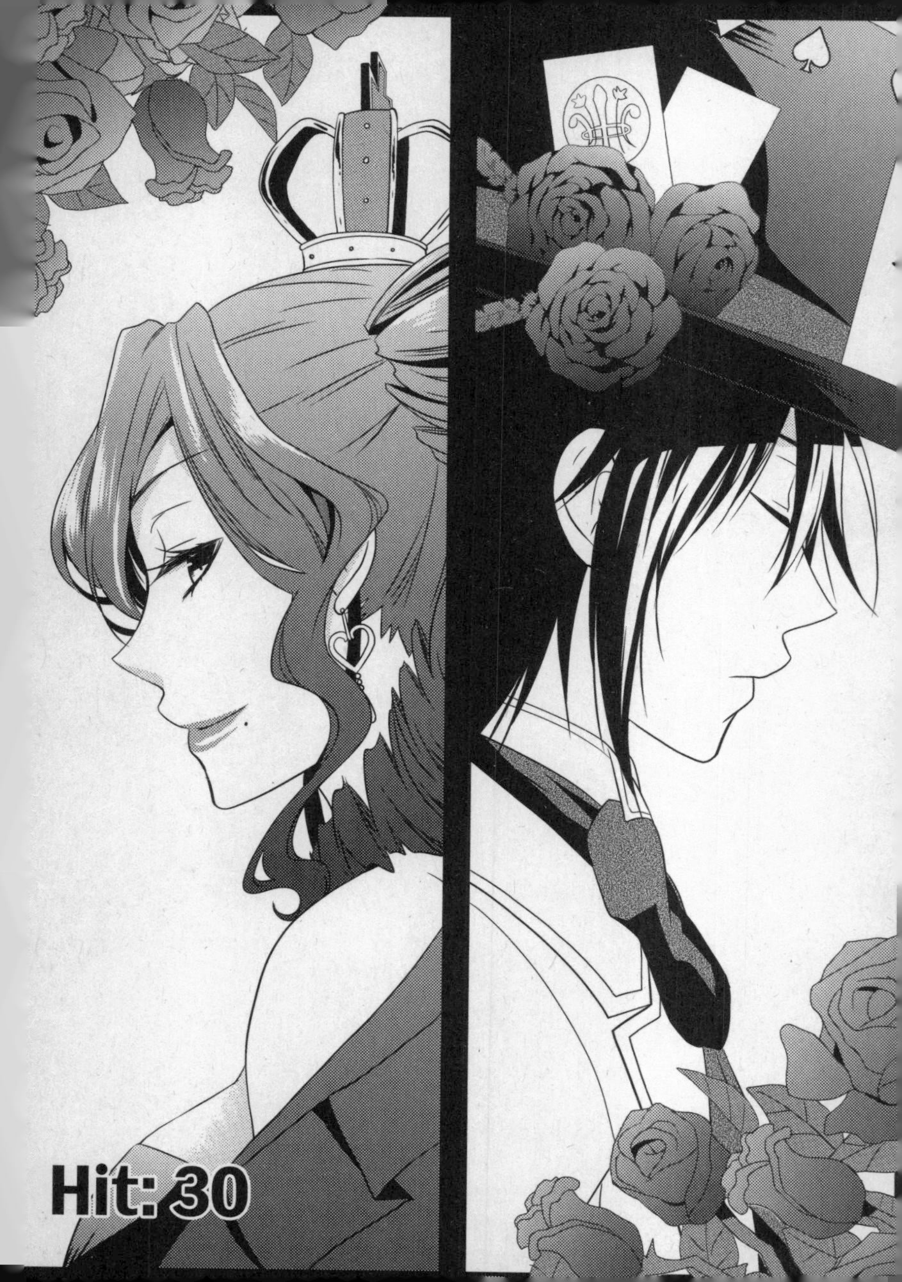
Hit: 30

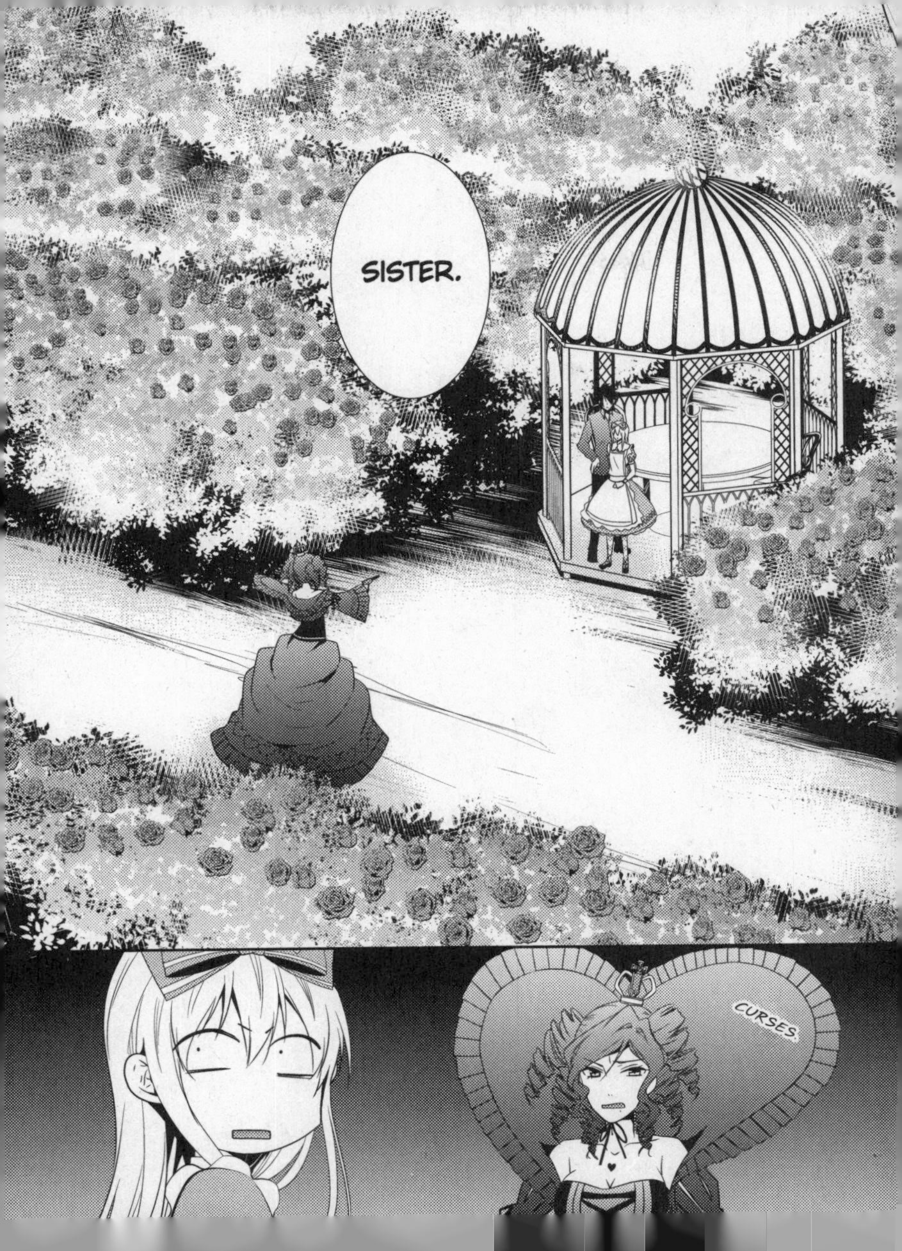
SISTER.
CURSES.

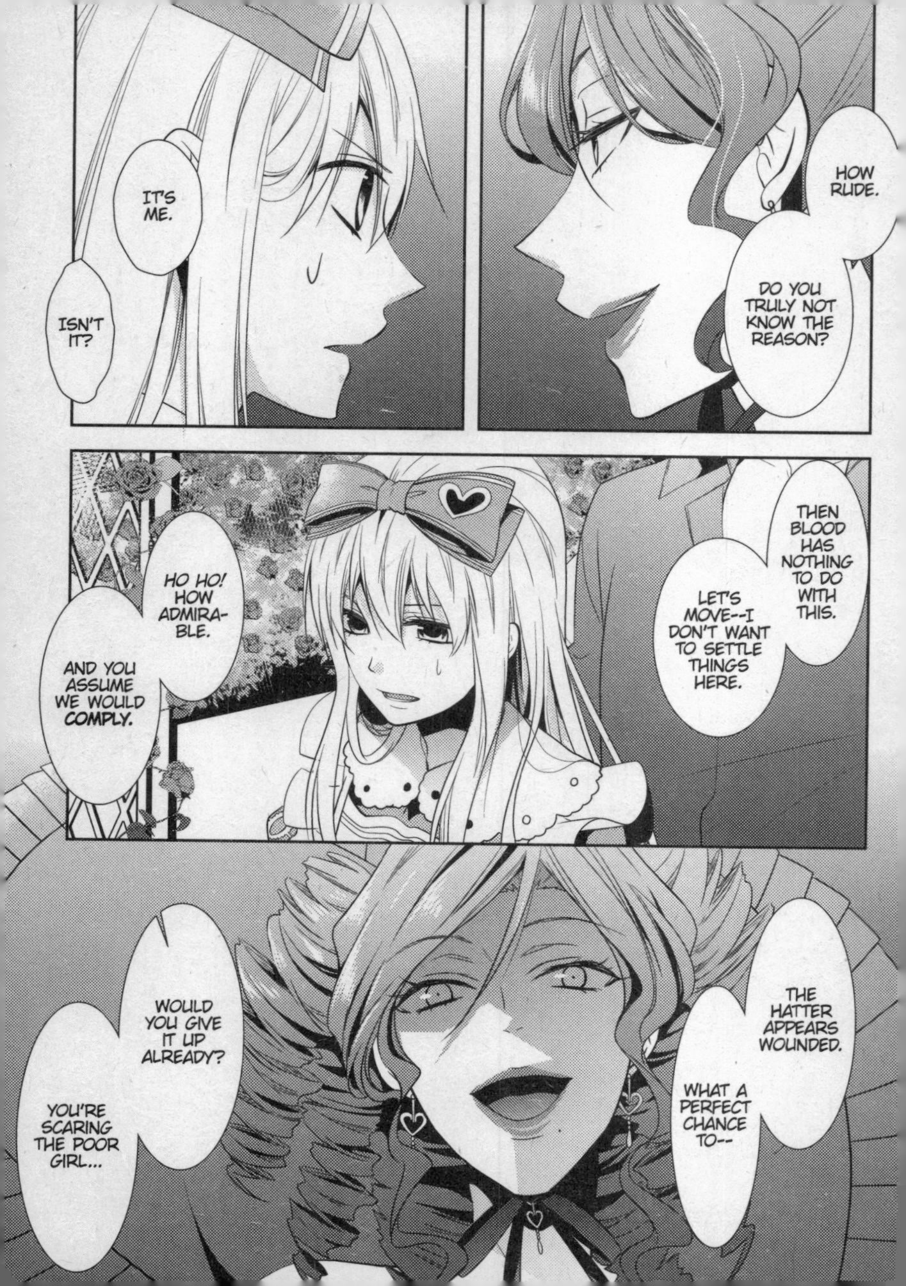
HOW RUDE.
DO YOU TRULY NOT KNOW THE REASON?
IT'S ME.
ISN'T IT?
THEN BLOOD HAS NOTHING TO DO WITH THIS.
LET'S MOVE--I DON'T WANT TO SETTLE THINGS HERE.
HO HO! HOW ADMIRABLE.
AND YOU ASSUME WE WOULD COMPLY.
THE HATTER APPEARS WOUNDED.
WHAT A PERFECT CHANCE TO--
WOULD YOU GIVE IT UP ALREADY?
YOU'RE SCARING THE POOR GIRL...

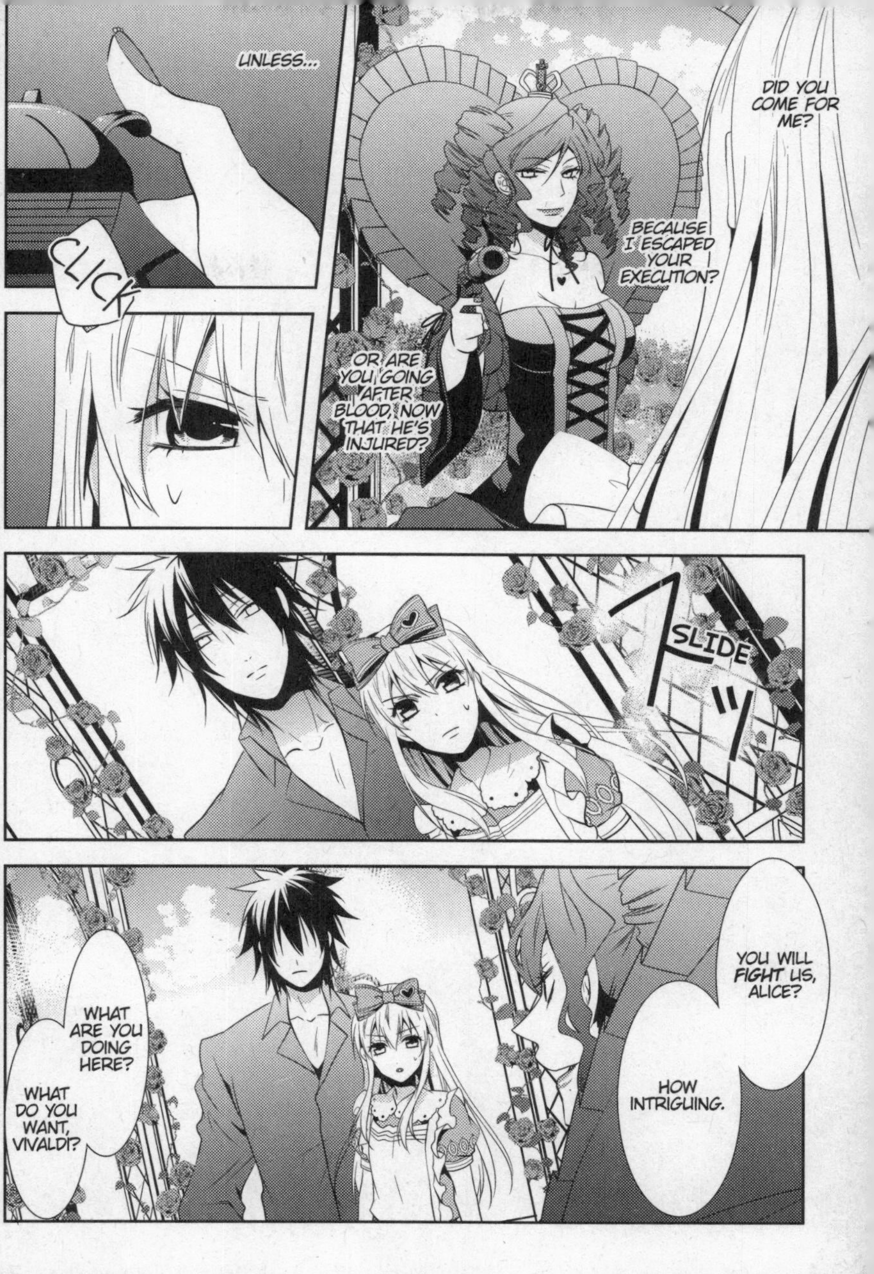
DID YOU COME FOR ME?
BECAUSE I ESCAPED YOUR EXECUTION?
OR ARE YOU GOING AFTER BLOOD, NOW THAT HE'S INJURED?
UNLESS...
CLICK
SLIDE
YOU WILL FIGHT US, ALICE?
HOW INTRIGUING.
WHAT ARE YOU DOING HERE?
WHAT DO YOU WANT, VIVALDI?

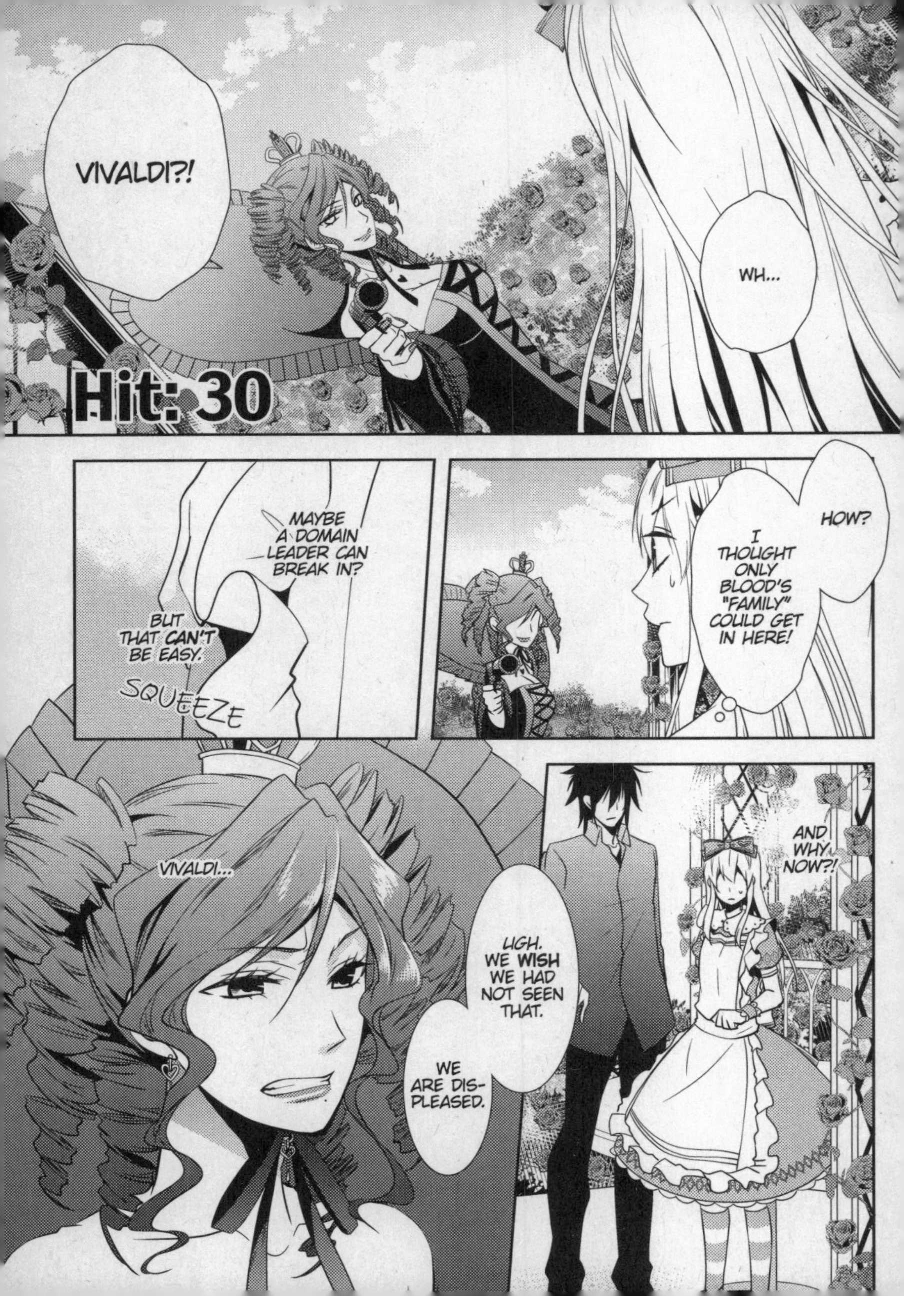
WH...
VIVALDI?!
Hit: 30
HOW?
I THOUGHT ONLY BLOOD'S "FAMILY" COULD GET IN HERE!
MAYBE A DOMAIN LEADER CAN BREAK IN?
BUT THAT CAN'T BE EASY.
SQUEEZE
AND WHY NOW?!
VIVALDI...
UGH. WE WISH WE HAD NOT SEEN THAT.
WE ARE DIS-PLEASED.

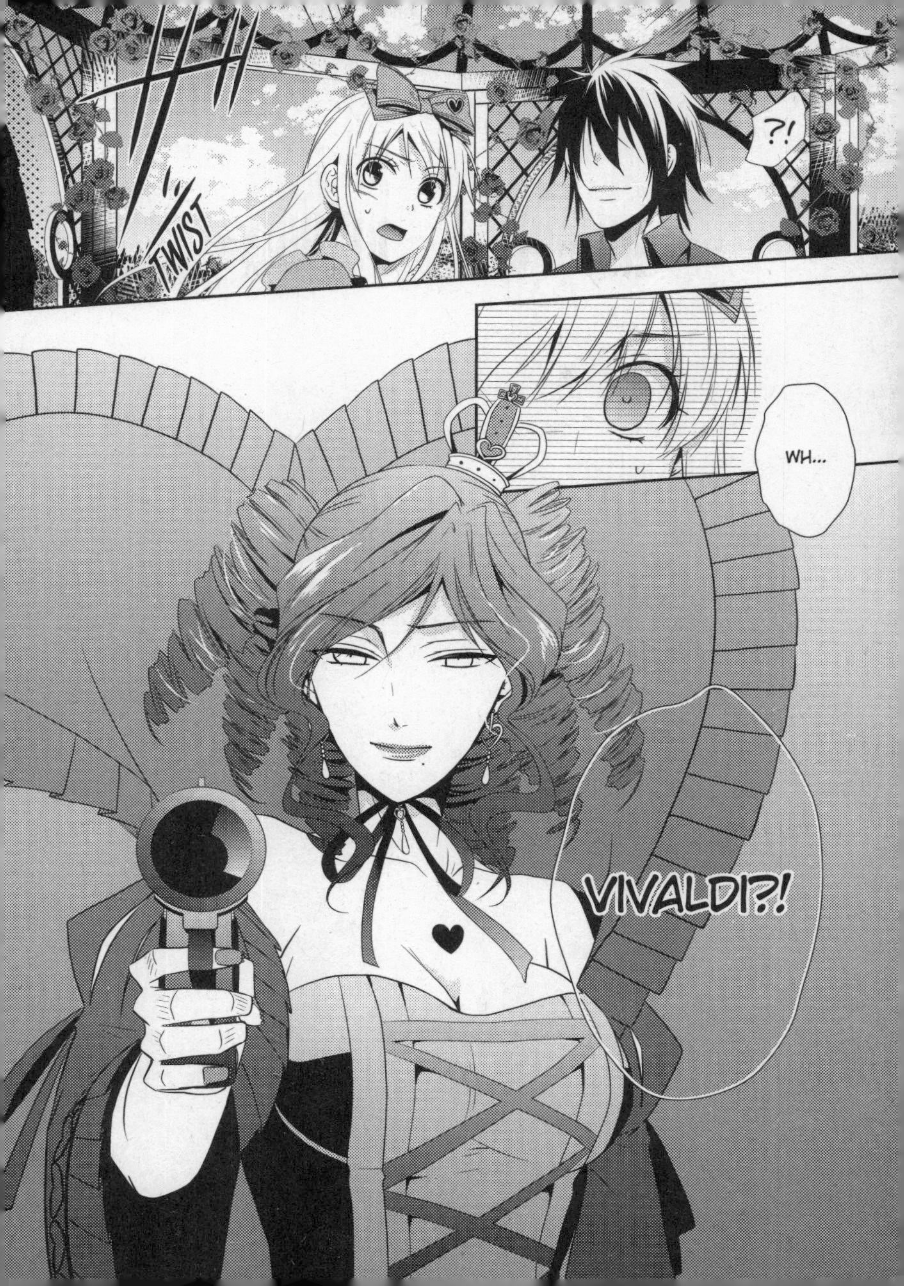
?!
TWIST
WH...
VIVALDI?!

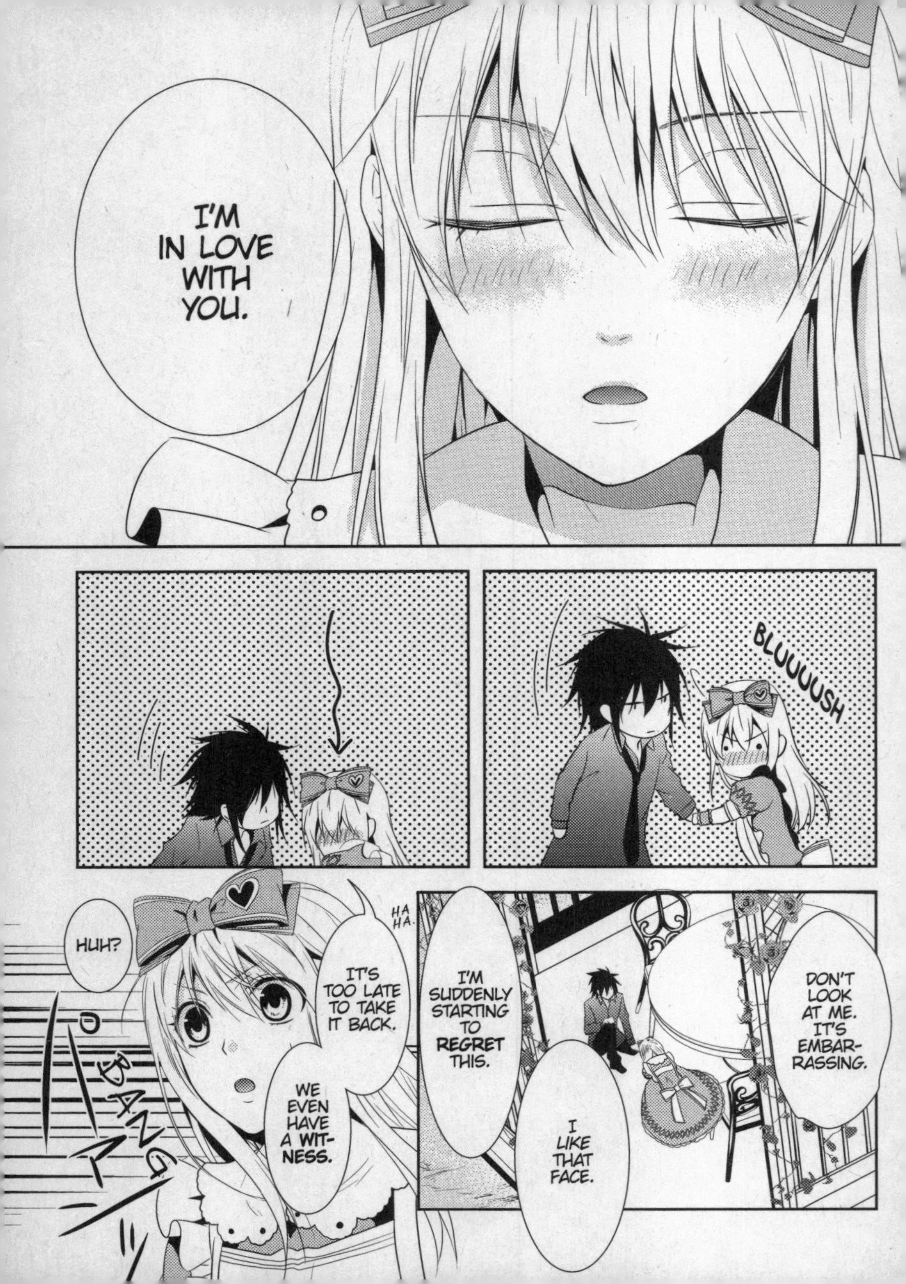
I'M IN LOVE WITH YOU.
BLUUUUSH
DON'T LOOK AT ME. IT'S EMBAR-RASSING.
I'M SUDDENLY STARTING TO REGRET THIS.
I LIKE THAT FACE.
HA HA.
IT'S TOO LATE TO TAKE IT BACK.
HUH?
WE EVEN HAVE A WIT-NESS.
BANG

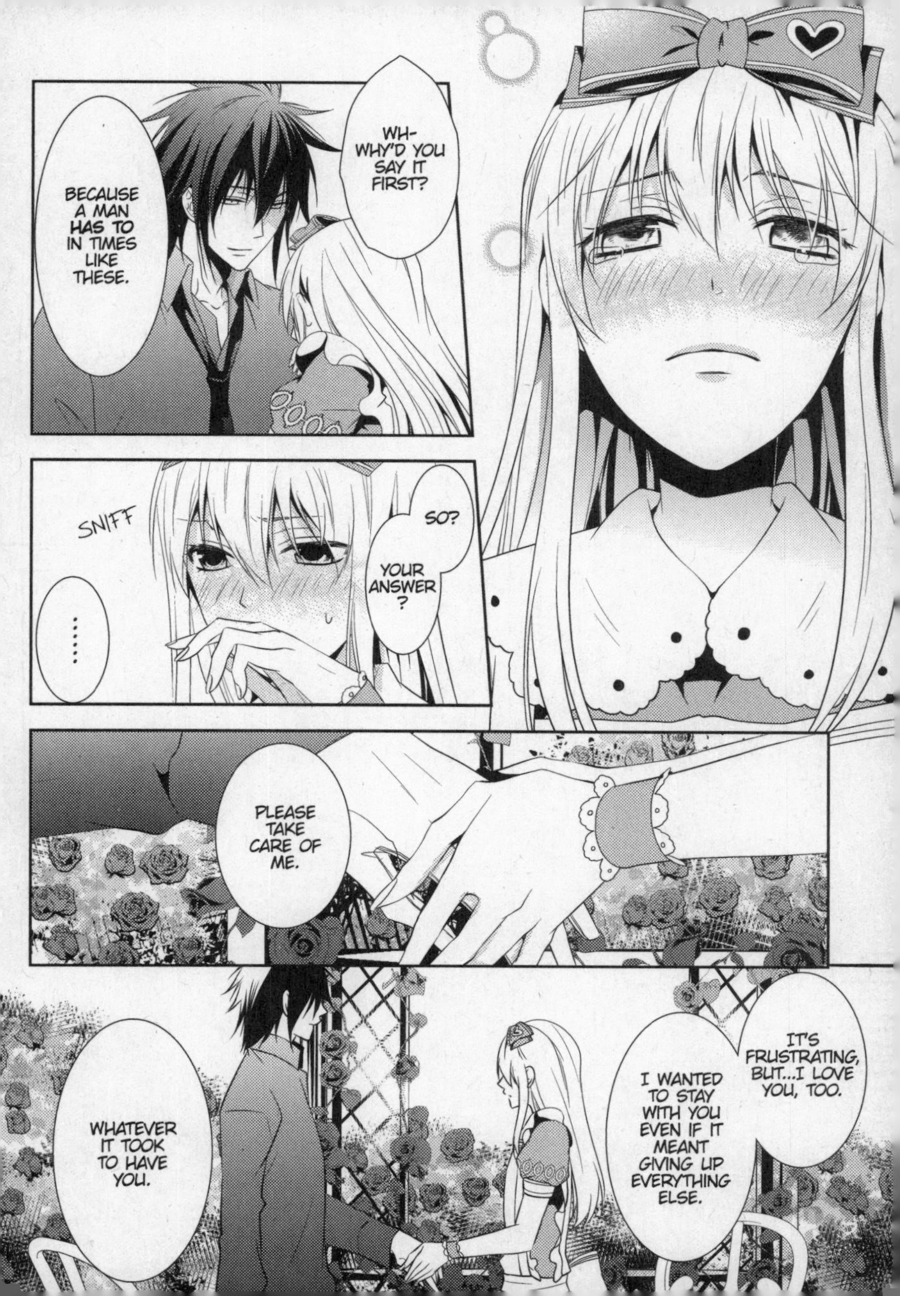
WH- WHY'D YOU SAY IT FIRST?
BECAUSE A MAN HAS TO IN TIMES LIKE THESE.
SO?
YOUR ANSWER?
SNIFF
......
PLEASE TAKE CARE OF ME.
IT'S FRUSTRATING, BUT...I LOVE YOU, TOO.
I WANTED TO STAY WITH YOU EVEN IF IT MEANT GIVING UP EVERYTHING ELSE.
WHATEVER IT TOOK TO HAVE YOU.

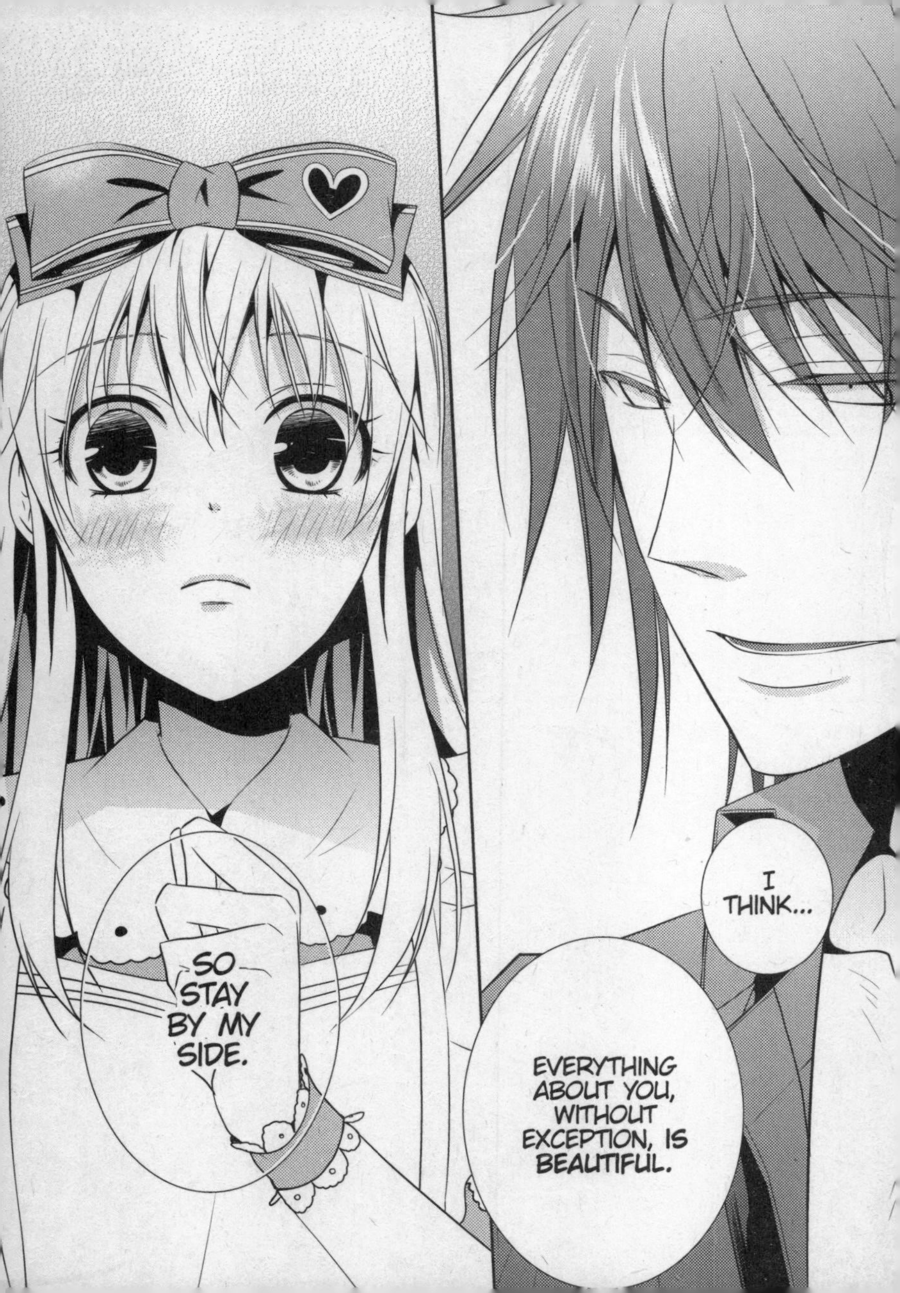
I THINK...
EVERYTHING ABOUT YOU, WITHOUT EXCEPTION, IS BEAUTIFUL.
SO STAY BY MY SIDE.

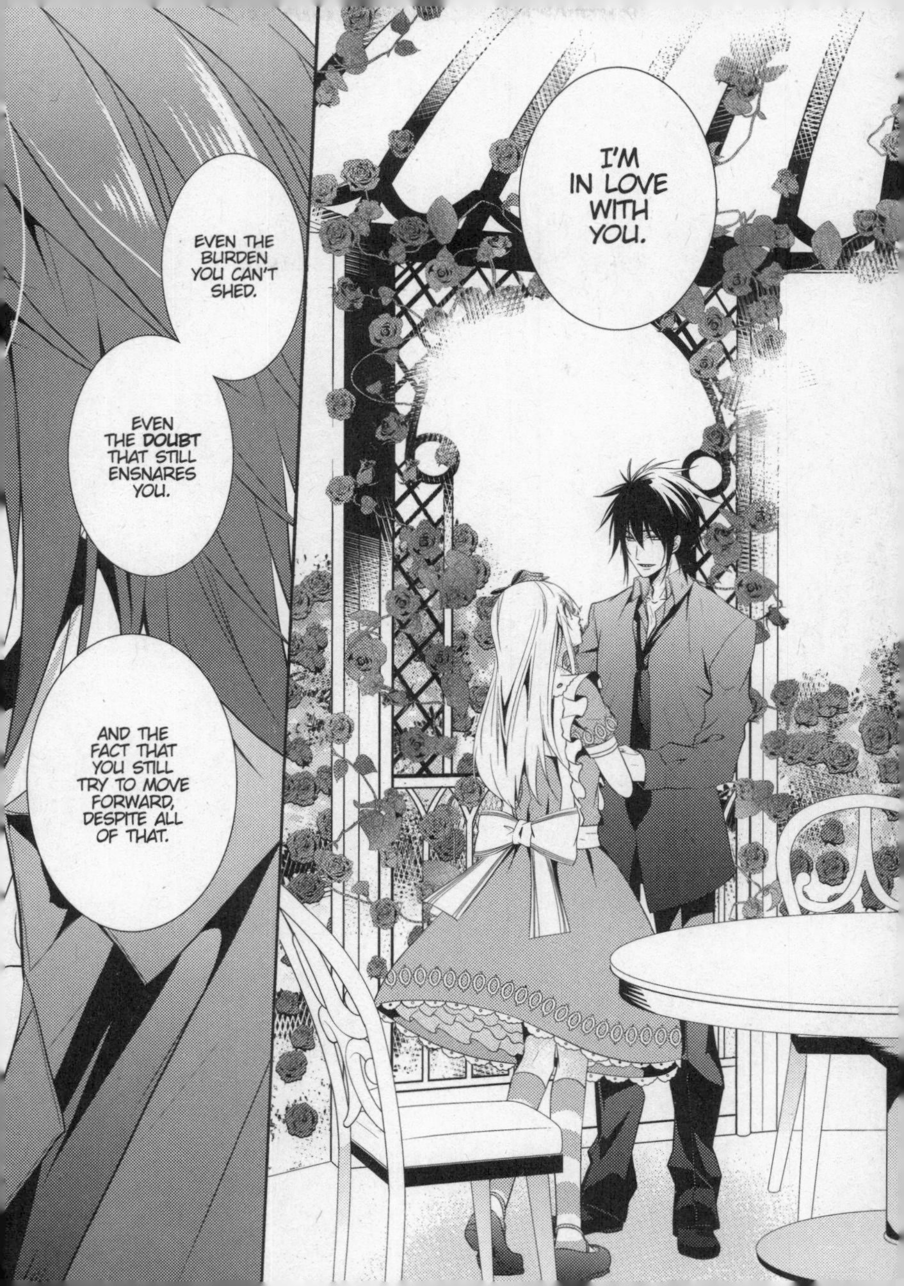
I'M IN LOVE WITH YOU.
EVEN THE BURDEN YOU CAN'T SHED.
EVEN THE DOUBT THAT STILL ENSNARES YOU.
AND THE FACT THAT YOU STILL TRY TO MOVE FORWARD, DESPITE ALL OF THAT.

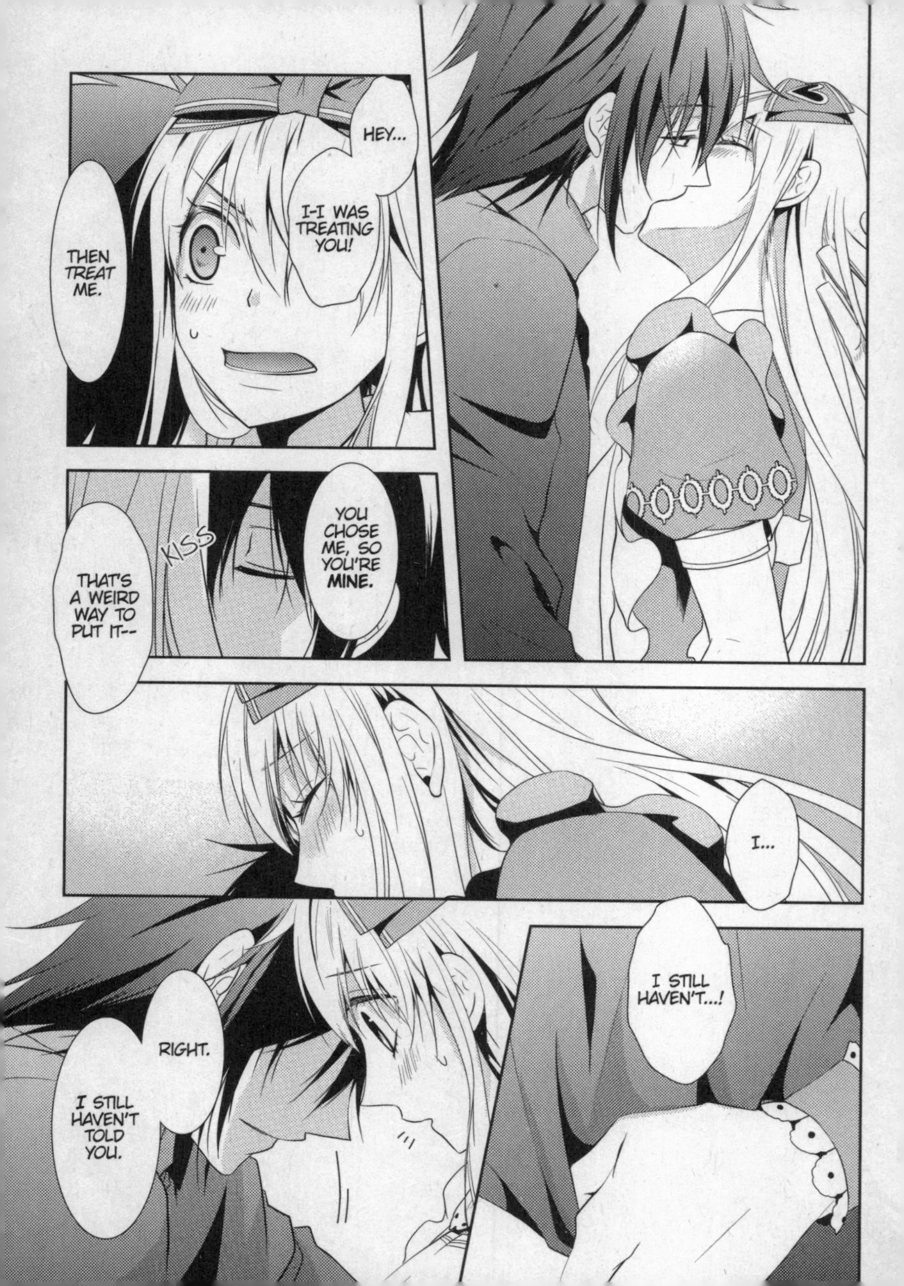
HEY...
I-I WAS TREATING YOU!
THEN TREAT ME.
YOU CHOSE ME, SO YOU'RE MINE.
KISS
THAT'S A WEIRD WAY TO PUT IT--
I...
I STILL HAVEN'T...!
RIGHT.
I STILL HAVEN'T TOLD YOU.

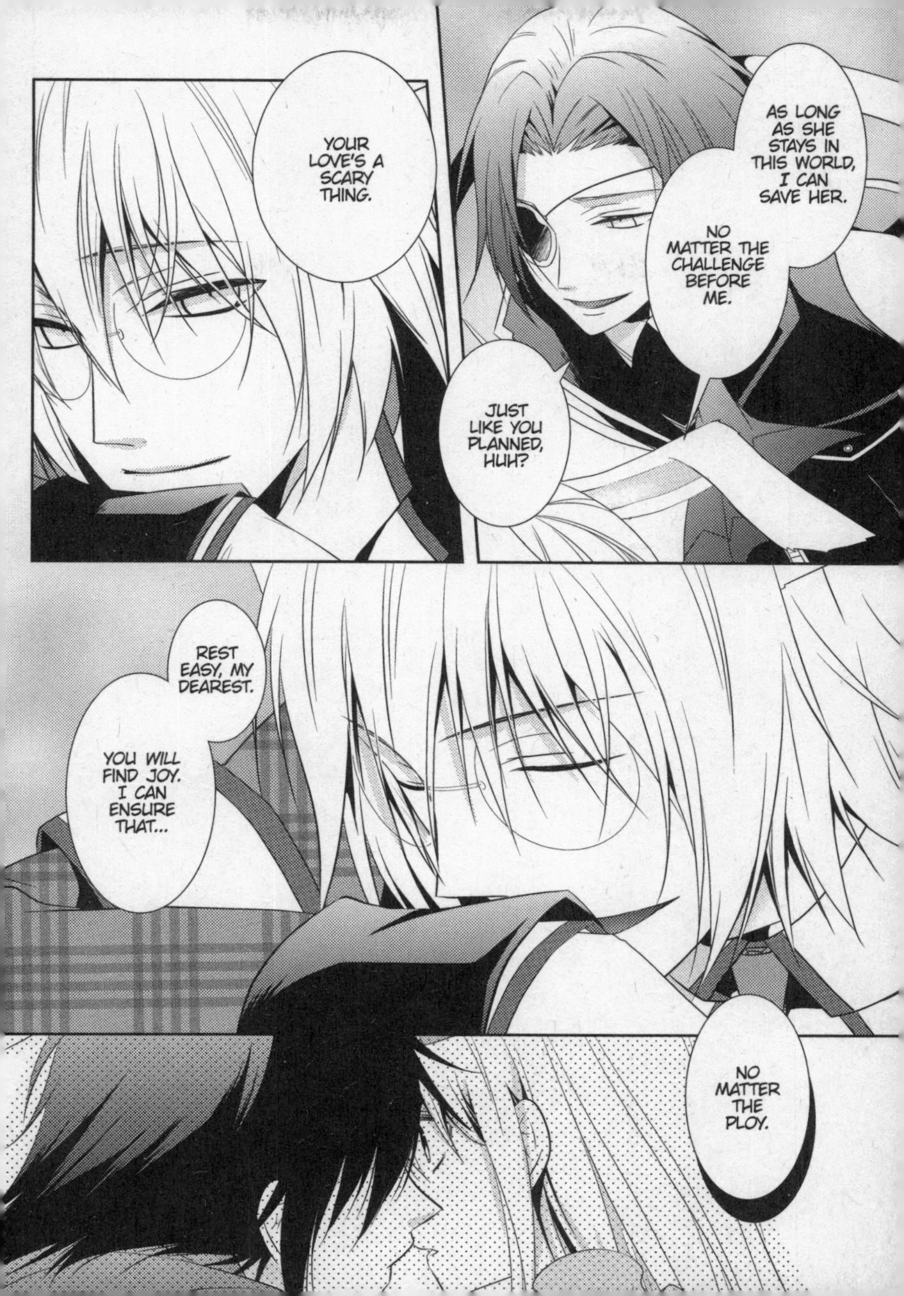
AS LONG AS SHE STAYS IN THIS WORLD, I CAN SAVE HER.
NO MATTER THE CHALLENGE BEFORE ME.
JUST LIKE YOU PLANNED, HUH?
YOUR LOVE'S A SCARY THING.
REST EASY, MY DEAREST.
YOU WILL FIND JOY. I CAN ENSURE THAT...
NO MATTER THE PLOY.

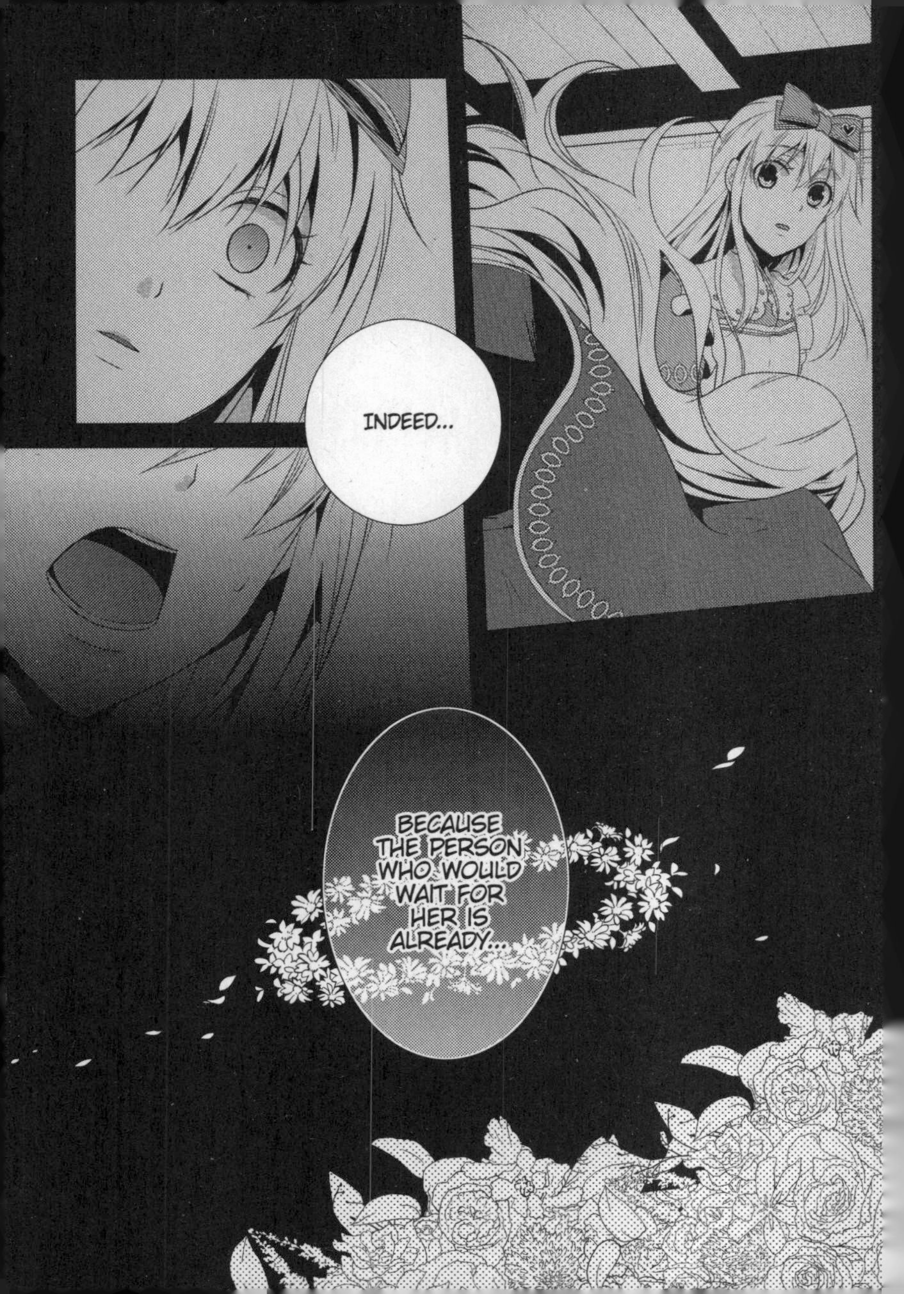
INDEED...
BECAUSE THE PERSON WHO WOULD WAIT FOR HER IS ALREADY...

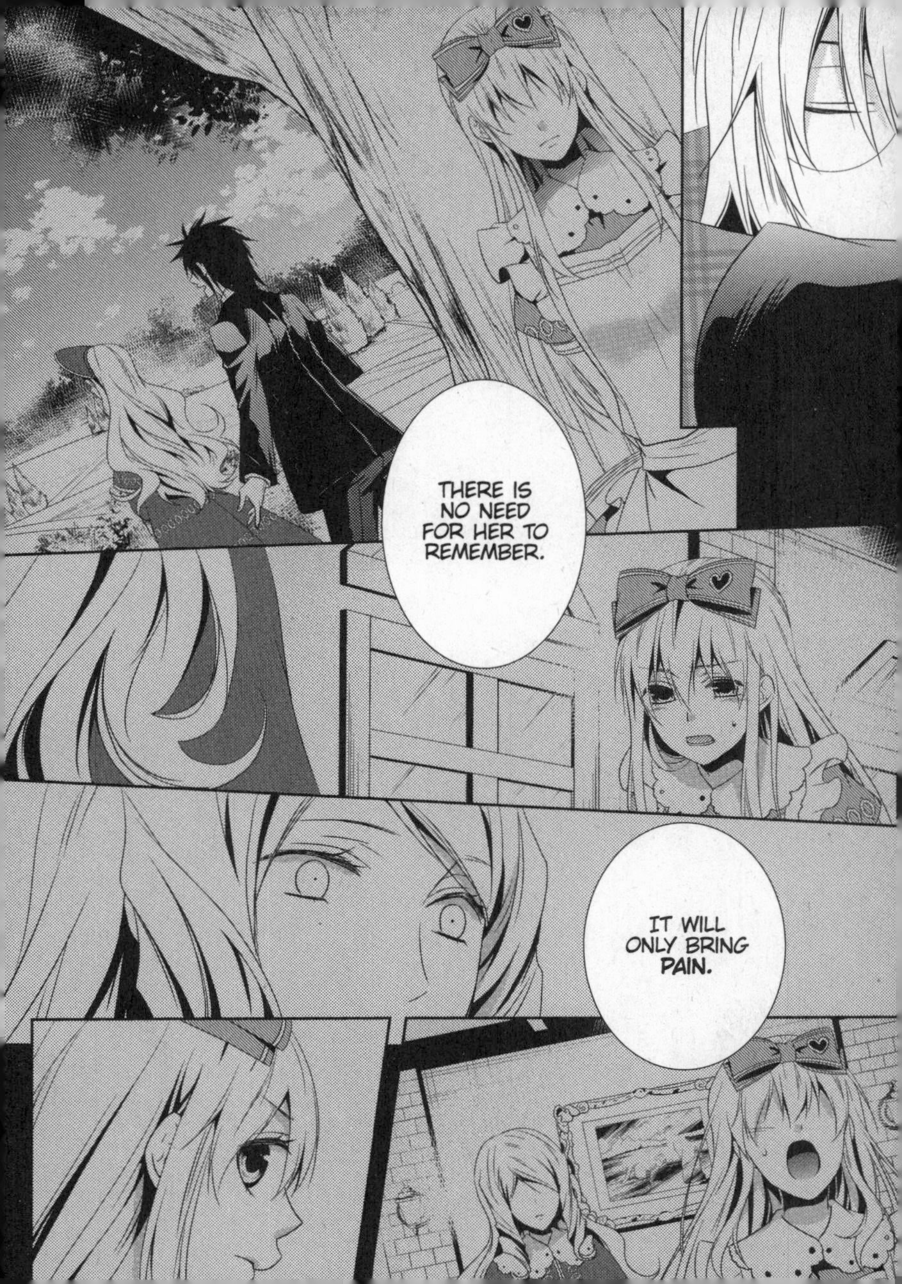
THERE IS NO NEED FOR HER TO REMEMBER.
IT WILL ONLY BRING PAIN.

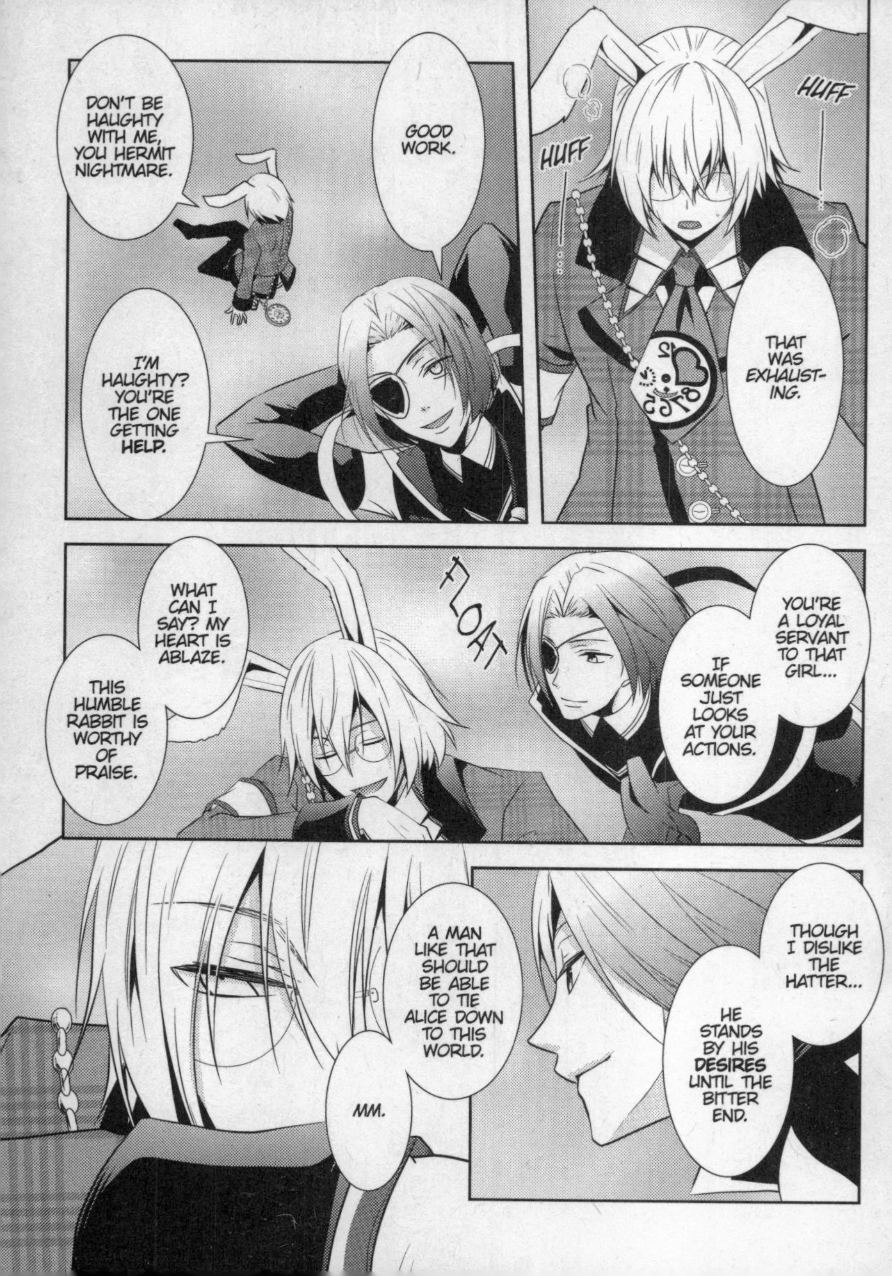
HUFF
HUFF
THAT WAS EXHAUSTING.
GOOD WORK.
DON'T BE HAUGHTY WITH ME, YOU HERMIT NIGHTMARE.
I'M HAUGHTY? YOU'RE THE ONE GETTING HELP.
YOU'RE A LOYAL SERVANT TO THAT GIRL...
IF SOMEONE JUST LOOKS AT YOUR ACTIONS.
FLOAT
WHAT CAN I SAY? MY HEART IS ABLAZE.
THIS HUMBLE RABBIT IS WORTHY OF PRAISE.
THOUGH I DISLIKE THE HATTER...
HE STANDS BY HIS DESIRES UNTIL THE BITTER END.
A MAN LIKE THAT SHOULD BE ABLE TO TIE ALICE DOWN TO THIS WORLD.
MM.

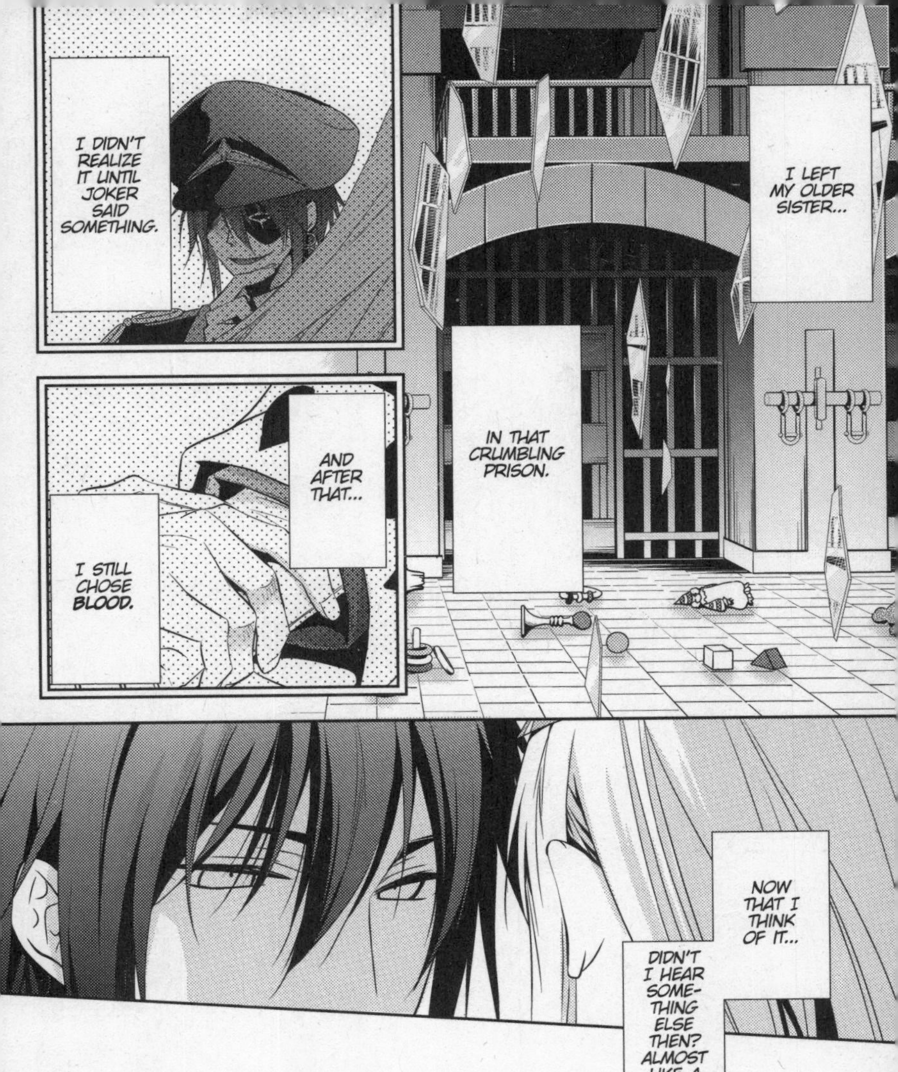
I LEFT MY OLDER SISTER...
IN THAT CRUMBLING PRISON.
I DIDN'T REALIZE IT UNTIL JOKER SAID SOMETHING.
AND AFTER THAT...
I STILL CHOSE BLOOD.
NOW THAT I THINK OF IT...
DIDN'T I HEAR SOMETHING ELSE THEN? ALMOST LIKE A GUNSHOT...

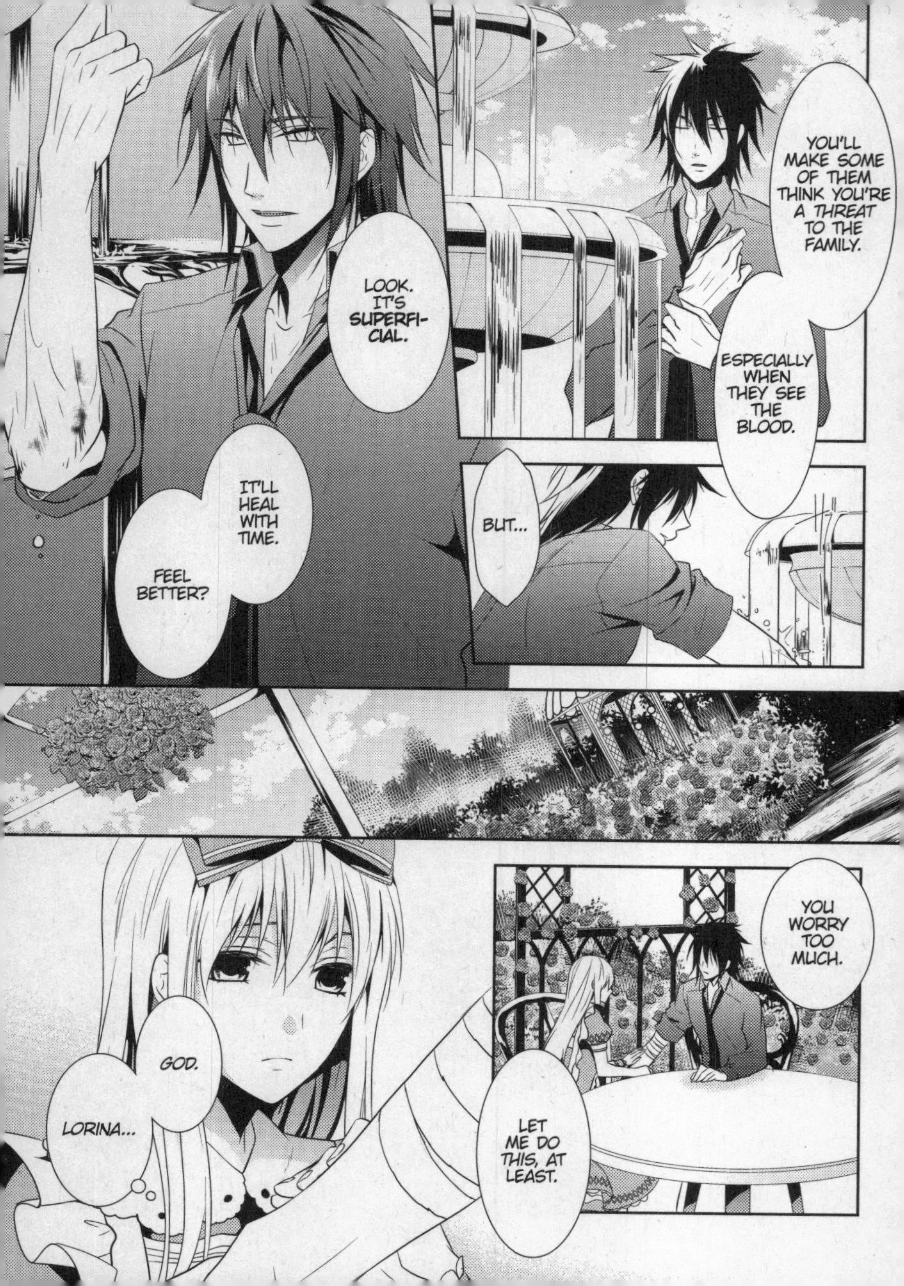
YOU'LL MAKE SOME OF THEM THINK YOU'RE A *THREAT* TO THE FAMILY.
ESPECIALLY WHEN THEY SEE THE BLOOD.
BUT...
LOOK. IT'S SUPERFICIAL.
IT'LL HEAL WITH TIME.
FEEL BETTER?
YOU WORRY TOO MUCH.
LET ME DO THIS, AT LEAST.
GOD.
LORINA...

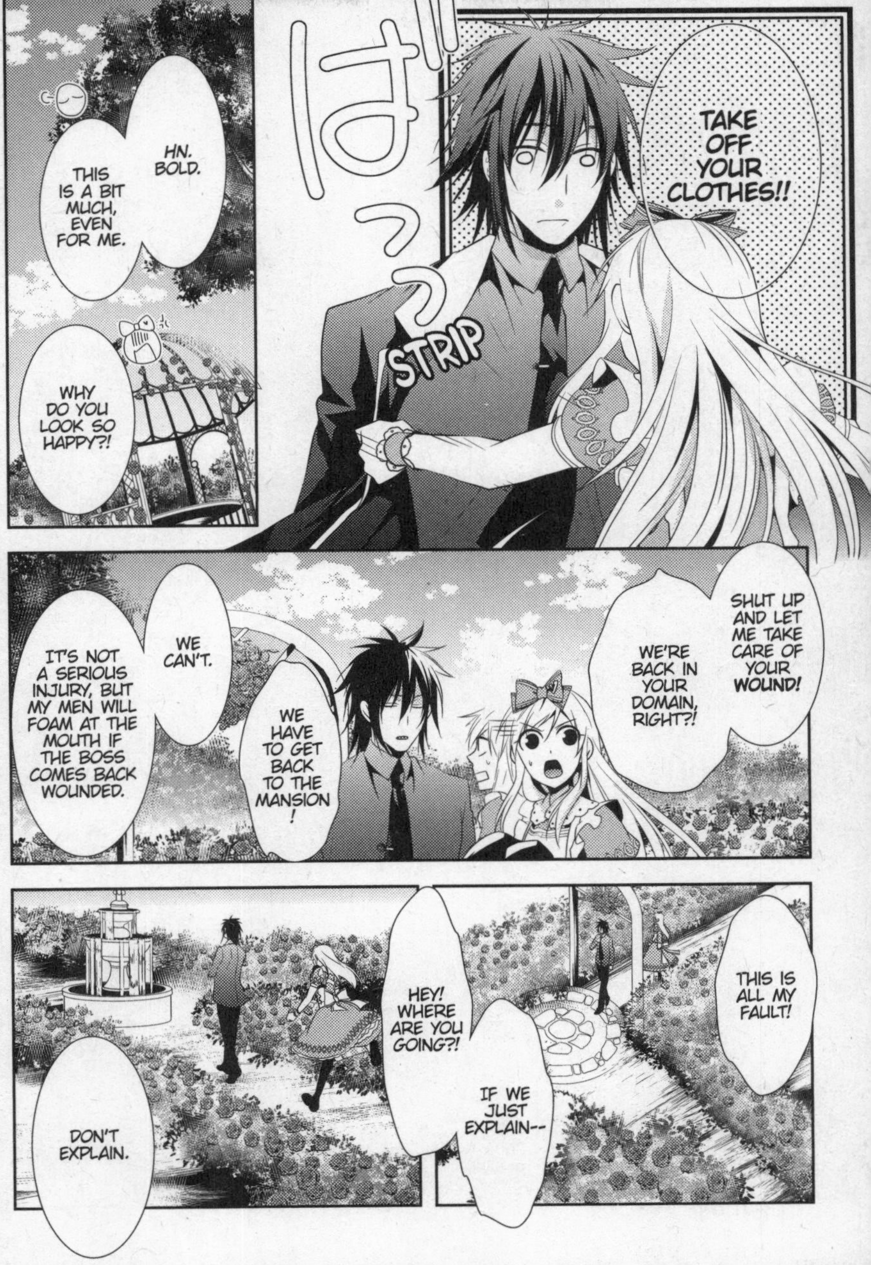
TAKE OFF YOUR CLOTHES!!
ばっ
STRIP
HN. BOLD.
THIS IS A BIT MUCH, EVEN FOR ME.
WHY DO YOU LOOK SO HAPPY?!
SHUT UP AND LET ME TAKE CARE OF YOUR WOUND!
WE'RE BACK IN YOUR DOMAIN, RIGHT?!
WE CAN'T.
WE HAVE TO GET BACK TO THE MANSION!
IT'S NOT A SERIOUS INJURY, BUT MY MEN WILL FOAM AT THE MOUTH IF THE BOSS COMES BACK WOUNDED.
THIS IS ALL MY FAULT!
HEY! WHERE ARE YOU GOING?!
IF WE JUST EXPLAIN--
DON'T EXPLAIN.

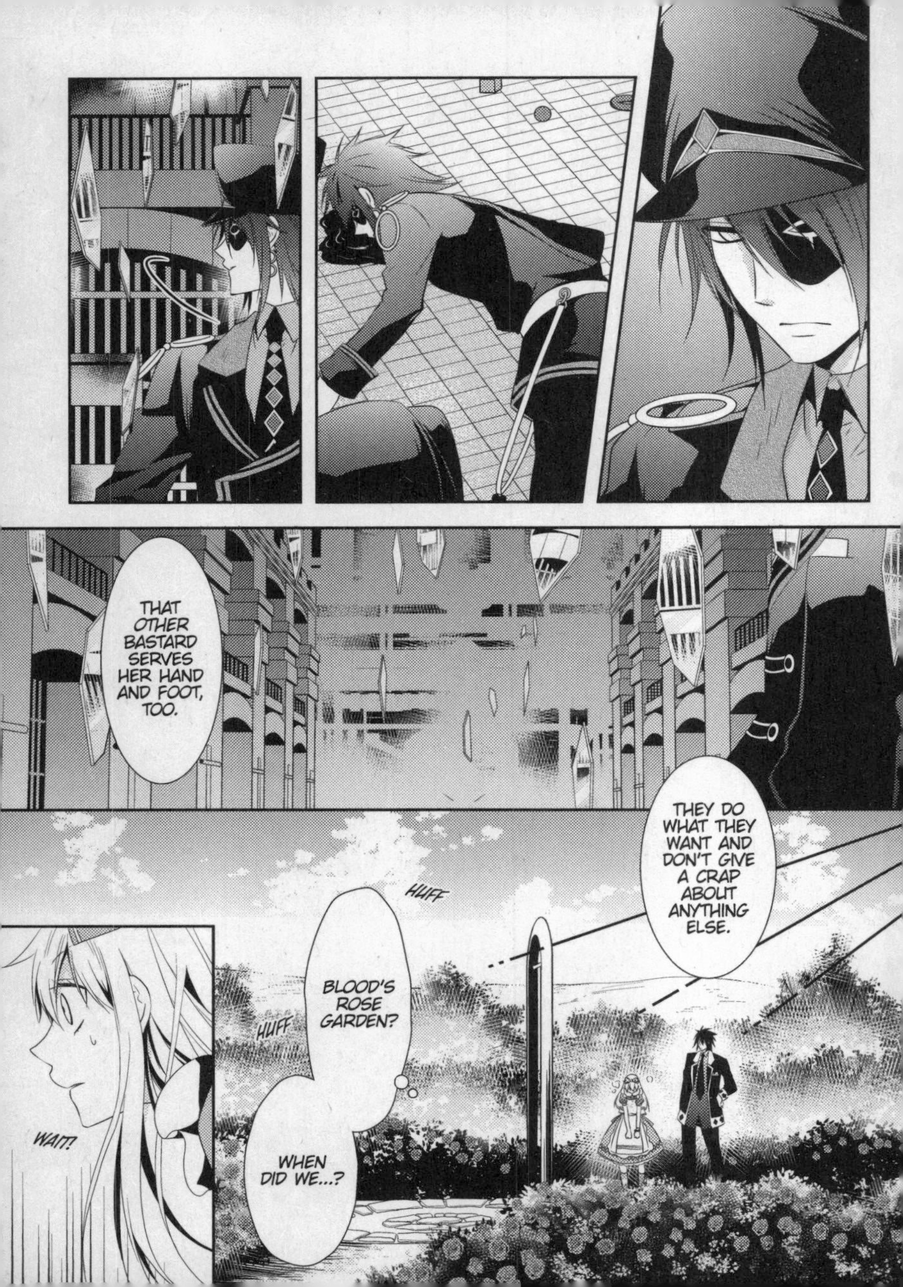
THAT OTHER BASTARD SERVES HER HAND AND FOOT, TOO.
THEY DO WHAT THEY WANT AND DON'T GIVE A CRAP ABOUT ANYTHING ELSE.
HUFF
HUFF
BLOOD'S ROSE GARDEN?
WHEN DID WE...?
WAIT!

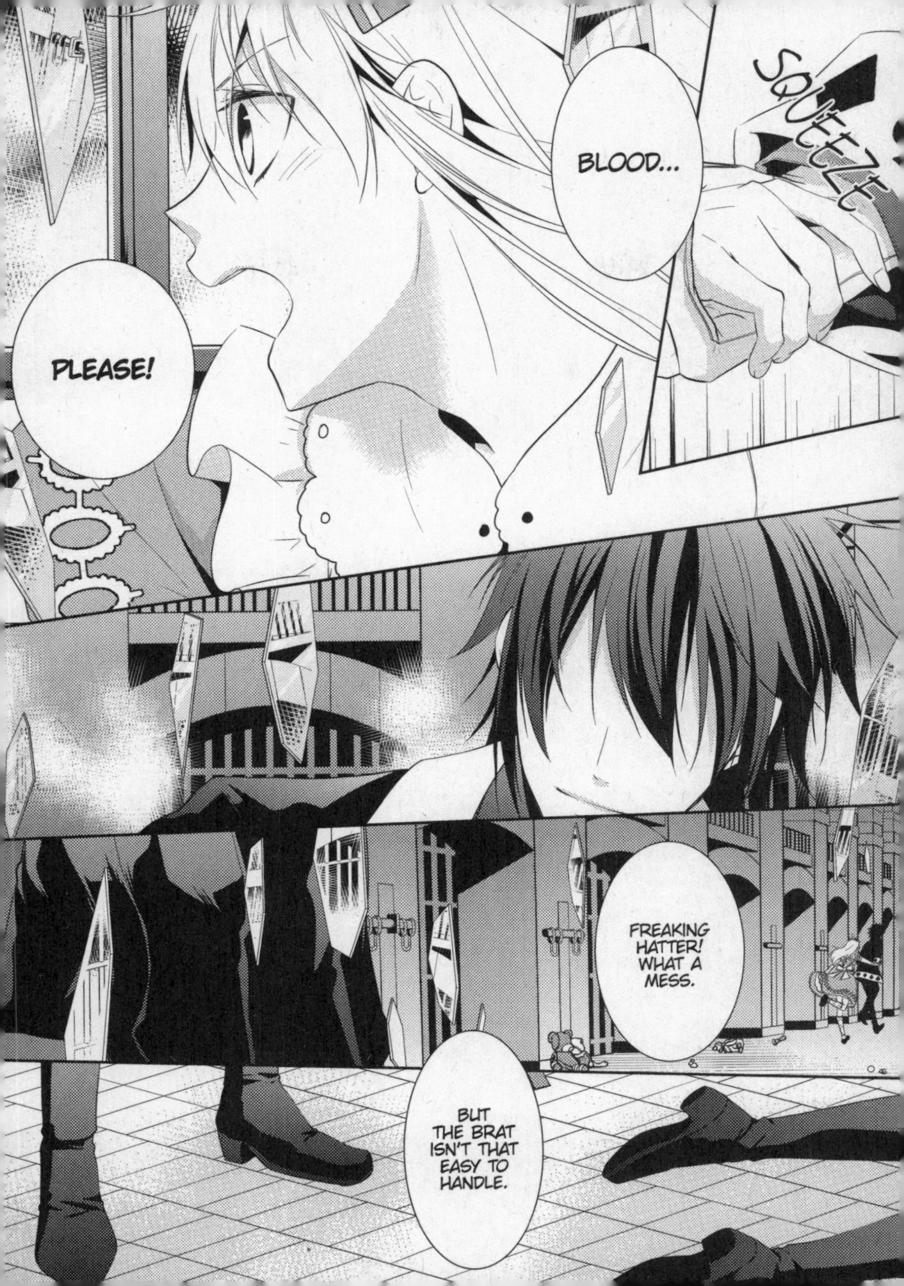
SQUEEZE
BLOOD...
PLEASE!
FREAKING HATTER! WHAT A MESS.
BUT THE BRAT ISN'T THAT EASY TO HANDLE.

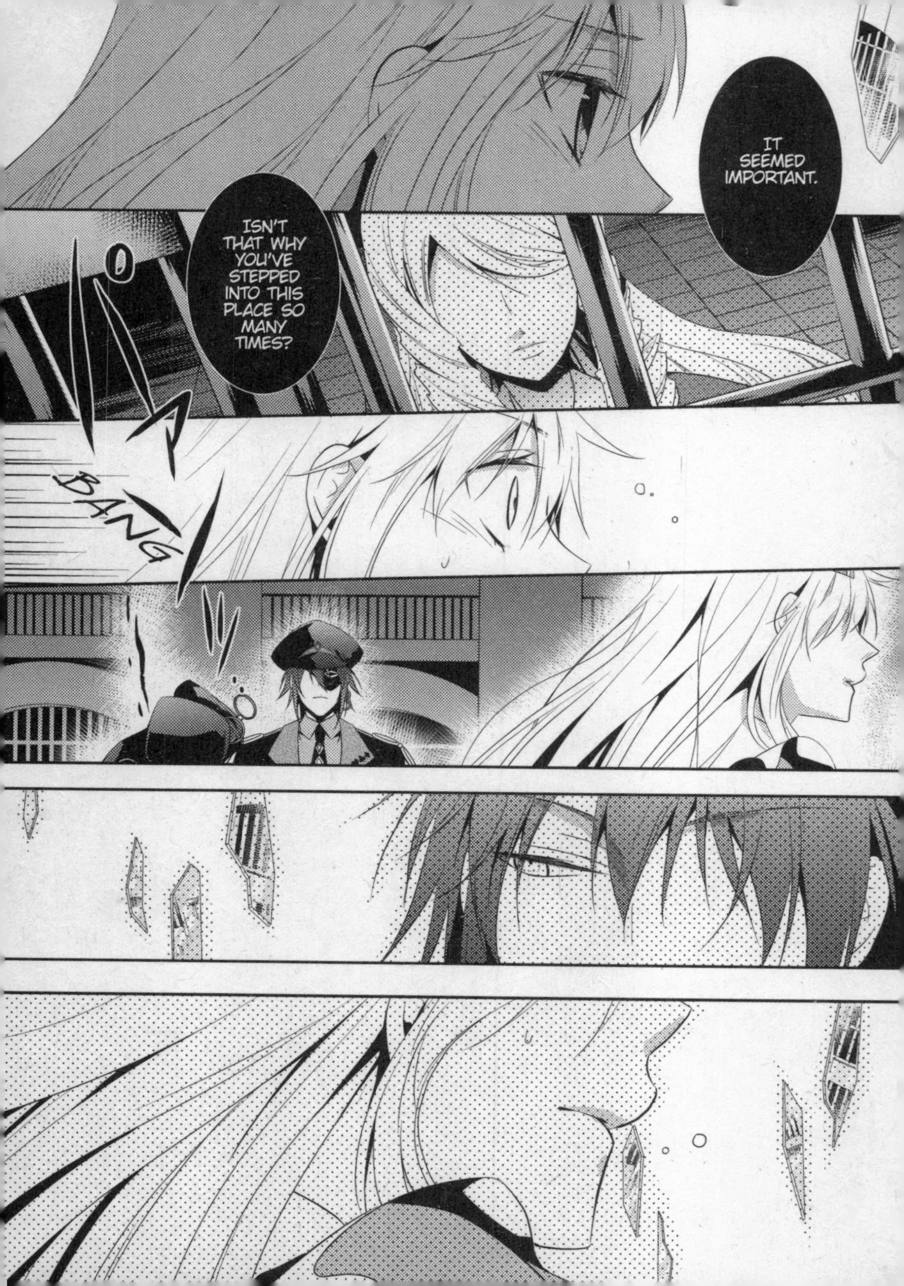
IT SEEMED IMPORTANT.
ISN'T THAT WHY YOU'VE STEPPED INTO THIS PLACE SO MANY TIMES?
BANG

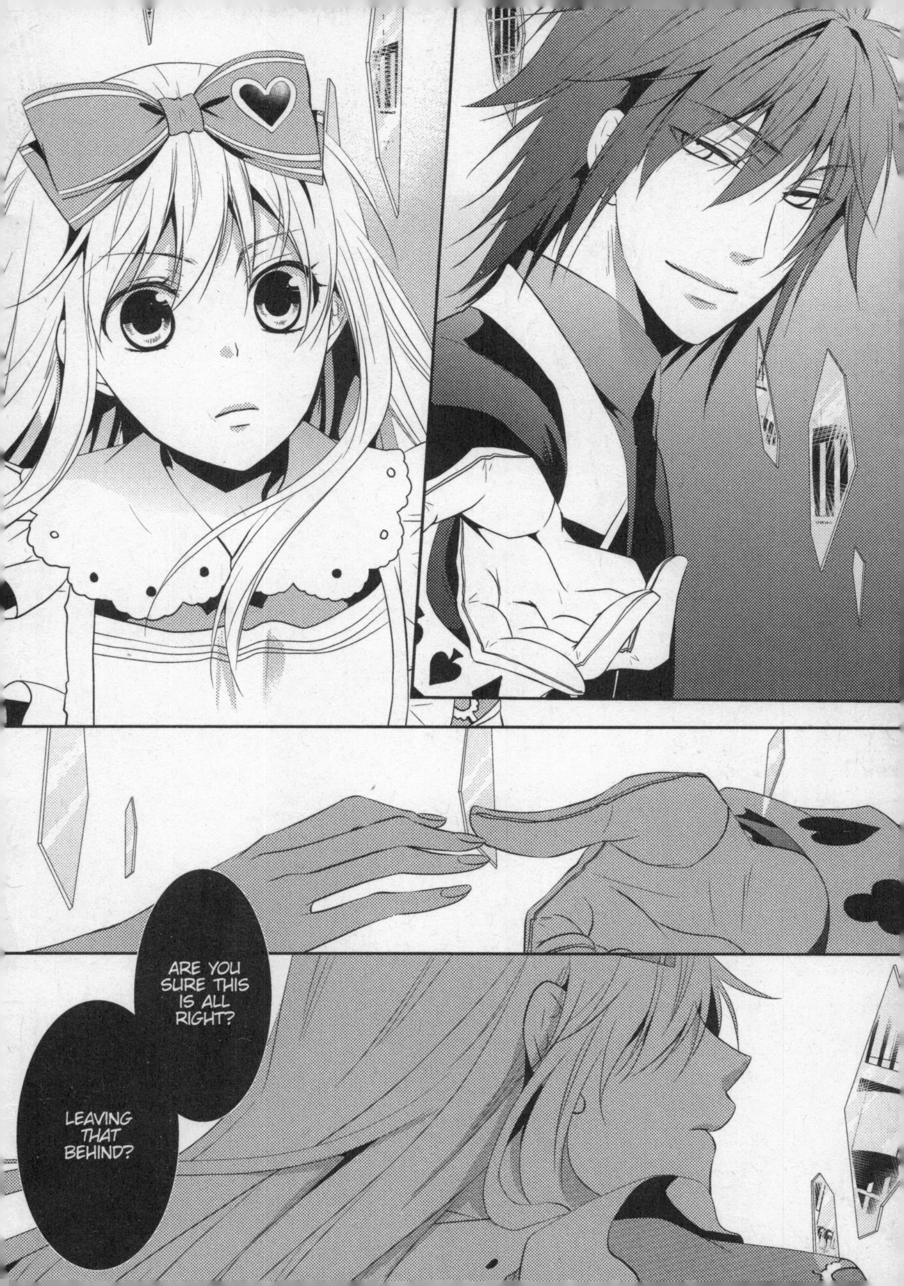
ARE YOU SURE THIS IS ALL RIGHT?
LEAVING THAT BEHIND?

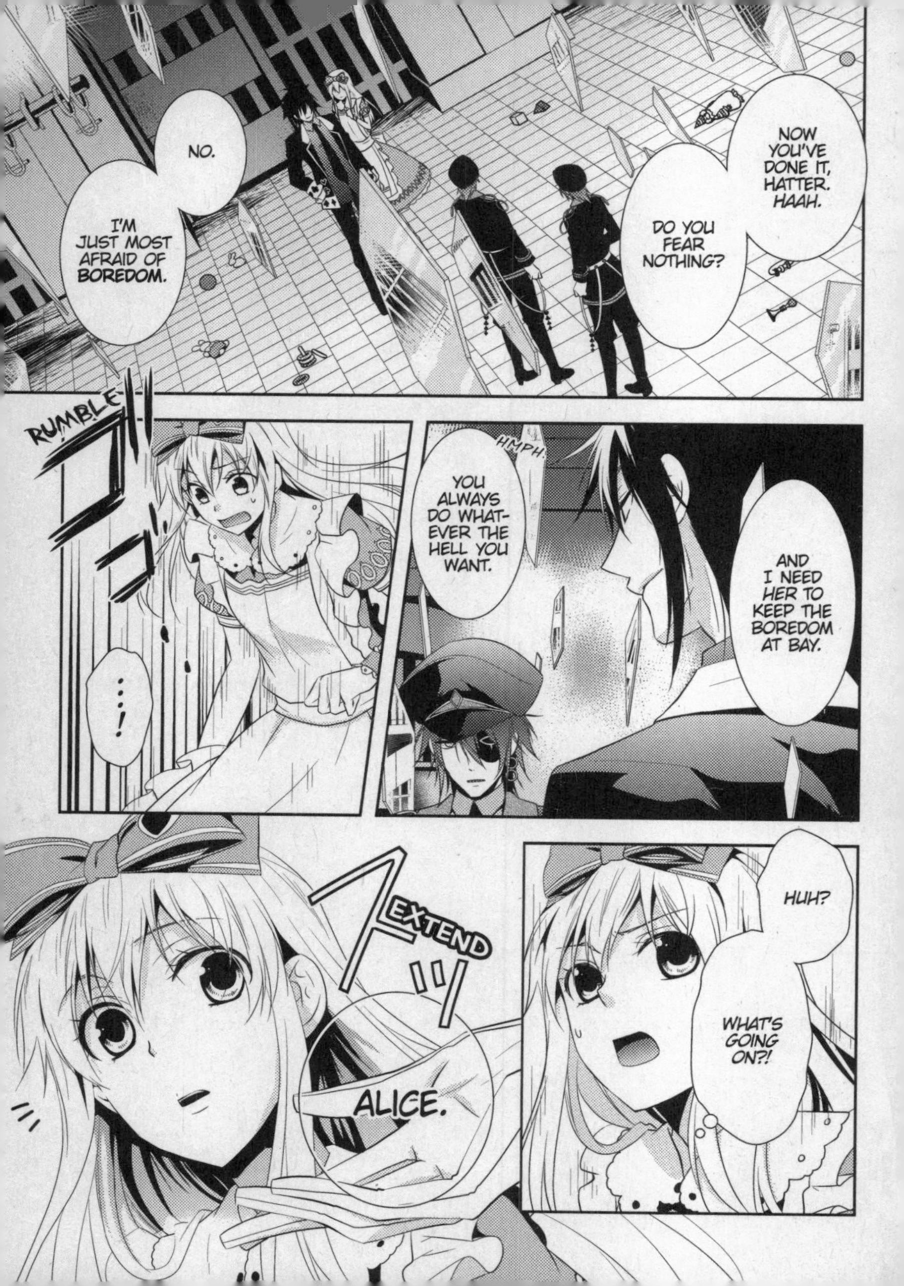
NOW YOU'VE DONE IT, HATTER. HAAH.
DO YOU FEAR NOTHING?
NO.
I'M JUST MOST AFRAID OF BOREDOM.
AND I NEED HER TO KEEP THE BOREDOM AT BAY.
HMPH.
YOU ALWAYS DO WHAT-EVER THE HELL YOU WANT.
RUMBLE
...!
HUH?
WHAT'S GOING ON?!
EXTEND
ALICE.

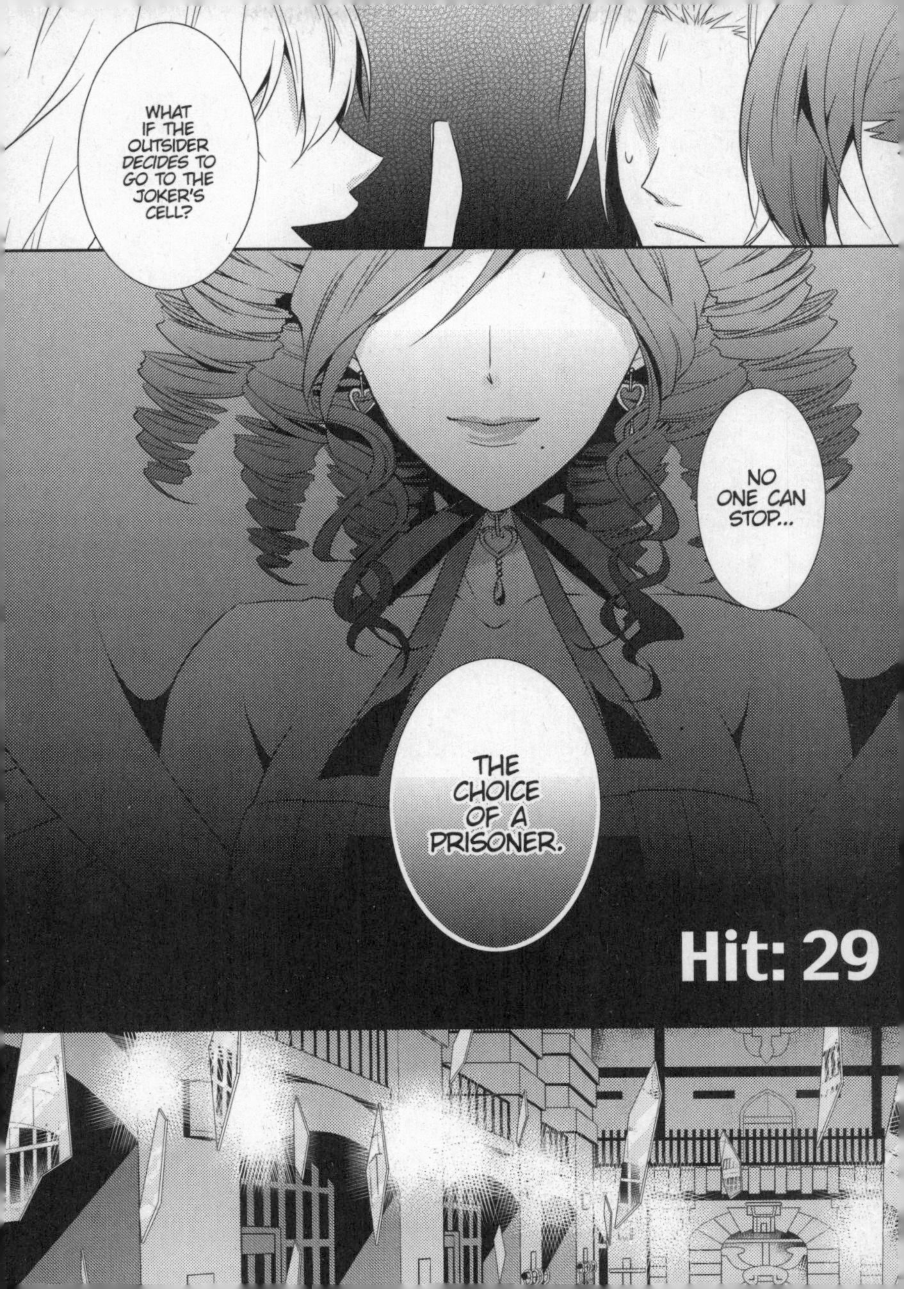
WHAT IF THE OUTSIDER DECIDES TO GO TO THE JOKER'S CELL?
NO ONE CAN STOP...
THE CHOICE OF A PRISONER.
Hit: 29

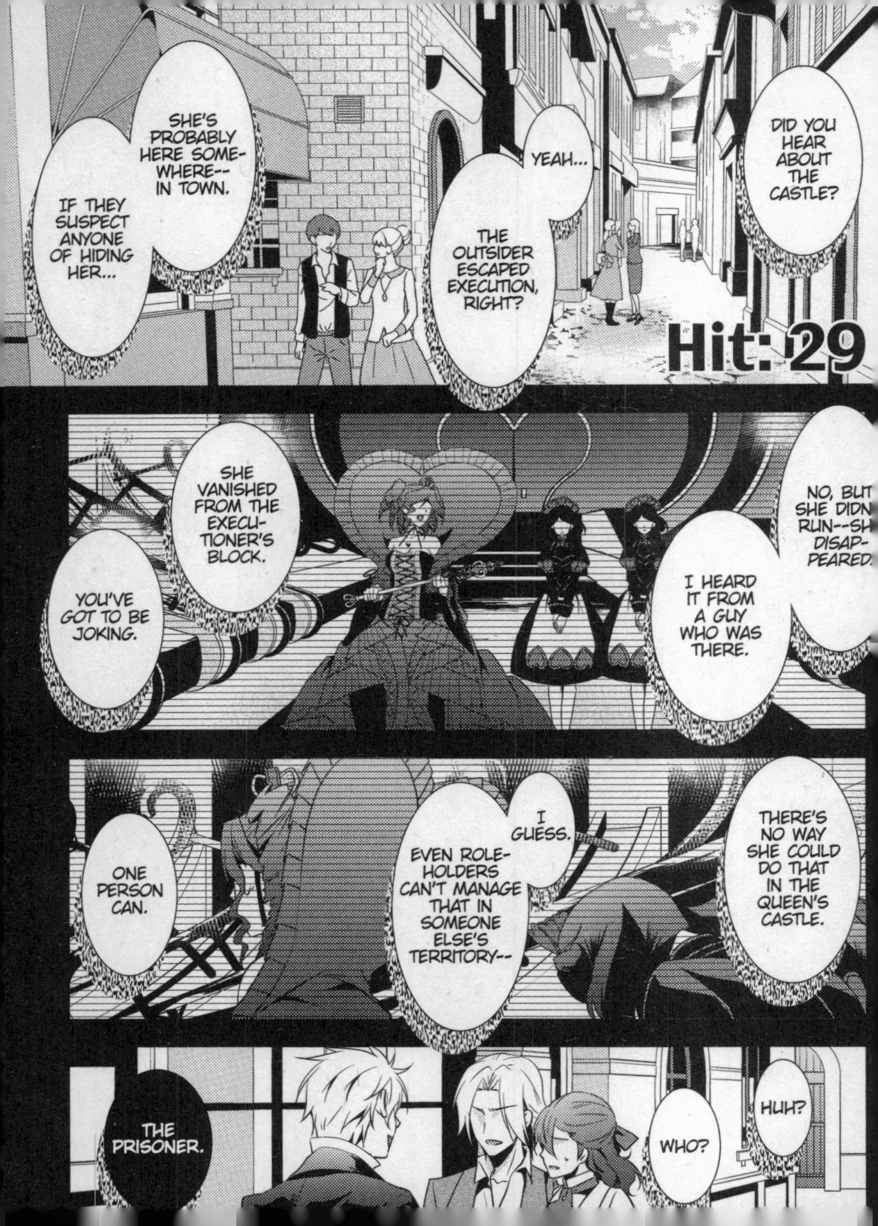
DID YOU HEAR ABOUT THE CASTLE?
Hit: 29
YEAH...
THE OUTSIDER ESCAPED EXECUTION, RIGHT?
SHE'S PROBABLY HERE SOME-WHERE--IN TOWN.
IF THEY SUSPECT ANYONE OF HIDING HER...
NO, BUT SHE DIDN RUN--SH DISAP-PEARED.
I HEARD IT FROM A GUY WHO WAS THERE.
SHE VANISHED FROM THE EXECU-TIONER'S BLOCK.
YOU'VE GOT TO BE JOKING.
THERE'S NO WAY SHE COULD DO THAT IN THE QUEEN'S CASTLE.
I GUESS.
EVEN ROLE-HOLDERS CAN'T MANAGE THAT IN SOMEONE ELSE'S TERRITORY--
ONE PERSON CAN.
HUH?
WHO?
THE PRISONER.

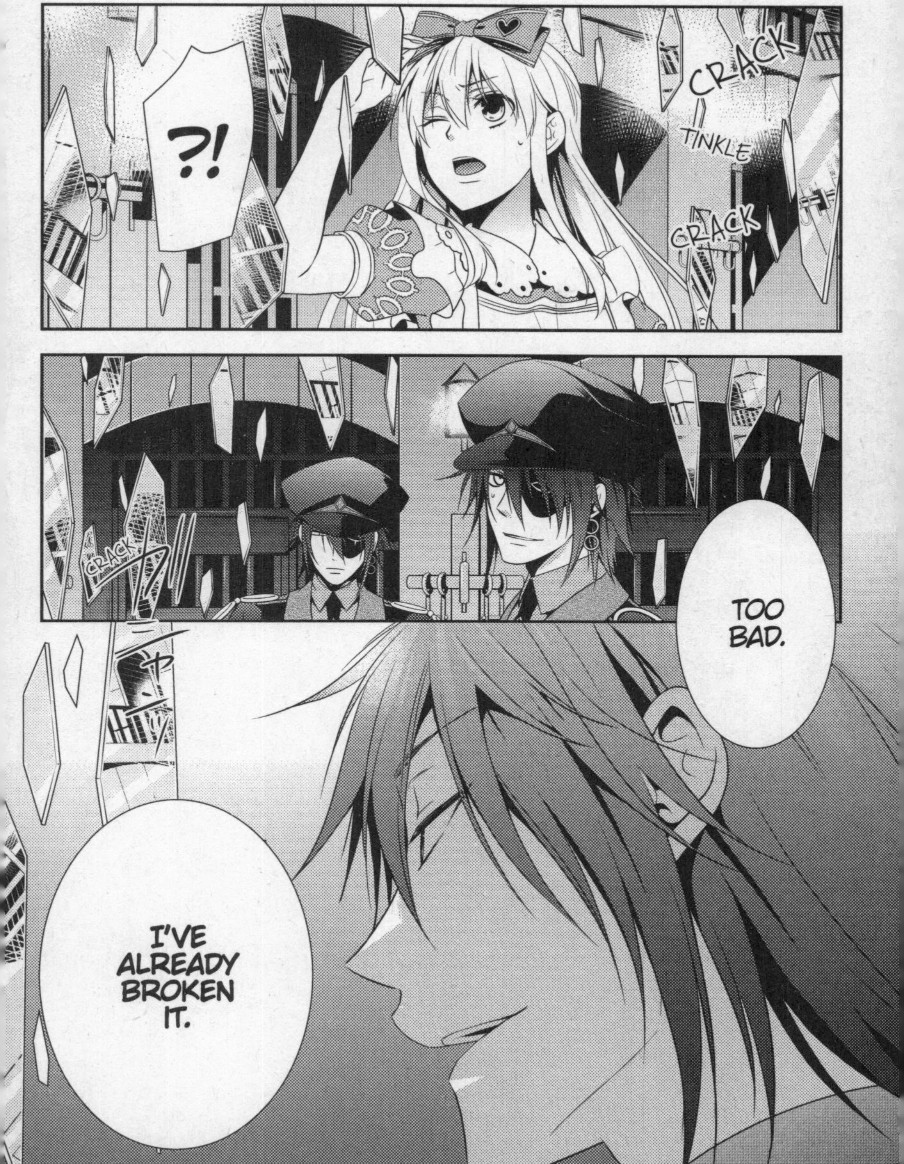
CRACK
TINKLE
CRACK
?!
TOO BAD.
CRACK
I'VE ALREADY BROKEN IT.

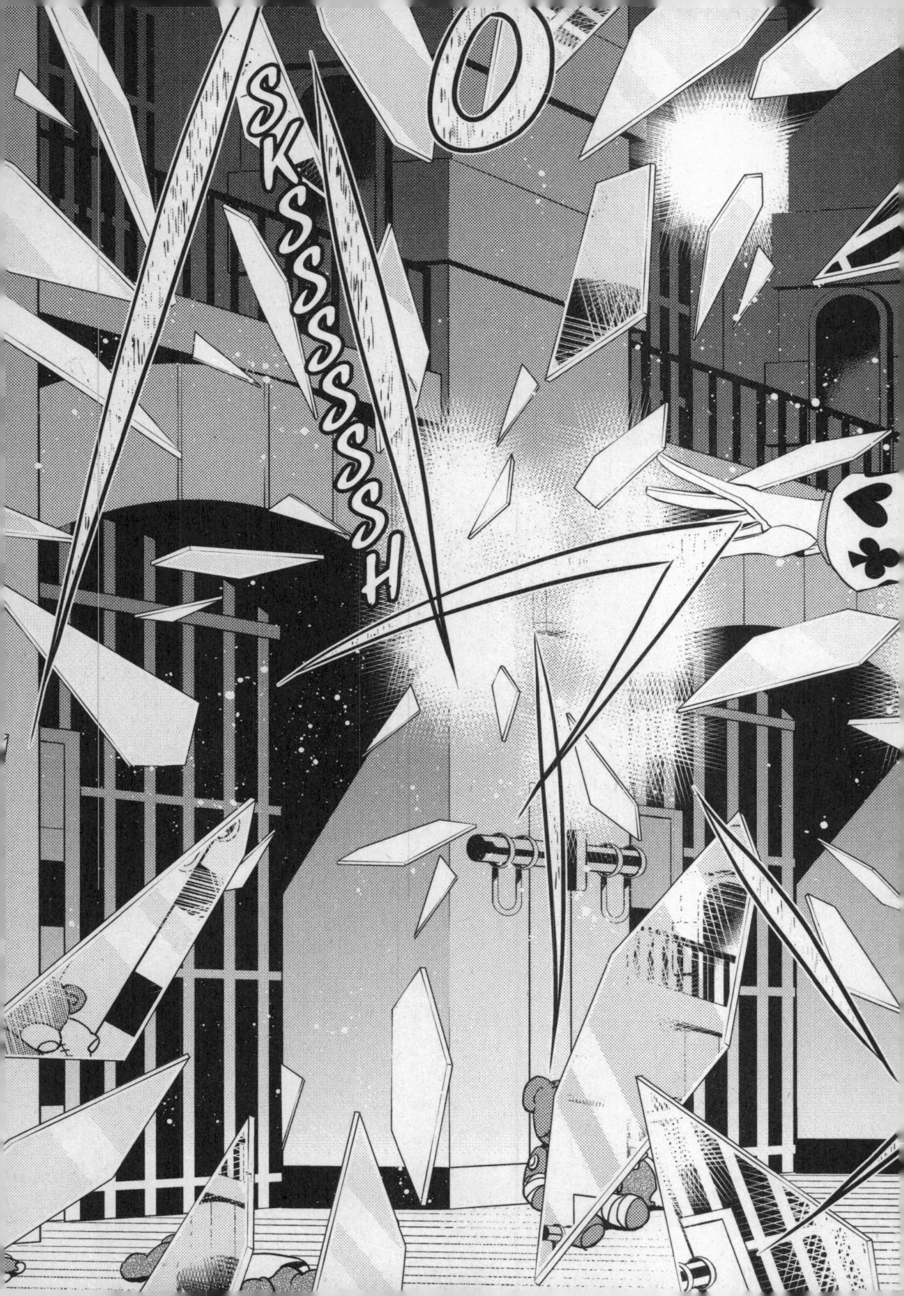
SKSSSSSSH

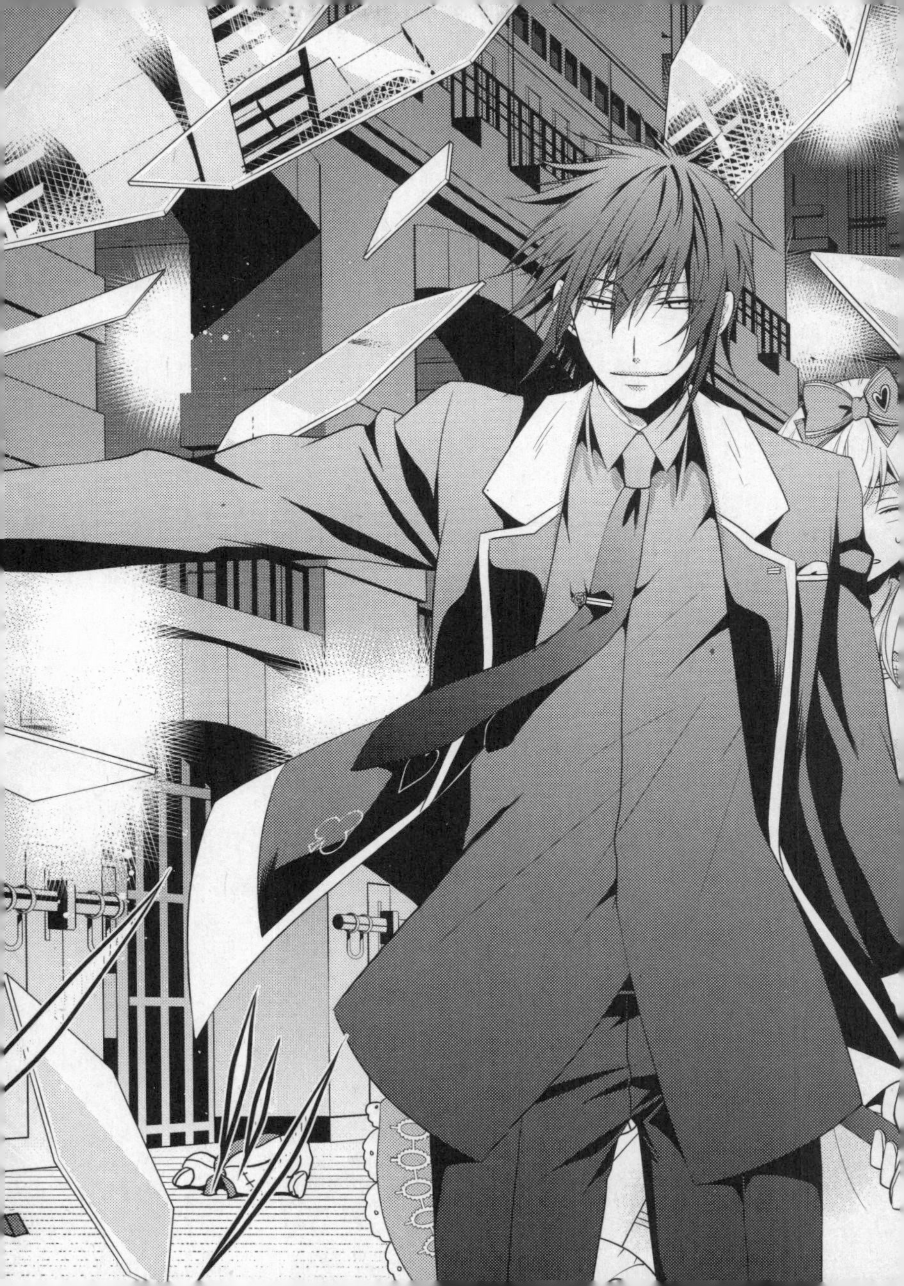

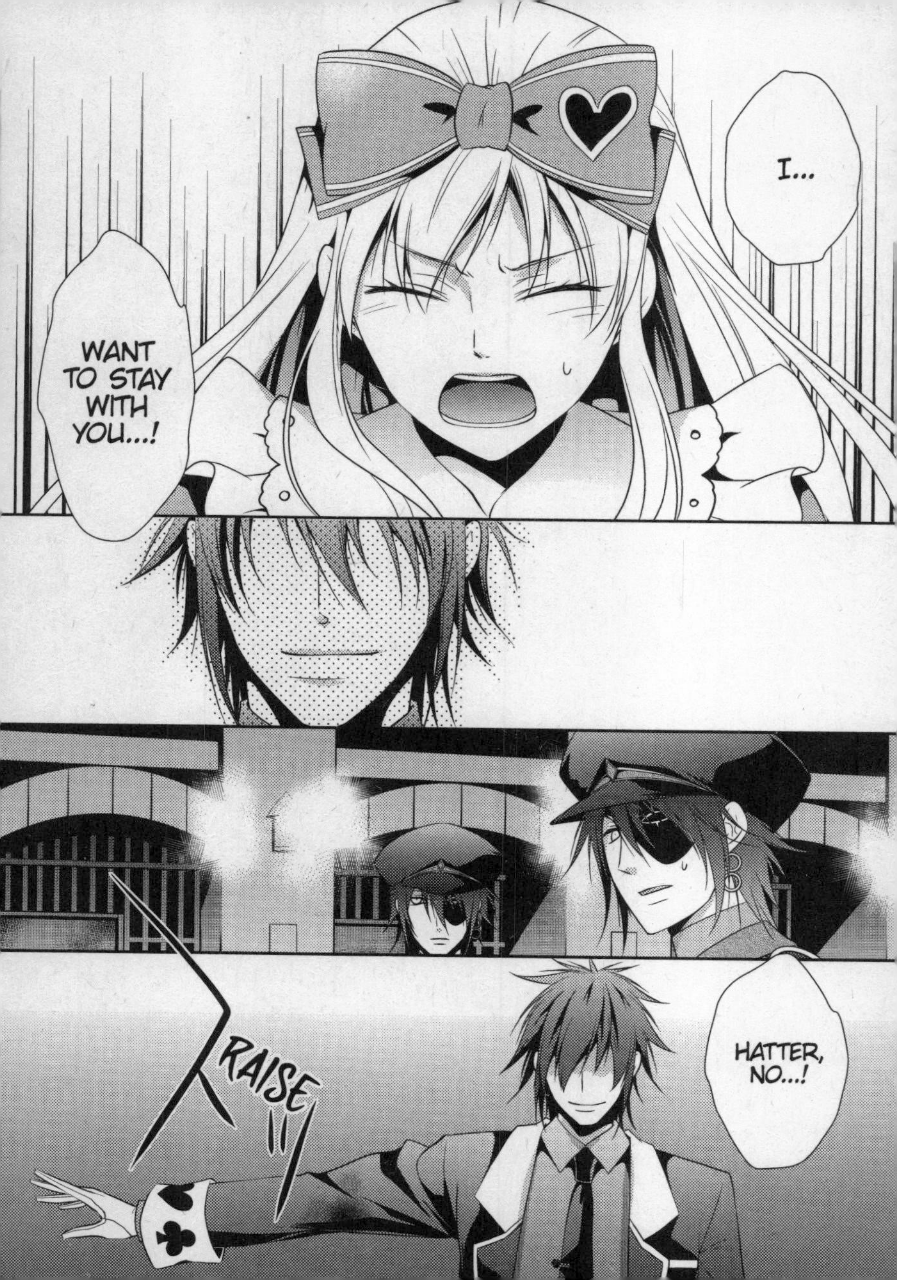
I...
WANT TO STAY WITH YOU...!
HATTER, NO...!
RAISE

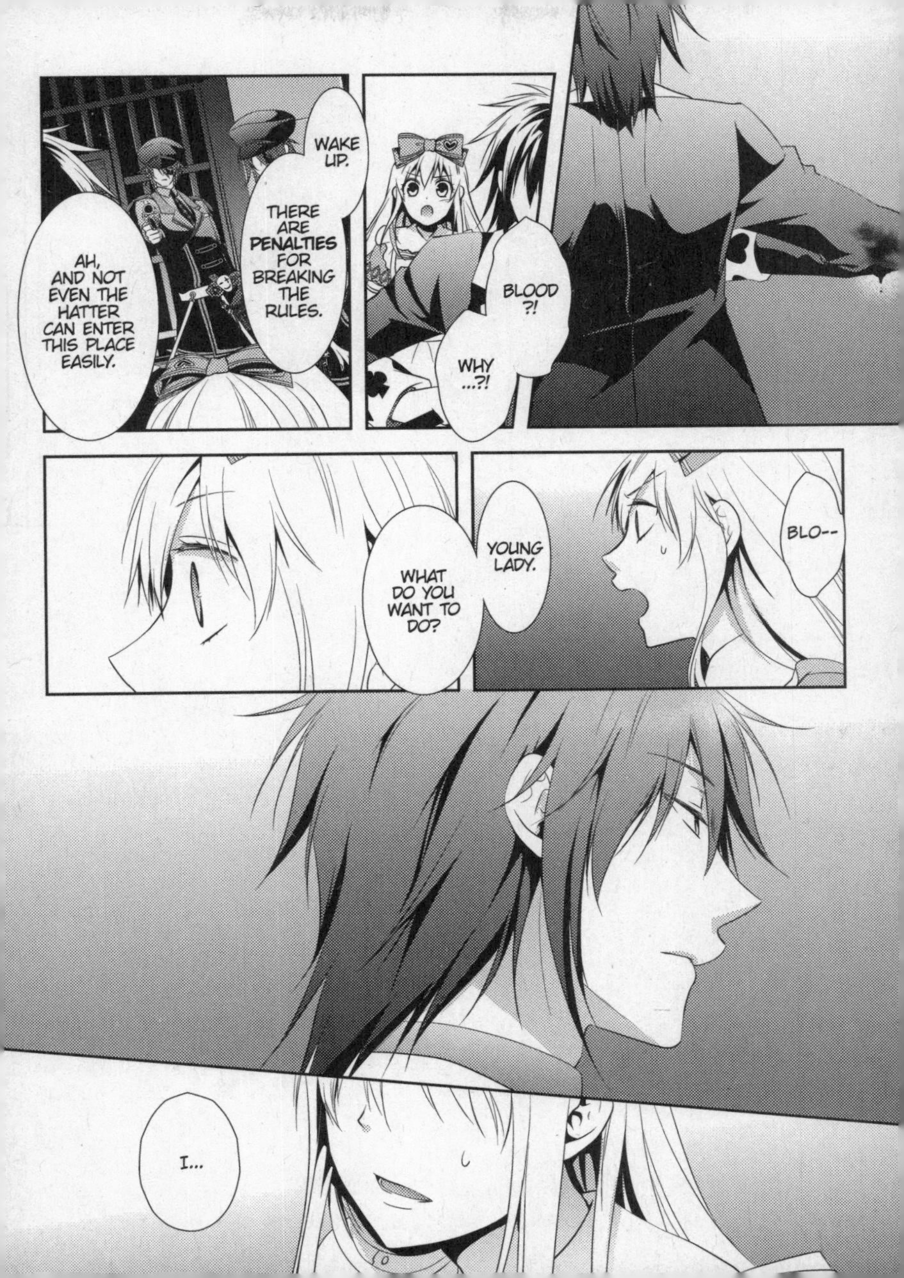
BLOOD?!
WHY...?!
WAKE UP.
THERE ARE PENALTIES FOR BREAKING THE RULES.
AH, AND NOT EVEN THE HATTER CAN ENTER THIS PLACE EASILY.
BLO--
YOUNG LADY.
WHAT DO YOU WANT TO DO?
I...

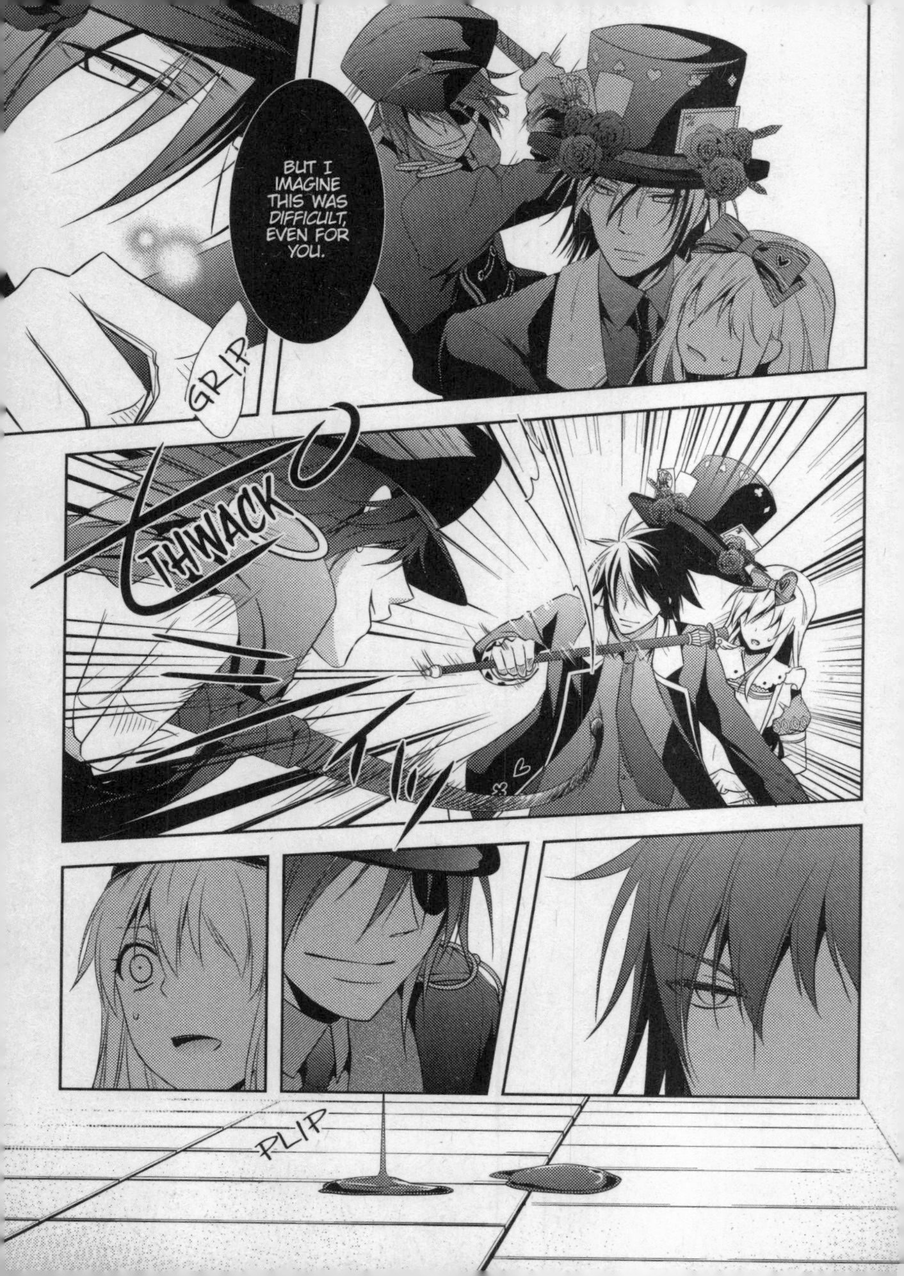
BUT I IMAGINE THIS WAS DIFFICULT, EVEN FOR YOU.
GRIP
THWACK
PLIP

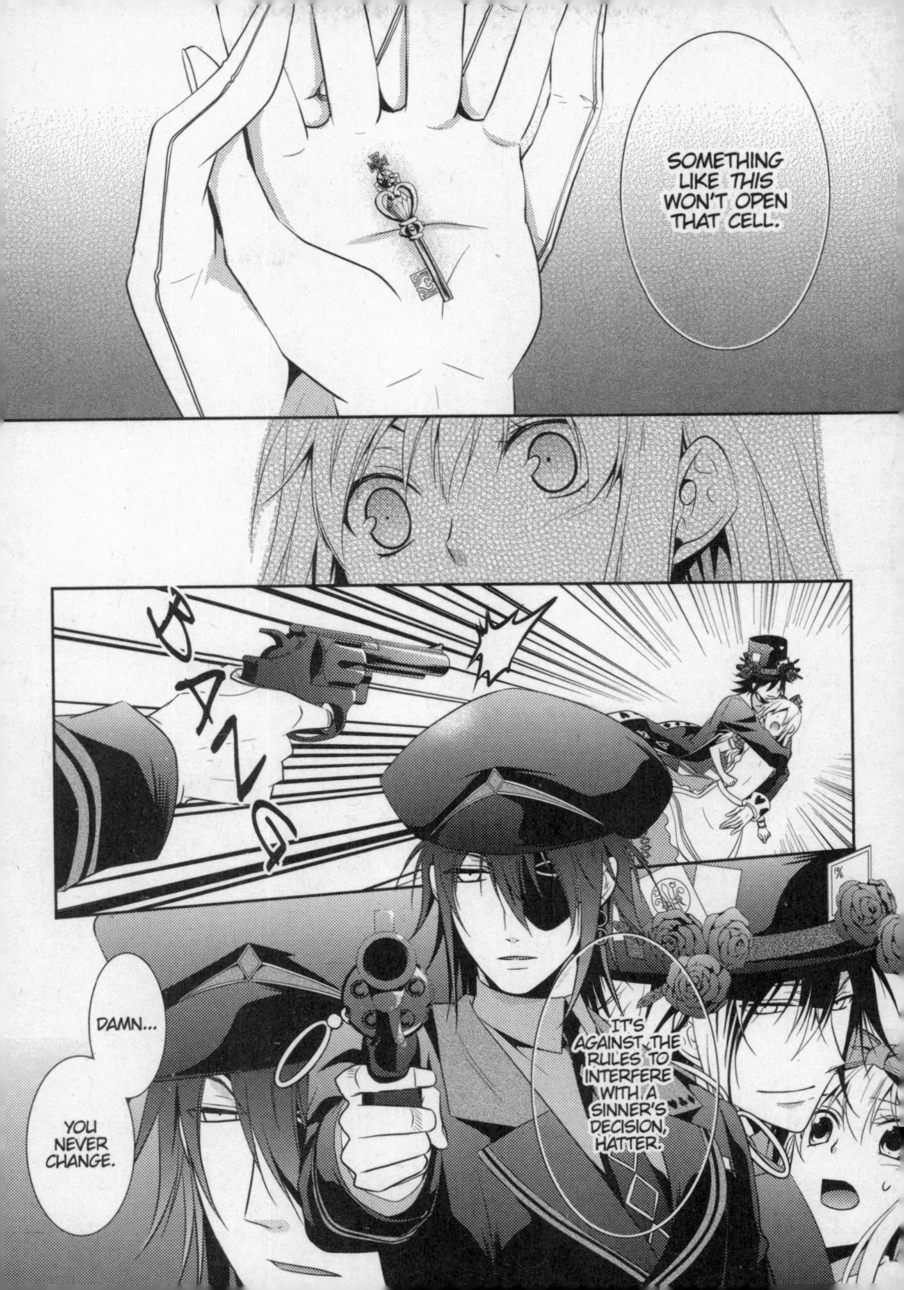
SOMETHING LIKE THIS WON'T OPEN THAT CELL.
BANG
IT'S AGAINST THE RULES TO INTERFERE WITH A SINNER'S DECISION, HATTER.
DAMN...
YOU NEVER CHANGE.

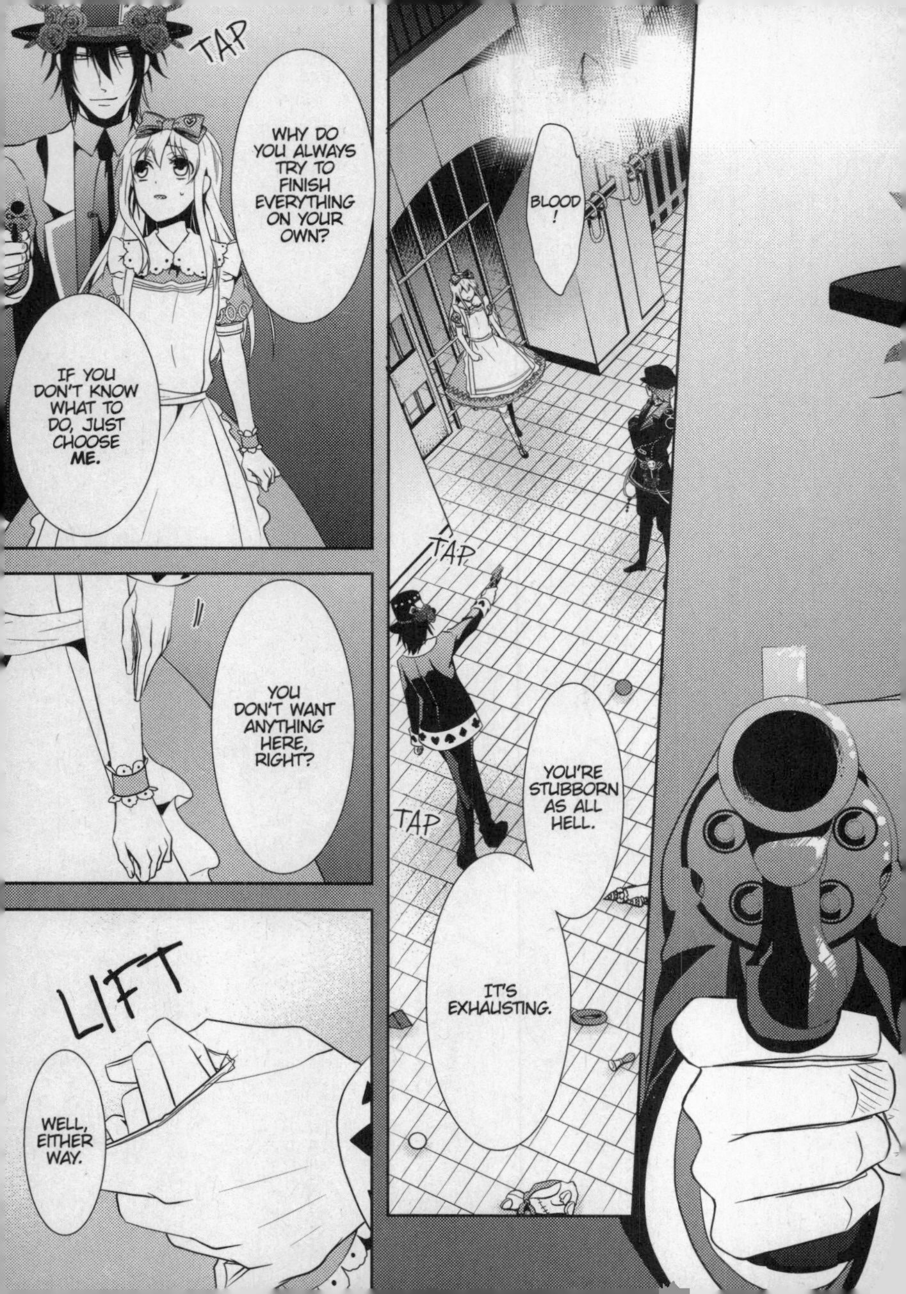
BLOOD!
TAP
YOU'RE STUBBORN AS ALL HELL.
TAP
IT'S EXHAUSTING.
TAP
WHY DO YOU ALWAYS TRY TO FINISH EVERYTHING ON YOUR OWN?
IF YOU DON'T KNOW WHAT TO DO, JUST CHOOSE ME.
YOU DON'T WANT ANYTHING HERE, RIGHT?
LIFT
WELL, EITHER WAY.

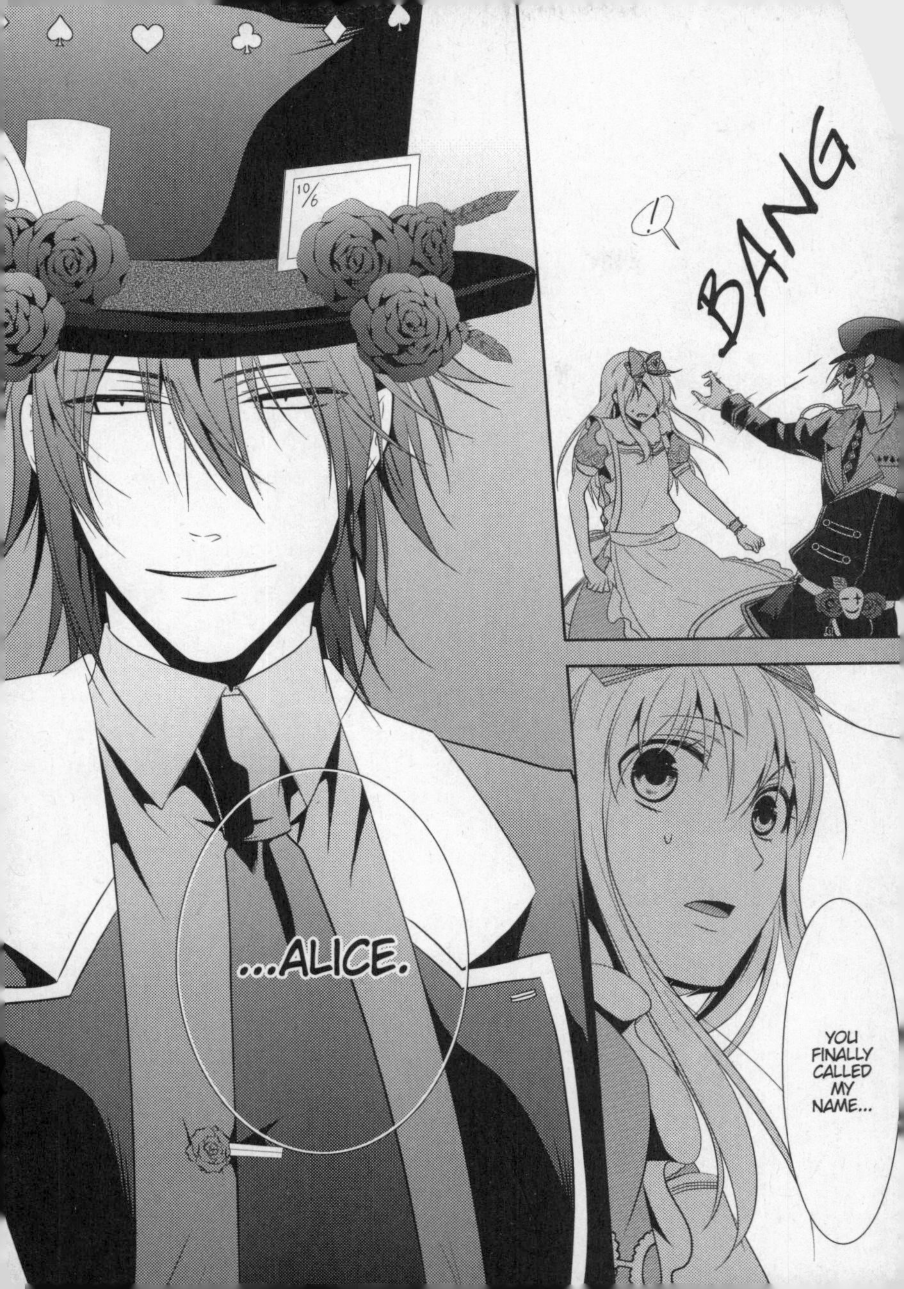
!
BANG
YOU FINALLY CALLED MY NAME...
...ALICE.

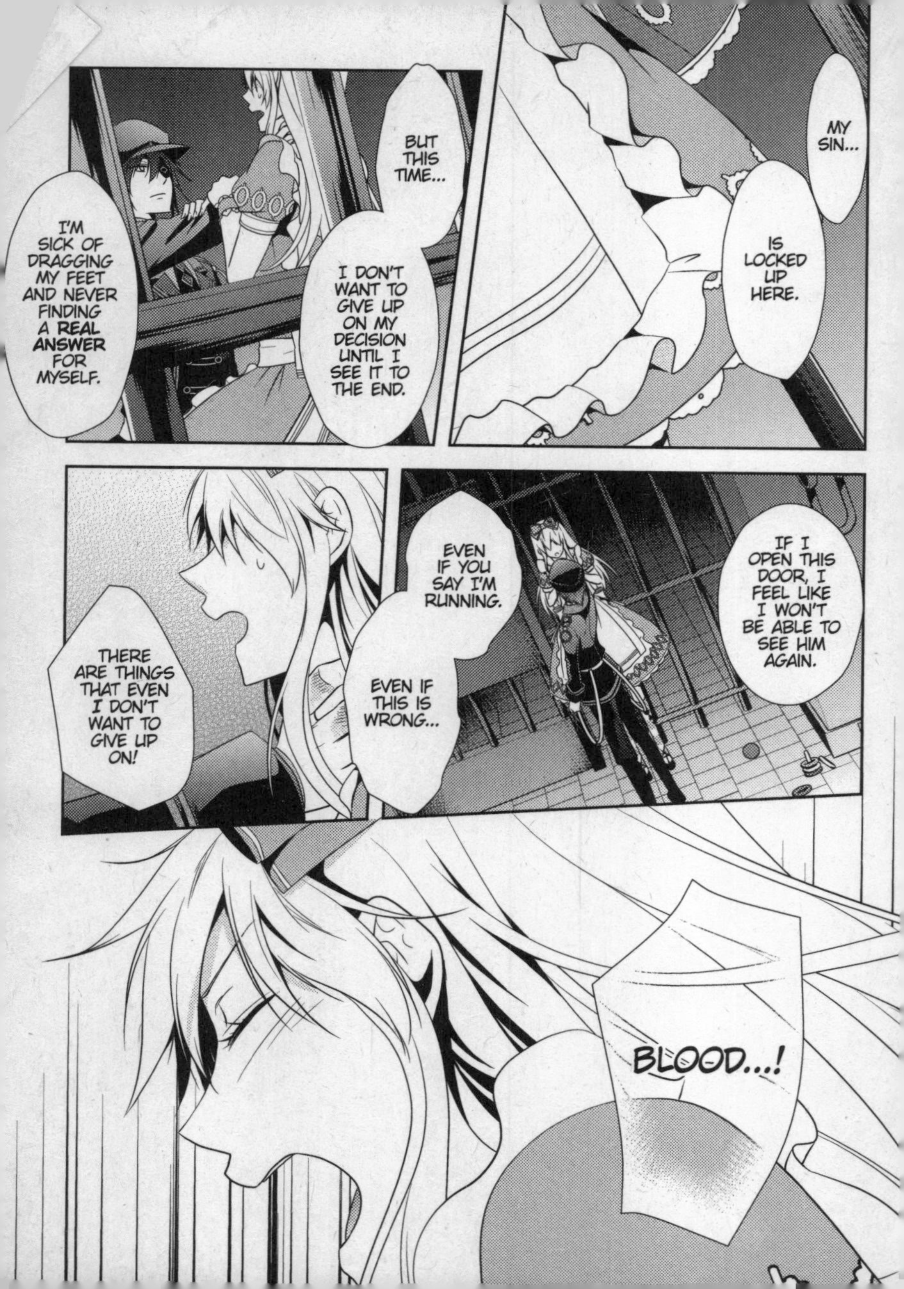
MY SIN...
IS LOCKED UP HERE.
BUT THIS TIME...
I DON'T WANT TO GIVE UP ON MY DECISION UNTIL I SEE IT TO THE END.
I'M SICK OF DRAGGING MY FEET AND NEVER FINDING A **REAL ANSWER** FOR MYSELF.
IF I OPEN THIS DOOR, I FEEL LIKE I WON'T BE ABLE TO SEE HIM AGAIN.
EVEN IF YOU SAY I'M RUNNING.
EVEN IF THIS IS WRONG...
THERE ARE THINGS THAT EVEN I DON'T WANT TO GIVE UP ON!
BLOOD...!

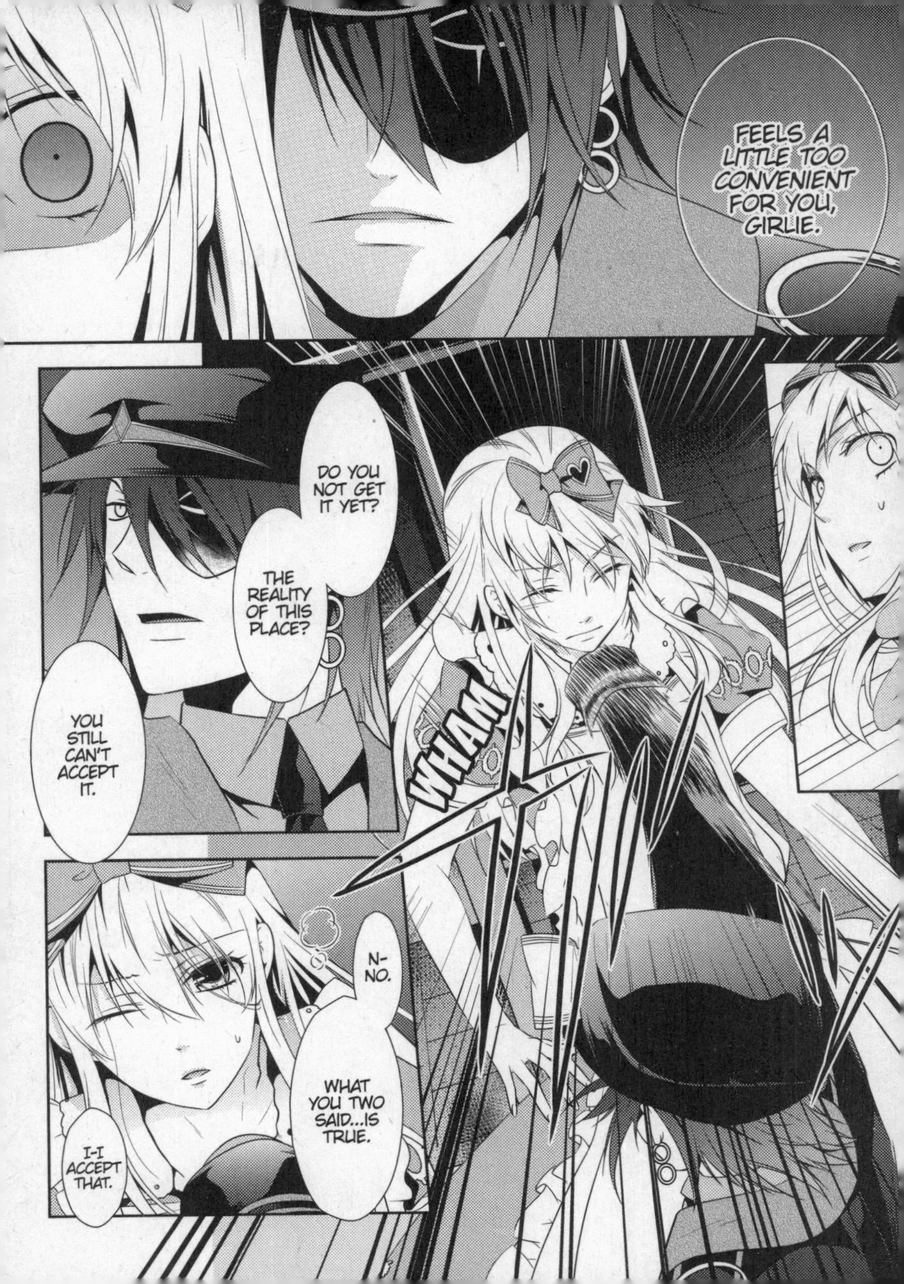
FEELS A LITTLE TOO CONVENIENT FOR YOU, GIRLIE.
WHAM
DO YOU NOT GET IT YET?
THE REALITY OF THIS PLACE?
YOU STILL CAN'T ACCEPT IT.
N-NO.
WHAT YOU TWO SAID...IS TRUE.
I-I ACCEPT THAT.

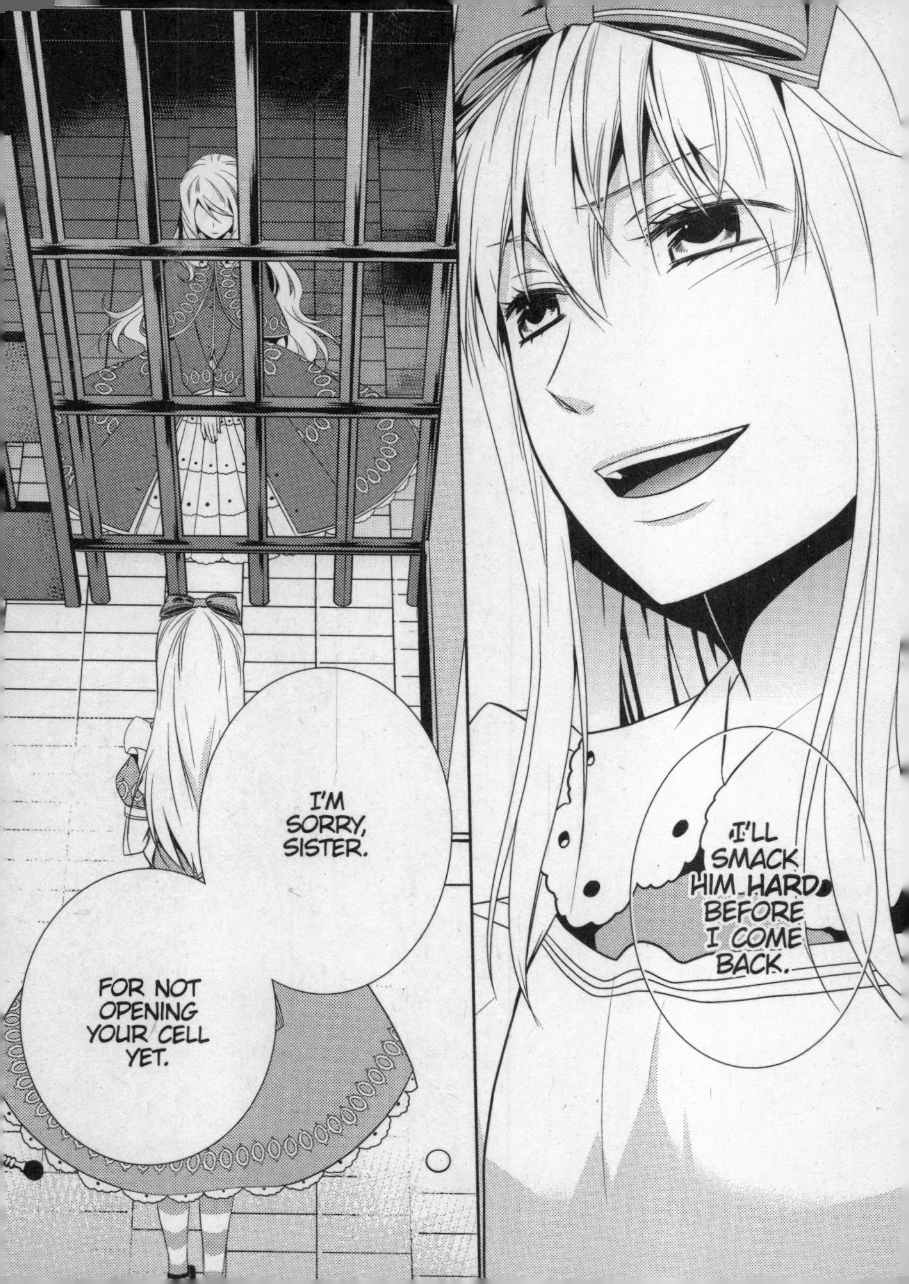
I'LL SMACK HIM HARD BEFORE I COME BACK.
I'M SORRY, SISTER.
FOR NOT OPENING YOUR CELL YET.

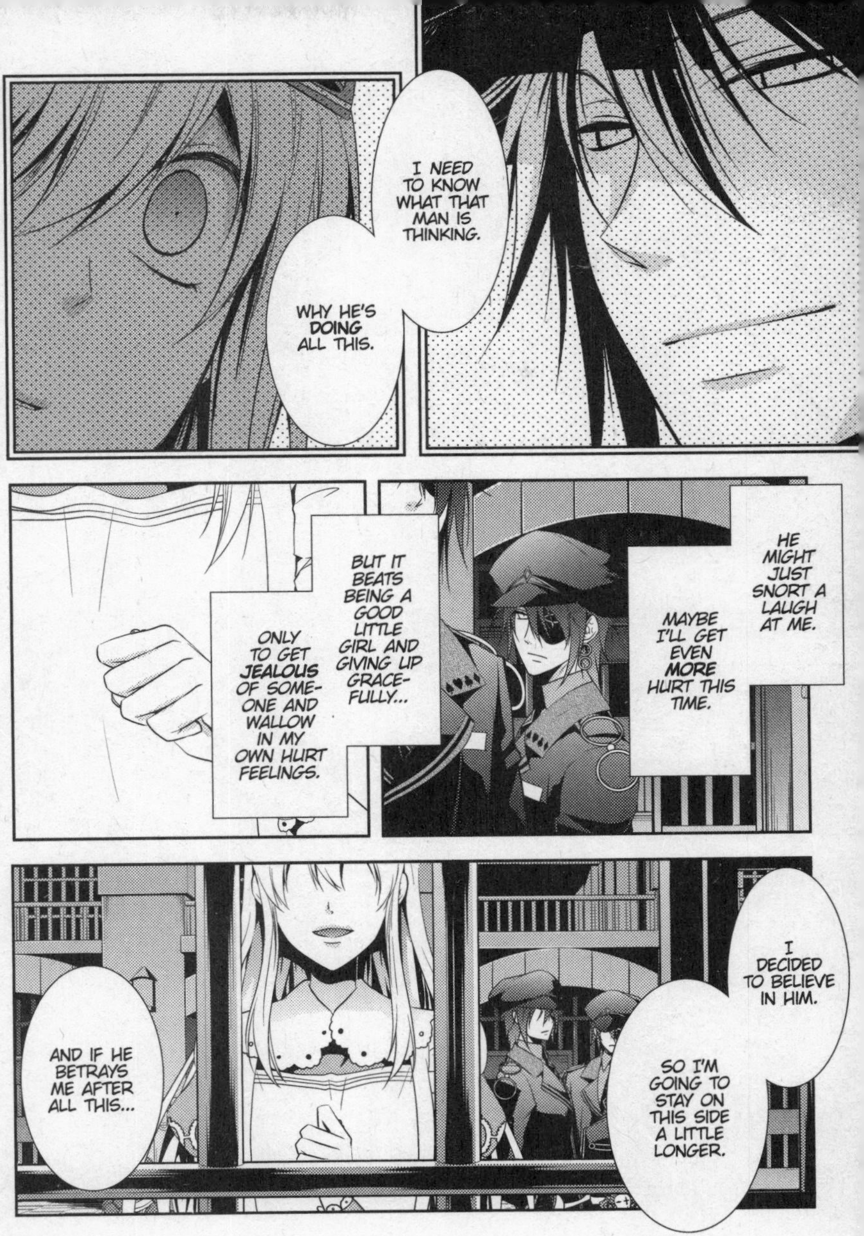
I NEED TO KNOW WHAT THAT MAN IS THINKING.
WHY HE'S DOING ALL THIS.
HE MIGHT JUST SNORT A LAUGH AT ME.
MAYBE I'LL GET EVEN MORE HURT THIS TIME.
BUT IT BEATS BEING A GOOD LITTLE GIRL AND GIVING UP GRACE-FULLY...
ONLY TO GET JEALOUS OF SOME-ONE AND WALLOW IN MY OWN HURT FEELINGS.
I DECIDED TO BELIEVE IN HIM.
SO I'M GOING TO STAY ON THIS SIDE A LITTLE LONGER.
AND IF HE BETRAYS ME AFTER ALL THIS...

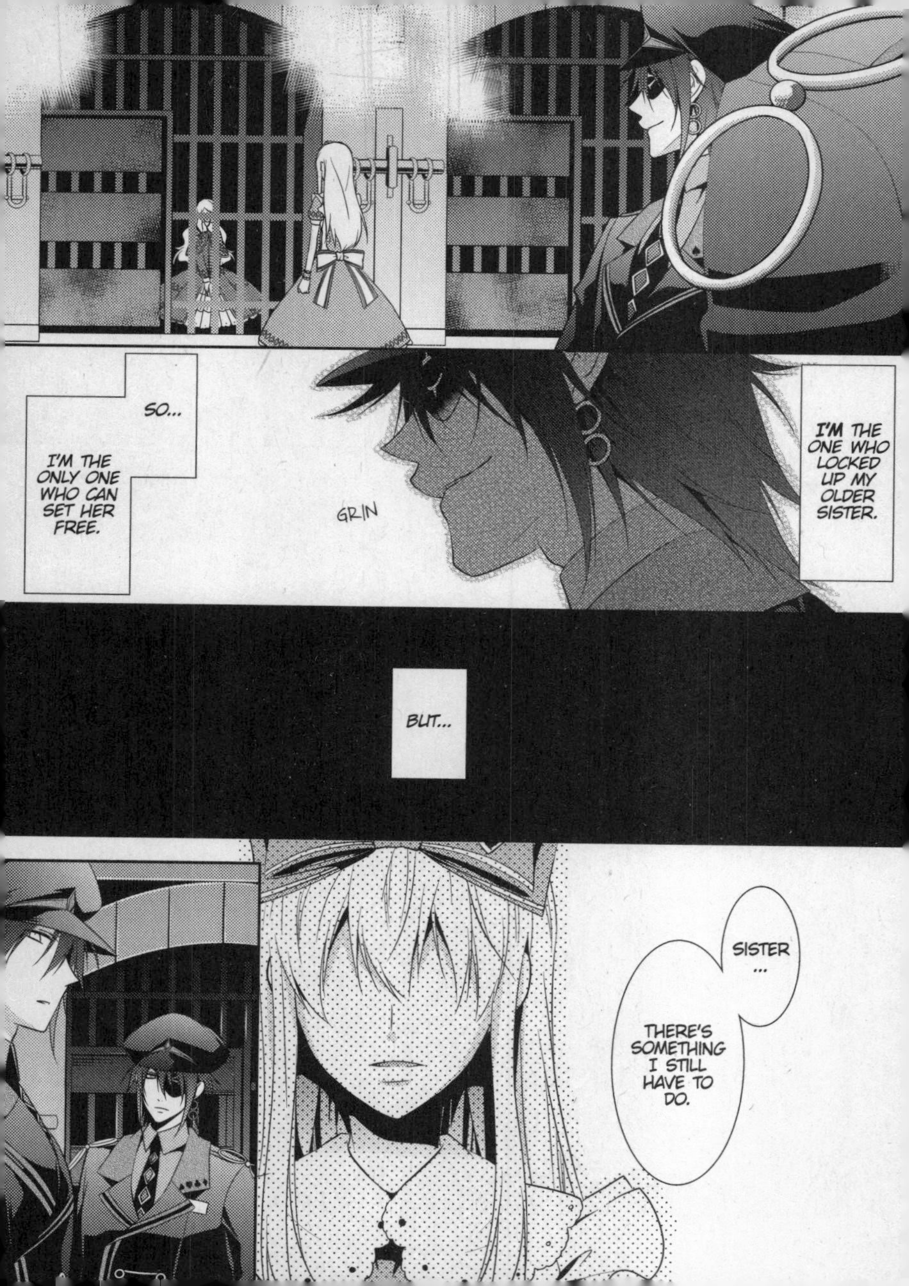
I'M THE ONE WHO LOCKED UP MY OLDER SISTER.
GRIN
SO...
I'M THE ONLY ONE WHO CAN SET HER FREE.
BUT...
SISTER...
THERE'S SOMETHING I STILL HAVE TO DO.

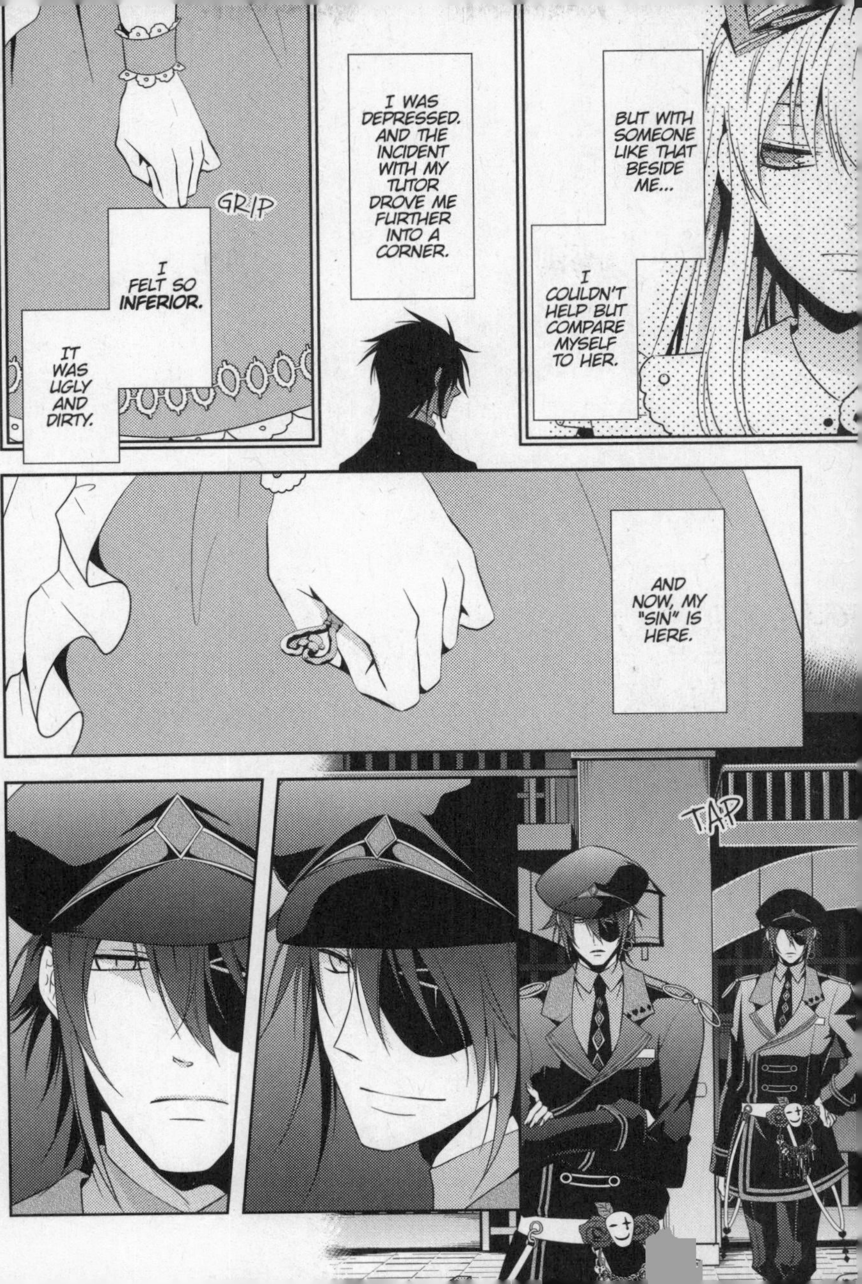
BUT WITH SOMEONE LIKE THAT BESIDE ME...
I COULDN'T HELP BUT COMPARE MYSELF TO HER.
I WAS DEPRESSED. AND THE INCIDENT WITH MY TUTOR DROVE ME FURTHER INTO A CORNER.
GRIP
I FELT SO INFERIOR.
IT WAS UGLY AND DIRTY.
AND NOW, MY "SIN" IS HERE.
TAP

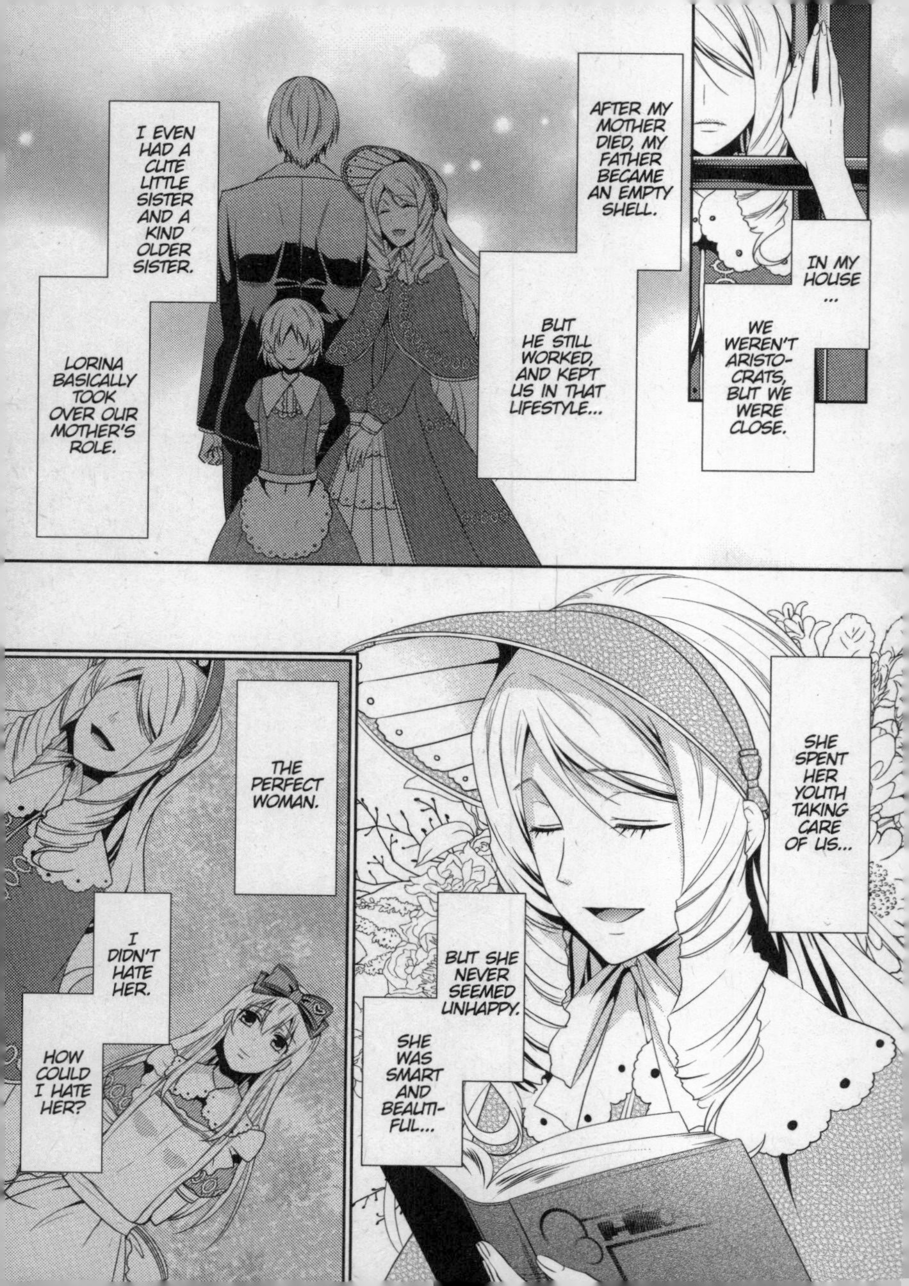
IN MY HOUSE...
WE WEREN'T ARISTOCRATS, BUT WE WERE CLOSE.
AFTER MY MOTHER DIED, MY FATHER BECAME AN EMPTY SHELL.
BUT HE STILL WORKED, AND KEPT US IN THAT LIFESTYLE...
I EVEN HAD A CUTE LITTLE SISTER AND A KIND OLDER SISTER.
LORINA BASICALLY TOOK OVER OUR MOTHER'S ROLE.
SHE SPENT HER YOUTH TAKING CARE OF US...
BUT SHE NEVER SEEMED UNHAPPY.
SHE WAS SMART AND BEAUTIFUL...
THE PERFECT WOMAN.
I DIDN'T HATE HER.
HOW COULD I HATE HER?

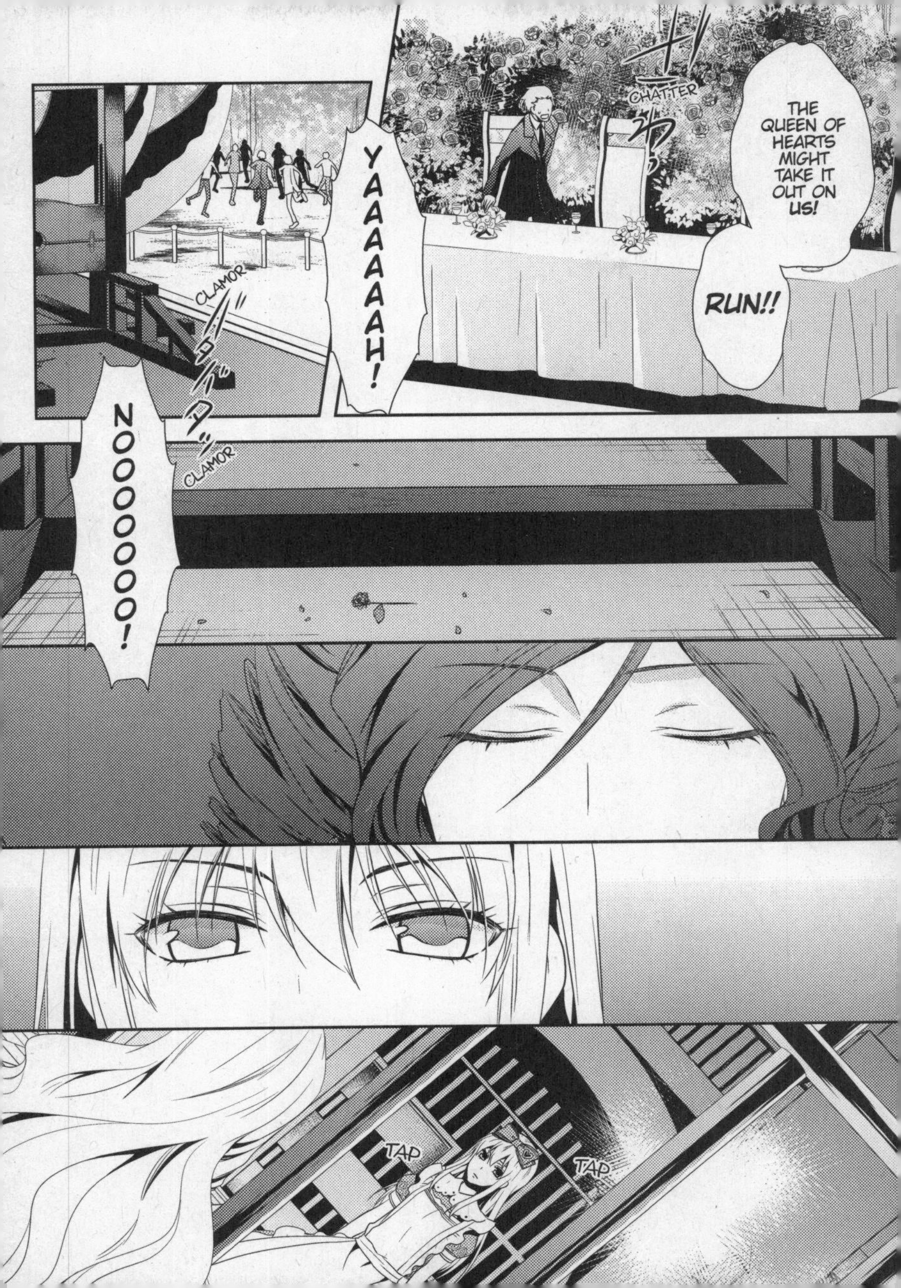
CHATTER
THE QUEEN OF HEARTS MIGHT TAKE IT OUT ON US!
RUN!!
YAAAAAAAH!
CLAMOR
NOOOOOOOO!
CLAMOR
TAP
TAP

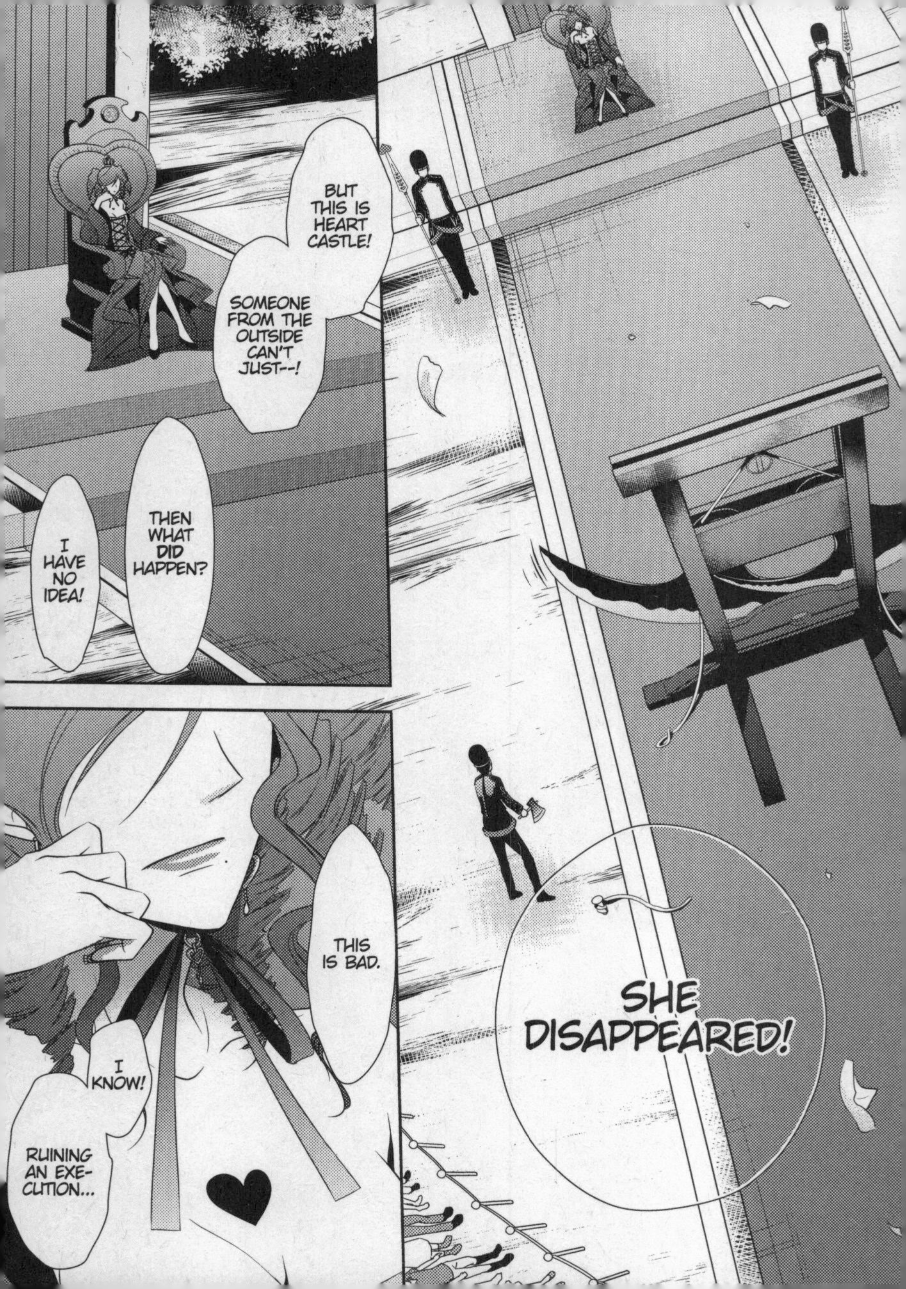
SHE DISAPPEARED!
BUT THIS IS HEART CASTLE!
SOMEONE FROM THE OUTSIDE CAN'T JUST--!
THEN WHAT DID HAPPEN?
I HAVE NO IDEA!
THIS IS BAD.
I KNOW!
RUINING AN EXE-CUTION...

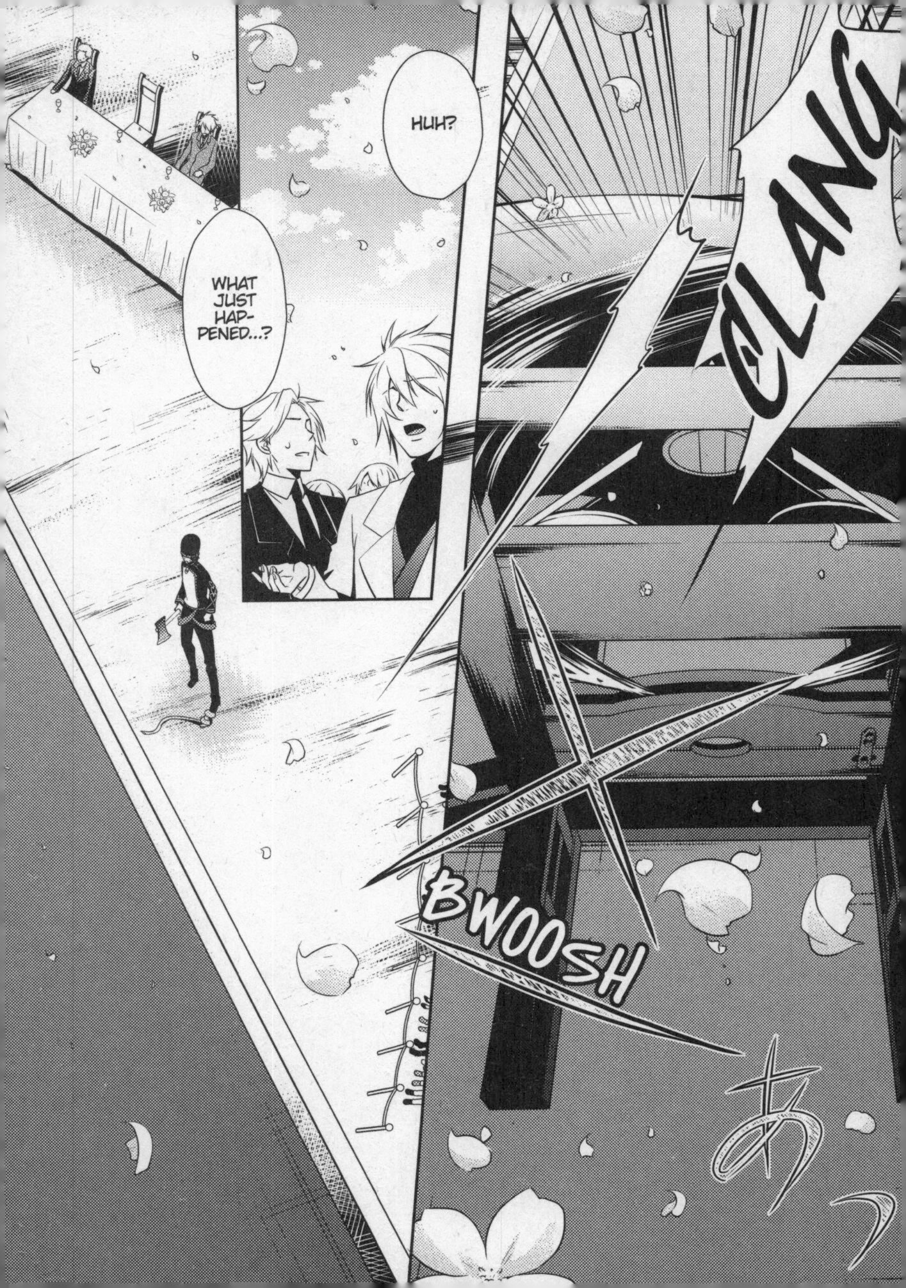
CLANG
BWOOSH
あっ
HUH?
WHAT JUST HAP-PENED...?

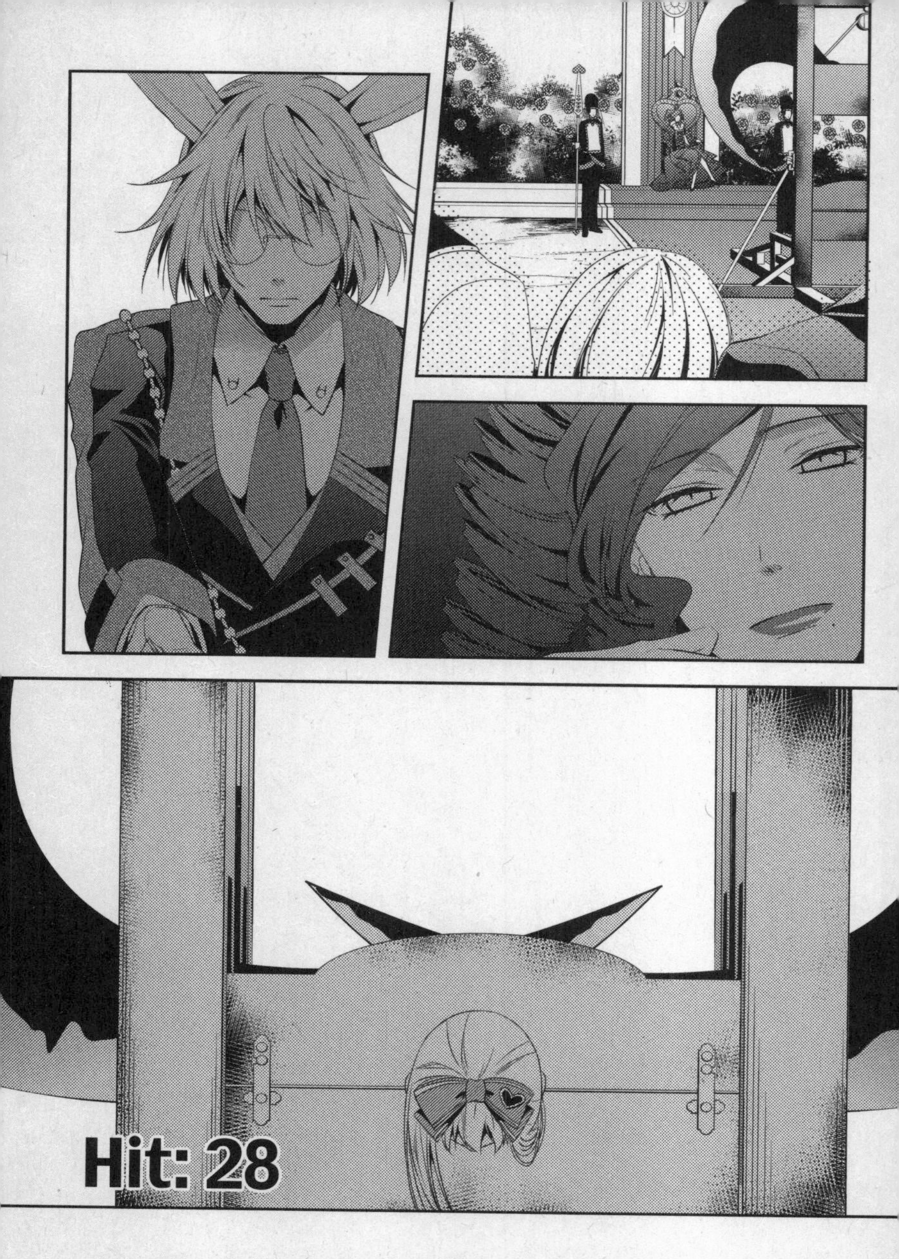
Hit: 28

SEVEN SEAS ENTERTAINMENT PRESENTS

Alice IN THE COUNTRY OF JOKER
CIRCUS AND LIAR'S GAME

art by **MAMENOSUKE FUJIMARU** / story by **QUINROSE**   VOLUME 7

TRANSLATION
Angela Liu

ADAPTATION
Lianne Sentar

LETTERING AND LAYOUT
Laura Scoville

LOGO DESIGN
Courtney Williams

COVER DESIGN
Nicky Lim

PROOFREADER
Shanti Whitesides
Lee Otter

MANAGING EDITOR
Adam Arnold

PUBLISHER
Jason DeAngelis

ALICE IN THE COUNTRY OF JOKER: CIRCUS AND LIAR'S GAME VOL. 7
Copyright © Mamenosuke Fujimaru / QuinRose 2014
First published in Japan in 2014 by ICHIJINSHA Inc., Tokyo.
English translation rights arranged with ICHIJINSHA Inc., Tokyo, Japan.

Seven Seas books may be purchased in bulk for educational, business, or
promotional use. For information on bulk purchases, please contact Macmillan
Corporate & Premium Sales Department at 1-800-221-7945 (ext 5442)
or write specialmarkets@macmillan.com.

Seven Seas and the Seven Seas logo are trademarks of
Seven Seas Entertainment, LLC. All rights reserved.

ISBN: 978-1-626921-16-0

Printed in Canada

First Printing: February 2015

10 9 8 7 6 5 4 3 2 1

FOLLOW US ONLINE: **www.gomanga.com**

READING DIRECTIONS

This book reads from *right to left*, Japanese style.
If this is your first time reading manga, you start
reading from the top right panel on each page and
take it from there. If you get lost, just follow the
numbered diagram here. It may seem backwards at
first, but you'll get the hang of it! Have fun!!

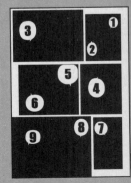

Alice in the Country of Joker

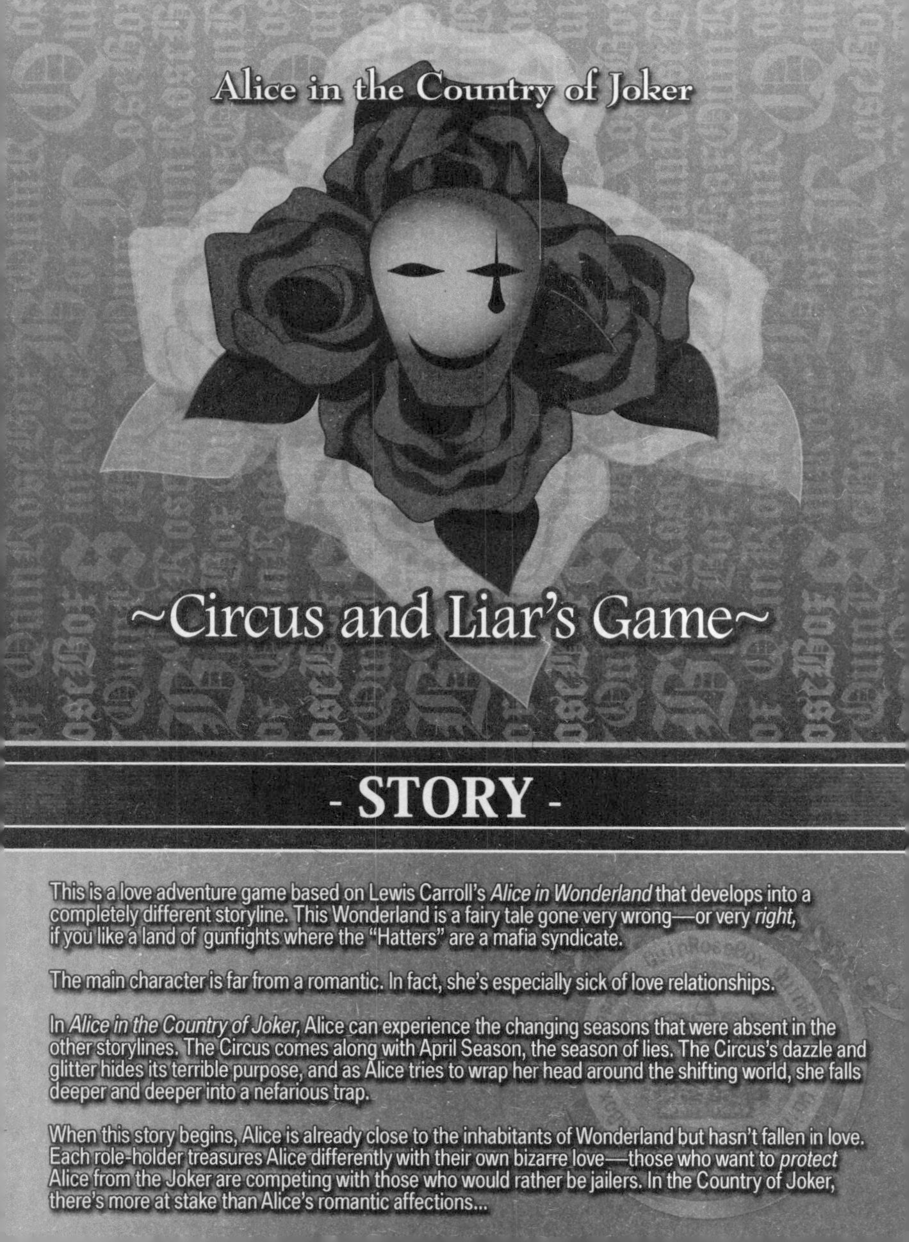

~Circus and Liar's Game~

- STORY -

This is a love adventure game based on Lewis Carroll's *Alice in Wonderland* that develops into a completely different storyline. This Wonderland is a fairy tale gone very wrong—or very *right*, if you like a land of gunfights where the "Hatters" are a mafia syndicate.

The main character is far from a romantic. In fact, she's especially sick of love relationships.

In *Alice in the Country of Joker,* Alice can experience the changing seasons that were absent in the other storylines. The Circus comes along with April Season, the season of lies. The Circus's dazzle and glitter hides its terrible purpose, and as Alice tries to wrap her head around the shifting world, she falls deeper and deeper into a nefarious trap.

When this story begins, Alice is already close to the inhabitants of Wonderland but hasn't fallen in love. Each role-holder treasures Alice differently with their own bizarre love—those who want to *protect* Alice from the Joker are competing with those who would rather be jailers. In the Country of Joker, there's more at stake than Alice's romantic affections...

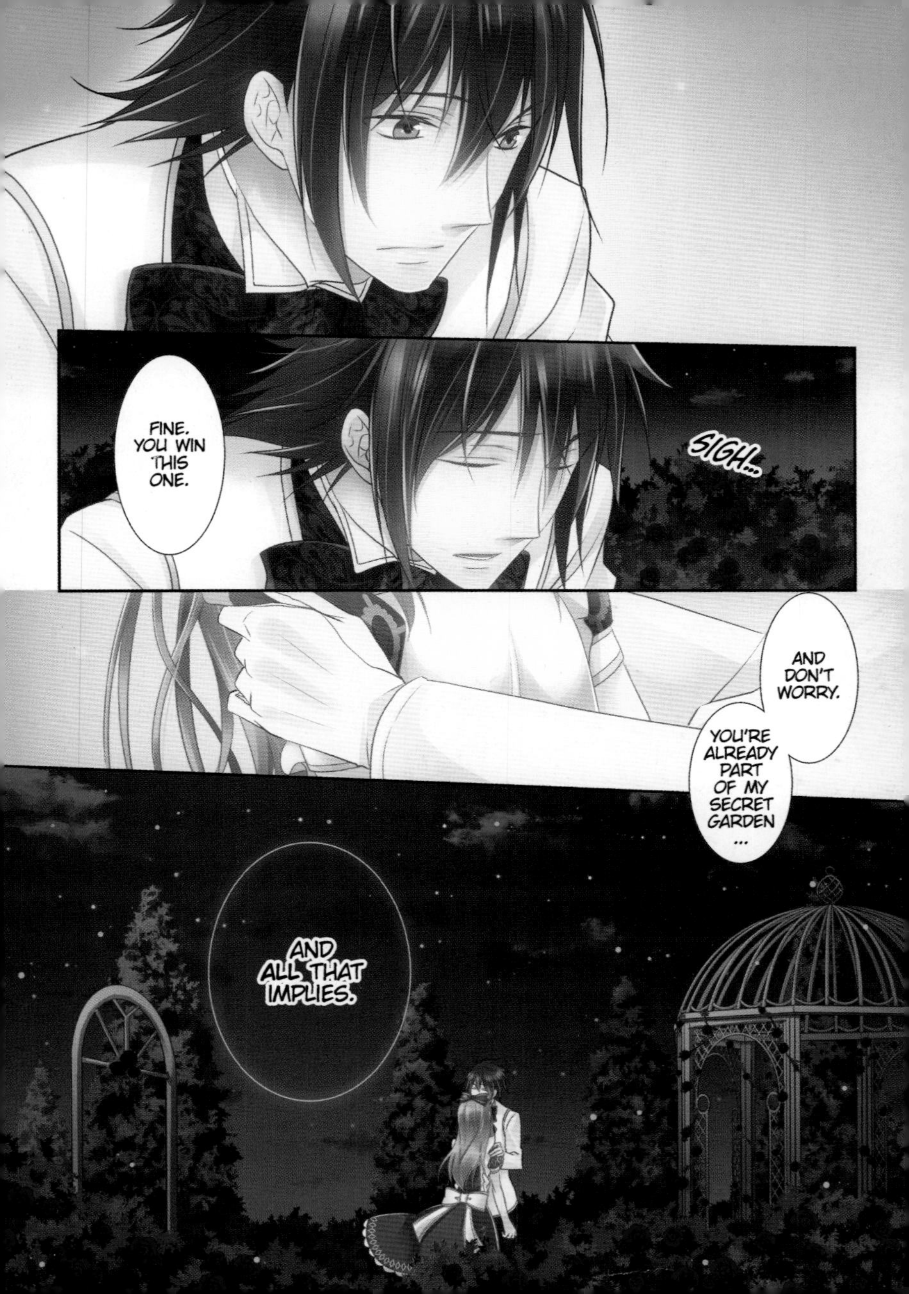
SIGH...
FINE. YOU WIN THIS ONE.
AND DON'T WORRY.
YOU'RE ALREADY PART OF MY SECRET GARDEN ...
AND ALL THAT IMPLIES.

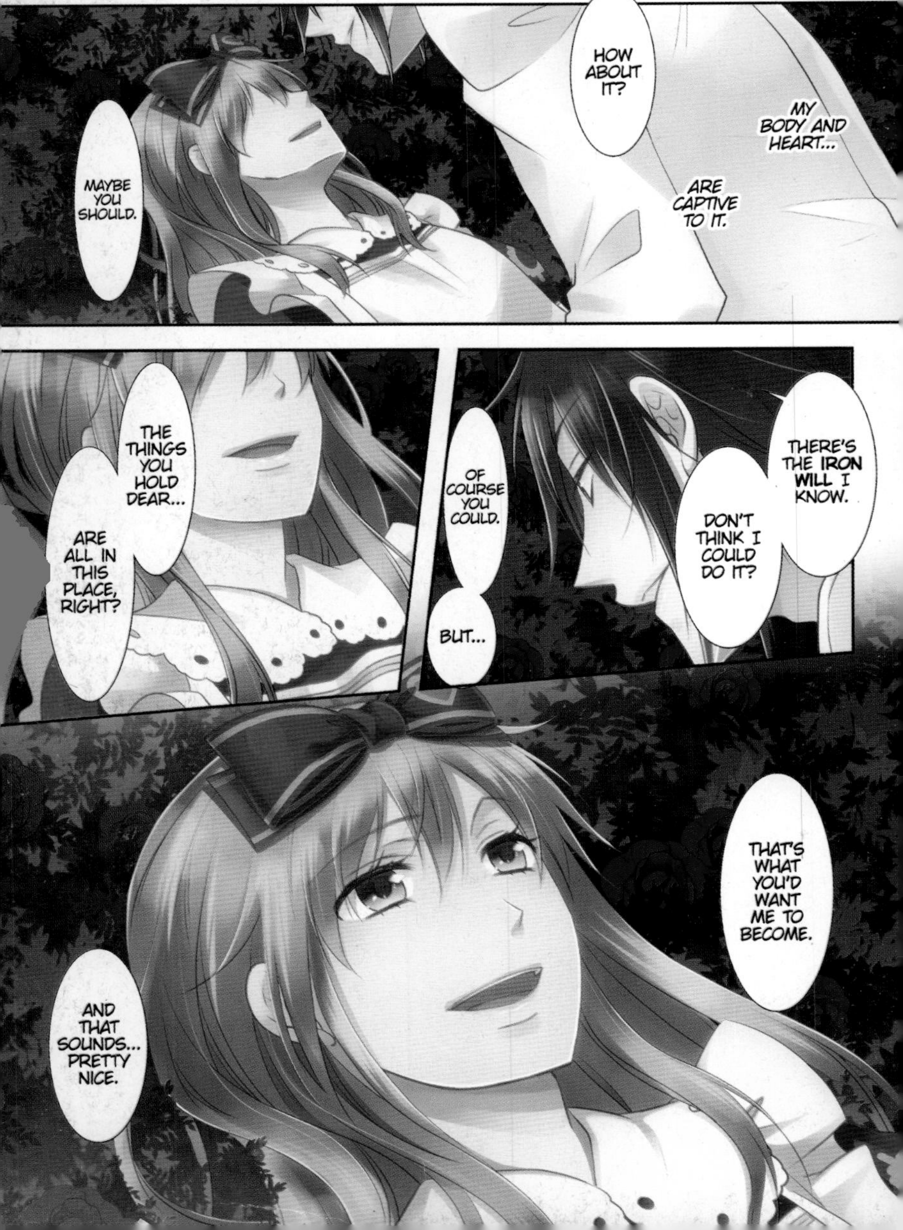
MY BODY AND HEART...
ARE CAPTIVE TO IT.
HOW ABOUT IT?
MAYBE YOU SHOULD.
THERE'S THE IRON WILL I KNOW.
DON'T THINK I COULD DO IT?
OF COURSE YOU COULD.
BUT...
THE THINGS YOU HOLD DEAR...
ARE ALL IN THIS PLACE, RIGHT?
THAT'S WHAT YOU'D WANT ME TO BECOME.
AND THAT SOUNDS... PRETTY NICE.